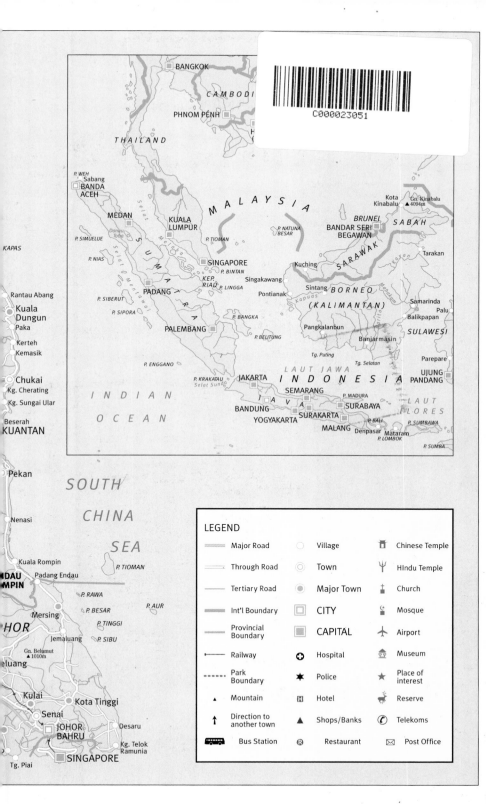

C000023051

BANGKOK

CAMBODIA

PHNOM PÉNH

THAILAND

P. WEH
Sabang
BANDA
ACEH

MEDAN

Danau
Toba

P. SIMUELUE

KAPAS

P. NIAS

Rantau Abang

P. SIBERUT

Kuala
Dungun
Paka

P. SIPORA

Kerteh
Kemasik

PADANG

P. ENGGANO

Chukai
Kg. Cherating
Kg. Sungai Ular

Beserah
KUANTAN

MALAYSIA

Kota
Kinabalu

Gn. Kinabalu
▲ 4094m

KUALA
LUMPUR

P. NATUNA
BESAR

BANDAR SERI
BEGAWAN

BRUNEI

SABAH

P. TIOMAN

SARAWAK

Kayan

Tarakan

SINGAPORE
P. BINTAN

Kuching

KEP.
RIAU P. LINGGA

Singakawang

Pontianak

Sintang

BORNEO

(KALIMANTAN)

Samarinda
Palu
Balikpapan

PALEMBANG

P. BANGKA

Pangkalanbun

P. BELITUNG

Banjarmasin

SULAWESI

Tg. Puting

Tg. Selatan

Parepare

P. KRAKATAU
Selat Sunda

JAKARTA

INDONESIA

UJUNG
PANDANG

LAUT JAWA

SEMARANG

P. MADURA

INDIAN

JAVA

BANDUNG

SURABAYA

LAUT
FLORES

OCEAN

YOGYAKARTA

SURAKARTA

MALANG

Denpasar

P. BALI

P. SUMBAWA

Mataram
P. LOMBOK

P. SUMBA

Pekan

SOUTH

Nenasi

CHINA

Kuala Rompin

SEA

P. TIOMAN

DAU
MPIN

Padang Endau

P. RAWA

P. BESAR

P. AUR

Mersing

P. TINGGI

Jemaluang

P. SIBU

HOR

Gn. Belumut
▲ 1010m

luang

Kulai

Kota Tinggi

Senai

JOHOR
BAHRU

Desaru

Kg. Telok
Ramunia

SINGAPORE

Tg. Piai

LEGEND

Major Road	○	Village	🏮	Chinese Temple
Through Road	◎	Town	☸	Hindu Temple
Tertiary Road	◉	Major Town	✝	Church
Int'l Boundary	☐	CITY	☪	Mosque
Provincial Boundary	■	CAPITAL	✈	Airport
Railway	✚	Hospital	🏛	Museum
Park Boundary	★	Police	★	Place of interest
▲ Mountain	H	Hotel		Reserve
↑ Direction to another town	▲	Shops/Banks	✆	Telekoms
🚌 Bus Station	®	Restaurant	✉	Post Office

PENINSULAR MALAYSIA
AND SINGAPORE

Edited by
WENDY MOORE

PERIPLUS
EDITIONS

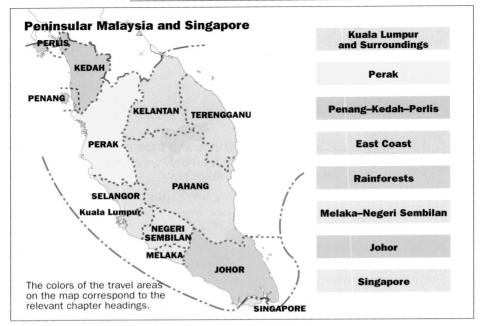

Peninsular Malaysia and Singapore

PERLIS
KEDAH
PENANG
KELANTAN   TERENGGANU
PERAK
PAHANG
SELANGOR
Kuala Lumpur
NEGERI SEMBILAN
MELAKA
JOHOR
SINGAPORE

Kuala Lumpur and Surroundings

Perak

Penang–Kedah–Perlis

East Coast

Rainforests

Melaka–Negeri Sembilan

Johor

Singapore

The colors of the travel areas on the map correspond to the relevant chapter headings.

© 1998 by Periplus Editions (HK) Ltd.
Second edition
ALL RIGHTS RESERVED
Printed in the Republic of Singapore
ISBN 962-593-179-1

Publisher: Eric Oey
Design: Peter Ivey
Production: Mary Chia, TC Su
Cartography: Violet Wong

We welcome comments and additions from readers. Please address all correspondence to:
Periplus (Singapore) Pte. Ltd.
5 Little Road #08-01
Singapore 536983.

International Distributors:
The Netherlands: Nilsson & Lamm BV, Postbus 195, 1380 AD Weesp
Germany: Brettschneider Fernreisebedarf, Feldkirchner Strasse 2, D-85551 Heimstetten
Indonesia: PT Wira Mandala Pustaka (Java Books - Indonesia), Jl. Kelapa Gading Kirana, Blok A14 No. 17, Jakarta 14240
Singapore and Malaysia: Berkeley Books Pte. Ltd., 5 Little Rd #08-01, Singapore 536983
U.K.: GeoCenter U.K. Ltd., The Viables Centre, Harrow Way, Basingstoke, Hampshire RG22 4BJ
U.S.A.: NTC/Contemporary Publishing Company (Passport Guides), 4255 W. Touhy Avenue, Lincolnwood [Chicago], Illinois 60646-1975

The Periplus Adventure Guides Series

BALI

JAVA

SUMATRA

KALIMANTAN *Indonesian Borneo*

SULAWESI *The Celebes*

EAST OF BALI *From Lombok to Timor*

MALUKU *Indonesian Spice Islands*

IRIAN JAYA *Indonesian New Guinea*

DIVING INDONESIA

SURFING INDONESIA

BIRDING INDONESIA

TREKKING INDONESIA *(1998)*

WEST MALAYSIA *and Singapore*

EAST MALAYSIA *and Brunei*

Cover: *A Malay girl dressed for a celebration at Kuala Terengganu. Photo by Alain Evrard.*
Pages 4-5: *In the shade of "chick" shopfront blinds. Photo by Jill Gocher.*
Pages 6-7: *A young Hindu penitent during the Thaipusam festival in Penang. Photo by Jean Leo Dugast.*
Frontispiece: *Young members of a tambourine band. Photo by Alain Evrard.*

Contents

12   CONTENTS

PART I

Land Where the Winds Meet

Dangling like a pendant from the tip of continental Asia, Peninsular Malaysia lies at the heart of Southeast Asia. Bordered in the north by Thailand, this verdant, tropical land stretches southwards 740km (460mi) to end at the Straits of Johor which separate the peninsula from the neighboring island republic of Singapore. Malaysia's Borneo states of Sarawak and Sabah lie to the east, 530km (329mi) across the South China Sea.

The peninsula has been well known since antiquity as it is straddled by the vital sea routes between India, the Middle East and China. It is also at the nexus of the monsoons. Ptolemy, the Greek astronomer, called it "The Golden Chersonese"; ancient mariners dubbed it "The Land Where the Winds Meet."

Early traders were lured by the products of the rainforests, the green mantle which still covers much of the country's mountainous interior, shrouding its elusive abundance of wildlife. The natural beauty of Peninsular Malaysia is one of the principal attractions for visitors today.

Inland from the popular coastal islands with their white sand beaches and aquamarine seas, are fertile alluvial plains punctuated by limestone hills containing ancient cave dwellings. The granite mountains of the Main Range, Banjaran Titiwangsa, form the peninsula's spine, splitting it into the culturally distinct regions of east and west.

While the west flourished during the tin mining and rubber booms, and economic migrants created an ethnically diverse population, the east kept its Malay identity and evolved in relative isolation from economic and colonial pressures.

The east thus retained many of the customs, crafts, arts and beliefs now hardly found in the west. These ancient traditions are actually on the increase in certain areas. Nowadays the west is connected to the east by new highways and access is no longer the month-long elephant trek it once was.

The peninsula's "golden age" occcured in the 15th century, when the great empire of Melaka was at its zenith. Much of modern-day Malaysia's political, religious and legal systems have their origins in that time. The empire fell to the Portuguese in 1511, then to the Dutch in the mid 17th century. But it was the British, from their strongholds in Penang and Singapore, who dominated the peninsula from the late 19th century.

Concrete evidence of the colonial era is found throughout the country in architectural form but most poignantly at the hill resorts of the Cameron Highlands and Fraser's Hill, where the cultural anachronism of afternoon tea in the gardens of a Malaysian mock-Tudor house becomes especially odd at 3,000 feet amid the rainforests.

Since independence in 1957 Malaysia has seen steady economic growth and a much higher standard of living following a number of industrialization programs aimed ultimately at gaining the country "developed nation" status by 2020.

Peninsular Malaysia's natural and ethnic diversity, coupled with the hospitable nature of its people and the efficient transportation infrastructure make traveling not only visually and culturally enriching but also socially stimulating and extremely easy.

Singapore, Peninsular Malaysia's dynamic southern neighbor, has seen phenomenal change over the past 25 years. Renowned for its airport, shopping and cuisine, the city state has a lot more than might initially meet the eye. Beneath a high tech Western veneer there lies a vibrant and unique society and the city state invariably rewards those who take the time to appreciate it fully.

Opposite: Celebrating her nation's independence from the British on Merdeka Day, a Malay girl holds a traditional decoration which derives from the flowering coconut palm. Photo by Radin Moh'd Noh Salleh.

GEOGRAPHY

Peninsula at the Tip of Mainland Asia

Malaysia's geography is characterized by stability and gentleness. None of the tectonic violence found in the neighboring regions occurs here. Earth tremors are rare and insignificant, there are no volcanoes, and typhoons and monsoons peter out before they reach the country's shores.

As if to emphasize this, forests cover the rugged hills of the interior with a lush blanket of foliage, softening harsh outlines and smoothing out rough edges. Even the land's major cash crops (rubber and oil palm) are trees, and it is this rich vegetation which invariably has the greatest impact on visitors.

The Malay Peninsula is a long and slender, slightly bulbous strip of land that extends southward from mainland Southeast Asia to the equator. The upper portion of the peninsula belongs to Thailand; the southerly half is known as Peninsular Malaysia, to distinguish it from the eastern Malaysian states of Sabah and Sarawak in Borneo. At the narrow Isthmus of Kra in Thailand, the peninsula's northernmost point, less than 50km (31mi) of land separates the Indian Ocean from the Gulf of Thailand and the South China Sea.

Ridges, domes, peaks and plains

A ridge of granite mountains forms the peninsula's north-south backbone. This is known as the Main Range, or more poetically in Malay as Banjaran Titiwangsa. Many of the range's peaks reach above 1,800m (6,000ft), including Gunung Korbu, the peninsula's second highest at 2,183m (7,160ft), as well as the hill stations at Cameron Highlands, Fraser's Hill and Genting Highlands.

At the northern end of Peninsular Malaysia, near the Thai border, other granite ranges and extensive hill country occurs. Towards the east coast is an H-shaped range of sandstone mountains, most of which lie within Taman Negara National Park, including the peninsula's highest peak, Gunung Tahan 2,191m (7,186ft). These sandstone mountains are generally steeper than the granite domes of the Main Range, with knife-edge ridges that jut upward sharply.

Extensive alluvial plains surround the mountains, and it is here that most agricultural settlements have developed. The materials forming these expanses of fertile land have resulted from the erosion of hill

R. MOH'D NOH SALLEH

slopes over the centuries, and the accumulation of marine sediments and sand created by the action of the ocean. Along the west coast, the trapping of silt by mangrove trees has created a natural landfill which has moved the coastline outward. Ptolemy recorded that in his day the coastal plain of the peninsula joined Sumatra, closing the Melaka Straits, but geological research indicates that this is not true.

The west coast plain is by far Peninsular Malaysia's most important economic region.

Tin has been mined extensively in Perak and Selangor for a century and a half, accounting in the late-19th century for more than a third of all colonial revenues. Timber is also a significant resource, and more recently the west coast plains have been the site of Malaysia's major rubber and oil palm estates. All of these have provided new jobs and created an infrastructure which is now developing at a rapid pace.

At scattered locations on the peninsula, especially where the foothills meet the coastal plains, clusters of limestone karst hills protrude like giant fingers from the earth. These curious topographical features, with vertical and overhanging cliff faces, are often depicted in traditional Chinese paintings, and it can come as a surprise to visitors that they also occur in Malaysia. Such tower karst formations do not have simple drainage from peak to base, but contain networks of sinkholes and channels, enabling water to flow in several directions. Examples of these clusters can be seen in Perak and Kelantan, Perlis and Kedah, including the Langkawi islands.

Rock lifestyles

Limestone is soft, which accounts for the existence of bottom cliffs. Through weathering, a block of rock will fall and leave a bare new face which in turn may be affected by water seepage, not just on the surface but up to 3m (10ft) or more into what looks like solid rock. These hills are often unstable due to such erosion.

They are nevertheless attractive places to live. The soft limestone also results in caves, carved out by the action of water over the millennia. The overhanging cliffs, which form the cave mouths, provide dry homes that have been exploited by man since prehistory. Many of the most famous archaeological sites in Malaysia occur in such surroundings, and today groups of squatters and smallholders live in similar dwellings; a way of life not without risk. In 1972, near Ipoh, 30 people living in shanties were killed by a rockfall.

The caves not only provide a home for man, but for a host of bats, insects and other animal life. Although Peninsular Malaysia also has some coastal caves in sandstone and other rock these are insignificant in comparison with the richness and abundance of the limestone caves.

The combination of tree cover, mountain ranges and the peripheral influence of continental monsoons govern a complex water regime. On the west coast there tend to be two peaks of rainfall a year, usually from April-May and October-December. On the east coast there is a much stronger, more dependable single wet season around October-January. These wet seasons are not monsoons, but occur during the turbulent inter-monsoon period when the wind changes direction from northeast to southwest.

On the west coast storms can be accompanied by sudden strong winds known as Sumatras. These build up under the influence of the southwest monsoon in the afternoon or evening over the coast of Sumatra, reaching

*Opposite: Limestone hills pitted with caves are a distinctive feature of rural Perlis. **Above, left:** Rainforest covers the foothills of the Banjaran Titiwangsa in Negeri Sembilan. **Above, right:** These fruiting pandanus thrive in the salty, sandy soils of the East Coast.*

the Malaysian coast early the following day. Elsewhere on the peninsula violent winds are rare and short-lived, generally blowing for the few minutes before a thunderstorm breaks.

Vegetation and precipitation

Montane forest above 900m (3,000ft) is typically cloud-covered and trees play a major role in stripping water from the atmosphere as the clouds sweep past. It is said that ten times as much water can be trapped by condensation than is gathered as rainfall. If so, montane forest must contribute disproportionately to the amount of water flowing down catchments.

Studies in Malaysia have shown that reduced tree cover can increase the amount of water flowing downstream. Because the loss of lowland trees reduces the leaf surface-area for evapo-transpiration, less water therefore re-evaporates into the atmosphere. This has been supported by similar research in many other countries. The neglected factor is that the amount of rainfall itself depends on vegetation cover. Although fewer trees in a small area increases water flow downstream—because overall rainfall is not affected—widespread loss of trees can prevent precipitation in the first place.

Mountains also contribute to rainfall, most of which is orographic, resulting in the typical rain shadows often seen behind them. The central peninsula from Jerantut south to Kuala Pilah is one of the driest regions in terms of total annual rainfall; both here and in Kedah/Perlis there can be periods of over a month with no rain at all.

The peninsula's main rivers are the Perak—which flows from near the Thai border, down through the west coast plain to the Melaka Straits—and the Kelantan, the Terengganu and the Pahang in the east, which flow into the South China Sea. It has been suggested that the east-flowing Pahang River once flowed westwards, along the course of the present day Muar River, into Melaka Straits. This change is thought to have occurred in the low-lying south of Pahang, in the peninsula's largest natural lake system—Tasek Bera—which is in fact a very slow-flowing complex of blackwater creeks.

Ancient riverine trading routes

Until at least the 19th century the peninsula's rivers provided the only efficient thoroughfares for long-distance inland transport and trade. The route along the Muar, through Tasek Bera and eastwards down the Pahang, provided the main means of crossing the peninsula. Another such ancient course traversed the south, following the Muar and Semberong rivers across Johor. Yet another led far up the Pahang river and out through Dungun in Terengganu. Although these routes were principally used for trade, they also served as military conduits during civil

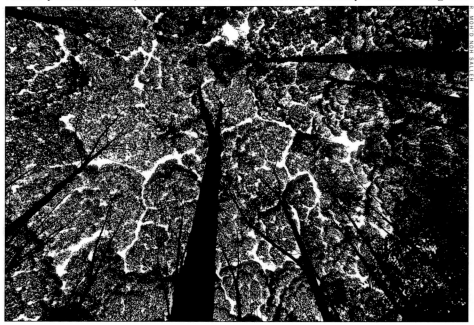

R. MOH'D NOH SALLEH

former tin mining companies turning to limestone quarrying. The Kinta Valley in Perak, once the hub of the world's tin industry, is now a major production center for cement, road chippings, marble and even the calcium which goes into toothpaste.

Although the presence of gold provided inspiration for the evocative titles of early travel books such as *The Golden Chersonese* (*see Further Reading*), it is present in such small quantities that it is seldom exploited. But the black gold, petroleum, is now a major revenue earner.

Despite the fact that Malaysia's first oil well, "The Old Lady," is onshore in East Malaysia, most of the current reserves lie far out to sea. Clusters of rigs can be seen off the coast of Terengganu and other big fields further north have yet to be opened up. Whereas it used to be normal practice to burn off the gas which escapes when oil is extracted, this too is now put to use in the colossal pipeline projects which will eventually link Malaysia, Singapore and Thailand in a regional energy network.

—*Geoffrey Davison*

conflicts between states.

Throughout the world there have been major changes in sea levels and these are traced largely by geographical features. Approximately 7,000 years ago the sea is thought to have been some 20m (66ft) below its present level. This would probably not have been low enough to join Malaysia to Sumatra, but there was certainly such a link during the more remote past. In the Pliocene period, over a million years ago, Malaysia, Sumatra, Java and Borneo were one single land mass.

Although there is some disagreement among geologists over higher levels, it is now generally accepted that by 5,000 years ago the sea had risen to 6m (20ft) above its present level in this part of the world. On some limestone hills in Kedah a shelf of undercut rock can be seen several meters above the ground where, in the prehistoric past, waves eroded the soft limestone. Sand dunes can also be found at several sites along the peninsula's east and west coasts up to 15km (9mi) inland.

As well as redefining the landscape, these geographical shifts contributed to the formation of resources such as tin and petroleum, and thus helped to enhance the country's economic well-being. While tin became a major source of revenue during the colonial era, the turbulence of the international tin market since the 1970s has resulted in many

*Opposite: Seen from the ground, this rainforest canopy displays "crown-shyness," where each tree-canopy is distinct from that of its neighbor. **Above:** A flowering ginger plant. **Below:** Carnivorous pitcher plants, thrive in the montane forests above 1,000m.*

WILDLIFE

Biological Riches of the Rainforest

In the evergreen jungles of Peninsular Malaysia, snakes seldom hang from branches awaiting innocent passers-by, and the tiger's roar or the trumpeting of elephants is a rare treat even for the seasoned explorer.

Yet the richness of the fauna which inhabits this small peninsula is statistically impressive. In a total area of only 132,828km^2 (51,285mi^2) there are over 203 species of mammal, 638 resident and migrant bird species, over 200 varieties of lizards and snakes, 92 species of amphibian and some 200 different types of freshwater fishes. The insect count is phenomenal: there are over 1,032 different butterflies, and an educated estimate of the moth species numbers 8,000. The number of beetles, stick insects, grasshoppers, cicadas, ants, termites and others has yet to be assessed.

Much of the wildlife—60 to 70%—lives in the humid evergreen rainforest and looking for these animals can pose a challenge to the uninitiated. You need to tune your eyes and ears to see and hear them. Many creatures are easier heard than seen, and can be readily detected by their distinctive songs and calls.

Tigers and panthers can sometimes be spotted or heard in Taman Negara and Endau Rompin where reasonable populations still exist. Elephants can occasionally be seen along the East-West Highway and in the wildlife reserves and national park. The Sumatran rhino—the world's most endangered animal—lingers on in Endau Rompin where there is a population of about 20 individuals.

The *seladang*, or wild ox, grazes in small clearings in Taman Negara, and a few remote wildlife reserves. To see any of these rare animals, special expeditions usually need to be mounted, yet with a bit of luck they may also be glimpsed in the wildlife parks.

The incredible diversity and richness of the rainforest is illustrated by the different species of plant life found in a small area. Two hectares of rainforest can house over 200 species of trees, and together with epiphytes, climbers, shrubs, herbs, fungi, and mosses, the number can exceed 1,000 species.

This range of plant life is the main factor determining the diversity of animal life. Plants not only generate a variety of foods for specific animals, but also provide a variety of microhabitats. Nooks and crannies are used by smaller invertebrates for shelter, and the hunting of these small creatures by insectivores generates a need for specialization and evolution which results in a corresponding richness in predator species.

Basic rules of survival

For most forest animals, being found in large concentrations spells trouble: they are more easily located by predators and the spread of disease in the population often results in epidemics. The solution of wildlife survival is to live scattered as individuals, and to meet occasionally to breed during favorable times when food is abundant.

The struggle for survival is never-ending, and the law of the jungle always in full operation. The fittest survive, while the weak and obvious get eaten. For those that are not swift and agile, there is a pressing need to hide and be unseen. Camouflage is the trick, stillness the key.

Insects often take on the form and shape of leaves, stick insects and inch worms resemble branches and twigs, and even their

R. IAN LLOYD

stationary postures mimic the host plant. Spiders that live on the tree trunks have mottled patterns and crouch to resemble the nodules on the bark.

Most animals in the forest are brown, enabling them to blend in with the tree trunks and leaf litter on the forest floor. The tiger makes use of its black stripes to break its well-known form among the grass and reeds. The tapir, with its distinct black and white patches, matches the forest in the moonlight with a mosaic pattern of light and dark, while squirrels and tree shrews dart and freeze in their forage for food to evade detection.

Watching them, watching you

By behavior, pattern and color, the animals in the forest conceal themselves from observers and predators alike. Watching wildlife demands immense patience and time. To see wildlife in the rainforest is to be part of the rainforest yourself.

Despite the development in the cities and along the coast, Peninsular Malaysia still has 55% forest cover and there are numerous wildlife areas. At hill stations such as Fraser's Hill and Genting Highlands, gibbons can be readily heard and squirrels and monkeys easily observed. At Taman Negara, deer, wild pigs, mousedeer, monkeys and monitor lizards can be sighted at the Park Headquarters at Kuala Tahan. Around the overnight hides, civet cats, tigers, wild cattle, tapirs, or other rare animals are sometimes sighted by the nearby salt-licks.

Endau Rompin State Park, although less accessible, provides similar adventure opportunities. Leaf monkeys are easily observed at the Kuala Selangor Nature Park just outside Kuala Lumpur, and the world's largest living turtle, the giant leatherback, comes ashore to nest at Rantau Abang in Terengganu between May and August. Singapore also has wildlife refuges, including the Bukit Timah Forest Reserve in the heart of the island.

In Peninsular Malaysia most wildlife is protected by law although hunting of some wild animals is allowed and regulated by the Department of Wildlife and National Parks. Malaysia and Singapore are both signatories to CITES, and trade in endangered species is strictly prohibited. Development has been rapid in recent years and the wildlife in most lowland forest areas is in retreat. Only gazetted conservation areas ensure the perpetuation and survival of this rich and unique fauna for the future.

—*Kiew Bong Heang*

Opposite: *This Malayan elephant was one of a trio which swam across the Johor Straits to an island off Singapore. They were returned to the Peninsula by the elephant-relocation unit.* **Below:** *The diminutive mousedeer is not a deer, but a distant relation of the camel.*

WWF MALAYSIA

BIRDS

Paradise for the Serious Ornithologist

Peninsular Malaysia's lowland tropical rainforest is the oldest and richest biological environment on earth. Over half of the 460 resident bird species are found mainly or exclusively in these forests. Their habitats have remained unchanged for millions of years, and the forest birds who inhabit them have evolved into many closely-related species. For example, there are 19 different bulbuls and 47 species of babblers.

Forest birds are typically sedentary, especially the insectivorous species such as babblers, flycatchers and woodpeckers. Males and females often pair for life and stay in a small area that constitutes their feeding ground and nesting territory. Only breeding once a year, they have much smaller clutches than similar birds in temperate lands.

Fruit-eating birds like hornbills, pigeons and barbets are more dynamic and often move up to the lower montane habitat to find fruiting trees. A fig tree in fruit is one of Malaysia's great wildlife spectacles, for 20-30 bird species may visit in a single morning, together with numerous mammals, including squirrels and monkeys.

No bird moves across the rainforests' entire vertical plane. Leafbirds and minivets stay high up in the canopies, trogons and broadbills perch at midstorey level, and pheasants and pittas rarely leave the forest floor. There are no hummingbirds, but keep an eye out for nectar-eaters like sunbirds, spiderhunters and flowerpeckers.

In the forest, birdwatchers have to be constantly alert. Often a bird appears briefly and there are only a few seconds in which to see it and make an identification before it disappears into the dense greenery. Knowing the calls of the birds is a great advantage.

The great diversity of species makes the Malaysian rainforest one of the best places in the world for serious ornithologists. At Taman Negara many lowland birds come out in the open at Kuala Tahan, and there is good viewing from trails and elevated hides. Other notable areas include Endau-Rompin, Templer Park near Kuala Lumpur, and the Pantai Forest Reserve in Johor.

Peninsular Malaysia is part of the Oriental zoogeographical region stretching from the Indian subcontinent to Wallace's Line east of Borneo and Bali. There are very few endemic

MORTON STRANGE

montane regions. The forest appears to be quiet and devoid of avifauna, and then suddenly it comes alive with birds like orioles, nuthatches and many different babblers.

Mangroves form another ecosystem of special interest to the birdwatcher. Johor still has some large expanses which are easily accessed from Kukup on the southwest coast. At Kuala Selangor near Kuala Lumpur, and at Kuala Gula in Perak there are protected patches of mangroves and also visitor's facilities. On the nearby mudflats, herons, storks

species in Peninsular Malaysia because it is part of the Sunda subregion which includes Thailand's far south, and the islands of Sumatra, Java and Borneo. During the last Ice Age, when sea levels were much lower than today, this area was joined, and as a result most of the fauna is shared with these surrounding areas. In Peninsular Malaysia only two species, the Malayan Whistling Thrush and the Mountain Peacock Pheasant, are considered true endemic species.

With rapid economic growth and development much of the lowland rainforest has been cleared, and birds have declined in numbers. In a 1988 world survey of threatened birds, Peninsular Malaysia had 12 resident species listed, and 10 were lowland rainforest birds. Four of the sensitive pheasants are in danger of extinction and others are very rare and seldom seen. Asian hornbills are also becoming harder to see and the Helmeted Hornbill is regarded as threatened with extinction. Other endangered birds include the Giant and Fairy Pitta, the Giant Swift and the peculiar Masked Finfoot that can still be seen near the Tahan River inside Taman Negara.

Hill stations and bird waves

In the montane rainforest the avifauna is so different that the birdwatcher might as well have traveled to a different continent. More than 70 bird species in Peninsular Malaysia are exclusively found between 1,000-1,500m (3,300-5,00ft), and a handful of upper montane specialists are found only between 1,300-2,100m (4,300-7,000ft).

Birdwatching at the hill stations, particularly Fraser's Hill, is an enjoyable and highly rewarding experience. The birds are easy to see because you are at eye-level with the low tree tops in the hilly terrain, and they are often colorful and vocal and seem to be more confiding than lowland forest birds.

All rainforest birds form "bird waves" but this phenomenon is especially typical of the

and migratory shorebirds feed at low tide. Most of these are widely distributed Palaearctic species. Including migrants, visitors and vagrants, 623 different species have been spotted in Peninsular Malaysia.

Birds seen around gardens and parks often originate from mangroves and coastal scrub. They are adaptable species and once they make the transition they become very numerous. Open-country birds which often visit gardens include munias, bee-eaters, starlings, kingfishers and shrikes.

Singapore's avifauna, listed at 326 species, is no different than Malaysia's, apart from a few species which are vagrants, or have escaped captivity, but it is a convenient place to birdwatch. Beautiful garden birds like the Black-naped Oriole and Crimson Sunbird are more widespread, and along the north coast near Serangoon, Mandai and Sungei Buloh estuaries, shorebirds and other migratory species can be easily spotted. Rainforest birds can be seen at Bukit Timah Nature Reserve and the Watercatchment Forest where trails lead in from Lornie Road, Upper Thomson Road and Mandai Road, but the species diversity cannot compare with that of Malaysia.

—Morton Strange

Opposite: *A female Olive-Backed Sunbird sips nectar from a bottle-brush flower.* **Above, left:** *The Thick-billed Pigeon.* **Above, right:** *The Asian Fairy Bluebird is often spotted at Fraser's Hill.*

PREHISTORY

Cave Dwellers and Forest Foragers

Through both prehistoric and historic time, Peninsular Malaysia has witnessed the presence of many different layers of human culture. Initially, early hominids of the species *Homo erectus* may have passed through here as they migrated to Java about one million years ago.But no traces of these early humans have been found in the peninsula and scholars are still divided as to whether the Chinese and Javan populations were the ancestors of modern East Asians and Australasians, or an extinct side line of evolution.

Our first clear evidence for human activity dates from perhaps 35,000 years ago, when makers of stone tools left their cores, flakes and hammerstones of quartzite at the site of Kota Tampan, near Lenggong in the Perak Valley (*see Kota Tampan, p. 87*). This site was probably on a lake shoreline when it was occupied and subsequently sealed under an

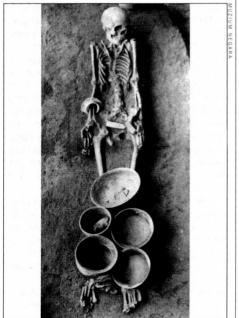

ash fall from a massive eruption of the Toba volcano in Sumatra about 31,000 years ago. At this time, the sea's surface was about 50m (164ft) below its present level owing to the trapping of water in the high latitude ice sheets. Kota Tampan was thus probably located much further inland than today, and perhaps in drier and open forest conditions.

By about 10,000 years ago the climate was warming to present temperatures and the Malaysian rainforests were becoming more equatorial. From this time until the appearance of agricultural populations in the peninsula about 4000 years ago, we find traces of hunting and gathering activities in limestone rock shelters right across the country, and in a few surviving shell mounds on the western coast. Archaeologists refer to this period as the "Hoabinhian" named after cave sites in northern Vietnam.

About ten rock shelters and two shell middens have produced good evidence for Hoabinhian living and dying; perhaps the best is Gua Cha in inland Kelantan which was occupied by Hoabinhians between about 10,000 and 3,000 years ago. The 2m (6.5ft) thickness of Hoabinhian layers at Gua Cha revealed many flaked pebble tools, riverine shellfish, and bones of cooked and eaten forest animals such as cattle, deer, pig, monkey and squirrel. The people also buried their dead in flexed postures in the cave floor, as they also did about 9,000 years ago in the cave of Gua Gunung Runtuh in Perak.

They came from the north

By 2000BC the peninsula had witnessed important economic changes; new populations with agriculture (probably rice and millet) and sedentary villages moved southwards from today's Thailand into Peninsular Malaysia. These people made burnished and cord-marked pottery, similar to that found in sites as far north as Kanchanaburi in central Thailand. They used polished stone adzes and spears with bone points, and wore stone bracelets, shell bead necklaces, and clothing of beaten barkcloth.

Large and wealthy burial grounds with fully-extended burials have been found on sites dating from this period in central Thailand, where there is also clear evidence of rice cultivation. Direct evidence for rice growing in Peninsular Malaysia has yet to be found, perhaps because most archaeological sites concentrate on rock shelters, away from likely early rice-growing areas. One such shelter is again Gua Cha where the

Hoabinhians were succeeded about 3,000 years ago by people who buried their dead with very finely crafted pots, stone adzes and stone bracelets. More finds from around 2,000BC have also been recently reported from Jenderam Hilir in Selangor.

People who made burnished and cord-marked Neolithic pottery like that discovered in Gua Cha continued to occupy the peninsula until around 500BC, if not later. Between 500BC and 500AD the archaeological record illustrates major changes. Bronze drums of Vietnamese manufacture ("Dongson" drums), bronze bells and a broad range of iron tools have been found across northern and central Peninsular Malaysia. Clearly, the ethnic patterning was transforming rapidly. The Malays, documented in Sumatra by 7th-century Srivijayan inscriptions, had perhaps arrived on the coasts of the Malay Peninsula with their interest in sea-borne trade. But if Malays were settling the coasts as early as 2,000 years ago, who was there before them?

The great ethnogenesis debate

Questions of ethnicity are hard to answer from the record of prehistoric archaeology. Prehistoric records in the southern peninsula are almost non existent; almost all our knowledge comes from the north and central regions and from southern Thailand. But even with this restriction we can still ask whose ancestors made the archaeological record over the past 10,000 years.

Ethnolinguistically, there are today three major population groupings; the Semang Negrito foragers of the northern interior rainforests, the Senoi cultivators of the southern interior (both the Semang and Senoi are known as Orang Asli and speak Austroasiatic languages in the Mon-Khmer subgroup, which also includes Khmer of Cambodia and Vietnamese), and the Austronesian-speaking groups in coastal districts and the far south of whom the Malays are the most numerous and widespread. The Austronesians are today one of the most widely dispersed major ethnolinguistic groups on earth, including populations as far apart geographically as the peoples of Madagascar, Aboriginal Taiwan, Indonesia, the Philippines, and all of Oceania beyond western Melanesia.

Although archaeologists and anthropologists like to disagree over questions of ethnogenesis, my own opinion is that the Semang forest foragers are the fairly direct descendants of the Hoabinhians, whereas the slightly more Mongoloid Senoi represent the

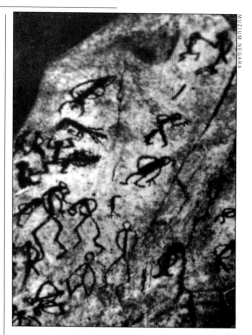

descendants of both the Hoabinhians and the Neolithic cultivators who entered the Malay Peninsula around 2,000BC from southern Thailand. The Malays and their Austronesian-speaking relatives (the speakers of so-called "Aboriginal Malay" or Orang Asli Melayu dialects) probably migrated into the peninsula from an original homeland in western Borneo between 2,000 and 3,000 years ago.

After their arrival it seems that many previously Austroasiatic-speaking groups adopted Austronesian languages. Malay linguistic origins are closely tied to related languages such as Iban and Selako in western Borneo. It is thus clear that the original direction of Malayic migration was from Indonesia into the Malay Peninsula, perhaps via eastern Sumatra, and not vice-versa. Malay proper—the language associated with Hindu Srivijaya and subsequent Muslim sultanates in Island Southeast Asia—perhaps only replaced the Mon language in the northern peninsular after the 12th century.

The Malay Peninsula has been a region which people have entered rather than left in prehistoric times, and it has absorbed its migrants and forged them into one of modern Southeast Asia's most diversified societies.

—*Peter Bellwood*

Opposite: *A Hoabinhian burial site at the Gua Cha, a rock shelter in inland Kelantan.* ***Above:*** *Prehistoric cave drawings in Gua Badak, Perak.*

EARLY HISTORY

Melaka and the Legendary Kingdoms

Due to a lack of documentation it is difficult to reconstruct with any real certainty the history of Peninsular Malaysia prior to the 15th century. Consequently, the centuries before 1400—the "pre-Melakan period"—are usually considered as being relatively less important in the evolution of modern Malaysia. Historians have tended to regard the rise of the great entrepôt of Melaka, on the west coast, as the starting point for Malay history.

Cultural foundations

However, the growth of Melaka from a quiet fishing village to a world-renowned emporium and center of Malay culture cannot be understood without knowing that beneath the splendor of its court and the vigor of its commerce was a strong foundation of governmental traditions that must have taken centuries to evolve. Malaysia's civilization does not

begin at Melaka, but instead stretches much deeper into the past.

Before the 7th century the empire of Funan—located in the Menan basin of the Indo-Chinese Peninsula near today's Kampuchea—was the first great power in Southeast Asian history. Smaller states in the Malay Peninsula showed support to this kingdom, but around the 6th century these mainland states, as well as other island states throughout Southeast Asia, liberated themselves and Funan started to decline in power.

Early powers in Southeast Asia

Political power then shifted from the Asian mainland to the islands of the Malay Archipelago. During the Funan supremacy the most popular crossing between the Indian Ocean and South China Sea was an overland route across the narrow isthmus of Kra in today's southern Thailand.

The rise of maritime empires meant sea routes via the Straits of Melaka became more popular and this contributed greatly to the development of ports in Sumatra and Java.

By the mid-7th century, two states emerged in Sumatra—Melayu (situated on the mouth of the Batang Hari) and Srivijaya. Inscriptions dated 686 to 688AD suggest that during this time Srivijaya was gaining power, and soon its influence swept across the straits to the Malay Peninsula.

The exact extent of Srivijaya's imperial

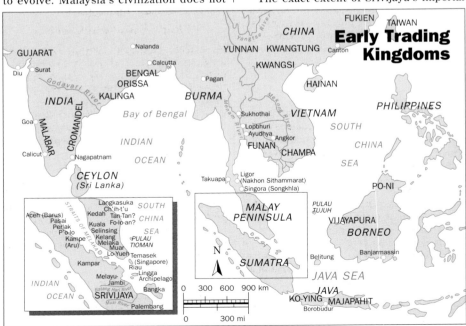

Early Trading Kingdoms

control is still vague and historians are also uncertain as to where it was situated, although it was most probably on the east coast of Sumatra.

The rise of Srivijaya

Srivijaya sent envoys to China bearing gifts, for Chinese friendship was crucial as Srivijaya depended upon the China trade. By 900AD Srivijaya's power in Southeast Asia was unchallenged and small states in Sumatra, the Malay Peninsula and Western Java were subjected to its maritime supremacy. Occasional threats to the empire included the attack on its capital by Dharmavansa, King of Java in the 990s, but these were easily handled by Srivijaya's massive counter attacks.

In its heyday Srivijaya commanded the entire East-West trade, and was so powerful that ships were forced to sail through the Straits of Melaka and call on its ports to pay toll and tribute. As late as the 13th century, Chua Ju-kua, the Chinese Inspector of Foreign Trade, wrote that all foreign ships passing the Straits were forced to pay toll under threat of outright destruction.

So what happened to Srivijaya? There is no single answer, but the erosion of friendly relations with China and India contributed to its fall. India's most powerful maritime power during this time was the Cholas, who were greatly interested in the China and Southeast Asian trade.

It is likely that the expansion of Srivijaya's power in Indonesian waters caused friction between the two maritime powers. The Cholas clearly envied Srivijaya's success and were essentially determined to get a piece of the action.

A crippling naval attack

In 1025AD, the Cholas launched a naval attack on all Srivijaya's major trading stations which certainly weakened the empire and following this many states attempted to free themselves from Srivijaya's control.

During later Sung times and in the Mongol period (1279-1368) the Chinese found that Siam offered better products that were much in demand, and gradually shifted focus away from Srivijaya. According to Marco Polo's reports, China then shifted its interests within Sumatra from Srivijaya to Melayu, which consequently became a more important trading center.

Gradually, the name Srivijaya lost its impact. A new star, the Majapahit empire, rose in Java and together with the Siamese

empire undermined the remaining power of Srivijaya

During this time, there were also other smaller empires on the Malay Pensinula such as Chih Tu, Langkasuka, and Tan Tan. Their exact dates are still unknown, but historians believe that they emerged roughly around the same time as Srivijaya, which overshadowed these smaller trading ports.

Envoys on elephant back

Most of these legendary kingdoms were nevertheless "civilized," with their own forms of government, and ceremonies which included those for welcoming visitors from abroad which showed that they had already made contact with other states. Historical records mention that envoys from China were treated with respect and that the messengers were carried about on elephants.

From the 5th century onwards, there also existed a renowned power called the Government of Old Kedah (Kerajaan Kedah Tua) situated at Lembah Bujang in the north of the peninsula (*see story "Lembah Bujang," p. 106*). Despite challenges from its neighbors, especially Siam, it continued expanding until its zenith during the 14th century.

Above: *Evidence of the Peninsular's pre-Islamic era, this Buddha statue was found at Lembah Bujang in southern Kedah, the site of Old Kedah, a Hindu-Buddhist kingdom.*

Another important regional administrative center and port of the time was Pengkalan Bujang, and merchant ships from India, West Asia and China stopped over at this well-known trading hub until the emergence of Melaka as the regon's major entrepôt.

Malaka: the origins

There are two main versions on the origins of Melaka. The most popular being that found in Sejarah Melayu, the court annals of the Melakan Sultanate. It begins with an impressive genealogy tracing the line of Melaka kings back to Alexander the Great—described as a Muslim king, Raja Iskandar—then follows the fortunes of his dynastic line in India and the Malay world until three of his descendants miraculously appear on Bukit Si Guntang in Palembang, Sumatra.

One of them, Sri Tri Buana, was made ruler and later left Palembang in the hands of his brothers and went in search of new lands. Their fleet first arrived at Bintan in the Riau-Lingga archipelago, and subsequently moved to the island of Temasek where Sri Tri Buana established Singapura or the "Lion City," named after a strange lion-like beast he sighted there. His descendants ruled Singapore for five generations, until the last ruler, Parameswara, was forced to flee to Muar when the Javanese attacked.

The account has it that one day while hunting north of Muar one of Parameswara's hounds was kicked by a white mousedeer. The ruler exclaimed, "This is a good place, where even the mousedeer are full of fight!" Because he was standing under a Melaka tree, he decided that the new settlement should bear that name.

China's powerful protection

In 1403, a Chinese fleet under Admiral Yin Chi'ng, arrived at the settlement on the Melaka River and brought Parameswara presents of silk woven with golden flowers and other valuable gifts, and asked him to pay tribute to their Emperor. Melaka's ruler saw China as a powerful protector against Siam and accordingly sent envoys with tribute to China in 1405.

The Emperor spoke in praise of him, appointed him King of Melaka and sent him a commission, a seal, a suit of silk clothes and a yellow umbrella, which were delivered to Parameswara in 1406. This event was the turning point in Melaka's history. From this point on it started to establish itself as an important trading port for China and traders

began to flock there.

Once Melaka embraced Islam in the early 15th century, the kingdom became transformed. The Sejarah Melayu regards the acceptance of Islam as a watershed in Melaka's history, an event which confirmed the kingdom's superior status.

As Melaka expanded territorially, it persuaded or compelled its vassals in the Straits area to accept Islam, and its growing prestige and commercial success also reinforced the process of Islamization throughout the archipelago. Muslim traders from abroad preferred to stop over at Melaka because of the protection they could expect from fellow Muslims, and the presence of a mosque meant that they could pray without outside interference.

Omnipotent sultans

The life of Melaka's people was centered around the royal court. The sultan had no council of advisors, and was totally free to declare war or peace on anybody, but he did, however, have informal consultations with those he chose. His main source of income came from taxes paid by foreign traders, and he also obtained wealth through conquests and tributes from vassal states.

Melaka was visited by merchants from all over the world who came to trade mainly in spices, silk, and tea. Since Melaka was recognized by China as the "sole distributor" for China's goods in Asia, it attracted an ever-expanding population. Most of them communicated in the Malay language and even today Melaka's Straits-born Chinese still speak a special form of Malay. Melaka's native population consisted of the Orang Laut (Sea People)—who lived on the coast and derived their income from fishing—and the Minangkabau from Sumatra who functioned as middlemen, buying native goods and then reselling them.

Laws and loyalty

The Sejarah Melayu hardly refers to the daily life of the people although there is mention of offences committed. However, the laws of that time provide an insight into the activities of ordinary folk during the 15th century. Basically there were two major laws.

The Hukum Kanun Melaka dealt solely with aspects of the agrarian society, and also recognized the status of slaves who had their own rights and were not to be treated harshly by their masters. The Undang-Undang Laut Melaka related to maritime rights like the power of a ship's captain, and the rights of his crew members.

Despite these laws, rulers enjoyed almost absolute power as the Malay masses generally accorded the ruler total loyalty. This was based on the concepts of *daulat* (sovereignty) and *derhaka* (disobedience). *Daulat* provided the ruler with power and privileges which placed him above society and criticism, and entitled him to undivided loyalty from his subjects. Meanwhile *derhaka* placed fear in the subjects if they were disloyal. If a subject rebelled against a ruler this would be considered *derhaka* and the culprit would be severely punished.

Zenith of the empire

During Sultan Mansur Syah's reign Melaka reached its peak and, according to the *Sejarah Melayu*, envoys were sent to Sumatra, Pahang, Minangkabau, Siak, Siam and Kampar. It also mentions that even though China was a very powerful country, it still had to bow to Melaka's greatness, and that when China's emperor suffered an incurable disease, he was advised by the medicine-man to drink and bathe with water that had been used to wash Sultan Mansur Syah's leg.

Mansur Syah's predecessor, Muzaffar Syah, established Islam as the state religion and defeated Siam in a battle near Muar with the help of his able *bendahara* (similar to a Prime Minister), Tun Perak and the leg-endary warrior Hang Tuah. The former was renowned for his administrative and diplomatic skills, and was regarded as the power behind the throne responsible for the defence and expansion of Melaka.

A sultan goes undercover

A later ruler, Sultan Alauddin Riayat Syah also strengthened Melaka as an empire after Sultan Mansur Syah had laid the foundation. He tightened up security by building more "police stations" and this brave ruler also disguised himself as a thief and went undercover to solve the town's robbery problems.

After the death of Bendahara Tun Perak, his position was taken over by his cousin, Sri Maharaja, a very able man of whom it was said that Melaka would not fall to any power as long as he was alive. However, he was not appreciated by Sultan Mahmud who had him and his family executed.

One account states that Sri Maharaja was better known to the foreign merchants than the Sultan himself. Not long after this incident, the Portuguese attacked Melaka, and the fall of the empire in 1511 marked the beginning of Western domination in the Malay archipelago.

—Zuraina Majid

Below: *British officers meet with a Perak chieftain at his Kuala Kangsar home in this mid-19th century etching.*

COLONIAL HISTORY

The Impact and Aftermath of the West

In August 1511 Melaka, the famed center for archipelago trade, was captured by the Portuguese in an effort to control the sea routes to the spice islands and to spread Christianity. They then proceeded to destroy Melaka's great mosque, drive out Muslim traders, build churches and a formidable new fort, while encouraging missionary activity.

The Portuguese had assumed they would inherit Melaka's former prosperity, but without Muslim patronage it never regained its former prestige. Meanwhile, the heirs of the former dynasty fled to the Riau-Lingga archipelago in the southern Melaka Straits, from where they repeatedly yet unsuccessfully sought to re-capture their previous capital. Despite their hold on the town, the Portuguese had no hope of dominating the Malay peninsula and their influence was largely confined to the area around Melaka.

With Melaka in non-Malay hands, new trading centers emerged along the Melaka Straits. From its capital, alternatively in the Riau-Lingga archipelago and along the Johor River, the former Melaka dynasty attempted to reassert its old hegemony, but it now faced competition from the Portuguese as well as the aggressive new Sumatran state of Aceh. From 1619 the Acehnese made a number of raids on Malay states. Pahang's previously flourishing trade was destroyed and for many years the tin-producing state of Perak was an Acehnese vassal.

At the beginning of the 17th-century, the arrival of the Dutch East India Company (VOC) seemed to offer Malays the hope of new allies against the Portuguese. But although Johor assisted the Dutch to take Melaka from Portugal in January 1641, the town did not return to Malay hands.

Like the Portuguese, the Dutch hoped to conclude monopoly agreements with Malay rulers which would give them exclusive access to lucrative products such as tin. Kedah and Perak's rulers entered into such contracts in expectation of Dutch help against Aceh and Siam, which had ambitions to extend its suzerainty down the peninsula. However, the VOC did not want to become involved in expensive wars, and hopes of assistance soon faded.

At the end of the 17th century Johor was clearly the most powerful Malay state, con-

R. MOH'D NOH SALLEH

trolling Pahang, Terengganu, Selangor and Siak in Sumatra. Aceh's power had fallen, and Perak was again independent. Meanwhile Kedah, Patani, and Kelantan acknowledged Siam's authority while still recognizing that they were part of the Malay world. In 1699, however, Malay respect for Johor as the heir to Melaka was shaken when the ruler was murdered by his nobles. Though the Bendahara (Prime Minister) assumed power, many condemned the regicide as a heinous crime and refused to accept the new order.

Demographic flux

The demise of the prestigious Melaka line coincided with large movements of non-Malays into the region. Minangkabau groups from Sumatra had earlier settled in modern-day Negeri Sembilan, but there had been no conflict with existing Malay polities. Chinese and Indians were present in small numbers, but remained confined to coastal settlements under the authority of Malay rulers. Bugis and Makassarese from Sulawesi, fleeing from prolonged wars in their homeland, proved less easy to absorb.

Malaya's sparsely populated lands were an open invitation to these refugees and by the first decade of the 18th-century numerous communities had appeared, particularly in Selangor. Well known as traders, the Bugis also had a formidable reputation as warriors. When a Minangkabau prince, claiming to be the son of the murdered ruler, seized control of Johor in 1717 it was a group of Bugis who ousted him.

Meanwhile, Terengganu, previously a Johor vassal, became independent, and in 1766 the Bugis of Selangor established a separate state outside Johor's authority. Further afield, the wars between Siam and Burma allowed Patani, Kedah, and Kelantan a new degree of independence.

Singapore and the British

The decline of the Dutch East India Company during the 18th-century was accompanied by the emergence of England as the world's foremost commercial power. Concerned with developing the China trade, the English had already occupied the island of Penang, previously under Kedah, in 1786. In 1819 Stamford Raffles, vehemently opposed to the extension of Dutch authority in the east, made an agreement with Johor permitting the English to establish a trading post on Singapore island. As momentous as the fall of Melaka, this event changed the course of Malay history.

Although the British never set out to colonize the peninsula, once established in Singapore it was regarded as lying within their "sphere of influence."

After this, British involvement in the Malay Peninsula increased. In 1826 Melaka, Penang, Singapore and Province Wellesley (a strip of land along the Kedah coast) were incorporated as the Straits Settlements. Population increased rapidly, especially in Singapore, which became a linchpin of English trade with China. Its prosperity attracted large numbers of Chinese migrants, fleeing from poverty and civil unrest. Soon they began to move into the peninsula, developing agricultural plantations and tin mines.

As Chinese and British economic involvement was increasing, a series of succession disputes broke out among Malay ruling families. Chinese secret societies and, indirectly, British financiers became caught up in these struggles as they backed one or another contender, hoping for favored treatment.

Conflict, intervention and treaties

But such assistance tended to prolong the conflicts, in turn encouraging British merchants in the Straits Settlements to appeal for British political intervention to restore order to trade. This was a persuasive argument because industrializing Britain needed tin which the Malay Peninsula provided.

In 1874, when one contender for the Perak throne asked for British help, the Straits Settlements Governor seized the opportunity to move in. The Perak prince gained British support in the form of the Pangkor Engagement in return for accepting a resident whose advice he was required to accept on all matters "except religion and custom."

By 1888 similar treaties had been signed with Selangor, Negeri Sembilan, and Pahang—and in 1896 they became the Federated Malay States (FMS) with Kuala Lumpur as the capital. Johor, because of its links with Singapore, was also closely tied to British economic interests, although the adroitness of its ruler meant it retained its independence until 1914.

Change came less quickly along the east coast. In Pahang a major rebellion against the British occurred in 1891, led by district chiefs protesting against a lessening of their former privileges. Colonial ambitions meant that

Opposite: This mid-19th century watercolor of Melaka's Town Square with the Stadthuys (to the right) and Christ Church (center)

Siam was under increasing pressure to relinquish its Malay vassals—Patani, Kelantan, and Terengganu—and in 1909 all except Patani were surrendered to the British in return for diplomatic privileges. However, in economic terms the east coast lagged behind the west, attracting less Chinese migrants and remaining more "Malay" in character.

By 1919 "British Malaya" was complete. Fundamental in the formulation of colonial government was the British view that although the Malays were likeable people, they were ill inclined to do the backbreaking work of developing tin mines and rubber estates. This was left to immigrant labor from China and India which doubled Malaya's population during the early 20th century.

In the process the Malays were locked out of the export-oriented sector of the colonial economy, and with the exception of the ruling elite, were denied opportunities for economic advancement. Despite lip service to the notion that Malays were the rightful political heirs, they received little training in government and civil servants were rarely given responsible positions.

Another colonial assumption which had far-reaching implications was that the Chinese and Indians were itinerants, and there was no need to provide a common school system for all. A small number of upper-class Malays, Chinese and Indians did receive an English education, but the majority acquired only basic schooling in the vernacular. Thus the opportunity to bridge differences between ethnic groups among the mass of the population was lost.

Ethnic divisions were further encouraged by the revolutionary movements in China which excited the Chinese community, and a number joined the Malayan Communist Party (MCP), formed in 1930. Indians took similar pride in the developing Indian independence movement, while Malays were caught up by the call for Islamic reform which urged Muslims to modernize education in order to compete with the West. Largely concerned with developing a unified economy and administration, the British gave little thought to the possibility of Malayan independence, and how a new nation would deal with deepening ethnic distinctions.

World War II and independence

Malaya's independence was precipitated by the outbreak of World War II. Japan attacked the peninsula in late 1941, and by February 1942 Malaya and Singapore were in Japanese hands. All British officials were imprisoned, and towards the end of the war there were hints that Japan might grant Malaya independence. Anxious to win local support, the Japanese generally treated Malays and Indians leninetly but because of Japan's conflict with China, the Chinese met systematic discrimination. It was therefore Chinese

groups, dominated by the MCP, which led wartime resistance against the Japanese.

As a result, when the war ended many British thought the Chinese should be rewarded with full citizenship. But it was difficult to erradicate suspicions resulting from years of separate ethnic development. The British government's proposal of a "Malayan Union" which would make Chinese and Indians citizens thus aroused unprecedented opposition among the Malays.

In 1946, a group of leading Malays formed the United Malays National Organization (UMNO). Basic to UMNO's platform was the upholding of "special privileges" which Malays should enjoy as the original occupants of the land, and the status of Malay Sultans. The Malayan Union was revoked in February 1948 and replaced by the Federation of Malaya which united the peninsula under one government. Singapore, heavily Chinese, was excluded because its incorporation would mean Malays would be outnumbered.

The Federation was seen as a victory for the Malays, and many Chinese became sympathetic towards the MCP's aim of establishing a Malayan republic. Mid 1948 marked the beginning of the Malayan Emergency, when the MCP embarked on a systematic campaign of violence directed against European interests. Since the communists were mainly Chinese, they received substantial help from their rural compatriots. From 1950 British

forces gained control by resettling these communities into "New Villages"—thus denying the MCP access to supplies. The Emergency officially ended in 1960.

A prime reason for the ultimate failure of the communist insurrection was a new political alliance between Malay and Chinese leaders and Britain's commitment to Malaya's independence. The formation of the Alliance, consisting of UMNO, the Malayan Chinese party (MCA) and later the Malayan Indian Association (MIA) gave hope for multi-cultural politics. By 1955 the Alliance and its call for independence had overwhelming support. A constitution was developed for the new nation which created a federation of states with a strong central government, retaining certain privileges for Malays. Singapore was again not included because of continuing fears of ethnic imbalance.

On 15 August 1957, under its first Prime Minister Tunku Abdul Rahman, Malaya was declared independent; two years later Singapore became internally self-governing. Both looked towards increasing prosperity, but still faced the problem of replacing ethnic loyalties by a common allegiance to a modern state.

—*Barbara Watson Andaya*

Opposite: *A colonial tin mine boss poses with his coolies at a Perak tin mine in the 1880s.*
Above: *Rubber planters dressed in amateur dramatics costumes, at Seremban in the 1880s.*

MODERN HISTORY

Independence and the Road to Tomorrow

The orderly transition to independence allowed the government under Tengku Abdul Rahman to turn its attention immediately to economic development. The new leadership avoided espousing radical economic and social change; the existing free market economy was maintained, and foreign investments encouraged. At the same time new federal programs were implemented to promote development in poorer rural areas which were largely Malay.

The first five years after independence were marked by impressive gains; schools and clinics were built while basic transport and communications infrastructure expanded across the country. The fight against the communist insurgency was slowly being won, and in 1960 the Emergency was officially ended.

Inter-ethnic cooperation within the Alliance was severely tested by the competing demands and expectations of its constituent communities. In 1959, UMNO and MCA (Malayan Chinese party) disputed over parliamentary seat allocation and education policy. The Alliance system of political accommodation survived when the Tengku stood firm and MCA backed down. In the national elections the Alliance retained power but the opposition made gains.

In early September 1963 Singapore, Sabah, and Sarawak joined Malaya to form Malaysia—twice the land area of Malaya. The multi-racial and multi-cultural character of the country became even more diverse with the inclusion of other distinctive indigenous groups from Sabah and Sarawak.

The formation led to regional tension. The Philippines insisted Sabah was part of the Sulu sultanate, while Indonesia interpreted the move as a new colonial manoeuver. Relations were severed on September 17th 1963 and Indonesia under Sukarno launched a campaign of confrontation (*Konfrontasi*) against Malaysia. The conflict came dangerously close to war as Indonesia infiltrated commandos into Malaysia.

Within Malaysia, differences between the Kuala Lumpur and Singapore leaders surfaced. The PAP (People's Action Party) under Lee Kuan Yew insisted on a more equalitarian policy, but the Alliance maintained that preferential provisions in government policies were necessary for the disadvantaged Malay

ARKIB NEGARA

community to progress.

The dispute worsened when the PAP contested the 1964 pariamentary elections. Two racial riots in Singapore in early 1965 convinced the Tengku that the island state had to leave the federation to avoid dangerous inter-ethnic conflicts. Singapore separated from Malaysia in August 1965 to become an independent republic. Two months later, a failed coup d'etat in Indonesia led to the phasing out of Sukarno and the confrontation against Malaysia came to an end.

Restructuring society

Within Malaysia, the debate on communally-related issues intensified as the 1969 parliamentary elections approached. The Alliance was returned but lost parliamentary seats and control of two states. Racial violence broke out a few days later resulting in heavy casualties. Parliament was suspended and the country was placed under emergency rule. The National Operations Council with Tun Abdul Razak as director virtually ruled the country between May 1969 and February 1971.

Parliament was reconvened in 1971 and Tun Abdul Razak became the new Prime Minister. Under him two important changes took place. Firstly, consensus politics within the ruling coalition, now renamed Barison Nasional, was broadened to include parties from Sabah and Sarawak as well as three others which previously were in the opposition. Secondly, a 20-year New Economic Policy was introduced aimed at eradicating poverty and restructuring society to eliminate identification of race with economic functions.

The government set targets using strategies of positive discrimination to increase Malay participation in the corporate sector, employment, and higher education. A national educational policy with Malay as the main language of instruction was begun at all levels of education. The implementation of NEP witnessed a significant social transformation as a rural to urban population shift took place.

A vision of the future

Dato Hussein Onn succeeded as Prime Minister when Tun Abdul Razak died in 1976 and the new Prime Minister maintained existing policies and direction. Increased revenue from oil ensured continued high economic growth. The ruling coalition retained commanding majorities in elections and coped effectively with emerging social and political problems such as state rights, religious extremism, student and peasant agitations, and intra-party factionalism.

In 1981, Dato Sri Dr. Mahathir Mohammed became Malaysia's fourth Prime Minister. Non-aristocratic in background and once sacked from the party for harshly criticising the Tengku, Mahathir set agendas to take the nation to new economic and political status. His style was regarded as authoritarian by critics as he sought to enhance the power and influence of the political executive and to define more strictly those of the traditional rulers, the judiciary, the unions, and various non-governmental organizations. In 1987 he narrowly survived a bitterly-contested challenge to his leadership of UMNO.

The winning of the 1990 general elections has greatly strengthened Mahathir's political position. Impressive economic performance and foreign investments have lent weight to Malaysia's projection of achieving developed country status by the year 2020. Vision 2020 has became a goal and a symbol as the country shifts slowly but perceptibly from narrow communal concerns and rhetorics of the past to seek a broader international role.

—Lee Kam Hing

Opposite: *Tunku Abdul Rahman (far left), the King and his consort escort the outgoing British Governor at independence.* **Below:** *The playing fields in Kuala Lumpur; the official venue for national celebrations, since independence was proclaimed here in 1957.*

ALAIN EVRARD

PEOPLES

Asia's Cultural Crossroads

At the center of the maritime trade routes between India, the Middle East and China, the Malay Peninsula has always been a cultural crossroads. In Melaka's heyday, the cosmopolitan port attracted an extraordinary diversity of merchants: chronicles of those times record that over sixty different languages were spoken in the streets. The current richness of Malaysia's cultural traditions has been influenced over the centuries by a combination of trade, religion, education, and colonialism.

The present population stands at some 22 million. The Malays and other native/indigenous groups form the majority at 59%, the Chinese number 32%, the Indians 8%, and the remainder is made up of Eurasians and Europeans.

Who are the Malays? The Federal constitution defines the Malays as *bumiputra*, or "sons of the soil," who speak Malay, profess Islam as their religion and adopt the Malay culture as their way of life. The bond with Islam is an integral part of the Malay personality; all Malays are Muslim and it is forbidden by law to convert them to other religions.

Although Muslim, the Malays retain certain animistic and Hindu beliefs. Some Malays believe in spirits and ghosts, make sacrificial offerings to appease the spirits, and use amulets for protection against evil deeds. Some Hindu marriage and birth rituals have also been assimilated into the Malay way of life and are now part and parcel of their cultural traditions.

Hindu heritage at the royal court

The Malay court and its regalia, which uses yellow as the royal color, are also remnants of their former Hindu heritage, as are some of the rituals performed during the installation of a sultan. Furthermore, the *pawang* or *dukun*, traditional magicians, are still popular even though Malay society is rapidly assimilating modern values and is exposed to an increasing amount of scientific knowledge. The Perak court retains a royal *pawang* who is said to possess the spiritual powers that safeguard the royal lineage and the throne.

Of the ancient Malay states which survive today, Kedah, Perak, Selangor, Johor, Pahang, Terengganu, Kelantan, Perlis and Negeri Sembilan still maintain the position and status

of a sultan or raja. The constitution also provides for the appointment of a paramount ruler or King. Every five years, depending on their tenure on the thrones of their respective states, one of the nine Malay rulers is instated as the Yang di-Pertuan Agung.

Though the position of the Malay rulers and King is merely ceremonial according to the Federal Constitution, they are still looked upon as the custodians and protectors of Malay culture, customs and Islam in their respective states.

The new dynamic renaissance in Islam has, to a certain extent, transformed the thinking of most Malays to be more "Islamic," but not fanatical. The current multi-racial fabric of Malaysian society with its divergent traditions and different religious roots have more or less checked extremism from various racial quarters.

Assimilated influences

In a context of modern development the Malays still cherish their great cultural attachments to Islam as a way of life (*addin*), their language (Bahasa Melayu or Malay), their culture and their sultan. These are important attributes in the make-up of the Malay personality which are often incomprehensible to others.

Culturally speaking, the Malays have assimilated traits from Hinduism, Islam and to a certain extent from the West, but they have also inherited the influences of the Minangkabau from West Sumatra (especially the people of Negeri Sembilan), the Javanese, the Achinese, the Bugis, and in Kelantan, Perlis and Kedah, the Thai influence is obvious in traditional dances and the *wayang kulit* (shadow-puppet play).

Islam nevertheless remains the dominant feature in the lives of most Malays. Education and practice have formed a strong foundation in establishing an Islamic heritage that governs their lives. Traders and missionaries brought Arabic script, the language of the Koran, to the shores of the Malay world. This in turn gave rise to the Jawi script which is used by Malays to this day, in addition to the more recent use of roman script.

Language and privileges

Bahasa Malayu is the official language of Malaysia but English is widely spoken and an important second language. Although Bahasa Malayu has been spoken throughout the Malay world for centuries, it unfortunately became less significant as a medium of instruction during the British colonial period,

Opposite: A school excursion to Kuala Kedah's historical fort is a happy occasion for these schoolgirls from Kedah state. *Below:* Although these Indian women are Malaysians by birth they still wear the saree, follow the Hindu religion and preserve many cultural traditions.

when the school system emphasized English as the vehicle of instruction and government. However, after Merdeka (independence), Malay replaced English as the official language, and today it is an important tool for retaining national unity.

Together with the indigenous peoples of Sarawak and Sabah, and the Orang Asli, the Malays are classed as *bumiputra*, who share special privileges laid down in the Federal constitution. These privileges were formulated to assist the *bumiputra* to compete with the other more advanced races—in particular the Chinese—in the fields of economy and education.

Legacy of colonial division

The relative backwardness of the Malays and other indigenous peoples was mainly due to the British colonial policy of "divide and rule" when the Malays were entrenched as poor peasants, fishermen and minor civil servants; the Chinese dominated the business world, and the Indians were mainly laborers in rubber estates, roadworks and railways.

However, the New Economic Policy adopted by the Malaysian government after the race riots of May 13th, 1969, greatly helped the *bumiputras*. Today the Malays are moving into the formerly Chinese bastions, and now play an important role in sectors such as banking, commerce, industry, education, science and technology.

The ancestors of the second largest group of peninsular peoples—the Chinese—mainly arrived as immigrants from southern China in search of greener pastures from the late 19th century onwards. Many started as laborers, small shopkeepers and merchants in Penang, Melaka, Taiping, Kuala Lumpur, and other tin mining towns. The influx of Chinese into the country introduced new cultural traits alien to the Malays. Chinese temples and rituals, dragon and lion dances and other festivals became part of the Malaysian cultural scene.

The concentration of Chinese in certain urban areas led to the formation of Chinatowns which can still be seen in practically every large town on the peninsula, including Malay-dominated states such as Alor Setar in Kedah, Kota Bharu in Kelantan, and Kuala Terengganu in Terengganu. These urban centers still reflect the cultural heritage of the country of their forebears.

Straits Chinese

There is little cultural assimilation of Malay culture into the mainstream of Malaysian Chinese heritage, with the exception of the Baba and Nonya (*see Babas and Nonyas, p. 168*) culture of Melaka, Penang and Singapore. These people, also known as the Straits Chinese or the *peranakan*, which means "born here" in Malay, speak a distinct Malay dialect among themselves and have no knowledge of Chinese languages.

In dress as well as in diet they have adopted the culture of the Malays. Most still follow Chinese religions however, and some are Christians. According to the *Sejarah Melayu*, "The Malay Annals," Sultan Mansur Shah, the Sultan of Melaka in the 15th century, married a Chinese princess, Hang Li Po. The princess and her entourage of 500 handmaidens sailed to Melaka, and their descendants are the present-day Babas and Nonyas.

Roots of Malaysia's Indians

The third-largest racial group, the Indians, were brought into Malaya, mostly from southern India, as contract laborers on the European rubber estates, railways and telecommunications works in the 19th century. Others established themselves as small traders and merchants, setting up business ventures in Penang, Singapore and other peninsula towns.

Since most of these traders were Muslim they found it relatively easy to assimilate into the Malay community through marriage as well as other religious activities. The descendants of these mixed marriages known as the *mamak* can be found mostly in Penang and Singapore. One of the most famous families of these mixed marriages is the Merican family of Penang whose descendants are spread all over Malaysia and Singapore. Even the Prime Minister, Datuk Seri Dr Mahathir Muhammad is of mixed blood, with an Indian Muslim father and a Malay mother.

The majority of the Indians, who are mostly Hindus, brought with them all the religious and cultural traits of Hinduism including the caste system. Although they make up only 8% of the population, their festival of Deepavali is a national holiday, and some states also have a public holiday on Thaipusam, when tranced penitents pierce their bodies with iron hooks and undergo a pilgrimage to their holy temples.

The celebrations symbolize the victory of good over evil and candles decorate every Hindu home during this festival. Like the Malays who celebrate their Hari Raya with open houses for visitors, the Hindus do the same for Deepavali.

"The Original People"

Besides the three major races there are also the Orang Asli, or the peninsular aboriginal peoples, known as the Senoi, Jakun, Negritos and other splinter groups which live mainly in the mountainous interior (*see story Orang Asli, p. 152*). Most of the Orang Asli settlers are agriculturists, while others work in the jungle collecting rattan and other forest products. A number of them work with the Aboriginal Department while others find employment as soldiers of the Senoi Praak, the nation's best jungle trackers. Others in Cameron Highlands work as laborers in the tea plantations and vegetable gardens.

Cultural values retained

Some of the Orang Asli have converted to Islam, while others have become Christians, but many remain animists. They still maintain the *tok batin* as the leader of their tribe, and traditional medicine men also play an important role. Many continue use the blowpipe and are skilled hunters, while others are creative craftsmen producing fine wood carvings (*see Mah Meri p. 69)*.

Although those who live near Malay villages have adopted much of the Malay way of life and their children are educated in Bahasa Melayu, they nevertheless continue to cherish their own culture.

—*Yahaya Ismail*

Opposite: *Schoolgirls of various ethnic parentage join together to celebrate their nation's Independence Day.*
Below: *These three schoolboys are part of the Peninsular's growing youth population.*

ALAIN EVRARD

RELIGION

The World's Great Faiths in Unison

Walk down any street in Peninsular Malaysia, or drive through the countryside and it is apparent that religion is very much part of everyday life.

From the tiny village *surau* to the tiled halls of the National Mosque, the amplified voice of the muezzin calls Muslims to prayer five times a day. Every morning, candles and joss-sticks are lit at the altars outside thousands of Chinese shops, flowers and fruit are presented at ancestral shrines, and the tinkling of bells signifies that the *puja* is about to begin at the neighborhood Indian temple.

Devotional diversity

Although Islam is the national faith, freedom to worship according to the religion of your choice is preserved in the constitution. The devotional make-up of Malaysia is as diverse as its population and all the world's great

religions are represented throughout the peninsula.

An old saying has it that "tradition comes down from the mountains, but religion comes from the sea," and this in part explains why Malaysia's apparently devout Muslims still cling to traditions that are obvious remnants of pantheist, or pre-Islamic, times.

The spirit world

In the beginning, spirits were everywhere. They inhabited rocks, trees, mountains, seas, rivers and lakes and had to be appeased for they were in control of all the natural forces. In agricultural societies it was a disaster if the rains failed to come, and traditional medicine men, known as *bomoh*, are still called upon to invoke the rains in remote villages during droughts. Their spells are preceded with Koranic verses, but their chants are still addressed to the nature spirits.

Some aboriginal Negrito and Orang Asli tribes have embraced Islam, yet many still practice the earth religion of their ancestors. The Negrito, for instance, believe it is dangerous to laugh at butterflies as these are often spirits of the dead. Even the Malays have a code of conduct for entering the jungle, or putting to sea, which ensures that the spirits are appeased.

Animist religions, however, only survived deep inland for when other religions came to the region it was "from the sea." Hinduism

arrived first, brought by Indian traders at least a millennium ago, and spread rapidly throughout the coastal ports which the merchants frequented.

Influences from abroad

India was then at its cultural zenith, and Malay sailors who had ventured across the Bay of Bengal brought back wondrous tales. Sanskrit texts in the Malay language show that astronomy, textile dyeing, the potter's wheel, monumental architecture, glass, and wet-rice agriculture all came to Malaysia from India. But most influential of all was Hindu philosophy and the concept of a god-like ruler possessing absolute power. Remnants of this era are still seen in the royal courts, in wedding ceremonies and shadow-puppet plays.

Buddhism was the second of the world's great religions to arrive on Malaysian shores. Although little lasting influence remains, tangible evidence survives in the 10th-century temple mounts at Kedah's Bujang Valley where the inhabitants' curious religion was a mixture of Shiva and Vishnu cults combined with Mahayana Buddhism, similar to other communities in Sumatra and Sarawak.

Islam moved across the Melaka Straits from Sumatra to the Malay Peninsula and was by far the most successful of the new faiths. In 1411, Parameswara, Melaka's ruler, embraced the faith, and the Malay population quickly followed suit, although historical evidence records that Islam was already established in Terengganu during the 14th century, predating the Melakan conversion. The faith of Mohammad didn't reach Southeast Asia on the blade of a sword, but was a peaceful conversion initiated by wealthy Arab and Indian traders. Psychologically it had great attractions; its revolutionary concepts freed men from the Hindu feudal bondage.

The celebrated Arab traveler Ibn Battuta visited Sumatra in 1323 and wrote of its rich trading kingdoms. He noted that the Muslim ruler was a "humble-hearted man who walks on foot to the Friday prayer."

Islam—the national religion

Six hundred years later the Malays are still fervent about their faith, and to be Malay is synonomous with being a Muslim. So intertwined are the two that when a person of another race converts to Islam they are said to have *masuk Melayu*, or "become Malay" which is synonymous with *masuk Islam*, "become a Muslim."

From the dawn call of the muezzin to the sonorous Allah hu-Akbar, "God is Great," of the evening prayer, Islam pervades all of

Opposite: *Dressed in sarongs and songkok hats, Malay men relax after Friday prayers outside a Malaka mosque.*
Below: *Smoke from joss-sticks fills the air at this temple in Georgetown, Penang.*

JEAN-LEO DUGAST

Malay life. At birth, the *kalimah shahadah,* the first principle of Islam—"There is no god but Allah and Mohammad is the messenger of Allah"—is whispered in the baby's ear. The other four principles, namely, to pray five times a day, to fast during the month of Ramadan, to pay the *zakat*—a charitable tax for the poor—and to make the pilgrimage to Mecca, are the pillars of the faith and form the basis of most Malays' lives.

Although Malaysia has its fundamentalists, Islam here is tempered with tradition. A BMW-driving executive still goes to the village healer for those ailments that the doctor can't cure. And before docking his boat at a popular holiday island, the Malay boatman mouths a silent prayer, asking permission from the island spirits to enter their domain.

A multitude of deities

It is a tribute to the racial tolerance of Malaysian peoples that such differing religions can survive side by side, for the Chinese and Indian faiths embody everything that is condemned by Islam. They worship more than one god and a multitude of idols, and eat pork which is forbidden to Muslims but there are few incidents sparked by religious difference.

Small Chinese and Indian communities have existed in the Malay Peninsula for centuries, notably in Melaka where some 300-year-old temples still survive, but the majority arrived during the British colonial period as plantation workers and traders.

Malaysian Chinese can be Taoists, Buddhists, Confucianists, or usually a mixture of all of these. Their festivals are among the most exciting events of the calendar. Spirits must be propitiated in order to bring good luck. Elaborate offerings are burnt at the Hungry Ghost Festival to ensure the ghosts are appeased.

Superstition and symbolism pervade all aspects of life. At the Lunar New Year, red—signifying prosperity—is lavishly splashed everywhere. Banners inscribed with good luck slogans are draped across houses, hotels and shopfronts. Lengthy noodles are eaten to ensure long life, and spectacular lion dances are staged to expel evil spirits.

Hinduism is the principal religion of Malaysia's Indians who form 8% of the population. Many were originally from Tamil Nadu in southern India, and this is reflected in their temples with magnificent towering archways, known as *gopuram*, which are lavishly decorated with human and animal deities.

A major Malaysian Hindu festival is Thaipusam, a celebration related to penance and atonement. Held in honor of Lord Muruga, whose traditional abode is in hills, penitents fast and pray, before taking part in processions to hill temples. While walking, they chant and/or carry an object, such as a milk jug or the famous massive *kavadis*, ornate frames supported by metal spikes inserted in the bearer's body. Some penitents are in a trance, and say they do not feel pain.

There are famous processions in Singapore and Penang, but the most spectacular attracting crowds of 800,000, is at Kuala Lumpur's Batu Caves where penitents climb 272 steps up a limestone cliff-face to a shrine inside a vast cavern.

Conquistadores and the cross

Christianity, the last major religion to reach the peninsula, arrived with the Portuguese when they conquered Melaka in 1511. They only held power for little over a century but the enclaves of Catholicism they left behind are still firmly entrenched. At Easter and Christmas time when the Portuguese Eurasians of Melaka open their homes for feasting and celebrations, their traditions, food, dances, and even their language form archaic remnants of their Portuguese past.

R. MOH'D NOH SALLEH

Left: *Seated on a decorated dais, in front of an "eternal flame" this Hindu couple are blessed by a priest on their wedding day.*

BOMOH

Magic and Traditional Healing

Being a Malay, a devout Muslim and a *bomoh*, Haji Osman believes that for every illness there must be an agent responsible for it, and that for all these sicknesses there must be a cure. Consequently, it is necessary to continuously seek ways and means to free oneself from the illness, a process known as *ikhtiar*.

In common with other *bomoh*—which loosely translates as a medicine-man cum magician—Haji Osman believes that everything derives from God, but that human beings are nevertheless responsible for the illnesses that befall them. People can become sick through irresponsible behavior, for example, which can be avoided by behaving properly. However, supernatural forces such as evil spirits—locally known as *hantu* or *penunggu*—can possess an individual whose soul is weak. Illness can also be caused by sorcery, which used to be rampant, but rare today.

A *bomoh* uses various healing techniques, the most popular being his ability to heal fractured bones. Many Malaysians believe that modern medicine is no match for treating fractures, and even those who have undergone western medical treatment often seek further help from a traditional healer. *Bomohs* are also well versed in the art of curing with herbal medicines.

Only a Malay who has received the calling can become a real *bomoh*, and he usually learns his art by serving as an apprentice to a well-known master. An individual can also become a *bomoh* through inheritance, and often the master will choose one of his siblings to learn his art. The chosen one can be any of his children, but to be eligible an individual must have certain physical and mental characteristics.

One specific requirement is the ability to remember and recite long incantations. This is extremely important because in every form of healing there are various mantras that need to be recited. Even medicine has its own incantations so as to ensure its effectiveness.

If a *bomoh* forgets his words this would ruin the healing process.

Incantations can be magical words or verses chosen from the Koran. However, most mantras begin with the name of God and end with the mention of the holy prophet Mohammad. This is to ensure that what is being done is always accomplished with the help of God.

Some *bomoh* treat a wide range of ailments, others specialize in healing certain illnesses, and some, like the *pawang* don't even involve themselves in healing. The *pawang hujan*, performs rituals to prevent rain, and the *pawang buaya* is called upon to catch crocodiles. Besides these, there is also the *bidan*—a female *bomoh* whose speciality is childbirth.

Although many *bomoh* are still active they are a dying breed. The aging specialist is often unwilling to hand over his secrets because he believes that today's youth lack the strong self-discipline that is needed to strictly observe the many taboos and prohibitions. Without this inner strength they may endanger their lives if they attempt to practice the *bomoh's* esoteric knowledge.

—Hashim bin Awang A.R.

Below: *Surrounded by ritual paraphenalia and an absorbed, usually predominantly male audience, streetside medicine-men are a common sight in the Peninsula's major towns.*

JEAN-LEO DUGAST

ADAT

Ancient Ways Passed Down Generations

To orthodox Malays it is important that the practice of *adat*, or traditional custom, is upheld at all times, for this is an essential part of life, a sentiment reflected in the old proverb, "*biar mati anak, jangan mati adat*," which translates literally as "lose a child rather than lose a custom."

The practice of traditional custom begins from before birth and culminates with death, and even though *adat* varies from state to state, and even from village to village, the following examples are basic customs which, with slight variations, occur across the peninsula.

Childbirth and circumcision

In most villages and rural areas, the seventh month of pregnancy is when the rocking of the abdomen, *lenggang perut,* is carried out. Certain materials are gathered and prepared, including seven different colored sarongs,

one *gantang* (about three kilos) of rice, a ripe unhusked coconut, cotton yarn, resinous *damar*, seven white candles, a betel-nut box, and lastly some massage oil. When these are ready the midwife invites the mother-to-be to lie down on a mattress over which the colored sarongs have been arranged.

After gently massaging her with the oil, the midwife takes the peeled coconut and rolls it seven times across the abdomen. On the last roll she allows it to fall to the floor. If it stops with the "eye" facing upwards it is believed the child will be a boy. To conclude the ceremony, the midwife grasps both ends of all the seven sarongs to form a cradle, and then rocks the woman a couple of times before pulling the sarongs out.

Hours before the child is born, the husband cuts a bunch of thorny *pandanus* leaves and hangs them beneath the house to trap any evil spirits that might harm the mother and her newborn baby.

Immediately after the seventh day, a feast is held during which time it is also customary to shave the baby's head, and give the child a name. The newborn is passed around to the guests who bless it with scented water before the head is shaved. The hair is then put into a young coconut filled with water and buried alongside a coconut seedling planted near the house, to serve as a reminder of the birth.

Another important *adat* which is still observed, is the *bertindek telinga*, or piercing

of a girl's ear lobes—when she is between five and 10 years old—and the *bersunat*, the boy's circumcision, when he is between eight and 12. On the auspicious day the boy is dressed in fine clothes, and carried around the village on a special dais. Before the ceremony begins, a few things are prepared for the arrival of the *mudin* who will perform the operation. These include about three yards of white cloth, one live rooster, a bowl of water, a banana stem, and a betel-nut box.

Once the boy has been prepared by the *mudin* and certain incantations or spells have been read, he is washed and then seated on the banana stem. After the lightning-quick operation, the *mudin* takes the live rooster, holds it above the boy and notes its response by looking at its feathers.

From this ritual, the *mudin* is supposed to be able to judge the boy's sexual prowess in the future. Thereafter, for the following three mornings, the *mudin* will dress the boy's wound until he is satisfied that he has recovered. Today, many parents take their sons to a clinic where the circumcision is performed by a doctor.

The wedding

By far the most popular *adat* is the marriage ceremony and customs. Although traditions differ from state to state, there are certain basic practices which most Malays adhere to, regardless of whether they come from rural or urban society. Parents go to great lengths to spend time and money on making the occasion a memorable one, and to ensure that the marriage ceremony and all the *adat* involved meets the expectations of their community.

The basic rules and customs of a marriage can be divided into three stages. Firstly, the parents will deputize a close relative as their representative to select a suitable partner for their son. When a bride has been chosen the engagement or betrothal takes place, when the go-between approaches the girl's parents for their consent.

Once the decision has been made, a ring and other gifts are sent to the bride, followed by a ceremonial feast. In a case of breach of promise by the man the gifts are all forfeited, but if the bride changes her mind then she has to return twice the number of gifts or double their value. This *adat* has been followed for generations, although many Malays these days pick their own partners.

Apart from agreeing on the dowry and wedding expenses, other items exchanged on the wedding day have to be agreed upon by

both parties. These include a ring, a complete bridal attire, good quality cloth (usually pure silk), a complete betel-nut set, cakes and fruits, and others. These are carried at the head of the procession accompanying the ceremonially-dressed bridegroom, to the bride's house, where the marriage is solemnised.

Before the *bersanding*, there are other minor rituals like hair-trimming and teeth-filing, as well as staining of the fingers with henna. After this comes the finale where the bride and groom are seated on a specially decorated *pelamin*, or dais.

Family elders and friends bless the couple by ceremonially feeding them yellow rice, and sprinkling them with *tepung tawar* (rice flour mixed with water), sliced petals and scented water. Having done this the guest is presented with a decorated egg symbolizing sincerity, purity and fertility.

There are numerous other customs, including traditional funeral *adat* which is still followed by all Malays; customs which relate to occupations, for example fishermen; and a wealth of traditions and customs observed by the royal families.

—*Mohd. Kassim Haji Ali*

Opposite: At a Melakan Malay wedding feast, guests given red-dyed eggs—a symbol of fertility. **Above:** The bride and groom perform the bersanding, a traditional "sitting in state" which derives from pre-Islamic times.

LITERATURE

Adventures, Epics and a New Identity

It was just after dark. The village folk started to gather around a thatched hut—a theatre stage of sorts. Flame flickered from bamboo torches, illuminating the stage, and the audience settled themselves on mats or on the ground while the storyteller began tuning his instrument.

For this particular tale, the *rebab*—a three-stringed upright fiddle—provided the accompaniment for the main characters who journey across rivers, hills and jungle, through romance, battles and intrigues, to at last arrive at their rightful kingdoms with stunning brides or miraculous magical potions.

Such was the mood and climate of traditional folklore—the root of the Malay literary tradition. In a society of limited literacy, storytelling was the norm. People with exceptional memory, wit, and the ability to render tales with intonation and rhythm, interspursed by poetry and punchlines, could make a decent living and acquire renown.

Fairy tales, fables and comedy

The vast repertoire of these local geniuses, included fairy-tales, adaptations of Hindu epics, local humor and fables. Malay fairy tales, known as *penglipur lara,* usually center around the journey of a prince in quest of love, truth, justice or miracles. The prince often leaves the comfort of his palace to suffer through difficult terrain, battling ogres, *jinns,* multiple-headed beasts and supernatural villains.

A favorite version involves a prince unaware, or robbed of his royal status. After almost unending ordeals he is rewarded with his bride, his rightful heritage, or the once elusive throne. The names of these popular fairy tales are always preceded by the word *hikayat,* meaning tale or romance, for example Hikayat Malim Deman, "The Tale of Deman the Navigator."

As Peninsular Malaysia was originally an animistic society influenced to some degree by Hindiusm, before the advent of Islamization in the 15th century, adaptations of the Hindu epics *Ramayana* and *Mahabhrata,* including the *Hikayat Seri Rama,* became part of traditional Malay literature.

In humorous tales-—another traditional genre—we meet idiotic simpletons such as Pak Pandir, and Mat Jenin. These characters

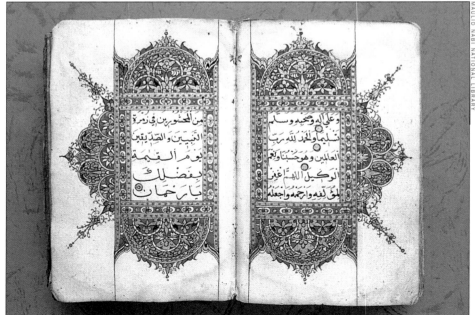

are commoners with simple minds and their endless misfortunes never ceased to provide amusement. Characters such as Si Luncai and Pak Belalang are also commoners, but they were smart and scheming, outwitting even kings.

Malay literature also features animal characters. Apart from local adaptions of Aesop's fables, the Malays have their distinctive beast epic in the Hikayat Sang Kancil. Sang Kancil is a dimunitive mousedeer, commonly known among the Malays as *pelanduk*. The antics of Sang Kancil include outwitting bigger beasts such as crocodiles and even humans. These fables, animal epics and humorous stories served to educate as well as entertain their peasant audiences.

An Islamic heritage

The coming of Islam brought two of the biggest treasures to Malay literary tradition: the rich collections of folk tales from Arabia and Persia, and the Arabic script, which was adopted and adapted to the Malay language. The effect of the latter phenomenon was the enrichment and enhancement of the Malay language itself. Arabic and Persian words were progressively Malayanized and remain part of the language today.

As the sultans were the first to embrace Islam their palaces (*istana*) became centers for Islamic knowledge and writings. Ministers and noblemen became literate and several writers of exceptional perception emerged. Written works on royal geneology, history and law evolved from this tradition.

Almost all the Malay kingdoms had a *hikayat* that depicted the history and tradition of their kings, and the code of law that governed the affairs of state. The most well-known is *Sejarah Melayu*, the so-called Malay Annals, which chronicles the Melakan Sultanate; others include the *Tuhfat al-Nafis* (for Riau), *Hikayat Merong Mahawangsa* (for Kedah), and *Misa Melayu* (for Perak).

European literary genres

As early as the 1500s, the Malay Archipelago came into contact with the formidable European powers of Portugal, Holland and England. The fall of Malaka in 1511 to the Portuguese marked a slow and steady change among the Malay people. When the Dutch and English demarcated their sphere of influence on the Malay world in the mid 1800s, the Malay Peninsula happened to be for the English, who proceeded to gain political and economic control over the Malays.

The social system changed and eventually English became the dominant language. One indirect effect of this was the introduction of western literary genres—novels, short stories and poetry. The British also established a formal education system, published newspapers, and encouraged the use of Roman alphabets in written Malay. Consequently the Malay language is among the few languages in the world that can be written in two different scripts—Arabic and Roman.

The pre-war period

The beginning of the 20th century, saw the emergence of Malay novels, starting with *Hikayat Faridah Hanum*, and followed by *Kawan Benar* and others. Also dubbed as Pre-War novels, these books were didactic and very moralistic. The writing style was very much influenced by traditional genres, thus the word "hikayat" was still appended to earlier titles. Women's emancipation and freedom to choose one's life partner were the mainstay of pre-war literary themes, be it in novels or short stories.

The turn of the century also marked the transition and change in form, style and purpose of Malay literature. Writing became the mouthpiece for the observant to voice their concerns over social ills and injustice.

Post independence to present day

Then came World War II and the Japanese occupation. The emergence of this Asian power gave impetus to the craving for independence, and via the circulation of newspapers, the written word became the vehicle of social reorientation. Short stories, poetry and novels gave a new sense of direction, identity and self-esteem to the Malays. Historians agree that the press and literature played a crucial part in bringing about awareness among the Malays.

Even after independence, Malay writers had to battle for supremacy and recognition due to the overwhelming influence of English in Malaysian social and commercial life. However, due to the implementation of the National Education Policy and the National Language Policy by the government, plus the enthusiasm of local writers and publishing houses, Malay literature is currently undergoing a popular revival.

—*Said Halim*

Opposite: This hand-written Maulud Nabi, a book of songs in praise of Prophet Muhammad, on display at Kuala Lumpur's National Library.

MUSIC & DANCE

Percussion, Puppets and Trance Dance

Malaysian music and dance is remarkably diverse due to the cosmopolitan nature of the population. Typical genres range from traditional Malay folk-dance dramas like *Mak Yong* to the *ngajat* dances from Malaysian Borneo. Choreogaphed movements also vary from simple steps and tunes in Dikir Barat to the complicated moves in Joget Gamelan.

Traditional Malaysian music is basically percussive. Gongs of various kinds provide the beat for many dances, and entire gong ensembles from the huge *kenong* to the small *bonang* are used in *gamelan* orchestras to accompany the graceful dance of Joget Gamelan. Besides gongs, there are drums of various sizes, from the large *rebana ubi* used to punctuate important events to the small *jingled-rebana* (frame drums) used as an accompaniment to vocal recitations in religious ceremonies.

The peninsular aborigines, known as Orang Asli (*see Orang Asli p.152*), have a great variety of tribal or ethnic music. Similar to other tribal groups in Southeast Asia, they use materials from their surroundings to create musical instruments like gourd and cane mouth organs, mouth and nose-blown flutes, wooden xylophones, and bamboo stamping tubes. They also use the knobbed gong characteristic throughout Southeast Asia.

Malaysian traditional music is functional and music-making is an inherent part of religious rituals, court ceremonies, and life-cycle celebrations. The solemn *nobat* court music serves the function of upholding the sovereignty of Malaysian kings and legitimizing their power or *daulat*.

Nobat originated from the Middle East and became part of the royal regalia when Islam was first introduced into the Malay Peninsula in the 13th century. Gracing the courts of Kedah, Perak, Selangor and Terengganu, *nobat* is only performed at ceremonies such as the ruler's installation, weddings or funerals. Its orchestra includes the *nehara* (kettledrum), *gendang* (double-headed drums), *nafiri* (silver trumpet), and an oboe. These instruments are considered sacred by Malaysian society and are highly revered.

Hinduism and Islam have also influenced dance and music in Malaysia. Stories from the Hindu epics, Ramayana and Mahabharata, form the main repertoire for several

dian, guitar and maracas. Like Nobat, Ghazal came from the Middle East and became an instant hit with the locals especially so because of its Arabic/Persian melody and the romantic lyrics. Today, it is performed at weddings, fun fairs, festivals, royal birthdays and other functions.

Malaysia is also renowned for its traditional dance. The repertoire is endless and includes many graceful dances including Joget Gamelan and Asyik which both originated from the court tradition and became popular

types of shadow–puppet plays—*wayang kulit.* The most popular being the Wayang Siam, performed in Kelantan on the East Coast. The epic Ramayana is about the adventures of Prince Rama, his beautiful wife, Siti Dewi, and the villainous rival, Maharaja Rawana, the ogre king. Nowadays these classical stories are seldom performed as puppeteers tend to prefer the diversions, or *ranting* (branches) of stories in which the principal characters encounter different hazards and enemies.

Accompanied by an ensemble of musicians who play three kinds of drums, a pair of small knobbed gongs, a pair of hanging gongs, a pair of small hand cymbals and *serunai* or reed oboe, the puppeteer, or *dalang,* stirs up great excitement and enthusiasm during his performances. The *dalang* is the sole pupeteer and his skills are enormous. His expertise includes the adept handling of all puppets, voice imitations for 40 to 50 different characters, cuing his musicians; singing and comedy; and creating the right sound effects for all scenes.

Music of the shamans

Besides accompaning puppet theaters and dance dramas such as *mak yong,* traditional music is also used in spiritualism. A shaman without music and sound is one without power. On the East Coast, Main Puteri is a popular trance-dance accompanied by a mak-yong ensemble which consists of a *rebab* (fiddle), two *gendang* (double-headed drums), and a pair of gongs known as *tetawak.* The chief performer, Tok Puteri, entranced by the music of the *rebab,* communicates with the spirits. Aided by his attendant, Tok Minduk, who is also the rebab player, he "sucks out" evil spirits from afflicted patients.

A popular form of folk singing is Ghazal, found mostly in Johor. Ghazal is the vocal rendition of love poems, known as *pantun,* to the accompaniment of various musical instruments such as the *gambus,* tabla, violin, accor-

folk performances once royal patronage ceased to exist. Joget Gamelan is a Malay folk dance accompanied by a *gamelan* ensemble which includes various kinds of gongs, xylophones, and drums.

These dances depict certain episodes of stories relating to the royal household. The costumes are elaborate and include a decorated headdress, a silk blouse, and an ankle-length skirt. Their accessories include a narrow belt with a large gilded buckle known as a *pending,* and a long silk scarf tied behind the buckle. The dancers hold the ends of the scarf with their fingertips and make graceful gestures as they dance.

Asyik, the oldest and most prestigious court dance was usually performed in the palace's inner private hall for exclusive ceremonies. The dancers were beautiful young girls who were trained from an early age in the palace compound and the dances imitated their daily activities like weaving silk thread, and winding yarn. Today, Asyik and Joget Gamelan have transcended the palace boundaries to become popular entertainments.

—Ku Zam Zam

Opposite: In Kelantan during festival times, teams compete on the rebana ubi, a large decorated drum. Above, left: Subtle hand moves are an essential part of Malay dance. Above, right: Gongs, drums and serunai accompanying a silat performance in Kelantan.

ARCHITECTURE

The Timeless Kampung Home

In the 15th century, Ma Huan and Fei Hsin, a couple of Chinese travelers, described the Malay house, and although it has evolved through the centuries to suit changing lifestyles, the basic shape and construction remains much the same. Perched on stilts, surrounded by rice-fields, and shaded by tropical fruit trees, these unique wooden structures merge aesthetically with the scenery throughout the country.

Wooden *kampung* houses are still numerous, but they are being threatened by architectural ideas alien to the Malaysian climate and way of life. Formerly, excellent building timber was easily obtainable from the jungle. Thatched roofs, known as *attap*, were made from *nipah* palm fronds which grew beside the rivers, and flooring was made by splitting the tough nibung palms. Today, agriculture and development encroach into the rain-forests and riverbanks and these materials are becoming harder to obtain and more expensive, forcing rural dwellers to turn to cheaper, less-suitable concrete homes.

Traditional wooden homes, with long windows open to the floor are ventilated by the slightest breeze. By contrast, windows in modern concrete homes are set too high for proper ventilation. The new houses are also built in rows which inhibits the airflow, unlike the kampung where homes are arranged so the breeze can circulate around them.

At the entrance of most traditional homes is a covered porch known as an *anjung*, often decorated with elaborate wood carvings, where guests are greeted. From here, stairs lead to a long covered verandah, known as the *serambi* where close friends and relatives are entertained, and where the family rest in the heat of the afternoon. Leading off the *serambi* is the *rumah ibu*, literally the "mother house," and the main living area. Often poorer families build this core house first and then add the *dapur* (kitchen) and other rooms later as the family prosper. Over generations, a small house can evolve into a mansion.

Evolving to suit the climate

Houses were built for the Malay lifestyle which centers around Islam and community life. Privacy was not high priority, in fact, there is no equivalent in the Malay language. Interiors are open with only a few partitions

R. MOH'D NOH SALLEH

and the full-length windows provide an easy view of the house interior. Inside older homes there is a sense of space and coolness; woven *pandanus* mats cover the wooden floors and furniture is minimal.

Furniture arrived with the Portuguese in 16th-century Melaka and their words *almari* for cupboard and *meja* for table still survive. Except in the houses of the nobility, furniture was scarce until the British colonial era, when it became more popular. Following this trend, house shapes changed and hipped roofs

appeared as higher headroom was needed for the European-style furniture.

Local influences also shaped the traditional house. In Perak and Kedah, homes are raised even higher than in the south. This was to be above flood levels, but also to protect from tiger attacks, a very real danger well into this century. Outside influences have also played their part in the different regional designs. Around Melaka, where 100-year-old homes are no rarity, there are architectural variations that occur nowhere else in the peninsula. Courtyards and curved, tiled staircases show Chinese and European influences—remnants of Melaka's rich cosmopolitan past.

In adjoining Negeri Sembilan, settled in the 16th century by the matriarchal Minangkabau from Sumatra, homes have curved roof ridges emulating the horns of the water buffalo, or *kerbau*, which symbolizes Minangkabau culture. Along the upper East Coast, which for centuries paid tribute to the Thai court, gable roof ends and wall panelling are similar to traditional Thai styles.

House-building rituals

Village life was, and in many places still is, a communal affair, with the entire kampung often participating in house-building. Certain rituals are observed before construction commences. A house site is carefully selected, for an inauspicious site may bring ruin to the

family. The *bomoh* chants and burns incense, and then the woman of the house measures a stick and a string of rattan to the length of her outstretched arms. The *bomoh* then ties the rattan to the stick and plants it at the site beside a full bucket of water.

The next morning they are measured. If they have shrunk the site is no good, but if they have grown it is suitable. Similarly, if the water has overflowed it is a good omen, but if it has lessened it is a negative sign. If one test proves positive then it is here that the *tiang seri,* the main column of the house, will be placed. The site is then cleared, but the surrounding trees and shrubs are left intact—the reason why traditional homes fit in so well with their surroundings.

The second ceremony is the raising of the *tiang seri,* or central column. All the components are prepared beforehand as the Malay house is a pre-fabricated structure first made on the ground, and later assembled on site. A rice-flour mixture, believed to frustrate evil, is sprinkled on the columns, and pieces of white, black, and red cloth, known as *bunga halang,* are placed atop the columns to ward off ghosts and malicious spirits. Coins are buried under the *tiang seri* to help ensure a prosperous future for the inhabitants, and to appease the *semangat,* or house spirit.

Although many Malays are urban dwellers, the kampung is where their heart really belongs. Many of them feel a special attachment to their ancestral homes where so many generations have lived and died, and hopefully these traditional homes will continue to adorn the Malaysian countryside for many more generations to come.

Opposite: The tiled front staircase of Melaka's old houses is a feature unique to the state.
Above, left: An elaborately-carved tiang seri *column, the central support of the Malay house.*
Above right: Art nouveau tiles, imported from Europe, are found on many Melaka houses.

FOOD

A Spicy Cultural Heritage

Peninsular Malaysia is a food-lovers dream, both in terms of value for money and variety. The most renowned culinary centers are Penang, Kuala Lumpur, Melaka and Ipoh, although many other towns, including Kota Bharu and Johor Bahru, specialize with their own regional cuisines.

On the road

Food from roadside stalls is still some of the best Malaysia can offer, despite the urban trend towards Singapore-style air-conditioned food centers.

Malayanized "Nonya" and various Chinese provincial cuisines are abundantly available—Penang and Melaka being the Nonya and Eurasian food centers—as well as Southern Indian food, but traditional Malay cooking is found throughout the peninsula.

Some Malay food is hot (*pedas*), but most is not, thanks to the extensive use of cooling, cholesterol-rich coconut milk (*santan*) in Malay curries—this gives them their typically *lemak* (milky, coconutty) appearance, texture and flavor. But the vital companion condiments are consistently spicy: no Malaysian meal is complete without *sambals*.

Hot stuff

There is a great variety of these hot sauces, ranging from the straight chilli-*sambal* to *sambal-belacan* (pronounced "blachan"), a potent and odorous dark red-brown paste of chilli and fermented shrimps (while not for the faint-hearted, it grows on you). Other accompaniments include sharp pickles, known as *acar* (pronounced "achar").

Further light and shade is added to Malay cuisine with the use of *assam* (sour) ingredients such as *serai* (lemon-grass) and *assam* itself, the tamarind fruit, besides the subtler, dusky-lemon flavours emanating from aromatic leaves such as the pandanus leaf, *daun ketumbar* (coriander), *daun limau perut* (lime leaves), or *daun kesom* leaves. Ginger and *lengkuas* (galangal) root, together with *bawang puteh* (garlic), give yet more depth.

Chicken, fish and prawns are the staple meats in the Malay diet, with beef (*lembu*) and lamb or goat (*kambing*) seen less often. (*Kangkong* greens, water convolvulus, traced with *sambal belacan* make an excellent side-dish complementing fish or prawn curries.)

R. MOH'D NOH SALLEH

One meat you will never see on a Malay table is pork (*babi*), taboo (*haram*) to all Muslims. However, both the Buddhist-Taoistic Nonya Chinese and the Christian Portuguese Eurasians of Malaysia have married pork with Malay cooking styles, creating unique dishes.

The glue that sticks all this good stuff together is of course rice (*nasi*). There are many interesting dishes which feature rice as their centrepiece—for example, *nasi lemak*, a simple but superb breakfast dish comprising coconut-and-pandan-leaf cooked rice; *sambal ikan bilis* (tiny crisp-fried *ikan bilis* fish, similar to anchovies, in a hot chilli paste), fried peanuts, strips of fried egg, sometimes a small fried salted fish, and cucumber.

Other rice-based dishes include *nasi kunyit*, a yellow rice—named after the *kunyit*, turmeric powder, coloring—cooked with coconut and *pandan*; and *nasi biryani*, a spicy rice usually served with chicken.

Graduating to the malodorous

Aficionados quickly graduate from easy-to-love standards—coconut-curry coated, tender beef *rendang*; *longtong*, a vegetable stew with rice-cake squares in coconut soup; and barbecued shashlik-like sticks of *satay* meats dipped in peanut-chilli sauce—to exotica such as the foul-smelling Durian, prickly of exterior but creamy-marshmallow inside, or the broad-bean-like green *petai* bean, a known kidney-cleanser (and wind-maker), eaten either raw with *samban belacan* or chopped and fried with chilli, sliced small red onions (*bawang merah*) and *ikan bilis*.

Laksa is a meal in itself, so don't bother to order anything else. There are two kinds, *laksa lemak* or *laksa assam*, the latter being a Thai-influenced Penang speciality. Both feature a thick coconut-chilli soup over a noodle and seafood base It is the wonderful convergence of flavors—lemon grass and pineapple, peppercorns with mint and lime leaves, chilli and coconut—that gives this dish its special character. In *laksa assam* the lemony tang is highlighted.

Battered bananas for breakfast

For a breakfast snack, sample *roti kaya*: pancake-like bread (*roti*) spread with egg-and-coconut jam (*kaya*). Similarly delicious are *pisang goreng*, or deep-fried battered bananas. Another snack or appetising side-dish, is the nearest Malaysian equivalent to pate, *otak-otak*, a pungent spiced fish paste neatly stapled inside banana-leaf wrappings.

Malay desserts are extremely creamy and sweet. *Cendol* (pronounced "Chendole"), and *bubur cha cha* are both coconut-milk based concoctions with the addition of *gula melaka*, (dark brown Melaka palm-sugar laced with coconut), green *agar-agar* (seaweed jelly "worms"), sweet potato and yam chunks, with red beans. *Pulut hitam* falls into the same category this gooey black rice porridge is served with *gula melaka* and coconut milk. *Gula melaka* itself is the name of a favorite sweet—a small pearl-sago pudding drowned in *gula melaka* sugar and coconut milk.

A grand finale

Ice kacang is a truly spectacular dessert—a veritable mountain of ice shavings streaked with violently red, green and brown syrups and laced with condensed milk. This heap hides a treasure-trove base of sweet beans, *agar-agar* sweet potato, sweet corn kernels and attap chee, the crunchy jelly-like fruit of a mangrove palm.

One Malay word you're guaranteed to need after your feast is *Sedap!*—delicious.

—*Ilsa Sharp*

Opposite: Dominated by women traders, Kota Bharu's Central Market showcases the fantastic array of fruits, vegetables and herbs that are the mainstay of Malaysian cuisine. **Below:** Rich and spicy meat and vegetable dishes on display at a Kelantan foodstall.

PART II

Introducing Kuala Lumpur

At dusk, when the domes and cupolas of the Moorish-style railway station are silhouetted against a golden tropical sunset, and the muezzin's sonorous call to prayer of "Allah-hu-Akbar" drifts from the minaret of the National Mosque, Kuala Lumpur looks and feels like a truly ancient city.

But KL, as Malaysia's largest city is fondly known, is in fact the youngest of Southeast Asia's booming capitals, its scant history spanning less than 150 years since the earliest-known settlement. Most Malaysian cities and major towns can boast older pedigrees, but none can match Kuala Lumpur's remarkable success. This rapidly-expanding, cosmopolitan city, home to 1.5 million, is the hub of the nation, and worthy of its nickname *Ibu Kota*—the "mother city."

Against a background of soaring office towers an Arabian-style mosque shaded by coconut palms now straddles the historic promontory at the confluence of the Klang and Gombak Rivers, the *kuala lumpur*, or "muddy estuary," where the city first began.

Mining, malaria and civil war

In 1857, a party of Chinese tin-miners who had poled upstream from Klang on the Melaka Straits, decided to set up camp where the rivers met, as the waters beyond were too shallow for easy navigation. The 87 pioneers unloaded their supplies on the riverbank, now known as Benteng, and their shanty town quickly expanded into the area of Medan Pasar, now a bustling banking hub.

The miners had been lured upriver by reports of prolific tin deposits in the upper Klang Valley and although the mineral riches were there, malaria took its toll. Mosquitoes bred rampantly in the stagnant waters of mining holes and after the first month only 18 of the original party survived.

Upstream at Ampang, an old Malay district, the mines were thriving. Lured by the luck of a few, and despite the horrific odds,

immigrants arrived in droves. Having escaped a life of grinding poverty in their native China there was little to lose and all to gain in the Nanyang—the southern land of promise.

Chinese secret societies operated as benefactors offering the immigrants a measure of security in return for a portion of their wages. Intense rivalry built up between these groups over the running of lucrative brothels and opium and gambling dens which dominated the leisure hours of the male-dominated shanty town. Two major groups, the Hai San and Ghee Hin were constantly waging gang wars, and coupled with the devastating epidemics and fires that periodically razed the fledgling town, the economic stability of the region was threatened.

Discontent among the Malay rulers over control of the lucrative mining revenues came to a head in 1867 when Raja Mahdi of Klang refused to remit his dues to Sultan Abdul Samad, ruler of Selangor. The Sultan enlisted the aid of his son-in-law, Tengku Kudin, a landless prince from Kedah, and also formed alliances with local chiefs.

Seizing the opportunity to exploit the differences between the secret societies, Abdul Samad appointed Yap Ah Loy, a tough, charismatic Hakka as the Kapitan Cina, the Chinese Headman of Kuala Lumpur. Yap pledged support with his powerful Hai San society. Their most bitter rivals, the Ghee Hin, sided with Raja Mahdi and the Selangor Civil War began.

The fighting was initially evenly matched, but as hostilities continued Tunku Kudin's group gained the advantage by securing the backing of the colonial government in

*Overleaf: Malaysia's highest-priced property overlooks the glittering thoroughfare of Jalan Sultan Ismail. Photo by Alain Evrard. **Opposite:** Her face framed by a telekung headscarf, this Malay girl takes part in the Independence Day celebrations in KL. Photo by Alain Evrard.*

Singapore which was keen to see the area return to economic prosperity

In 1871 when Raja Mahdi's men pirated a Chinese Penang vessel off Kuala Selangor, this was all the excuse the British needed to intervene. Gunboat diplomacy thus turned the war in Tunku Kudin's favor. Raja Mahdi, an esteemed warrior, was much more popular with the Malays than his rival, but as historian Barbara Watson Andaya writes; "The outcome of the Selangor wars demonstrated to Malays that even an unpopular or weak prince could gain power with British assistance."

From chaos to growth

After the war, with Kuala Lumpur in shambles, many Chinese were ready to quit, but

under Yap Ah Loy's tough rule the clan wars were quelled, the mines restarted, and the town boomed when tin prices doubled in 1878.

The British were eager to get their piece of the action and in 1880 Selangor's British Resident moved the state capital from Klang to the riverbank opposite Yap Ah Loy's Chinatown.

With the arrival of Frank Swettenham, who later became the Resident General of the Federated Malay States (FMS), the town underwent a transformation. Thatched huts were replaced by brick buildings and less than 40 years after the pioneering miners stepped ashore, Kuala Lumpur became the capital of the FMS.

The next two decades witnessed a farsighted building spree that gave the city its enduring Moorish influenced architecture which owes its existence to C.E. Spooner, the state engineer, who talked the architect, A.C. Norman, out of his planned Renaissance style as he felt it was not a fitting design for a Muslim country.

As the hub of British power on the peninsula, Kuala Lumpur continued to grow rapidly. The city was unaffected by World War I, but when Malaya was invaded by the Japanese on December 8th, 1941, Kuala Lumpur soon fell. However, its architecture escaped major bomb damage as the British retreated further south.

Surrender and freedom

On returning three years later, the English encountered a different mood. The educated Malays wanted nothing less than independence. Nationalism had been steadily growing throughout the century, but had been given extra impetus by the humiliating surrender of the British. Finally, on August 31st, 1957, the Union Jack was hauled down for the last time and the capital resounded to the cheers of *merdeka* —"freedom".

Many years have passed since Independence and although the city has changed beyond belief, KL still retains a colonial feel. At the Royal Selangor Club there are BMWs in the car park and members stroll around with cellular phones, but cricket is still played every Sunday. Out along Jalan Ampang, notorious for its traffic jams, huge old raintrees still shade 19th-century tinbaron's mansions that survive between the mushrooming condominiums.

KL also shares problems inherent to any rapidly developing third-world nation. Suburbs carve up the surrounding hills, roads are clogged with 10 times more traffic than they were designed for, and in the windless season before the monsoon, the city gasps under a haze that rivals Los Angeles'. But when the rains descend the city is reborn. The winds blow the smog out across the Melaka Straits and you can see the rainforested hills looming above the city like a primeval backdrop.

Right: *The copper-domed, Moorish-inspired, Sultan Abdul Samad Building was the colonial government's power base for the Federated Malay States.*

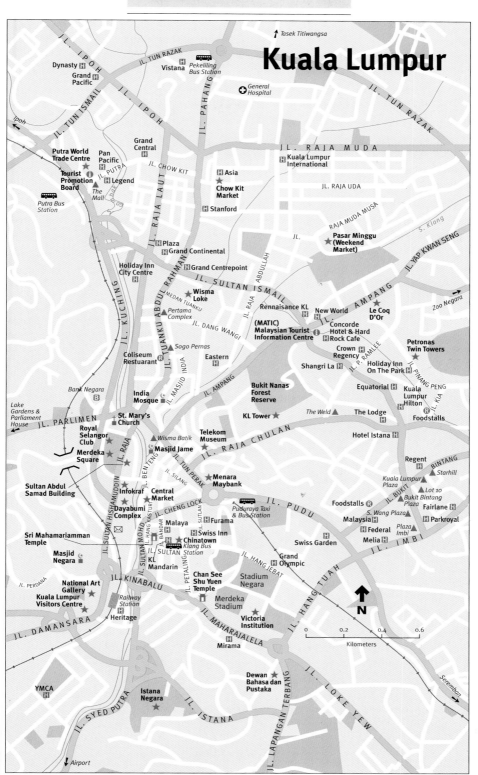

Kuala Lumpur

↑ Tasek Titiwangsa

Dynasty
Grand
Pacific

Vistana Pekeliling
Bus Station

JL. TUN RAZAK

JL. IPOH

JL. IPOH

JL. TUN ISMAIL

JL. PAHANG

Ipoh

General
Hospital

JL. TUN RAZAK

Grand
Central

Putra World
Trade Centre

Pan
Pacific

JL. CHOW KIT

JL. RAJA MUDA

Kuala Lumpur
International

Tourist
Promotion
Board

JL. PUTRA

Legend

The
Mall

Asia

Chow Kit
Market

JL. RAJA UDA

Putra Bus
Station

Stanford

JL. RAJA LAUT

RAJA MUDA MUSA

S. Klang

JL.

Plaza

Grand Continental

Pasar Minggu
(Weekend
Market)

JL. YAP KWAN SENG

Holiday Inn
City Centre

Grand Centrepoint

JL. TUANKU ABDUL RAHMAN

JL. SULTAN ISMAIL

JL. RAJA ABDULLAH

Wisma
Loke

MEDAN TUANKU

Rennaisance KL

New World

Le Coq
D'Or

JL. AMPANG

Zoo Negara

JL. KUCHING

Pertama
Complex

JL. DANG WANGI

(MATIC)
Malaysian Tourist
Information Centre

Concorde
Hotel & Hard
Rock Cafe

JL. P. RAMLEE

Sogo Pernas

JL. MASJID INDIA

Eastern

Crown
Regency

Petronas
Twin Towers

Coliseum
Restuarant

Shangri La

Holiday Inn
On The Park

JL. PINANG

Bank Negara

India
Mosque

JL. AMPANG

Bukit Nanas
Forest
Reserve

Equatorial

Kuala
Lumpur
Hilton

JL. PENG

JL. KIA

Lake
Gardens &
Parliament
House

JL. PARLIMEN

St. Mary's
Church

KL Tower

The Weld

The Lodge

Foodstalls

Royal
Selangor
Club

JL. RAJA

JL. BEN-TENG

Telekom
Museum

JL. RAJA CHULAN

Hotel Istana

Merdeka
Square

Wisma Batik

Masjid Jame

JL. TUN PERAK

Regent

BINTANG

JL. SILANG

Menara
Maybank

Kuala Lumpur
Plaza

Starhill

Sultan Abdul
Samad Building

JL. SULTAN HISHAMUDDIN

Infokraf

Central
Market

JL. CHENG LOCK

JL. PUDU

Lot 10

Bukit Bintang
Plaza

Foodstalls

JL. BUKIT

Fairlane

Dayabumi
Complex

JL. HANG KASTURI

JL. SULTAN MOHD.

JL. BANDAR

Malaya

Puduraya Taxi
& Bus Station

S. Wang Plaza

Malaysia

Federal

Plaza
Imbi

Parkroyal

Sri Mahamariamman
Temple

Furama

Swiss Inn

Chinatown

Swiss Garden

Melia

JL. IMBI

Masjid
Negara

KL
Mandarin

SULTAN

Klang Bus
Station

Grand
Olympic

National Art
Gallery

JL. KINABALU

Chan See
Shu Yuen
Temple

Stadium
Negara

JL. HANG JEBAT

JL. PERDANA

Kuala Lumpur
Visitors Centre

Railway
Station

JL. PETALING

Merdeka
Stadium

JL. HANG TUAH

N

JL. DAMANSARA

Heritage

JL. MAHARAJALELA

Victoria
Institution

Mirama

0   0.2   0.4   0.6

Kilometers

YMCA

Istana
Negara

Dewan
Bahasa dan
Pustaka

JL. LOKE YEW

JL. SYED PUTRA

JL. ISTANA

JL. LAPANGAN TERBANG

Serembn

↓ Airport

KL SIGHTS

Walking Tours Around the Mother City

With its ever-changing skyline and constant traffic jams, Kuala Lumpur can initially appear a difficult city to get around. Yet at its very heart there is a plethora of sights easily circumnavigated on foot. More convenient and infinitely preferable to crawling through the stop-start traffic cocooned in a taxi, walking about the city center also immediately immerses the traveler in the sounds, smells, sights and sensations of life in this unique equatorial capital.

Historically, the city was bisected by the Klang River, with the colonial administrative hub centered around Merdeka Square (Dataran Merdeka) on the west bank, and the commercial region (Chinatown) on the east side. North of the confluence of the rivers is the Jalan Masjid India area, a multi-cultural district known as "Little India". East of the central district is the "Golden Triangle,"

renowned for its luxury hotels and shopping complexes, and in the wooded hills to the west of downtown are the Lake Gardens (Taman Tasek Perdana).

A swathe of green playing fields formerly known as the *Padang*, and now revamped as **Merdeka Square**, is a fitting place to begin a tour of KL. Not only was it the apex of British life in the tropics, but it has remained very much at the center of city life ever since.

The colonial hub

On Saturday nights when the road is closed to traffic, the square is a favorite venue for KL's youth who flirt by the colonial fountain under the world's tallest flagpole.

Overlooking the square is the copper-domed **Sultan Abdul Samad Building,** the forerunner of the capital's unique Moorish-style architecture which flourished between the 1890s and 1920s. A 41-meter-high clock tower and arched colonnades characterize this former Secretariat building, now the High Court, built between 1894 and 1897. To the left is old City Hall with its black domes in the same architectural style, and to the right is yet another Moorish-style building, featuring striped brickwork and keyhole archways, now the home of Infokraf, a permanent exhibition of modern Malaysian handicrafts.

A *stengah* at the Spotted Dog

On the far side of the square is the black-and-

R. MOH'D NOH SALLEH

white Tudor-style **Royal Selangor Club**, commonly known as the "Spotted Dog," the favorite watering-hole of the colonial era. The nickname either refers to the mixed-race membership or to a dalmatian which a former member used to tie up at the steps, but no one knows for sure. On the spacious verandahs you can still sip a *stengah*, half whiskey and water, and enjoy a curry tiffin lunch; but only if you're lucky enough to know a member.

Directly behind the Club on Jalan Tangsi is the beautifully restored PAM (Malaysian Institute of Architects) Building which was once the townhouse of Loke Chow Kit, a department store baron. Later it functioned as the Kuala Lumpur Resthouse. Fittingly, this colonial gem built in 1907 also houses the Heritage Trust, which spearheads the struggle to preserve the nation's architectural legacy.

Other important buildings around Merdeka Square include the Gothic-style St. Mary's Church (1907) designed by A. C. Spooner, the versatile architect famed for his Moorish style; and the neo-Renaissance style KL Memorial Library opposite Infokraf.

Architectural landmarks

Dominating the landscape to the south is the elegant, glistening-white Dayabumi Complex, a dramatic Islamic-inspired skyscraper. Beside it is the General Post Office. Further down Jalan Sultan Hishamuddin is another prominent landmark, the **National Mosque** (Masjid Negara). Built in contemporary style in 1965 it features a massive, umbrella-shaped dome and a 73-meter minaret.

On any Friday, the Muslim prayer day, thousands of KL's faithful shed their work clothes and don a *songkok*, the velvet, fez-like cap and checkered sarongs to give thanks to Allah in the marble-floored Great Hall. Visitors can also take time out to admire the aesthetic architecture of the nearby Islamic Center, which houses an impressive collection of ancient Muslim manuscripts.

From here, walk back down Jalan Perdana to the roundabout. The grandiose stone building on the right is the Railway Administration Headquarters, built in 1917—the last of the glorious Moorish government offices to be constructed.

Directly ahead is its even more impressive neighbor, the **Kuala Lumpur Railway Station,** an architectural smorgasbord of domes, cupolas, and colonnaded archways. Travelers have waxed lyrical of its charms since its completion in 1911. Paul Theroux called it "the grandest station in Southeast Asia", but Cuthbert Woodville Harrison, writing in the 1920s was not so impressed, saying that "if not too late, the Federated States railway department ought to deal severely with the architect!"

Renowned cultural collections

Past the Railway Headquarters is the **National Art Gallery**, formerly the Majestic Hotel, which now houses the country's art treasures, and further down on Jalan Damansara is the **National Museum** (Muzium Negara) characterized by its sweeping Minangkabau-style roofs. Its predecessor was destroyed by badly-aimed Allied bombs meant to hit the nearby railway yards. The present museum, renowned as one of Southeast Asia's best, opened in 1963. As well as rich ethnographic and archaeological collections, Muzium Negara is best known for its colorful dioramas depicting cultural events, including a Straits Chinese wedding and a Malay circumcision ceremony.

KL's largest park

From here, a walkway leads under Jalan

Opposite: Unusual pediments and wrought-iron balustrades decorate the early-20th century PAM Building, once a Chinese tycoon's mansion. Above: Youthful participants in a Chinese fan-dance apply last-minute make-up in front of the Tudor-style Royal Selangor Club.

Damansara to **Taman Tasek Perdana,** formerly known as the Lake Gardens. KL's most popular and largest green-lung (173 acres) provides a welcome respite from the equatorial heat and boasts an excellent Bird Park with vast walk-through aviaries including a hornbill enclosure complete with rainforest trees.

Other attractions include an Orchid Gardens and a Deer Park where visitors can glimpse the diminutive mousedeer renowned in Malay fairy tales. Overlooking the gardens is Carcosa Seri Negara, an elegant colonial mansion once the home of the colonial governors and now refurbished into Malaysia's most expensive hotel.

Chinatown

Since the city's founding, the center of commercial activity has always been the grid of streets which evolved around where Yap Ah Loy, the charismatic Chinese master of KL, held sway in the late 19th-century. Roughly bordered by Jalan Petaling and Medan Pasar, Chinatown is an eclectic collection of southern-Chinese style shophouses, coffee-shops and temples overshadowed by looming high-rises.

Vendors spill out onto the sidewalks, motorcyclists weave crazily through the honking traffic, and the pedestrian crowds bare witness to Kuala Lumpur's multi-cultural population. Family businesses still flourish in turn-of-the-century shops decorated with plaster bas-reliefs of flowers, birds and dragons. Chinese druggists—*sinseh*—weigh up seeds and barks to cure everything from acne to flagging sexual powers; grocers do a roaring trade in oriental delicacies like sharks' fins, sea slugs, and edible swallow s' nests.

Prophets of the future—an indispensable adjunct to Asian life—abound. Under the arches of the five-foot-ways which shade shoppers from the heat, you can take your pick of traditional Chinese fortune tellers or Indian palmists.

For those concerned with more earthly

occupations there are a host of eating houses. Dim Sum breakfasts here are authentic, as is the chicken rice, *nasi ayam*, at Kim Hong's, one of the many tile-floored, marble-tabled coffee shops in Jalan Bandar (Jalan Tun H.S.Lee) where the working-class patrons still wear singlets and wooden clogs.

Nearby, is the **Sri Mahamariamman Temple**, KL's oldest Hindu shrine. Outside the entrance arch, elaborately decorated with dozens of deities, women deftly thread jasmine flowers into garlands which serve as

offerings to the gods. Sari-draped Indian girls file inside to the sound of bells as the Brahmin priest conducts the morning *puja*.

Hidden behind Jalan Bandar, is the Tze Ya Temple built by Yap Ah Loy who was himself added as an additional deity on his death in 1885. Its unusual location is apparently in accordance with auspicious *feng sui*—geomancic principles.

A fine temple and a notorious murder

At the Jalan Kinabalu end of Petaling Street is the city's most elaborate Chinese temple, the Chan See Shu Yuen. Built in 1906 it features a pottery, Kwangtung-style roof profusely adorned with terra-cotta figures from Chinese mythology. Nearby, next to the Traffic Police Headquarters, is the **Victoria Institution**, KL's oldest school (built in 1894) where a celebrated murder took place in 1911. The headmaster's wife claimed the victim was a rapist, but he later turned out to be her lover. Somerset Maugham used the tale for his short story "The Letter," which was made into a movie starring Bette Davis.

Come evening, Jalan Petaling metamorphoses into an open-air night market. Under a ceiling of striped umbrellas, pedestrian hordes jostle past cassette hawkers and pork-floss vendors—the night air pungent with cooking aromas and filled with a cacophony of sounds. Blind buskers on Yamaha organs compete with Malaysian heavy-metal and

Cantonese opera. Here, you can score fake Rolex watches and Gucci T-shirts, as well as bargain-basement clothes and footwear.

On the edge of Chinatown, fronting the Klang River, is one of KL's most popular hang-out, the Art Deco-style **Central Market.** Built in the 1920s, this pastel-colored edifice was once the capital's "wet" market, haunt of fruit-sellers and fishmongers. Saved from demolition by some forward-thinking bureaucrats, the market has been refurbished into a lively maze of shops and restaurants.

Artistic enclave

The city's artists and craftsmen have congregated here, and at any given time shoppers can watch glass-blowers, batik-painters, portraitists, fortune-tellers and even catch a traditional dance performance or a shadow-puppet play. There are dozens of food stalls on the mezzanine and top floors, but for a regional treat, join the crowds and head for Abdul Majeed Khan's Kampung Pandan Restaurant for the specialty of the house: fish head curry. After dark, the Riverbank Restaurant and Bar plays host to the best of regional jazz.

At the back entrance, past where beret-clad artists immortalize their customers in oils, a walkway connects with the colorful new Central Square, which houses local designer boutiques specializing in batik and casual wear, an American-style ice-cream parlor and an upstairs cinema.

Around Jalan Masjid India

Follow the riverbank upstream, cross Leboh Pasar Besar, formerly Market Street, venture out across the old metal bridge and look upriver. It is a rewarding vista, for here, astride the promontory where the Klang and Gombak Rivers meet, is one of Asia's most aesthetic buildings, the **Jame Mosque.** Three silver domes, pink and white-banded minarets, and graceful arched colonnades adorn this turn-of-the-century edifice which, until the opening of the National Mosque, was the principal place of worship for the city's Muslims.

Visitors are welcome except at prayer times, and travelers dressed immodestly can don a robe for a small donation. To the left of the mosque is Batik Malaysia which specializes in hand-drawn and traditional stamped batik. Opposite here, follow Jalan Melaka to Jalan Masjid India, a lively hub of shops and restaurants dominated by traders from the Indian sub-continent. Like Aladdin's cave, glit-

Opposite left: A 19th-century fountain adds a colonial touch to Merdeka Square.
Opposite right: The former home of Malaysia's first prime minister now houses a tourist information office and theater.
Below: Space is at a premium in this cupboard-sized mamak shop.

tering saris drape from the ceilings of the shops crammed with a dazzling array of brassware and stainless-steel cooking utensils. Roadside vendors selling snacks and cakes jostle for position along with flower hawkers, garland makers, buskers, and traditional medicine men.

Clothing, food and antiques

Opposite the Masjid India mosque are Malay shops specializing in traditional clothing; the silky pantsuits called *baju Melayu*, white prayer veils for women, *jamu* medicine from Java, prayer rugs from Turkey, and a fantastic array of headgear ranging from Mujahiddin-styles from Pakistan to PLO-style red-and-white turbans. Some of KL's best and cheapest food is found in this area where outdoor eating stalls specialize in buffet-style "pay for what you take" Malaysian curries with traditional herbal salads.

Take any of the side lanes to Jalan Tuanku Abdul Rahman, one of the city's busiest trading streets well-known for its department stores, fabric shops, cheap hotels, and the famed Coliseum Restaurant which was once the haunt of Somerset Maugham. Further along, turn into Jalan Medan Tuanku for Wisma Loke, a baroque-style mansion which is now an art and antique gallery. Once the home of Loke Yew, a business baron, it was the first private residence in KL to be lit with electric light.

Mansions of the Golden Triangle

Outside downtown, bordered by Jalan Ampang, Jalan Tun Razak and Jalan Imbi is the area known as the "Golden Triangle" where most of the luxury hotels, shopping complexes and embassies are situated. Here are the famous 451.9 m-high **Petronas twin towers**, the world's tallest twin towers, designed by renowned architect Cesar Pelli. Take a ride up another vertical superlative: the 421m-high **KL Tower**, which has views of the city from an observation platform and a revolving restaurant. This telecommunications tower sits in KL's last green lung, the Bukit Nanas Forest Reserve.

The twin towers overlook Jl. Sultan Ismail/Jl. Kia Peng, an enclave for KL's trendy, boasting neck-to-neck nightspots and international eateries. A popular club is the Theatre Upstraits, specializing in revue and comic acts. Around the turn of the century the rich *towkays* (business bosses) built their mansions along Jalan Ampang, and some still survive.

The most famous is Le Coq D'Or, a palatial residence, now a restaurant, which was built by a lovesick tin baron to impress his neighbors who had denied him marriage to their daughter because of his earlier poverty. Another beautifully-restored mansion is the former Tuanku Abdul Rahman Hall now housing the Malaysian Tourist Information Centre (MATIC) and a theatre.

Heading Northeast

On the corner of Jalan Tun Razak, is one of KL's most unusual contemporary structures, the unique Tabung Haji—a skyscraper shaped like an hour-glass which is the center for organizing pilgrimages to Mecca. From Jl. Ampang, head north to the Royal Selangor Pewter factory in Setapak, where you can see how pewter is made, take photos of the world's largest tankard, and buy quality Malaysian souvenirs.

On the way there is another park for people-watching. The pretty **Taman Tasik Titiwangsa**, a rehabilitated mining pond, is popular with joggers, canoeists and families.

On the southern fringe of the city, off Jalan Syed Putra, is Istana Negara, a white-domed palace surrounded by spacious lawns which is the home of Malaysia's King, the Yang Di Pertuan Agung.

Left: *A Muslim shopkeeper sells alcohol-free perfumes used before worship at the mosque on Jalan Masjid India.*

PASAR MALAM

Shopping Under the Stars

The movies, pubs, and discos may draw a sizable evening crowd, but by far the most popular night-time amusement, not only in Kuala Lumpur but throughout the country, is the *pasar malam*, or "night market". At dusk, streets are closed to vehicular traffic, hawkers set up their stalls on the pavements, and the fun begins.

At these nocturnal bazaars, vendors sell an incredible array of ready-cooked food, fruit and vegetables, meat and fish, household goods, clothing, shoes, cassettes, tools, hardware, dry-goods, watches and electronics. In fact, the range is so extensive, that many locals do all their necessary shopping at the *pasar malam*.

A venerable social institution

Don't be fooled into thinking that purchasing is the only reason why Malaysians flock to the night markets, for it is just as much a place to socialize, pick up a girl, show off your latest dress, or just hang out and watch the action. Parents with half a dozen pyjama-clad kids in tow are not an unusual sight. For locals, the *pasar malam* is practically a sacred institution, and for travelers, it is the best introduction there is to real, unadulterated Malaysian life.

One of the great attractions to night shopping is that the equatorial climate is not conducive to strolling around the streets by day. Housewives usually go to the market early-morning. As the day heats up, smartly-dressed businesspeople head for the air-conditioned supermarkets, but the most serious shoppers save themselves for the balmy evenings when they can shop in earnest at the *pasar malam*. These days, an increasing percentage of city women work, and the night markets are perfect for working mums who have no time in the day to shop.

Pasar malam are only held in the same place one night a week, but there is at least one happening every night of the week in the Kuala Lumpur city area. An exception to this rule is the street market in Jalan Petaling, Chinatown, an exciting, noisy affair which is held every night of the week. But, markets in the Malay-dominated areas, or even in the suburbs are the most authentic, and have the best variety of food.

Sunday market on a Saturday night

The most famous is the **Pasar Minggu**, also known as the Sunday Market, which is held along Jalan Raja Muda Musa in Kampung Bahru, the oldest Malay *kampung* in the inner city. Don't be fooled into thinking that this market is held on Sunday: Malays follow the Islamic system which marks sunset as the end of the day. So the Sunday Market is actually on Saturday night.

Jalan Tuanku Abdul Rahman in the heart of downtown also closes to traffic on Saturday night and the sidewalks are lined with hawker stalls. Other locations are Jalan Angsana, off Jalan Tun Sambanthan on Wednesday night, Kampung Datuk Keramat on Friday night, and Taman Tun Dr. Ismail on Sunday night. However, there are dozens of other locations which often change nights so it is best to check with the tourist information offices who keep up to date on the venues.

Below: *At the night market, Malaysian-style "fast-food" is stir-fried in large convex frying pans known as kuali.*

R IAN LLOYD

Old Royal Forts and Hill Resorts

Selangor, the state which surrounds the Federal Territory of Kuala Lumpur, is often overlooked by travelers, but in the rugged northern mountains and the populous western plains are a wealth of interesting places to visit. Some, like Batu Caves with its cliffside temple, and the hill resorts of Fraser's Hill and Genting Highlands, are well known, but others, like the old royal capital of Jugra, and the hilltop fort at Kuala Selangor are far off the beaten tourist tracks.

By car, the western excursions can all be done as day trips. Fraser's Hill, however, with its bracing climate and colonial ambiance is an ideal spot to spend a few days recuperating from the often stifling heat of the lowlands.

To a cave shrine and forest reserves

Approached by climbing 272 steps up the side of a limestone massif, **Batu Caves**, 13km (8mi) north of the city, is the site of a century-old Hindu shrine. Located inside the cavernous Temple Cave, where stalactites drip from the 100-meter-high (328ft) ceiling.

The sacred shrine is a favorite venue for devout Indians particularly at the annual Thaipusam festival held in February, when 100,000 pilgrims make the arduous ascent. Thousands of devotees, in penance for past sins, enter a trance state and shoulder massive *kavadi*—symbolic frames with metal spikes attached to their flesh—and some penitents even pierce their tongues and cheeks with trident-shaped skewers.

North from Batu Caves, the Main Trunk Road climbs out of the Klang Valley through a pass to Templer Park. This forest reserve is popular with picnickers and offers excellent rock-climbing on Bukit Takun, a solitary limestone peak, surrounded by a golf club, but access is restricted to the national rock-climbing association. The neighboring Kanching Forest Reserve (Hutan Lipur Kanching), 1km (0.6mi) further on, is still peaceful. Trails wind through the dense rainforest beside the scenic Kanching Falls which cascade from the mountains in a series of tiers.

Turn off at Kuala Kubu Baharu, 62km (38mi) north of Kuala Lumpur, for Fraser's Hill (Bukit Fraser), an old colonial retreat, 39km (24mi) further on. An alternative route to the lorry-clogged main road is the recently-built road from Batu Caves to Ulu Yam

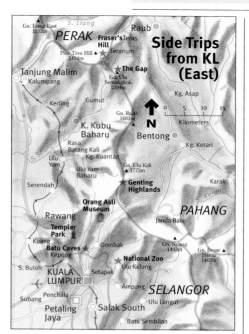

other getaway hill resort, renowned for its casino, night-life and luxury hotels, is a total contrast to Fraser's vestiges of colonialism, for except for its stunning mountain-top location and surrounding jungle-covered hills it feels more like an Asian-style Las Vegas. Visitors either love it or hate it.

To reach Genting, 50km (31mi) northeast of KL, take the Karak Highway and turn off at Genting Sempah for the dual carriageway which winds up to the 1,800-meter-high (5,905 ft) resort. An alternative route, and one that offers a more in-depth look at the countryside is the Old Pahang Road, the original road across the mountains leading to the East Coast.

The Orang Asli Museum, 1km (0.6mi) further on, has an excellent collection of tools and handicrafts of Malaysia's indigenous "original people," some of whom live in the surrounding villages.

From here, the road climbs through a series of hairpin bends to the Genting Highlands turnoff on the left. Continue along the old road on the right for Janda Baik, a serene valley retreat popular for picnics, or follow the road to Bentong past a roadside waterfall and a stream with steaming hot springs.

Bahru which skirts the edges of a man-made lake and winds through rainforested hills.

Once on the old British-built Gap Road which snakes up the ranges to the top of the watershed, the traffic is left behind. Giant bamboo and tree-ferns overshadow the road, and a wraith-like mist enshrouds the forested hills. At the top of the pass, is the Tudor-style Gap Resthouse, an isolated remnant of the colonial era. From The Gap, an 8km (4.9mi) single track one-way road, which operates 40 minutes in each direction, connects with Fraser's Hill. Travelers can await the gate change while enjoying tea and cakes in the Resthouse dining room.

Colonial remnants and Vegas glitz

Perched on a series of seven hills, a cool 1,524m (5,000 ft) above sea level, **Fraser's Hill** is named after its first European resident, a hermit muleteer who mysteriously disappeared. Visitors can stay at English-style stone bungalows complete with ivy-covered walls and gardens of chrysanthemums, and even enjoy tea and scones in front of a log fire—a paradox in these equatorial realms.

Bird life is prolific along the forest trails, and once a year a bird spotting contest is held which attracts an international following. Other attractions include tennis courts, and a 9-hole golf course—one of the few public ones in Malaysia.

Genting Highlands, Kuala Lumpur's

Opposite: Middle Eastern and European architectural influences combine in the eclectic Istana Bandar, a royal palace at the former Selangor capital of Jugra.

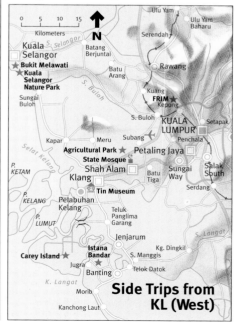

Westward to Klang

The Federal Highway west of KL leads past the satellite town of Petaling Jaya and its vast industrial sprawl to Shah Alam, the state capital of Selangor, some 20 km (12.4 mi) from Kuala Lumpur.

Dominating the landscape is the spectacular, blue and white State Mosque (Masjid Sultan Salahuddin) featuring a massive, computer-designed dome and reputedly the world's highest minarets. Continue past the mosque for the Malaysian Agricultural Park at Bukit Cerakah where local crops are exhibited and children can enjoy the suspended rope walk through the jungle.

The former state capital of Klang, 12 km further down the Federal Highway, is experiencing boomtime due to the modernization and expansion of its port, Pelabuhan Klang, but maintains its charm. In the town's old quarter is the Gedung Raja Abdullah, an old tin warehouse built in 1856 which was besieged and overtaken by Raja Mahdi during the Selangor Civil War.

Recently, while the building was being renovated for its new role as the Tin Museum, some early drawings were discovered beneath the old limewash. Other sights around the historic town include the Istana Alam Shah, an old palace; the Art Deco-style Sultan Sulaiman Mosque on Jalan Raja Timur; and the neo-classical government offices on Jalan Istana.

Along Route 5

South of Klang (17 km/10.5 mi) on Route 5, turn off at Teluk Panglima Garang for Carey Island, home of the Mah Meri wood-craftsmen, (see page 69). Further on, a scenic *kampung* road links Jenjarum with Jugra, the old 19th-century royal capital of Selangor.

At the hilltop Makam di Raja (Royal Mausoleum) are the graves of past sultans, and at nearby Bandar, amongst the coconut palms, is the exquisite Istana Bandar, the former palace of Sultan Alauddin Shah, which has been recently restored to its turn-of-the-century glory. This creative ruler, who apparently worked on the palace's original decorations, was also responsible for the elegant, Moorish-style mosque which bears his name, just down the road from the palace.

Follow Route 5, 46 km (28.5 mi) north of Klang for Kuala Selangor, another old royal capital beside the estuary of the Selangor River. Strategically sited on Bukit Melawati, a hill overlooking the town, are the ruins of Kota Melawati, originally an 18th-century fortress built by the Dutch in an ineffectual bid to control the tin trade, and later taken over by the pioneering Bugis for Sulawesi who used the fort as a base to establish the first Sultanate of Selangor.

Bugis graves and wildlife watching

Also on the hill, shaded by magnificent raintrees, is a royal mausoleum containing the graves of the first three Bugis sultans; the original execution block; a lighthouse; and some old cannons which overlook the expansive wetlands at the base of the hill which is now the Kuala Selangor Nature Park. Home to leaf-monkeys, herons, and sea-eagles, the mangrove forest is also a favored stopover for migratory birds which can be easily viewed from observation hides.

To avoid the often horrendous traffic on the Federal Highway, return to Kuala Lumpur via Sungai Buloh to Kepong where there is the beautifully-maintained forest of FRIM (Forest Research Institute of Malaysia), and the Forest Museum.

Below: One of the many cascades at the Kanching Forest Reserve, a rainforest retreat on Kuala Lumpur's outskirts.

R MOH'D NOH SALLEH

MAH MERI

Creators of Ancestor Carvings

Dominated by a vast oil-palm plantation, Carey Island in Selangor, 60 km west of KL, is home to a group of Orang Asli craftsmen. Apart from the Jahut people of Pahang the Orang Asli are the only other aboriginals in Peninsular Malaysia who create traditional wooden carvings.

Ethnographically, little is known of the Mah Meri, a sub-branch of the Senoi who speak a Mon-Khmer language and number around 1,400. However, elders at Kampung Sungai Bumbon, where most of the craftsmen live, maintain that their ancestors migrated to their present island home from either Johor or the islands near Singapore.

Pion anak Bumbon, the best-known wood carver, spends most days at the back of his house, sitting cross-legged on a carpet of rose-colored wood chips, quietly working on his sculptures. "Our pregnant women are not allowed to walk here," he remarks, "for the old people believe this may cause the child to be born with features resembling the spirit from which the chips are carved."

With a curved *parang* (machete) he hacks off pieces of the reddish wood which is soft to carve, but turns hard when it dries. He then selects a chisel from the array at his feet and using a hand-hewn mallet, shapes out the features of a *moyang*—literally "ancestor"—and the generic name for all the spirit images.

Well over a hundred *moyang,*, each representing a different spirit, encompass the gamut of Mah Mehri animist beliefs. Famous examples include Moyang Bahai, a demonic-looking dragon with a young girl swinging from its jaw; the spiral-shaped Moyang Puting Beliong, the spirit of the waterspout, who assists those who need water; and a powerful frog holding an evil scorpion aloft—the Moyang Katak dan Kala—which illustrates an ancient Mah Meri tale.

There are also dozens of different *topeng*, or masks, which are also *moyang*, and each has a different legend. These stories are invariably bound up in the natural arena of swamp, jungle and sea—the Mah Meri world.

Using sandpaper—quicker than the traditional palas leaf—Pion's wife, Kantar anak Kassim, smooth-finishes a magnificent Moyang Tenong Jerat Harimau. This legendary tiger can only be seen by people with the power to see the unknown, such as a *bomoh*, a traditional medicine man, who formerly used the *moyang* for curing sickness.

The *bomoh* would go into trance in order to pick the most appropriate *moyang*, and after receiving enlightenment, would instruct the carver to make an appropriate small image. Ritual offerings of eggs, rice and a chicken were then presented, while he called on the spirit to help him cure the patient. After the ceremony the *moyang* was thrown away for it was believed to have removed the sickness and was therefore contaminated. This is the major reason why few carvings of this type remain.

Today, the craftsmen carve for collectors of primitive art and there is no lack of orders. Some scholars are skeptical of tourism and the negative effects it has on indigenous peoples, however the carvers themselves enjoy their work and feel that they arefulfilling a vital function by preserving their cutural traditions in the face of social change.

Below: Pion anak Bumbon, a Mah-Meri master-craftsman, roughs out a "monkey in chains."

R. MOH'D NOH SALLEH

PART III

Introducing Perak

Translated in Malay, Perak's name means "silver," however Peninsular Malaysia's second largest state, which sprawls over 21,000 square kilometers of the northwest, has always been associated not with silver, but with tin. During the 1890s when the Kinta Valley reached its zenith as one of the economic jewels in the British Empire's crown, this region possessed the richest alluvial tin deposits in the world.

The tin ore originated from the granite ranges of the Barisan Titiwangsa, the mountainous chain that forms the state's eastern border. Over the ages these deposits were washed down to the valley floor. There's still plenty of mineral wealth under the ground but these days, with tin prices in the doldrums, many mines have closed down and Perak's economy has diversified.

Surrounded by curious, loaf-shaped limestone peaks pitted with Buddhist cave temples, Ipoh, the capital—"the city that tin built"—is now a thriving industrial hub. It still retains much of its colonial architecture however, as does Batu Gajah to the south.

Recent archaeological discoveries at Kota Tampan, near Lenggong in Upper Perak, confirm that man has lived there since the Stone Age. The limestone caves provided shelter beside the 400km (248mi) long Sungai Perak, the peninsula's second longest river, which has always been the state's major artery.

Legends tell of a Hindu Malay kingdom called Gangga Negara which thrived near Bruas in the northeast, however, the state's recorded history stems from the founding of its sultanate by Sultan Muzaffar Syah, a son of the last ruler of Melaka, in around 1528. The sultans set up court in their wooden palaces along the riverbank, and graves of past sultans can been seen near Kampung Gajah. The present sultanate still resides in the royal capital of Kuala Kangsar renowned for its gold-domed Ubudiah Mosque.

Control of the river trade which plied to the mining lands upriver had always been lucrative, and throughout history there were always outsiders looking for a slice of the action. During the turbulent 17th and 18th centuries, local Malays warred with the Achehnese, Bugis, Thais and the Dutch. From the early 19th century, the first Chinese miners filtered into the state, starting a wave of economic migration that would ultimately change the entire face and fortunes of the region.

In 1862 Chinese gang wars broke out in the troubled mines of Taiping and by the 1870s when a succession dispute to the throne added to the region's woes, the British had an excuse to intervene. The hastily-signed and misunderstood Pangkor Treaty saw a British Resident being installed, then promptly assassinated. However, following the execution of the Malay ringleaders, who later became heroes of nationalism, the state had no choice but to buckle down under the colonial thumb, and in 1896 became one of the four Federated Malay States.

Today, Perak's multi-cultural population stands at just over 2 million—an ethnic mix of 45% Malays, 40% Chinese, and 14% Indians whose descendants arrived as laborers during the rubber boom.

Perak is slowly realizing the potential of tourism, but in Ipoh's old Chinatown; in the royal capital of Kuala Kangsar; and in Taiping's serene Lake Gardens, meeting up with other travelers is still a novelty. It's more likely, however, in the cool Cameron Highlands, which although in Pahang, is included in this chapter as the only approach is by road from Perak.

Overleaf: Taiping's Lake Gardens, a former tin mine, transformed during colonial days into Malaysia's loveliest public gardens. Photo by Radin Moh'd Noh Salleh. *Opposite:* Midday prayers at Kuala Kangsar's celebrated Masjid Ubudiah. Photo by Radin Moh'd Noh Salleh.

IPOH & KINTA VALLEY

Time-Capsule Towns that Tin Built

Although Ipoh, Perak's capital city, owes its existence to the profitable tin deposits of the surrounding Kinta Valley, the city's unusual name derives from its earlier existence as a river landing for traders dealing in jungle produce. The *ipoh* or *upas* is a tree which yields a poisonous sap used by the Orang Asli on their blowpipe darts. One such tree still survives in the railway station gardens.

From village to mining hub

Cave drawings found at nearby Tambun indicate that the valley has been home to man since prehistoric times. Written history records that a village existed here in the 15th-century when a Sumatran sea captain ventured upriver to a place called Gunung Ceroh, the highest navigable point on the Kinta River, probably near where Ipoh now stands.

When the British first intervened in 1874, the valley was under the rule of the Dato' Panglima Kinta, one of the eight territorial chieftains under the umbrella of the Perak Sultanate. De Morgan, a French tin prospector, published his Kinta Valley map in 1886, and marked Ipoh as a "Malay village" with a population of a few hundred. By 1890, following a massive influx of immigrants, it had become the largest town in the Kinta Valley, the colonial administration hub and the center for tin-collecting and smelting.

Today Ipoh, with 420,000 inhabitants, sprawls into the surrounding limestone hill-country. However, much of its industry and new suburbs are on the outskirts, leaving the old center with many colonial buildings and the original Chinatown relatively untouched.

A tour of the colonial heart

An obvious starting point for a walking tour of the old town is the Moorish-style **Ipoh Railway Station**, built in 1917 with silver domes on its rooftop and colonnaded archways. Upstairs at the Station Hotel, once a favored hostelry for colonial planters and tin barons, a 183-meter-long (600ft) verandah affords marvellous views of the city against a backdrop of limestone hills.

Opposite the railway station is the elegant **City Hall** (Dewan Bandaran) built in neo-classical style, and beside it the High Court; both were built in the late 19th-century. In the back of City Hall is the Perak Tourist Infor-

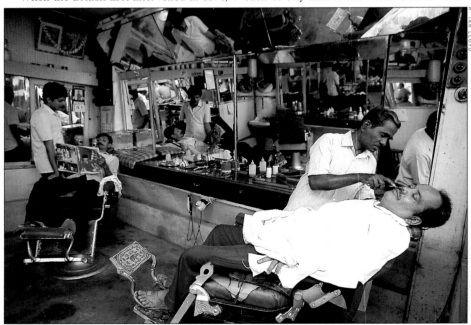

mation Center, and opposite is Gerai Nasi Kandar Hussein, a food center specializing in Indian-Muslim curry and rice dishes.

On the adjacent grassy square is the **J.W.W. Birch Clock Tower** built in 1917 to honor Perak's first British Resident, assassinated in 1875. Around the tower, a formerly controversial frieze illustrating the growth of civilization shows how insensitive the colonial administrators were to local culture; likenesses of prophets, forbidden in Islam, are among the depicted figures.

Further down Jalan Panglima Bukit Gantang Wahab is the Tudor-style **Royal Ipoh Club**. The club overlooks the tree-lined Padang, the playing fields which were an indispensable part of British life in the tropics. These days, early-morning footballers and joggers work out accompanied by the whirr of grass cutters.

Across the road, flanked by Royal Cuban Palms, is the imposing facade of **St. Michael's School**, a turn-of-the-century mission school. Pigeons roost in alcoves above the plaster statues of saints and at feeding time flock to the courtyard of nearby Masjid India, a North Indian-style mosque with scalloped archways.

On the far side of the Padang is the old Hong Kong and Shanghai Bank featuring Corinthian columns and a circular rooftop gazebo. Nearby, on Jalan Sultan Yusof is the FMS Bar—short for Federated Malay States—a favorite drinking haunt of the colonial era which still survives in almost original condition.

Old Chinatown

Follow Jalan Sultan Yusof up to Jalan Dato Maharaja Lela: the grid of streets around here comprise the first Chinatown which evolved from the 1880s when the district chieftain sold lots of land to Chinese merchants at $M25 a block. The old Georgetown Dispensary here is only one of at least 40, late-19th and early-20th century shophouses now listed as historical buildings.

Traditional split-bamboo blinds, known as *chiks*, colorfully painted with the shops' products and names, shade the "five-foot-ways" (covered sidewalks). Behind the *chiks* are dry goods shops selling grains displayed in rattan baskets, Chinese medicine shops which store herbs and roots in wooden drawers painted with calligraphy, and at the Star Printing Works old hand-operated printing presses are still in use. Along Jalan Leech, coffee shops with marble-topped tables

Opposite: *Old-fashioned barbershops, usually run by Indians, are a popular and necessary adjunct of Ipoh's social life.*
Below: *Paintings of mythical dragons and Taoist deities adorn the limestone walls, and gilded Buddhas preside over altars at the Perak Tong cave temple.*

abound, selling Ipoh chicken koay teow, curry mee, and other noodle dishes that Ipoh is famous for throughout Malaysia.

Cave temples

In the suburbs and countryside surrounding Ipoh the limestone hills are pitted with dozens of Buddhist shrines and temples, some dating from the 19th century. Six kilometers (3.7mi) south on the Kuala Lumpur trunk road at Gunung Rapat is **Sam Po Tong**, the region's biggest and oldest cave temple. Founded by a Buddhist monk in the 1890s it has landscaped gardens with symbolic statuary and a traditional Chinese archway lead to the cathedral-sized cave chamber famed for its Buddha statues and sacred tortoise pond.

Just before Gunung Rapat, with its large Mercedes Benz symbol on the summit—a gift from the German car-makers in appreciation of record-breaking sales to Ipoh's tin millionaires—turn into Jalan Raja Musa Mahadi. Follow the signs to **Gua Kek Look Tong**, the newest and most meditative of the cave temples. Set in a spectacular limestone cliff face, this massive cave is also known as the Brass Temple after its gleaming deities. A pot-bellied Laughing Buddha sits framed in the back entrance of the cave gazing out at a panorama of forested limestone hills, green valleys and a lotus-covered pond. The calm of this particular temple is enhanced by cool breezes, and

stalactites and limestone formations left in their natural state.

Beside the old Kuala Kangsar road, 6km (3.7mi) north of Ipoh is the lavish **Perak Tong** where huge wall paintings of Chinese deities have given rise to the nickname "The Tunghuang of the Peninsula" after the famed cave paintings in China. Built in 1926 by a Chinese Buddhist monk, Perak Tong also features a 15-meter-high (49ft) Buddha statue and a staircase which climbs 385 steps to the top of the cave; sadly the view of the surrounding countryside is spoiled by nearby industrial sites.

Life after tin

A 1910 guidebook described the Kinta Valley as "practically one huge tin mine," but travelers these days would be hard-pressed to find an operational tin mine in the region. There is, however, plenty of evidence of the valley's past riches: the sand hills and lakes of former workings scar much of the landscape.

While Ipoh's future without the mines was always assured, there are many old mining towns scattered throughout the valley—such as Kampar, Gopeng, Papan and Batu Gajah—which just went to sleep after the mines closed down. Consequently several of these towns continue to survive as time capsules from the turn of the century.

Few visitors ever reach little-known Papan just off Route 5, 13km (8mi) south of Ipoh, a perfectly-preserved mining town keeps getting into the spotlight. Conservationists want Papan to be designated as a historical site to save it from a zealous mining group which has plans to demolish the entire town to exploit the mineral riches beneath it. But the conservationists have time on their hands: the present depressed value of tin doesn't make this a viable proposition.

In this semi ghost town on a road to nowhere—which was probably what saved it from modernization—is a main street of original shop houses built around the turn of the century, their pastel-colored stucco walls faded from decades under the tropical sun. Except for the odd coffee shop, hardly any commercial activity disturbs the town's somnolence.

Raja Bilah's Istana, Papan's most historic building, is behind the shophouses on the right as you come into town. An entrance archway with the date 1896 leads through a walled garden to this original two-storey mansion built of brick and wood. Beautifully-carved barge boards hang from a Chinese-

Map of Ipoh showing: Kuala Kangsar, Jl. Raja Musa Aziz, Ipoh, YMCA, Taman D. R. Seenivasagam, Regalodge, St. Michael's School, Indian Mosque, Lotte, Syuen, Royal Ipoh Club, Padang, Railway Station & Hotel, City Hall, Masjid Negeri, Central Market, Excelsior, GPO, Masjid Panglima Kinta, Ritz Kowloon, Ritz Garden, Express Bus & Taxi Stand, Batu Gajah, Kuala Lumpur. Jl. Dato Panlima Gantang Wahab, Jl. S. P. Seeniva Sagam, Jl. Sultan Iskandar Shah, Jl. Dato Maharaja Lela, Jl. Sultan Yusof, Jl. Leong Boon Swee, Jl. Bendahara, Jl. Raja Ekram, Jl. Dato Onn Jaafar, Jl. Raja Musa Aziz, Jl. Sultan Idris Shah, Jl. C. M. Yusuf, Jl. Iskandar Sultan Shah, Sungai Kinta. N. 0, 0.25, 0.5, 0.75 Kilometers.

When building ceased the jungle soon took over. A rooftop courtyard for parties, an underground wine cellar, and a lift were all planned for the palatial Moorish-style home. Nowadays banyan roots encircle the columns, woodpeckers nest in the recesses, masonry capitals lie abandoned like ancient Greek ruins, and graffiti from decades ago adorns the plaster walls of the bedrooms.

Wearing a solar-topee, spats, a planter's jacket, and his pistol by his side, Kellie is immortalised on a rooftop freize on the near-by **Sri Maha Mariamman** Temple, easily recognizable among the Hindu deities. One story relates that he built the temple after a number of his labourers mysteriously died while building his house.

Another version tells that Kellie donated a substantial sum towards construction after his prayers for a child were answered. The current watchman at the temple has added his own bizarre twist to the legends by claiming that Tuan Kellie was in fact given poison by his dissatisfied construction workers and that this, not pnuemonia, was the real cause of his death.

tiled roof and a peek through the windows reveals an original interior complete with antique art nouveau furniture. The house is still owned by the Raja's descendants but is only opened by prior arrangement.

Turn off at Pusing for **Batu Gajah**, a former colonial administration center 20km (12.4mi) from Ipoh. The main street is typical of Perak's tin-mining towns: rows of old Chinese shophouses with decorated *chik* blinds line the road, and women dressed in sarongs bicycle home from the market with baskets full of fresh vegetables.

The English always favored building on higher ground and a road winds to the top of a nearby hill, past old colonial bungalows and century-old tropical trees to the regal **District Courthouse**, built in 1892 during the reign of Sultan Idris. The Palladian facade painted in striking black and white, features plaster bas-reliefs of strange eye-like shapes, decorated gables, and a covered walkway.

Above: Young Muslim girls dressed in their school uniforms take a rest under the pastel-colored archways of Ipoh's Masjid India.
Below: Abandoned before its completion, Kellie's Castle, near Batu Gajah, was the folly of a rich English rubber planter.

A planter's folly

Outside of Batu Gajah on the road to Gopeng is an even more impressive building, the mysterious, unfinished folly of William Kellie Smith, known as **Kellie's Castle**. A four-storey tower dominates the massive brick mansion which would have been Malaya's most ambitious planter's home if it had ever been completed. But Kellie died while on holiday in Europe in 1926.

PULAU PANGKOR

Emerald Bays, White Sand Beaches

Over a century ago, Isabella Bird, a most adventurous writer, sailed up the west coast of Peninsular Malaysia, venturing into spots that Westerners had barely glimpsed—let alone a single white woman. One evening her motor launch dropped anchor off the coast of Perak beside The Dindings, the British colonials' name for the Pangkor Island group. At that time the islands were notorious because of the recent murder of an Englishman, but even this sinister event didn't cloud Miss Bird's evocative description of these isles in her book *The Golden Chersonese*:

"The sun was low and the great heat past, the breeze had died away, and in the dewy stillness the largest of the islands looked unspeakably lovely as it lay in the golden light between us and the sun, forest-covered to its steep summit, its rocky promontories running out into calm, deep, green water, and forming almost landlocked bays, margined by shores of white coral sand backed by dense groves of coco-palms whose curving shadows lay dark upon the glassy sea."

From east to west

Since those days Pulau Pangkor, and all of Malaysia, has changed beyond belief, but there is something about this Victorian description, a feeling, a mood, that still lingers on Pangkor's quiet northwestern shores and its offshore islets.

Lumut, an easy-going riverside town is the jump-off spot for Pulau Pangkor, and also offers a colonial-style Resthouse, and a country resort. Despite the presence of Malaysia's largest naval base, the town has a relaxed ambience. From here it's a half-hour ferry ride past the navy docks and across the Manjung Straits to Pangkor, the main settlement on the island.

In Pangkor everyone eats in the seafood restaurants, and this is also where to hire motorbikes and bicycles. However, most visitors overnight at Pasir Bogak, 1km (0.6mi)

across the island on the western shores where all the best beaches and accommodation are found. Facing the white sand beach is a range of lodgings from smart hotels to little thatched-roof chalets. Throughout the week the beach is quiet and pleasant, one can bathe in the green waters and sunbake on the sands in peace, but on weekends it seems like half of Perak has flocked to the seashore and that's the time to escape to the quieter shores of the northwest.

Deserted shores

Bicycles are a popular form of transport, but the island is deceptively large and the roads in the north are hilly and rugged, so if you're not physically fit it's better to hire a motorbike. North from Pasir Bogak the road winds around the coast to Teluk Nipah, a pretty bay with shaded and usually deserted beaches. Tucked into the northern corner is Coral Bay which is popular with snorkelers, although Isabella Bird's experience of "watching scarlet fish playing in the coral forests" is little but a dream these days in the islands of the Melaka Straits.

Further northward the road heads inland through the jungle. In the early morning, monkeys swing through the treetops and hornbills can be seen gliding above the rainforest canopy. Pangkor's most famous beach, Pantai Puteri Dewi—"The Beach of the Fairy Princess"—is now off limits to the public and

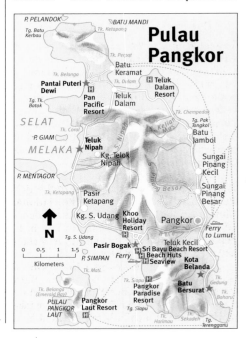

forms part of the luxury Pan Pacific Resort in the far northwest of the island.

According to local legend the name derives from the fate of a Sumatran princess. Worried because her betrothed had failed to return home from battle, she sent out a search party which discovered his grave on Pulau Pangkor. She leapt to her death from the nearby cliff on hearing the news.

Boat builders and Dutch history

When one tires of too much sun and sea, the east coast provides plenty of interesting diversions beside its excellent seafood restaurants. At Sungai Pinang Kecil, boat-builders still make wooden fishing boats in traditional style. Further south, along the prettiest kampung road on the island, just past Kampung Teluk Kecil where gaily-painted wooden houses stand on stilts above the sands, is a 300-year-old Dutch fort.

Kota Belanda, was built by the Dutch as a foothold in their bid to monopolize the rich Perak tin trade. Restored by the National Museum in 1973, this brick bastion surrounded by coconut palms, was the scene of many fierce battles between the Dutch, the Malays and the Bugis from Sulawesi.

At Teluk Gedung, just past Kota Belanda is a large boulder known as the Batu Bersurat—"The Inscribed Stone." Carved on it are the words "Ifcralo 1743," various initials, and a picture of a child being attacked by a tiger. According to local folklore the soldiers stationed at Kota Belanda carved the inscription on the stone as a memorial to a Dutch boy who disappeared and was believed to have been eaten by a tiger.

Offshore isles

On Pulau Pangkor Laut is scenic Emerald Bay where Spencer Chapman in his book *The Jungle is Neutral* made his submarine getaway during the Japanese Occupation. The beach is now the exclusive domain of the Pansea Pangkor Laut Resort. This idyllic resort island off the southwest tip of Pulau Pangkor is reached by ferry from either Pasir Bogak or direct from Lumut. Two other isles, Pulau Mentagor and Pulau Giam, both off the west coast, are good for snorkeling and escaping the crowds.

The offshore islets are seen at their best when silhouetted by Pangkor's magnificent sunsets—conveniently viewed from Pasir Bogak Beach. Sitting on the shoreline at dusk brings to mind Isabella Bird's final thoughts on Pulau Pangkor: "Peace brooded over the quiet shores, heavy aromatic odors of night-blooming plants wrapped us round, the sun sank suddenly, the air became cool, it was a dream of tropic beauty."

Above: The firey sea and sky of a Melaka Straits sunset silhouettes a deserted islet, viewed from Pulau Pangkor's western shore.

CAMERON HIGHLANDS

Tea Estates and Colonial Retreats

Bamboo thickets and towering tree ferns arch overhead giving the serpentine road a tunnel-like appearance as it climbs out of the sultry lowlands. From above the rainforest canopy, the tree-tops look like bunches of green broccoli. Thatched-roof huts perch at the roadside and sometimes you can glimpse their inhabitants—the indigenous Orang Asli—going hunting with their blowpipes.

Ascending Malaysia's spine, the Titiwangsa Range, the cloying equitorial heat is replaced by coolness. As the road crosses into Pahang state, the somber green of the rainforest gives way to bright green hedgerows of manicured tea bushes which characterize the Cameron Highlands, Malaysia's premier hill station.

Perched at an altitude of between 1,500 and 1,800m (4,921-5,905ft) the region was first discovered by its namesake, William Cameron, a government surveyor, in 1885.

In 1925, an official decision was made to develop the highlands. Lured by the cool climate, colonial government administrators, planters and businessmen built fashionable retreats while farmers began clearing the land. This all came to an untimely halt, however, during World War II when the Europeans were forced to return home. After the war, just as the region was getting back on its feet, the 12-year Emergency against the communist insurgents intervened: the highlands were declared a "black" zone and off limits to the public. But since the 1960s the highlands have steadily increased in popularity and tourists—domestic and international alike—now flock here to wear sweaters, sit by log fires, go for bracing walks, and most of all to escape the lowland temperatures.

From Tapah, 59km (36mi) from Ipoh, it's a winding 46km (28.5mi) climb to Ringlet, the first and lowest highlands town. Just north of here beside the Sultan Abu Bakar Dam is the Tudor-style Lakehouse Hotel. Another 14km (8.7mi) further and 305m (1,000ft) higher is Tanah Rata, the hub of the highlands, where old country homes snuggle against the hillsides. Many of the town's old grocery shops, with gold lettering on their stained glass windows advertising long-obsolete wares, are still run by Indian shopkeepers whose descendants first made their way to the Highlands 60 years ago to work on the planta-

JILL GOCHER

tions. Beyond Tanah Rata, trails wind out into the surrounding hills. Half-hour strolls lead to Robinson and Parit Falls where the famed butterfly—Raja Brooke's Birdwing—is often spotted. Other treks range from two-hour hikes to grueling all day mountain climbs, but whatever your level of fitness the cooler temperatures make any jungle walk a joy instead of an ordeal.

Further north, **Ye Olde Smokehouse** a 50-year-old Tudor-style hotel is the ultimate retreat, with its ivy-covered stone walls and English-style gardens. Inside are cosy fireplaces, overstuffed chintz lounges and a reading room full of back copies of England's *Country Life* magazine. Rooms are expensive here, but if you want to experience the life of a colonialist in the tropics this is the place to do it. The next best thing to taking a room is to treat yourself to a Devonshire tea in the garden restaurant.

North of Brinchang, the highlands' highest town, is the Sungai Palas Tea Estate, where bonsai tea bushes cover the hills, and Indian girls snip the tiny shoots on near-vertical slopes. Both Sungai Palas and Boh Estates are still run by descendants of J.A. Russell, an Englishman who took a gamble during the 1930's Depression and applied for a land grant to start a tea plantation. These estates were carved from the jungle and some towering rainforest trees still remain, like giants from the past. Just before the northeast monsoon blows up around November there is a so-called "dry" season when the roses bloom and the skies turn a deep cornflower blue. This is the best time to visit Robertson's Rose Gardens to view their flowers and stock up on homemade rose jam.

Past Sungai Palas, on the way to Gunung Brinchang along Peninsular Malaysia's highest road, a lookout provides a sweeping vista of tea plantations on one side and jungle-clad hills on the other. Further up, the forest changes to oak and laurel and mosses cover the trees and ground. At the summit, vegetation is stunted and matted by the force of the wind, but hardy rhododendrons with spotted pitcher plants hanging from them thrive. The mountain sides drop away almost vertically, but the thick vegetation below gives an illusion of cushioning safety.

The curious case of Jim Thompson

Although much has been cleared since the 1950s when Spenser Chapman wrote of "the terrifying vastness of the Malayan jungle," in his book *The Jungle is Neutral,* there are still

tracts of primeval wilderness which could swallow a man without trace.

The Cameron Highlands' most celebrated mystery involves just such an incident. In 1967 the American "Thai-silk King," Jim Thompson, disappeared after retiring to his room for a nap. The event prompted the biggest search in Malaysia's history. Moonlight Cottage, the bungalow he stayed at on his ill-fated holiday still survives above Tanah Rata. No one knows what happened. Theories include a jungle suicide, communist kidnapping, a CIA hit job (Thompson had earlier ties with them), or a tiger attack, but no clues have ever come to light to confirm any of these.

In the bracing air of this region temperate vegetables, flowers and fruit thrive, and around the hills north of Brinchang are valleys of intricately-terraced and beautifully kept market gardens. Mountain springs are tapped and gravity fed through the terraces to water the spring onions, cabbages and other vegetables that can't survive on the lowlands. Further north, the hills are lined with flower and cabbage farms all the way to Blue Valley, a remote tea plantation, far off the normal tourist trail.

Opposite: Over-stuffed chairs, European bric-a-brac, and open log fires maintain the colonial ambience at Ye Olde Smokehouse, which overlooks the golf course at Tanah Rata.

Cameron Highlands

PERAK RIVER

Through the Valley of the Kings

The Perak River Valley, known in Malay as Hilir Perak, is a traditional rural area with many unspoilt villages, little-known historic sites and peaceful riverine scenery little changed for decades, as well as Malaysia's answer to the Leaning Tower of Pisa.

Leaving Kuala Lumpur for Teluk Intan (166km/103mi), travelers can either turn off at Bidor on the main north road, or take the coastal route via Kuala Selangor.

The tilting tower of Teluk Intan

Formerly known as Teluk Anson (after an officious colonial public servant) this riverine town reverted to its Malay name of Teluk Intan after independence, although some still refer to it by the old title through force of habit. Teluk Intan thrived in the days when river travel was the only means of access to the rich upstream tin-mining fields. But since

road and rail took over, this town, like so many others on the river, was left behind.

The centre of Teluk Intan is dominated by a pagoda-shaped clock tower which tilts—proof that the low-lying town is sinking. Built by a rich Chinese contractor in 1885, the quaint 27-meter-high (88ft) tower is a curious mixture of oriental and colonial architectural styles. The eight-tiered roof is decked with Chinese tiles and the very English-looking clock often shows the wrong time. There are carved gables and a winding staircase that leads to a metal tank on the seventh tier which used to serve as the town's water supply.

Around the streets that encircle the clock tower are century-old shophouses with rows of verandah columns inscribed with Chinese calligraphy. On Jalan Pasar there's a bustling covered market, and colorful statues of Hindu deities adorn the Chettiar Temple behind the clock tower.

One block towards the river from the clocktower is the ageless Restoran Yussoffia, a Muslim-Indian restaurant in a pastel-colored old shophouse decorated with bas reliefs of Arabic writing and Islamic symbols. Their cuisine is as memorable as the decor—try the delicious mutton *murtabah*—Indian pancakes with a spicy meat filling served with curry sauce. There are also good Malay food stalls beside the river, a favorite place to watch the sun go down. Downstream from the town the Sungai Perak lazily loops its way

to the estuary at Bagan Datuk and out into the Melaka Straits.

Elephant village and royal graves

Out of town, cross the Sungai Bidor for Kampung Gajah (26km/16mi), passing rice paddies where wooden homes perch above the flooded fields and pink lotus bloom in the canals. Kampung Gajah means "the elephant village" and in the old days was heavily-populated with *Elephas maximus*. They were a favored method of transport throughout the Lower Perak district, especially among the ruling class, and historical photos show parties fording the Perak River, and prospecting for tin on elephant back. In the swampy forests to the east, an isolated herd still survives, far from their more numerous kin in the central ranges.

Nicknamed "**The Valley of the Kings**," the region between Kampung Gajah and Parit, 65km (40mi) to the north, is the original home of the Perak Sultanate. Dozens of old royal graves dating from the 16th century are found along here, indicated by distinctive road signs, painted royal yellow and bearing the name of each sultan and his number in the dynastic line. Sultan Muzaffar Syah, the founder of the Perak Sultanate, and his wife, are buried at Teluk Bakong, 11km (6.8mi) south of Bota Kanan, and their graves are marked with intricately-carved headstones known as *batu nisan*.

Death of an Englishman

There are other important tombs at Pulau Tiga, Kampung Jawa, Kampung Melayu and Pulau Besar. At the latter village is also another famous grave, that of J.W.W. Birch, the first British Resident of Perak, murdered in 1875 while using a bath house at Pasir Salak, further north.

Birch's assassination was condemned by the colonial government, but later historians are of the opinion that Birch was a tactless administrator who had little regard for Malay laws and religion. He was posting signs of controversial new laws which limited the local chiefs' powers when he was killed.

Just after Kampung Gajah, turn left across the Sungai Perak, and immediately left again along a tiny road which winds past traditional Malay homes made of oiled wood with long shuttered windows, scalloped and latticed eaves and rising-sun carvings on the gables. At Pasir Salak, 2km (1.2mi) along the road, is a historical complex with a reconstructed 120-year-old Rumah Kutai—traditional Perak

house. A memorial marks where Birch met his fate, and a monument in the form of a *kris* dagger commemorates Datuk Maharaja Lela, Datuk Sagor and their followers who lead the uprising against the British and who have since been established as heroes of Malaysian nationalism.

Just before Bota Kanan is the Pusat Pembiakan Tuntung Perak, a center for breeding river turtles which is open to the public. From the crossroads, Route 5 goes to Ipoh (east) or Pulau Pangkor (west). Continue north up the river valley for Parit past traditional houses shaded by orchards of durian trees.

The prickly "queen of fruits" is also favorite fare for tigers and it's said that this is why Parit houses were built so high off the ground. Huge raintrees shade this former royal town where a wooden Malay-style Resthouse overlooks the river, and a footbridge spans the Sungai Perak to a recreational park on an island.

From Parit, travelers can go to Ipoh (31km/19mi) or head to Kuala Kangsar, Perak's current royal capital, by taking the winding, less popular route through rubber estates and sleepy villages along the west bank of the river.

Opposite: *Cats, village women and schoolgirls take advantage of this resting spot outside a sundry store in Teluk Intan.*

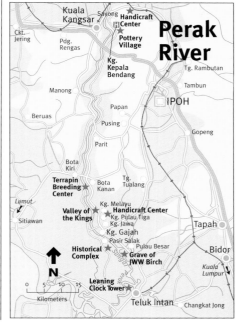

KUALA KANGSAR

Perak's Riverside Royal Capital

Ever since the 1740s when Sultan Muzaffar Syah III quarrelled with his brother and moved his court upriver, Kuala Kangsar has been the royal capital of Perak. Overlooking a bend of the languid Sungai Perak, against a distant backdrop of purple mountains, this picturesque town with its golden-domed mosque and royal palaces still retains much of the tropical ambience that moved a Victorian writer to admit that "I like Kwala Kangsa better than any place that I have been at in Asia..."

In those days the royal town was a few days journey on elephant-back over the mountains to Ipoh, but now travelers either arrive by train or via the 42-km (26mi) expressway which climbs out of the Kinta Valley, tunnels through a rainforested mountain and descends into the Perak River Valley.

Straddling the Kangsar River, which emp-

ties into the Perak, the town's administrative and commercial hub is sited on the north bank, and the royal residences on the south. Chinese and Indian businesses prevail, and the English have also left their mark in the town's many colonial-style buildings, but all these influences have scarcely touched the Malay essence of Kuala Kangsar.

For all the royal sights follow Jalan Istana south along the riverbank. Rambling, tropical trees bedecked with birds'-nest ferns, shade the riverside park—a relaxing spot for watching the wooden ferryboats ply back and forth across the river to Sayong, a kampung renowned for its distinctive pottery (see p. 86). In the windy season, boys fly large moon-shaped kites from the sandbanks on the opposite side of the river.

The turn-of-the-century mansion across from the park was formerly the British Resident's home, but is now a girl's school. This building replaced the old wooden bungalow where Hugh Low, the British Resident, together with his pet apes, entertained Isabella Bird, author of The Golden Chersonese. This book makes fascinating reading for travelers intending to visit Kuala Kangsar (see Further Reading, p. 280).

A fine mosque

Downriver is the Resthouse, where the views from the dining-room verandah are much the same as in 19th-century etchings. From here,

R. MOH'D NOH SALLEH

Jalan Istana winds up a rise, past neo-classical Istana Hulu, the former palace of Perak's 28th sultan, built in 1898. Kuala Kangsar's famed **Masjid Ubudiah** now comes into view, its golden onion domes gleam in the sunlight atop an "Arabian Nights"mosque of white and black marble. Sultan Idris laid the foundation stone in 1913 , but construction was delayed because World War I slowed up imports of the Italian marble which had had to be reordered after the first shipment was destroyed by the sultan's elephants who ran amok while in rut.

When the mosque was eventually finished six years later, Sultan Idris had died and it was opened by his successor, Sultan Abdul Jalil. Nowadays young girls chant from their Korans on the cool marble floors; boys play rounders on the verandah; and at prayer times, sarong-clad villagers wander informally in to pay their respects to Allah. Beside the mosque is the Makam Diraja, the royal mausoleum, and across the road is a well-known *madrasah*, a religious school which specializes in teaching Arabic. Many students go on to study at Middle Eastern Universities.

Regal residences

Continue along Jalan Istana for the grandiose Istana Iskandariah, the official home of the Perak Sultanate, currently occupied by Sultan Azlan Shah. Commanding a hilltop position overlooking the river, the 1930s palace is a combination of Saracenic and Art Deco styles. Viewed from the town jetty upstream, the palace's white towers topped with golden mosaic domes look fantastically mediaeval looming above the tropical greenery.

Beyond the Iskkana Iskandariah is yet another royal residence, the Istana Kenangan, now the **Royal Museum**. This whimsical palace is one of the few remaining royal residences built in traditional style. Early craftsmen used no nails, and this gem of Malay woodwork features carved panels, friezes and barge-boards, and woven wall panels of split bamboo. Open every day except Friday, the museum houses royal regalia and heirlooms. An interesting collection of historical photographs shows royalty on elephant back, and moustachioed British gents sternly posing beside sultans dressed in brocade sarongs with *kris* daggers in their waistbands.

In the past, the villages around the royal palaces were where the royal artisans lived and worked, and past Istana Kenangan, at Kampung Padang Changkak, a few black-smiths using traditional methods still forge *parang* (machetes), and *kris*. Kuala Kangsar is also famous for its gold-thread embroidery on velvet, called *tekatan*, and although some village women are still adept at this needle-craft, they usually only work on commissions. However, at the Kraftangan complex at Enggor, 20km (12.4mi) before Kuala Kangsar on the old Ipoh road, *tekatan* and many other traditional Perak crafts are still being practised and are on sale at the showroom.

On the north side of town, schoolboys play rugby on the spacious Padang of the prestigious **Malay College**, where the register reads like a "*Who's Who*"of Malay public life. Built by the British in 1905 to train royal offspring, the residential college is now open to all academically-qualified boys.

Opposite, is the Pavilion Polo Iskandar, an unusual octagonal tower built of wood and supported by brick columns, where Sultan Iskandar (1918-1938) used to relax between chukkas of polo. Continue along Jalan Tun Abdul Razak, past the hawker selling delicious *rojak petis*—fruit salad with peanut sauce—to the District Offices. The large rubber tree here is one of the first experimental trees planted over a century ago and a forerunner of the crop that changed the face and fortunes of Malaya.

Opposite: Minarets striped in black marble surround the glowing main dome of the celebrated Masjid Ubudiah at Kuala Kangsar.

Kuala Kangsar

1 Istana Kenangan
2 Istana Iskandaria
3 Masjid Ubudiah
4 Royal Mausoleum
5 Istana Hulu
6 Resthouse
7 Former British Residency
8 Rubber Tree
9 Polo Pavilion
10 Malay College
11 Railway Station
12 Bus Station

SAYONG

Pottery Village

Ferry

N

not to scale

POTTERS OF SAYONG

Ceramics Cooked to Perfection

Rabaah Pandak Bidin, housewife and potter, doesn't know how long the people of Sayong have been making their distinctive gourd-shaped pots, known as Labu Sayong. But, she does know that her family have been involved in the ceramics business "forever"—which means at least four generations.

Sayong is a traditional Malay enclave directly opposite Kuala Kangsar on the east bank of the Sungai Perak. Wooden ferries ply across the river to the Sayong jetty. By road, Sayong is approached by turning off at the bridge before Enggor, 19km from Kuala Kangsar. There is a government handicraft center at Enggor, but turn right to head for Kg. Kepala Bendang, the original Sayong potters' village. After 3km, turn left at a sign which says, 'Koperasi Industri Kg. Kepala Bendang.' The potters' village is 2.5km further on, easily recognizable by the workshops and showrooms built under their homes built on high stilts and rows of pottery drying in the sun.

Villagers now produce teapots, vases, urns and curios, but their biggest seller, and the reason the village acquired renown, are the gourd-shaped water vessels known as *Labu Sayong*. Although many families now own refrigerators, these jars are still used, for they keep drinking water at a cool, but not icy, temperature. It is believed that water stored in this way is good for the constitution.

These days, the pottery is made in moulds and finished on the pottery wheel. "We're all family here, no outsiders," says Rabaah's sister, Chah Ngah Syed, who uses a river stone to polish a vase while her sister incises designs into the still-pliant clay using a tool with a nib-like point.

Reminiscent of Malay woodcarvings, the designs are simple, but effective. The potters use patterns which occur in their everyday life; ferns, flowers, leaves and a design known as *kubah masjid*—the dome of the mosque. Nothing is drawn beforehand. The design is simply started at any point on the pot, which is turned while incising the pattern, and the end of the design always joins exactly with the beginning—a knack which takes years of practice to acquire.

After the pots have been polished and decorated they are dried in the sun then baked in brick-lined kilns set apart from the houses. Wood fuel is used and the firing time is dependent on the heat of the fire and the weather; there are no temperature gauges to judge by. Rabaah regards the process simply like cooking. She checks the pots after eight hours and if they are not "cooked" then they are left in longer.

Although the potters now make terracotta-colored as well as the original black wares, the latter are still the best known. The glaze is acquired by burying the kiln-hot pots in a mound of *sekam* (rice husks)—the heat emanating from the pot chars the husks which turns the glaze black.

A decade ago business was slow, and it seemed as though plastic was taking over, but with increasing tourism and a growing popularity, the traditional crafts are now undergoing a revival and the future of the potters of Sayong looks assured.

Below: *A young potter incises a leaf-like design around the base of a Sayong jar.*

KOTA TAMPAN

Solving a Stone Age Mystery

The status of Kota Tampan as a Palaeolithic site was the subject of furious debate among archaeologists specializing in Southeast Asia for over a decade. One theory, proposed by a British team of Sieveking and Walker (archaeologist and geologist respectively) dated the site as Middle Pleistocene (200,000-500,000 years old) and thus the only early Stone Age site in Peninsular Malaysia. But this was a controversial theory and subsequently disputed by scholars from the US, Europe and Australia.

In 1987, such doubts, and a lack of tangible evidence, prompted a team from University Science Malaysia, Penang, to search for sites in the Kota Tampan area that would help solve the riddle of whether or not early man did live there and if so, when.

Kota Tampan, a village some five kilometers (three miles) from the town of Lenggong in Perak was the focus of our operation. Excavations at one particular site began to reveal exclusively stone artifacts. The dense accumulation of quartzite chunks, flakes, and chips, together with small quartzite boulders and some tools, was puzzling at first. However, later it became clear that we had found anvils and hammer-stones (the "equipment" for making stone tools), cores (the raw material for tools), waste from stone-tool production, and finished and unfinished stone tools themselves.

What we had discovered was in fact a Stone-Age "factory" with all its evidence left intact and undisturbed. This meant that we had hit upon the centre of Palaeolithic life, as stone tools were the focus of their material culture. An undisturbed site means that the evidence is firm, and thus, the site had the potential of not only settling earlier disputes, but also of providing more evidence on the Palaeolithic era as a whole.

The spatial arrangement of artifacts observed during the excavation suggested that the artifacts were in-situ, and that we

were the first to view them after the site had been sealed over by ash from a volcanic eruption in Toba, Sumatra. This ash provided us with the age of the site. Petrographic examination of 12 soil samples taken from the artifact-bearing levels and the level above, revealed that all the samples contained a varying proportion of partially weathered volcanic ash. When chemically matched to the ash from Lake Toba's last eruption it was found to date from around 31,000 years ago.

The presence of ash above and in between the artifacts suggests a contemporaneity of events connecting the volcanic eruption and the last use of the site. The presence of large numbers of unfinished tools and blanks seems to indicate that the catastrophic eruption caused the sudden abandonment of the site. This gives us a rare opportunity of being able to know the exact point of abandonment and its cause.

Kota Tampan has already provided much-needed evidence of the various methods of making Palaeolithic stone tools. Another of the site's important contributions to Southeast Asian archaeology is the identification of tool-making "equipment" which when found out of context is unrecognizable. Since the whole region was a cultural entity in earlier times, the site has provided a vital missing link, not just in Malaysian prehistory, but also that of Southeast Asia as a whole.

—*Zuraina Majid*

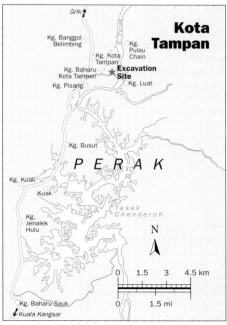

TAIPING

"Town of Everlasting Peace"

At mid-morning in the coffee shops of Taiping customers fervently place bets: not on horse-races or "four-digit" lotteries, but on a game of chance peculiar to this town. The local gamblers are putting money on what time the afternoon rain will begin. That it will arrive is a virtual certainty for Taiping lays claim to being the wettest town in Peninsular Malaysia. This daily shower makes for cool nights and fresh mornings, and also provides another reason to hang about the town coffee shops which serve up some of the country's tastiest and cheapest cuisine.

Tin and opium gang wars

Located 36km (22mi) north of Kuala Kangsar, the "Town of Everlasting Peace" as Taiping's name translates, was anything but peaceful in the mid-19th century when it was at the center of gang wars between rival Chinese clans fighting over tin holdings. Their bitter feuds, known as the Larut Wars, seriously affected the region's lucrative tin and opium production and eventually led to British interference and the inevitable appointment of a Resident. The clans were split up—the Hai San to Taiping and the Ghee Hin to neighboring Kamunting.—and after that calm prevailed.

From 1848, when Long Jaafar, the district Malay chieftain, had started giving the Chinese mining rights, the population expanded rapidly. A few decades later a traveler remarked that Taiping was "an important Chinese town, with a street about a mile long, with large bazaars and shops making a fine appearance, being much decorated in Chinese style."

Approaching Taiping today, much still rings true from this Victorian description. Mauve-colored hills rise abruptly behind the still-predominantly Chinese town which has some fine 19th-century architecture, the scenic Lake Gardens, and Malaysia's oldest railway station, museum, and hill resort.

Taiping is an easy and absorbing town to wander around, with many decorative old shops and houses adorned with art nouveau tiles, plaster bird and flower reliefs, and wooden nameboards painted in gold calligraphy. The original Town Market on Jalan Pasar is one of the last wood and wrought-iron markets still functioning on the peninsula. On the market's perimeter are hawker stalls which

R. MOH'D NOH SALLEH

offer cheap and tasty noodle dishes. Opposite, on the walls of an old Indian restaurant an antique clock proclaims "Bismillah Eating House Established 1900." This traditional establishment on Jalan Besar serves excellent *murtabah* and *roti canai*.

Taiping's multi-cultural population worships along Jalan Kota where within two blocks are the Old Taiping Town Mosque, the Sri Nagamuthu (Hindu) temple, Seng Tong Chinese Temple and the Indian Mosque. On Jalan Stesen is the old zinc-roofed railway station, which retains a steam-train water pump, signs hung in wrought-iron brackets, and wooden swing doors on the Station Master's Office. Further along Jalan Stesen, shaded by huge raintrees, is the King Edward VII School built in 19th-century colonial style.

Back on Jalan Kota, are the **District Offices**, another architectural gem built in 1879, which feature a distinctive Palladian facade and rooftop pediments. The offices were designed by Francis Caulfield, who was also the architect of the similar-styled Batu Gajah Courthouse. Further north on Jalan Taming Sari is another fine example of colonial architecture: the Muzium Perak, Malaysia's oldest museum built in 1886. Its fascinating displays include an elephant's skull, a tapir's skeleton, stuffed mousedeers, a rattan elephant *howdah*, Malay weapons and coats of mail, and traditional crafts and costumes.

Lake Gardens and Bukit Larut

Opposite the museum, follow the walls of Malaysia's oldest jail and turn right for the renowned Lake Gardens, a chain of lakes and lotus ponds with islands of palms and feathery bamboo. These century-old parklands, created from abandoned tin-mines, are at their best at dawn and dusk when *tai-chi* exponents exercise on the spacious lawns, and joggers and walkers take to the canopied roads shaded by the peninsula's most magnificent raintrees. On the massive, moss-covered branches grow orchids, creepers and at least 15 different fern species.

Follow Jalan Air Terjun through the Lake Gardens for Bukit Larut, formerly called Maxwell's Hill after the British Resident who first proposed the idea of a hilltop retreat in the late-19th century. Early visitors made their ascent in chairs carried by coolies. These days, land rovers climb the winding 9km (5.6mi) road through towering rainforest to the 1,035-meter-high (3,395ft) resort which has changed little since colonial days. Old-style wooden resthouses provide basic fare and accomodation amongst terraced lawns, pine trees and dahlia gardens. There's not much to do here, but that's part of the attraction. Early morning, before haze envelops the coast, the view spans from Pulau Pangkor in the south to Penang in the north. The nearby forests offer good opportunities for watching birds and spotting gibbon and wild boar.

Outside Taiping

Kuala Sepetang, formerly Port Weld, 11 km (6.8 mi) west of Taiping, is a bustling fishing port in the midst of a mangrove forest which can be viewed from a wooden walkway built above the wetlands at the Forest Park. Matang, a picturesque kampung on the way to Kuala Sepetang, is a traditional Malay stronghold where an old walled enclosure is all that remains of Kota Ngah Ibrahim, a fort which figured prominently during the Larut Wars of the 1860s.

Ngah Ibrahim was later exiled to the Seychelles by the British for his involvement in the killing of the British Resident J.W.W. Birch. Maharaja Lela, one of the other conspirators, and later a hero of Malay nationalists, was hung from a tree that still stands in the fort grounds.

Opposite: Draped in ferns and mosses, these century-old raintrees planted during the British colonial days, form an arch over the road at Taiping's Lake Gardens.

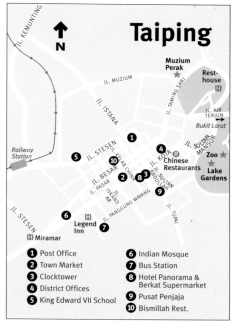

Taiping

Muzium Perak ★

Rest-house ⊞

JL. MUZIUM

JL. KEMUNTING

JL. ISTANA

JL. TAMING SARI

JL. AIR TERJUN →

Bukit Larut

JL. SULTAN MANSOR

Railway Station

JL. STESEN

❶

❹ ⊞ Zoo ★

Chinese Restaurants

Lake Gardens

❺ ❿ JL. BESAR

JL. KELAB CINA

JL. KOTA

JL. SULTAN ABDULLAH

❷ ❽ ❸

JL. PASAR

JL. ISTANA AIR

❾

JL. PANGGUNG WAYANG

JL. TUPAI

JL. STESEN

❻ ⊞

Legend Inn ❼

⊞ Miramar

❶ Post Office
❷ Town Market
❸ Clocktower
❹ District Offices
❺ King Edward VII School
❻ Indian Mosque
❼ Bus Station
❽ Hotel Panorama & Berkat Supermarket
❾ Pusat Penjaja
❿ Bismillah Rest.

PART IV

Introducing Penang, Kedah and Perlis

An elderly tourist overheard mentioning that "after I visited Penang I also went to Malaysia," may have got his geography muddled up, but such is the fame of the nation's best-known destination that he can be forgiven his blunder. Located off the northwest coast, this turtle-shaped island, a mere 24km (15mi) long by 12km (7.5mi) wide, is renowned for its beaches, spicy cuisine, elegant colonial architecture, bazaars and temples, as well as its independent-minded, multi-cultural population.

Penang has long inspired travelers to wax lyrical of its charms. In the 1930s, a fastidious New Yorker appalled by other Asian cities noticed that in Penang, "Europeans lived by choice" and that the island "by virtue of its climate, its scenery, its inhabitants, its many amenities, is livable and human." Later, Penang gained fame as a favorite stopover on the Asia hippy trail. Today, although "The Pearl of the Orient" has lost a little of its lustre through rampant urbanization it still has a magnetic appeal.

In 1786, Captain Francis Light, an adventurous English trader in the service of the East India Company, persuaded the Sultan of Kedah to sign over Pulau Pinang, "The Isle of Betel-nut Palms" in return for protection against enemies. This promise was never honored, but there was little Kedah could do against the might of the British Empire.

Penang thrived as an entrepôt for the lucrative tea and opium trade between India and China. Georgetown port was crammed with *praus*, junks, and steamers bringing the Chinese, Burmese, Javanese, Arabs, Malays, Sikhs, Madrassees, and Klings: the ancestors of today's cosmopolitan population. Penang's importance declined with the rise of Singapore, but it boomed again during the tin rush of the 1850s and the turn-of-the-century rubber boom. The island continues to dominate the economy of the northwest today.

Kedah, "The Nation's Rice Bowl," and pocket-sized Perlis, the two northwestern states which border Thailand, are as unknown as Penang is famed, although the idyllic isles of Pulau Langkawi are currently the rising stars of Malaysian tourism. Compared to Penang, and especially Georgetown, a very Chinese city, the northwest states are still largely agricultural and Malay-dominated.

Traditional villages are surrounded by paddy fields, and life still follows the rhythm of the harvest. Few tourists ever spend time exploring the northwest—except for Pulau Langkawi—and this region is a delight for travelers who enjoy being a novelty.

Kedah lays claim to being Malaysia's oldest state. The present royal family trace their roots back to pre-Islamic times, and in the south at Lembah Bujang are remains of 7th century Hindu/Buddhist temples. In 1821, Kedah was conquered by the Thais who ruled the state for the next 25 years.

Remnants of those times linger in the state capital of Alor Star, where 19th-century royal palaces show distinctive Thai architectural influences. The Sultan was later reinstated, but the region was under Thai suzerainty until 1909 when Kedah was transferred to Britain. However, they successfully controlled their own affairs and British influence was minimal.

Limestone massifs pitted with caves, loom above the rice paddies and sugarcane fields of tiny Perlis, Malaysia's smallest state. Originally part of Kedah, the state—wedged against Thailand in the northwestern corner—was separated in 1842 when the Thais handed Perlis to Raja Syed Hussein whose successors have ruled there ever since.

Overleaf: Viewed from Penang Hill, the peninsula's main range provides a backdrop to Southeast Asia's longest bridge.
Opposite: This Georgetown chef defty demonstrates the art of making roti canai—an Indian griddle-cake. Both photos by Jill Gocher.

PENANG TOWN SIGHTS

A Stroll Through Old Georgetown

A labyrinth of streets, lanes, and alleyways which weave through a sea of red-tiled roofs makes Georgetown's old center a marvellous place to explore on foot. If the heat gets too much, or a tropical storm descends, a trishaw, locally known as a *becak*, is the perfect alternative. Many of the downtown streets date from the original town plan, and bear names of early administrators like Light and Farquhar, or survive as testimony to their original inhabitants like Lebuh Chulia, where the Chulias—Indian Muslims from the Malabar Coast—first settled.

Nowadays "street" is translated to the Malay *lebuh*, "road" to *jalan*, "lane" to *lorong*: Love Lane thus becomes Lorong Cinta. Some names have been changed by zealous town planners, such as Lebuh Pitt which recently became Jalan Masjid Kapitan Kling, after its famous mosque. Residents, however, often still use the old names.

A historic site may be the main reason to head down a certain street, but in Georgetown it is often what is glimpsed or experienced along the way which makes a walk in the old city most memorable: an old woman waving incense before an altar; a pavement palmist engrossed in his art; a trishaw piled high with smiling children; or the aroma of fresh coffee from a wayside stall.

Edifices from a more leisurely age

A good starting point is from the domed Clock Tower at the crossroads of Lebuh Light and Lebuh Pantai. A Chinese tycoon presented it to the city as a gift on Queen Victoria's Diamond Jubilee in 1897. Facing the seafront Esplanade, is Fort Cornwallis, built on the site where legend has it that Francis Light ordered his ships to fire cannonloads of silver coins into the thick jungle to inspire the natives to clear the land faster.

Apparently this ploy was used to keep the laborers busy while awaiting a shipment of axes from Melaka. The story doesn't mention whether they used *parang* machetes to hack at the jungle, or their bare hands. Only the stone walls remain and some fine cannon, including the 16th-century Seri Rambai (facing north) which is said to aid childless women if they place flowers in the barrel.

Around the Padang—the large playing fields where the colonials played cricket,

bowls and croquet—are many important buildings from the British era. To the west are some elegant, grey and white buildings built in the late Victorian style which formerly housed the municipal offices. On the southern side is the classical-styled Dewan Negeri (Penang State Assembly Building), and further up Lebuh Light is the old High Court (Mahkamah Tinggi). Relax on the seaward side of the Padang where hawkers sell *rojak* and cold drinks.

Continue along Lebuh Light to the Convent of the Holy Infant Jesus which occupies the site of Francis Light's original dwelling. Domestic science students still use part of what is believed to have been his kitchen. Venture past the convent's Georgian facade and into the interior where arched collonades, cloisters and couryards dating from 1852 lend a Spanish colonial touch. Old Eurasian nuns in beige habits pray at the art nouveau chapel with its honeycombed ceiling and carved pews, as sunlight streams in through the stained-glass windows.

West along Lebuh Farquhar is the celebrated **E & O Hotel** (Eastern and Oriental) built in 1884, now undergoing renovation. Famous literary guests like Noel Coward and Somerset Maugham once dined in the still-functioning Grill Room and the Hollywood movie queen Rita Hayworth apparently sunbathed in her deckchair by the seafront. It was originally owned by the Armenian Sarkies brothers, who also established Singapore's Raffles and Rangoon's Strand. Past the E & O is an old walled cemetery where century-old frangipani trees with gnarled trunks litter their scented flowers over archaic tombs including that of Penang's founding father, Francis Light. The inscriptions on the headstones give a glimpse of the harshness of life for those early settlers.

Turn back along Jalan Sultan Ahmad Shah for the **Cheong Fatt Tze Mansion**, a rambling old home with faded stucco walls on the corner of Lebuh Leith. Recently restored, this 31-room residence built in 1870 is one of the last three—the other two are in Medan and Manilla—of its style surviving outside of China. It is still a private residence and visitors have to be content with a peek through the iron gates at its massive walls, wrought-iron verandahs and traditional Chinese tiled roof adorned with porcelain motifs. Inside, out of sight, are elaborate carved doorways, tiled courtyards and a spiral staircase.

Opposite the mansion is St. Xavier's Institution, an old Catholic School, and further along Lebuh Leith, in dazzling white, is the Cathay Hotel. Its plaster reliefs are painted lime-green and China blue, and the vast

Below: One of the oldest churches in the East, St.George's Anglican Church, built in 1817.

JILL GOCHER

tiled lobby and spacious rooms are reminders of a more leisurely age. Turn left into Lebuh Mentri, where the old shophouses still retain their art nouveau tiles and carved woodwork, then take a left into Lorong Cinta with more decorated shophouses, corner coffee shops and Chinese clanhouses, back to Lebuh Farquhar. On the corner is the Gothic-style Cathedral of the Assumption with its twin spires, and down the street, the **Penang State Museum and Art Gallery** is crammed with fascinating memorabilia from Penang's past, including historical paintings dating from the early 1800s and exhibits on the Chinese triad wars in 1867.

Historic houses of worship

On the corner of Lebuh Pitt, shaded by massive angsana trees which shower the grounds with a "golden rain" of blooms every April, is St.George's Church built in 1817. A historical air pervades Southeast Asia's oldest Anglican church constructed in superb Georgian style.

The matching pavilion in the grounds is a monument dedicated to Francis Light. From here, walk down Lebuh Pitt to the smoke-enshrouded Kuan Yin Temple which honors the Goddess of Mercy, the favorite deity of Malaysian-Chinese. Pigeons swoop about the courtyard where beggars wait for alms from businessmen who come to pay homage to another popular deity—the God of Prosperity.

Renovated and redecorated since its inception in 1800, the temple still retains its original tiled roof elaborately decorated with symbolic porcelain figures. Opposite, wander down Lebuh China, the original "Chinese Street," and turn into Lebuh King which has some impressive old Chinese clan houses. At No 32, the 19th-century Tua Peh Kong, legendary scenes are carved into the granite wall panels and the roof ridges are adorned with tiled motifs.

Further south, Lebuh King becomes a "Little India" and in the early morning the pavements are taken over by tea and *roti* sellers. On the corner of King and Chulia, what looks like a small mosque is in fact a white-domed shrine to the Nagore Durgha, a saintly Muslim from southern India. Indians in checkered sarongs relax on the cool marble floor and tucked in around the perimeter are a cupboard-sized *mamat* stall crammed with cigarettes and other sundry items, and a tiny store where a hatter makes velvet fez-like caps known as *songkok*. On neighboring Lebuh Penang, Indian money-lenders known as *Chettiar* still dress in their toga-like *dhoti* and sit on wooden floors to conduct their business. In adjacent textile shops, parrot-colored saris drape from the ceilings and brassware gleams in the sunshine.

On Lebuh Queen, the elaborate archway of the Sri Mariamman Temple is invariably occupied by hundreds of pigeons which

perch on the limbs, heads, and tridents of the dozens of Hindu deities. At the entrance arch, known as a *gopuram*, sari-clad devotees twist flowers into garlands for the gods. Within the temple, built in 1833, are shrines to the major deities and to the Nava Grahas—the nine planets of Indian astrology.

Return to Lebuh Pitt for its dominant attraction, the Kapitan Kling Mosque, built in 1916 to replace the original 1801 building constructed by the East India Company's Muslim troops. The Klings (a term now considered

derogatory) were the Indian Muslim traders from the Coromandel Coast and many of the mosque's patrons today are descendants of these early adventurous businessmen. In a tiny, covered lane beside the mosque some of these same Indians dish up perhaps Penang's tastiest *nasi kandar*—rice and curries—with a distinctive South Indian flavor.

Into the world of the clans

Walk further down Lebuh Pitt, past the shops selling lacquered tiffin-carriers, costumes for lion dances, and temple paraphenalia, to the corner of Lebuh Armenia, where Lebuh Pitt becomes Lebuh Cannon. The street's name derived from the clan wars of 1867 when the Tua Peh clan rioted and the British fired cannons to disrupt them. The Tua Peh clanhouse is still situated near this junction. Follow Lebuh Cannon to tiny, cobblestoned Lorong Cannon on the left. Pass under the archway, past the 19th-century Chinese town houses which line both sides of this narrow passage into Cannon Square.

This large courtyard, paved with granite, is the site of "The Dragon Mountain Hall," better known as the **Khoo Kongsi**, Malaysia's—and possibly Southeast Asia's—most elaborate clanhouse. Entry is free, but a pass to enter the Kongsi must be obtained from the signposted offices on the right. Every available surface of the building, both exterior and interior, is either gilded,

carved, enamelled, tiled, or painted. Reputed to weigh a massive 25.4 tonnes (25 tons), the roof is adorned with dragons and flowers made of porcelain tiles. An image of the Khoo clan's patron saint, a renowned 3rd-century Ch'in general, takes center stage in the main hall. In the left room resides the God of Prosperity, and to the right are carved and gilded ancestral tablets of the Khoo clan—Chinese bearing the Khoo name—dating back to 1840.

The forerunner of this clanhouse was even more elaborate, but on the eve of its completion in 1898 it burnt to the ground. "An act from above," was the unanimous verdict, as Penangites considered the ornate clanhouse too fantastic for the use of mere mortals and the gods responded accordingly. Across the courtyard, unnoticed by most visitors, is the stage for the *wayang*—Chinese operas staged for the gods. The theatre features beautifully-carved wooden doors and massive, circular roof beams.

Bustling street bazaars

Backtrack through Lorong Cannon, turn left, and at the end of the street facing Lebuh Acheh is the Masjid Melayu, the Malay Mosque founded in 1808 by a rich Muslim from Acheh in Sumatra. The distinctive minaret is in Egyptian style while the tiled roofs are traditional Javanese design. Follow this street up to Lebuh Carnarvon where craftsmen still turn out huge Chinese coffins made from tree trunks. Other shops specialize in paper Mercedes and replicas of domestic appliances which are burnt at Chinese funerals for the dead to use in their afterlife.

Opposite: Bargain hard with the fast-talking salesmen at the leatherware stalls off Jalan Penang. *Above, left:* Trishaws trundle past Masjid Kapitan Kling in Georgetown. *Above, right:* Garish pink buns are a favorite offering at the Festival of the Nine Emperor Gods.

Lebuh Carnarvon—especially around the old colonial market at the corner of Lebuh Campbell—is at its best in the early morning when the entire street becomes a market. Trishaws mass at the entrance awaiting housewives laden with their day's shopping. Stalls are not in any order, it is more like organized chaos. A butcher hacks up pork beside a mango seller, whose sales patter is drowned out by a neighboring stall which advertises "Buddha Cassettes Sold Here." Piles of fresh greens are stacked beside brooms and brushes. The rasp of a sugar-cane crusher making juice, competes with the sizzle of bean shoots fried with noodles, and the haggling of old women as they sort out sea slugs and barter over salted eggs.

Follow Lebuh Campbell, past the gold-smiths with their shops full of gleaming wares, presided over by mostachioed Sikh guards with rifles; past Jalan Pintal Tali, better known as Rope Walk, to Jalan Kuala Kangsar—yet another bustling morning market. Here, chickens await their fate, and hogs' heads hang from butchers' hooks. Nonyas throng the cake stalls which sell *nonya kuih*, pastel-colored delicacies made of rice flour and coconut cream. Bunches of Chinese sausages, like red candles, hang in the door-ways of dry-goods shops where the pavements are filled with baskets of dried fish. A cloth merchant surrounded by bolts of cot-

ton, flings out a couple of meters of pink fabric for a customer's appraisal and across the way, housewives dip their arms, elbow-deep into buckets to test the firmness of last night's squid catch.

More market action centers around Jalan Penang; at the covered emporium of stalls known as Chowrasta Bazaar; at Picadilly Bazaar which specializes in cloth; and the pavement leather stalls at the beginning of Lebuh Chulia. Turn left on Jalan Penang for the hard-to-miss, 65-storey, KOMTAR building which dominates this end of Georgetown. Inside there are air-conditioned fast-food joints, department stores and cloth-ing boutiques, but somehow it doesn't quite fit in with the rest of the city—and for smart shopping save your money for Kuala Lumpur's malls.

Georgetown has countless more attrac-tions; there are dozens of lanes like Lorong Toh Aka off Lebuh Carnarvon with 19th-cen-tury, pastel-colored townhouses which still display their traditional calligraphic sign-boards; there are the antique shops on Lebuh Bishop; the Victorian-style commercial build-ings and shipping companies along Lebuh Pantai; and the old Chinese clan piers at Pengkalan Weld—just to name a few.

Thai temples and tropical gardens

Further afield, on the outskirts of the city reached by either a pleasant walk or a short taxi ride, is the area known as Pulau Tikus. Follow Lebuh Farquhar west into Jalan Sultan Ahmad Shah (Northam Road), which is shad-ed by giant raintrees. Opulent, domed and turretted mansions—former residences of Straits Chinese tycoons—line both sides of this avenue which used to be nicknamed "Millionaires Row."

At the roundabout, turn left for the seafront Persiaran Gurney (Gurney Drive), a very popular evening eating spot famous for its roadside stalls selling *laksa*—a fish and noodle soup garnished with basil—and its Chinese hawker centers and seafood restaurants. Go straight across the round-about into Jalan Kelawai, and continue until Lorong Burma. Here, the renowned Thai temple, Wat Chayamangkalaram, houses a 32-meter (105ft) Reclining Buddha. A notice warns visitors against "photo-takin,", wearing hat or shoes, and to "beware of shoe thieves." Statues of fabulous serpentine creatures coil along the entrance path guarded by mythical Thai "birdmen."

The building which houses the Buddha is

R. IAN LLOYD

of little artistic merit, but behind, unnoticed by most devotees, is an aesthetic stupa, adorned with reliefs of Thai temple dancers which was built in 1900. Directly across the lane, is the lesser-known Burmese Temple where white stone elephants guard the gateway. Inside, where an aura of serenity pervades, are filigree metal archways, a Burmese-style stupa.

Running parallel to Lorong Burma is Lorong Bangkok, a charming lane flanked on both sides by a complete ensemble of pre-war terrace houses in the same architectural style, undisturbed by any other development. Each two-storey house is painted in matching creams and yellows, and features Chinese tiled roofs, stained-glass doors and windows, and arched and columned verandahs. Wander up to Jalan Burma and into the Pulau Tikus township—heart of the *baba* and *nonya* (Straits Chinese), Eurasian and Thai communities—where there is an interesting morning market and many excellent food stalls and restaurants featuring *nonya* and Thai cuisine.

From Pulau Tikus town it is about 2 km (1.25 mi) to Penang Botanic Gardens. Follow Jalan Burma to Jalan Gottlieb, turn left passing the Penang Chinese Girls' School on the right and through an avenue of stately Cuban Royal Palms which have smooth grey trunks like Roman columns. Turn right at Jalan Kebun Bunga, where the road is lined with huge, century-old *angsana* trees. On the right

is the **Nattukkottai Chettiar Temple**, Penang's largest Hindu temple, and a center for the annual Thaipusam festival when penitents pierce their flesh with sacred skewers and shoulder decorated structures known as *kavadi*. Over the entrance arch are colorful plaster statues of deities flanking a peacock.

Multiplying monkeys

Along the road to the gardens, groups of monkeys gather. They used to be a major attraction at the gardens and a source of much revenue for the peanut sellers. However they bred so profusely that gang wars broke out when they became aggressive, and so now feeding is not permitted inside the gardens, hence their very dominant presence just outside the gates.

Paths lead alongside the stream and up to a waterfall—the gardens are also called Waterfall Gardens—and a trail starts from here to Penang Hill. There are some fascinating tropical trees here, including the cannonball tree, with its enormous spherical fruit; the brilliant, pink-flowered Thai *bungor* tree; and the *penaga*, or ironwood tree, which caused Penang's early colonial land-clearers such anguish.

Opposite: Junior members of a Chinese street opera group dress up in outsized satin robes.
Below: Mythical winged dragons guard a globe at the Burmese Temple in Lorong Burma.

PENANG ISLAND

Around the Pearl of the Orient

In the afternoon we drove outside the city, through groves of coconut-palms and gardens wonderfully green, to swim in a blue bay and sip drinks on the verandah of a comfortable club.

Patrick Balfour
Grand Tour—Diary of an Eastward Journey

Although not quite as idyllic as this 60-year-old description, Penang's coast still offers plenty of opportunities to indulge in similar sensory and aesthetic pleasures, as well as others as varied as a funicular railway ride to a cool hill retreat, a temple guarded by sacred vipers, classical Malay villages, and a farm of 3,000 butterflies.

The 70km (43mi) journey around the island is an easy day trip by car or motorcycle which can be hired at very competitive prices opposite the hotels at Batu Ferringhi. Buses also make the trip, but there are many changes and it is a slow business. Bicycles are also fine for the north coast, but the winding hilly country through the western part of the island makes for tougher going.

The northern beaches

Heading out of Georgetown, follow Jalan Sultan Ahmad Shah which turns into Jalan Kelawei and then at the next roundabout turn into Jalan Tanjung Tokong. Along here, squeezed into the suburban sprawl, are some Chinese market gardens where neat rows of greens are tended by weathered old men in conical hats. When the road again joins the coast there are some small Malay roadside stalls that serve *laksa* and other Penang Malay specialities, as well as a good view back around the bay to Georgetown.

Further west, Tanjung Tokong and Tanjung Bunga were once bucolic fishing villages, but are now part of Georgetown's satellite suburbs. From here, the beaches begin, as do the luxury holiday resort complexes carved into the hillsides which loom above the serpentine road that has changed little in 20 years—although the surroundings and the volume of traffic have certainly kept pace with the times.

The beaches improve the further west one travels, but the bay overlooked by the Ferringhi Beach Hotel is clean and good for swimming. Around the next point, 14km (8.7mi) from Georgetown is Batu Fer-

ringhi—Malaysia's best-known beach. Its shoreline is dominated by luxury hotels and restaurants, souvenir shops, car-hire booths and moneychangers lining the road in front of the resorts.

Pockets of Malay kampungs, and a couple of small guesthouses—remnants of the 1960s when Batu Ferringhi was a laid-back hippy hangout with thatched huts—still survive around the back of the shops and along the western end of the beach. Despite its brash veneer, and the fact that there are lots of bet-

ter beaches in Malaysia, Batu Ferringhi has a certain magnetic appeal.

Elderly tourists on package tours—highly visible in their newly-acquired batiks and suntans—flock in from Europe and Australia. Children also adore the beach for the water is warm and inviting and there is always plenty of action going on such as para-sailing and windsurfing. From the beach you can see an outcrop of rock called Lovers Isle, with the mountains of Kedah shrouded in the distance by blueish mist, both lend an air of the exotic to the scene, especially as night draws near.

Restaurant prices are considerably higher here than in Georgetown, but many of the hotels serve superb food and on weekends they are often booked up by discerning Penangites themselves. It's a good idea to avoid the northern beaches at weekends for the bays and beaches become crammed with picnickers and holidaymakers. But, come Monday, the beaches are quite deserted, particularly Lone Crag Beach, a shaded bay 3km (1.9mi) north of Batu Ferringhi.

To the end of the world

Teluk Bahang, the most westerly town on the north coast, was until recently a quiet fishing village completely devoid of high-rise hotels. However, even now with the inevitable addition of yet another monolithic resort, the local inhabitants still rely more on fishing than tourism for their living, and the village

has lost little of its calm allure.

At the far end of the beach a wooden jetty heads out to sea where a flotilla of fishing boats is moored. There's plenty of maritime activity here, particularly at dusk when fishermen in small wooden sampans shuttle between ship and shore ferrying ice, bait and fish. The eastern end of the beach, away from the village, is good for swimming and sunbathing. Sunsets along this coast are particularly memorable—fishing boats silhouetted in a firey sea.

Next to the jetty, a trail leads from the aptly-named "End of the World Restoran" into the Pantai Acheh State Park, and along the roadless coast all the way to the lighthouse at Muka Head, a two hour trek. Another trail branches off to the southwest and heads through coastal forest—good for birdwatching and monkey-spotting—to end up at lonely Keracut Beach where there are toilet facilities and basic shelters.

The uncrowded west

Heading south from Teluk Bahang, watch out for the Batik Factory on the left where visitors can see batik cloth being produced. A little further on, 1km (0.6mi) from Teluk Bahang, is the **Penang Butterfly Farm**. Around 3,000 butterflies, including 50 Malaysian species, live out their fortnightly lifespan here, flitting amongst luxuriant ferns and sipping nectar from tropical blooms.

In the large, netted enclosure there's a man-made waterfall, ponds full of vermillion carp, and butterflies everywhere. A notice on a glassed-in display of butterfly pupae tell

*Opposite: Coconut palms shade the pool at one of Batu Ferringhi's luxury beachside hotels. **Above:** Catamarans and beach-boys are permanent fixtures along Penang's northern beaches. **Overleaf:** At the Penang Butterfly Farm this tropical butterfly makes a meal of flower nectar.*

visitors to "look out for those which may emerge at any moment." There is a huge, adjoining souvenir shop, blissfully air-conditioned to entice visitors to linger longer; some fascinating displays of scorpions, and such oddities as the world's largest moth and heaviest beetle.

At the Rimba Rekreasi (Recreational Forest), just past the Butterfly Farm, trails wind through the rainforest and a Forestry Museum contains exhibits on Malaysian forests and the logging industry. From here, the road climbs up through old rubber estates and into higher country where durian trees tower overhead.

In the fruiting season, farmers work hard at clearing the undergrowth, preparing for

JEAN-LEO DUGAST

the ripe durian to drop. These orchards are zealously guarded, for Malaysians have an obsessive passion for their most expensive and malodorous fruit.

Titi Kerawang to Teluk Bahang

Streams come tumbling down from the highlands, and just off the road at Titi Kerawang, is a waterfall and a natural swimming pool—deliciously cool after the tepid sea. From the crest of the road there's a panoramic view across the lonely west coast; coconut plantations fringed by mangroves reach all the way down south to Pulau Betung, a tiny offshore islet.

The route winds down through nutmeg

and clove orchards, past the turnoff to Pantai Acheh—a fishing village renowned for its pungent shrimp paste, past Sungai Pinang—a traditional rural Chinese village, and into a scenic region of Malay kampungs. Wooden homes on stilts, with frilly curtains flapping in the long glassless windows, are shaded by coconut palms and fruit trees and surrounded by neatly-swept, sandy yards and flowerpots full of pink bougainvilleas.

At Balik Pulau, Penang's "Durian Capital," 32km (20mi) from Georgetown, there's a main street of pastel-colored shophouses, and the town has a rural air unlike the rest of the island. Leaving here, the road forks at Genting. The right-hand route ends up at **Pulau Betung** where boats can be hired to explore the deserted beach of Pasir Panjang.

From Genting, the main road climbs up again through another range of hills, through more orchards and bamboo thickets, and then down to Teluk Kumbar, a fishing village on the south coast. A picturesque road turns off from here and follows the coast past wooded bays to Gertak Sanggul.

Although the beaches are muddy at low tide, there are marvellous sandy spots to escape the crowds, picnic, and watch the fishing boats come and go. Boats returning from the offshore fishing grounds come roaring into the bay creating curved walls of spray. After they anchor, the fishermen row into shore to collect their wives who help sort the fish and provide welcome drinks and snacks. At Teluk Bahang, beside a long jetty and rows of fishing boats, a tiny seaside restaurant serves up inspired *mee udang*—fried noodles with giant tiger prawns.

Holy venomous vipers

Continue to Bayan Lepas, the last of the traditional Malay villages before the start of the industrial complexes and surburban sprawl. Just before town a road leads through Kampung Seronok, with more Malay houses, and then to Batu Maung on the coast. Here, a shrine commemorates a hollowed-out impression on a rock believed by some Chinese to be the footprint of the great Admiral Cheng Ho who came ashore during his famous 15th-century voyages.

Once surrounded by rice paddies, the Snake Temple now sits beside the highway in the midst of factories and housing developments. Climb the entrance stairs, past the curio and drink sellers. Once inside, not much has changed in decades.

Incense-shrouded, with beams blackened

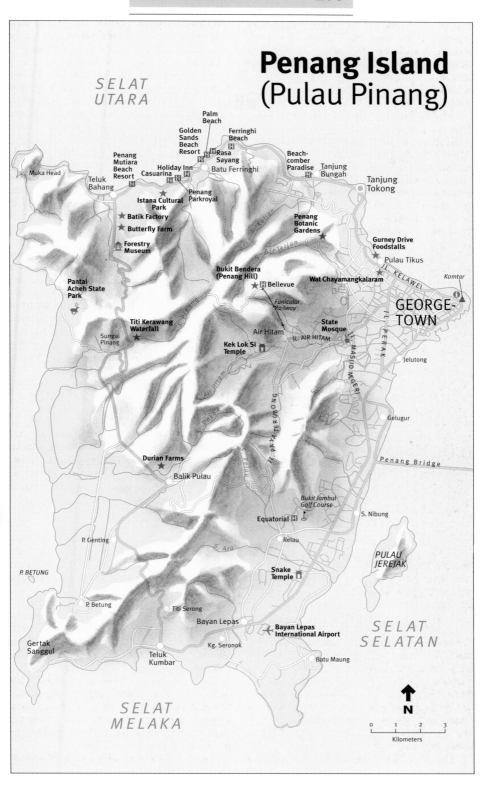

Penang Island (Pulau Pinang)

SELAT UTARA

SELAT MELAKA

SELAT SELATAN

Muka Head

Teluk Bahang

Penang Mutiara Beach Resort

Holiday Inn Casuarina

Palm Beach

Golden Sands Beach Resort

Rasa Sayang

Ferringhi Beach

Batu Ferringhi

Beachcomber Paradise

Tanjung Bungah

Tanjung Tokong

Istana Cultural Park

Penang Parkroyal

Batik Factory

Butterfly Farm

Forestry Museum

Penang Botanic Gardens

Gurney Drive Foodstalls

Pulau Tikus

Pantai Acheh State Park

Bukit Bendera (Penang Hill)

Bellevue

Wat Chayamangkalaram

Komtar

GEORGE-TOWN

Funicular Railway

Titi Kerawang Waterfall

Sungai Pinang

Air Hitam

State Mosque

JL. AIR HITAM

Kek Lok Si Temple

Jelutong

Gelugur

Durian Farms

Balik Pulau

Penang Bridge

Bukit Jambul Golf Course

Equatorial

S. Nibung

PULAU JEREJAK

P. Genting

Relau

P. BETUNG

Snake Temple

P. Betung

Titi Serong

Bayan Lepas

Bayan Lepas International Airport

Gertak Sanggul

Kg. Seronok

Teluk Kumbar

Batu Maung

0 1 2 3
Kilometers

N

from soot, the temple looks similar to many Chinese shrines, but with a difference, for here lazily draped around the altar are dozens of poisonous yellow and green-striped pit vipers, including some baby specimens which look like overgrown earthworms.

A wrought-iron stand behind the main altar, is what a temple assistant calls "the maternity ward"—where the pregnant snakes prefer to hang out. The vipers' drowsiness is apparently caused by the incense smoke which renders them relatively harmless, but at night they move freely around the temple and eat eggs which are left out for them.

Soon after its foundation in 1850 for the worshippers of the Taoist deity Chor Soo Kong, **The Temple of the Azure Cloud**—its correct title—was visited by these vipers who have made it their home ever since. Worshippers see the snakes as holy representations of the the deity and it is said that the population increases significantly in July, Choor Soo Kong's birthday month.

An interesting notice in the main hall, by order of the board, warns that "Mediums are forbidden to fall into a trance in the Snake Temple or its precincts to avoid causing inconvenience to worshippers or visitors." Marked with daubs of red paint on their heads, specially-milked, non-poisonous

vipers are draped around daring visitors' necks for souvenir snaps by the resident photographer.

A giant among temples

Following the main highway north, take the coastal loop to Georgetown to view Asia's longest and the world's third-longest bridge. The Penang Bridge, built at exhorbitant cost, spans the 13.5km-wide (8mi) straits which separate the island from the mainland.

Further north at the modern State Mosque (Masjid Negeri), turn up Jalan Air Hitam which leads to both the funicular railway up Penang Hill, and **Kek Lok Si Temple**, Malaysia's largest Buddhist Temple crowned by the lofty "10,000 Buddhas Precious Pagoda."

Around the back of Air Hitam market a covered walkway lined with souvenir stalls selling plastic Bhuddas, t-shirts and a variety of other gaudy items aimed mainly at Malaysian tourists, climbs up to the temple complex where there are ponds full of sacred tortoises—their backs painted with red calligraphy—and halls crammed with Buddha statues.

At gilded altars, devotees shake bamboo containers full of "I Ching" fortune sticks, and Buddhist nuns with shaven heads hand out the pre-printed prediction cards. For an impressive panorama of the surrounding countryside, climb to the top of the 30-meter-high (98ft) pagoda through its seven tiers, in Chinese Thai and Burmese fashion. Inspired by a visiting Buddhist abbot's apparition—he envisaged the surrounding hills as a crane with outstretched wings, the symbol of immortality—local Buddhists chose the sight for a temple. Construction started in 1890 and took 20 years to complete.

Behind the Kek Lok Si Temple, a road winds 3km (1.8mi) to Air Hitam Dam which is a popular picnic and jogging spot with its reservoir perched at a cool 233m (764ft) above sea level.

Tea on a hilltop

Penang Hill's official name is Bukit Bendera (Flag Hill), but no one ever calls it that. Follow the signs to the railway station from the roundabout just before Air Hitam. By bus from Georgetown take a green (Lim Seng Seng Bus Co) bus to Air Hitam and then change to the shuttle bus which runs to the railway terminus. Queues can be long and frustrating during public and school holidays but at most other times, especially early morning, there are few crowds. Services start at 6.30am and run until 9.15pm, and later until 11.15pm on Wednesday and Saturday nights.

Railway construction began in 1899 but the maiden journey was a fiasco due to an engineering fault. The train finally got into action in 1923 and has been ferrying passenger up the steep gradient through bamboo thickets and rainforest ever since. The half-hour journey passes a Chinese temple dedicated to the Jade Emperor, clumps of pitcher plants which can't survive in the lowlands, and English style bungalows to the top station at 731m (2,400ft).

At the summit, the air is noticeably cooler and can drop to 18 degrees centigrade. From the terrace of the Bellevue Hotel—where early morning visitors can enjoy an English breakfast complete with silver tea service—there is a sweeping vista of Georgetown and toy-sized boats weaving through a glittering sea.

Strawberry and Tiger Hills

In the early decades of this century, Herman Hesse, the celebrated German novelist, apparently hiked up to this very spot for a drink at the Crag Hotel—the forerunner of the Bellevue. Energetic walkers still make the 8km (5mi) walk (3 hours) which begins

at the Moongate in the Botanic Gardens.

Penang's founder, Francis Light, was responsible for forging the original trail to the top and even though he was only in the colony for a few years he managed to build the first bungalow—setting a trend which is still followed today by moneyed Penangites—and even grew strawberries from cuttings he had imported from his Suffolk home.

At the aptly-named Strawberry Hill there is a Tea Garden, and a small Hindu temple and a mosque. A map posted at the hotel shows the layout of the many trails which wind around the hills. The popular, and easy 3km (1.9mi) stroll to Tiger Hill passes mock-Tudor stone cottages where swallows nest in the eaves, Indian gardeners trim hedgerows, and sunbirds dart about among the flowering shrubs.

Smaller trails along stone paths wind about the forested hillsides and all you can hear from the city of half a million inhabitants at your feet is a barely audible hum. From Penang Hill, Georgetown seems like another world away.

Opposite: The climb to the top of the "10,000 Buddhas Precious Pagoda" is the ultimate goal for pilgrims to the Kek Lok Si Temple.
Below: Joss-sticks, and sacred papers for burning are among the offerings for sale at the Snake Temple near Bayan Lepas.

LEMBAH BUJANG

The Valley of Hidden Temples

A 7th-century Sanskrit drama describes it as Katha, the Tamils knew it as Katahara, and a Chinese missionary who visited in 671AD called it Chieh-Cha, but they were all talking of the same place—Kedah. Scholars believe that this legendary kingdom was in the Bujang Valley where archaeological sites containing dozens of Buddhist and Hindu temple remains prove the existence of settlements from the 5th century. The valley is on the southwest side of Gunung Jerai, a 1,300m (4,265ft) mountain which was an important navigational aid for early sailors.

These are not spectacular ruins, being mainly sandstone and brick temple platforms, but they are fascinating nonetheless for they are among the only tangible remnants of the Malay Peninsula's pre-Islamic past. Archaeological activities began 150 years ago when James Low, a colonial civil servant, dis-covered the "relics of a Hindoo Colony, with ruins of temples," but it wasn't until the 1930s that an authoritative exploration was made by Quaritch-Wales and his wife who excavated and studied 20 of the 30 known sites.

Early theories speculated that these were Indian colonies, but archaeologists now believe that a prehistoric Malay settlement at Sungai Muda developed into a landfall for ships from India, and that by the 7th century it had evolved into an entrepôt. Buddhist inscriptions and images indicate Indian contacts from the 5th century, and the abundance of Chinese ceramics and Middle-Eastern glassware from the 8th century shows that the port was by then internationally renowned.

This Buddhist phase operated well into the 9th century, but towards the end of the century the area around Pengkalan Bujang came into prominence and with it the emergence of Hindu temples. This era lasted until the coming of Islam in the 14th century.

The whole area comes under the purview of the excellent Muzium Arkeologi Lembah Bujang (Archaeological Museum), which is reconstructing the temples and also has a display museum showcasing finds from digs including sculptures, bronzes, ceramics, and models and photographs. Nine temples have been reconstructed and the museum staff is happy to act as guides to the four closest ones if you ring beforehand.

TO ALOR SETAR

North Through the Rice Bowl

A blur of green rice fields glimpsed through the windows of an express bus is all most travelers ever see of southern Kedah while they rush through to Pulau Langkawi. But those who take time to explore this quiet agricultural region will discover timeless villages, superb scenery, historical sites and lots of curious looks from the friendly Kedah people.

If you can afford it, hire a car, for along the 93km (58mi) route from Butterworth to Alor Setar, the best scenery and sites are off the main road. Leaving Butterworth, follow the main road north past the suburbs and the airforce base. The rice fields start just before the Kedah border, where the Merdeka Bridge spans the Sungai Muda. A sea of paddy fields stretches to the horizon with wooden houses, surrounded by coconut palms and fruit trees, perched on islands of higher ground. Over half of the nation's home-grown rice comes from Kedah.

During the planting season women dressed in batik and conical hats made of woven palm fronds wade through the flooded fields planting out rice seedlings. Although many of the ancient customs have died out some survive. In order to ensure a plentiful crop, old midwives are still called upon to plant the first seedlings. In the old days, many magic spells were used, no strangers could enter the chosen seed bed, and when the crop was ripe for harvest the village magician would select suitable rice stalks for the "rice baby" which was given a symbolical birth. It is rare in these days of automation to witness these rituals, but they are still performed in remote hamlets.

Legendary trading ports

Turn off at Tikam Batu, for Kota Kuala Muda, a small town 8km (5mi) along the road, where an old brick gateway plastered with faded election posters is all that remains of the fort of Kuala Muda, built in the 18th century when this riverside port attracted spice and tin merchants from Europe, China, India and the Middle East. It's hard to imagine that this sleepy hollow was once a cosmopolitan trading center.

North of town is Pantai Merdeka, a popular beach overlooking the estuary of the Sungai Merbok. Along the way are dozens of traditional Malay houses, some still with thatched *atap* roofs and woven bamboo walls. The beach is not great for swimming, but there are good views across the estuary with the solitary peak of Gunung Jerai looming in the background.

Back on the main road north is Sungai Petani, the region's main commercial town, surrounded by rubber estates which are now giving way to plywood factories and industrial estates. In the main street is an unusual Moorish-style Hong Kong and Shanghai Bank. There are lots of restaurants and food stalls, for this is the junction town for the East West Highway. North of town, turn off at Bedong for the **Lembah Bujang Archaeological Park and Museum**. This road is also an alternative route to Alor Setar, following the scenic coastal rice-farming district, and a more pleasant journey than the

*Opposite: Sandstone plinths from Hindu-Buddhist temples front a photographic display of archaeological digs at Lembah Bujang's Muzium Arkeologi. **Below:** Outside Kota Kuala Muda, a farmer rotary-hoes his rice paddy.*

R. MOH'D NOH SALLEH

main road which is often crammed with diesel-belching lorries.

To the home of the Fanged King

At Merbok, turn off for Lembah Bujang, a further 2km (1.2mi) beyond. Outside of town take the Yan road which winds around the base of cloud-wreathed Gunung Jerai. Across the Melaka Straits are deserted offshore islands and along the coastal road are picturesque rice-growing kampungs. At Yan, drive to the beachfront, where even though it's too muddy for swimming, there's sea breezes and food stalls serve homemade Kedah-style *laksa*—fish and noodle soup, and deliciously cool *leng ci kang*—an icy drink made with barley, jelly and preserved ginger.

At 1,200m (3,937ft) the massive limestone outcrop of Gunung Jerai, the legendary home of Raja Bersion "The Fanged King," dominates the region. Access to the summit where there are overnight chalets, a restaurant and a Forestry Museum is from Guar Chempedak on the highway, or from the coastal route, turn off at Yan Kecil.

Private cars or government-run jeeps make the winding 13-km (8mi) climb to the top of the peak where views extend across the patchwork of rice paddies, over the Melaka Straits to Penang. Jungle paths wind through forests of rhododendrons and giant ferns—home to mousedeer, long-tailed macaque, slow loris and giant squirrels.

R. MOH'D NOH SALLEH

North of Yan at Sungai Limau, is the colorful Sultan Abdul Halim Mosque built early this century with cream and red scalloped archways. Further on at Kangkong, boys and chickens play in mounds of paddy husks and beside each home is a small replica of the house, where the family rice is stored.

The coastal route ends at a T-junction where the right fork goes to Alor Setar (9km/5.6mi) and the left to Kuala Kedah, Kedah's principal port, and the southern gateway to Pulau Langkawi. Rows of fishing trawlers with bright red cabins line both sides of this bustling river and smaller boats crisscross to the far bank where the Kota Kuala Kedah, the remains of an old fort, is located.

Upstream, a new bridge spans the water, but the easiest approach to the fort is to take a 20 cent boat ride from the jetty on the seaward side of the ferry terminal. The river heaves when a big Langkawi ferry takes off, and continually churns with the traffic of fishing boats, but surprisingly, amidst all this action, dolphins are still sighted playing in these estuarine waters.

Small terracotta bricks make up the walls of the fort which features an imposing gateway with a keystone archway dating from 1771. This brick fort replaced earlier wooden fortifications which were the scene of a battle with the Portuguese in the 17th century. Legend has it that this is where Sultan Abdullah met Francis Light when he ceded the island of Penang to him. However, when the Thais attacked in 1821, the British failed to honor their promises of assistance and the fort was conquered.

These days, goats scramble over the walls, courting couples sit on the old cannon, and teenagers race to the top of the lighthouse. Come sundown, everyone leaves and heads for the numerous seafood restaurants perched on stilts beside the river. Here, over a plate of chilli crabs or baked grouper, diners can enjoy the added spectacle of a fiery Melaka Straits sunset.

East West Highway

The spectacular East West Highway which traverses the central mountain ranges linking the northern West Coast to Kelantan on the East coast is approached by either turning off at Kuala Kangsar in Perak which is 108km (67mi) from Grik where the highway proper begins, or by the popular northern route which starts at Sungai Petani in Kedah, 35km (21mi) north of Butterworth. This road connects to Grik through the towns of Baling and

Keroh in the far east of Kedah. The East West Highway runs 124km (77mi) from Grik in Perak to Jeli in Kelantan, and the road continues from there to Kota Bharu.

Elephants may be the world's biggest land mammals, but in the dense rainforest their size doesn't make them any easier to see. However, on the East West Highway, you will see Malaysia's only "Elephant Crossing" sign west of Pulau Banding. If you are incredibly lucky you may even catch a glimpse of these shy creatures.

After 11 years in the making, at a cost of $M400 million, when the East West Highway opened in 1982 it was under a night-time curfew for there were still rogue bands of communist terrorists—leftovers from the Emergency of the 50s and 60s—roaming this rugged border region between Thailand and Malaysia. Since early 1990, however, when the last of the remaining communists surrendered, the highway has been open 24 hours a day, although army posts still remain as the operation of finding all the booby traps still goes on.

In a roundabout way, this has worked to the benefit of the wildlife for the forests have been off limits to loggers for decades and much of the rainforest is still in its virgin state. Many elephants who have seen their former territories become plantations have now been happily relocated into the forests around Tasek Temengur, a man-made lake

formed when the Perak River was dammed.

From Grik, the highway cleaves the mountain tops then descends to Temengur Lake and across a bridge to the island of Pulau Banding. Commanding a view of the lake and the surrounding mountains is a comfortable resthouse, perfect for a quiet night's stopover and the base for fishing excursions and boat trips to the lake's interior for possible elephant sightings.

East of the lake, the highway ascends to the top of the 1,031-meter high (3,382ft) watershed, where the air is fresh and bracing and the views across Perak to the south and up to Thailand in the north are magnificent. Descending on the eastern side of the ranges, the highway crosses into Kelantan state.

At Batu 14, just over a metal suspension bridge, are the Sungai Pergau waterfalls, where the boulder-strewn river hurtles down to the lowlands. Further downstream, the river widens and flows past a solitary limestone massif, Gunung Reng, which is pitted with caves said to have been the settlements of prehistoric Stone Age tribes. From Jeli, where the highway ends, it is another 113km (70mi) to Kota Bharu, the capital of Kelantan.

Opposite: *A fish trapper outside the walls of Kota Kuala Kedah, an 18th-century fort.*
Below: *Viewed from the East West Highway, Gunung Reng towers above the Pergau River.*

R MOH'D NOH SALLEH

ALOR SETAR

Kedah's Courtly Capital

In Malaysia, where there are no great seasonal changes, the greenery which surrounds the towns looks similar throughout the year. But Alor Setar is an exception. The vast sea of rice fields which surrounds Kedah's capital in the northwest of the state changes dramatically with the seasons of cultivation.

When the paddy is growing, the landscape is bathed in a wash of brilliant green. Later, it takes on a golden hue when the grain is ripe. After the harvest, the fields are a bare virginal brown, and finally when the alluvial plains are again flooded for the next planting, Alor Setar is surrounded by reflections of clouds mirrored in the irrigated fields.

Alor Star (the "e" is often dropped), the commercial hub of the far northwest, may be experiencing a building boom in the wake of a fast-moving economy, but the town still retains much of its rich cultural heritage,

some splendid examples of royal architecture, and unpolluted skies which are the envy of the industrialized southern cities. Traditions and culture date back to the 4th century when the legendary kingdom of Langkasuka, held sway over much of today's northern Malaysia and southern Thailand.

The royal orchestra

Most of Alor Setar's historical sites are in the center of downtown. The obvious start for a tour of this courtly capital, is a curious three-tiered tower called the Balai Nobat, which houses the *nobat*. These sacred instruments of the royal orchestra comprise three drums, a gong and a flute, were presented to the Sultan of Kedah by Melaka's Sultan Mahmud Shah in the 15th century. Nowadays the orchestra only plays for royal inaugurations, weddings and funerals. Travelers wishing to view the *nobat* must make prior arrangements with the State Government Office opposite the Balai Nobat.

Close by, is the Balai Besar (The Large Audience Hall) a stately, open-sided building decorated with wood carvings, art nouveau wrought-iron, and upturned roof finials reminiscent of Thai architecture—remnants of the days when Kedah was under Siamese suzerainty. The 18th-century Balai Besar was demolished in 1904 to make way for the present structure which was built to stage the elaborate ceremonies for the marriages of

R. MOH'D NOH SALLEH

Sultan Abdul Hamid's five eldest children, which ran for an unprecedented 60 days.

Beside the Balai Besar, a triple-arched gateway leads into the walled compound of the Istana Kota Setar, the former royal palace and now the Muzium Di Raja (**Royal Museum**) built in 1763. The palace was renovated after the Bugis attacked in 1771, and again following the Thai occupation from 1821 to 1842.

When the new palace was built at Anak Bukit, just outside of Alor Setar, the Istana

Kota Setar was taken over by voluntary organizations, but was restored to its original form in 1983 when Sultan Abdul Halim opened the Royal Museum to commemorate his 25-year reign of Kedah.

A royal dais, a bridal chamber, and videos of recent royal weddings can be viewed in the Front Hall; while the Middle Hall displays regal costumes, the family tree, and stamp collections, photographs and historical documents. However, the most fascinating collection is in the Astaka Hall at the back, where Sultan Abdul Halim's African hunting trophies, including a black rhinocerous' head and a set of elephants' tusks, adorn the walls. Other interesting exhibits include historical photographs of royalty in traditional dress, a royal *buayi* (swinging cradle), finely-tooled spears, and elephant's foot stools—a bizarre Victorian fashion.

A superb Moorish mosque

Ever since the 12th century, when the ruler of Kedah, Maharaja Derba Raja II, embraced Islam and took the title of Sultan Muzaffar Shah, the state has been a bastion of the faith. It is fitting that the most prominent building in Alor Setar—discounting a couple of new box-like highrises—is the majestic **Masjid Zahir**, a Moorish-style mosque, built in 1912. Located on Jalan Pekan Melayu, opposite the Balai Besar, this white and beige mosque features arched collonades, onion-shaped

domes, and intricate plaster reliefs including medallions with Arabic inscriptions.

Opposite Masjid Zahir, at the southern end of the town's historical hub, is the neo-classical, Balai Seni Negeri, the State Art Gallery. Arched verandahs, decorated gables and columns with floral capitals adorn this elegant former courthouse constructed in the best colonial fashion in 1912. Works by Kedah-based artists, photographers, and craftsmen are displayed at the gallery, open every day from 10am to 6pm, but closed from noon to 2.30pm on Fridays.

Out of town

Follow the Lebuhraya Darulaman, the main trunk road, north of town for 2km (1.2mi) to the Muzium Negeri (State Museum), a Thai-style building built in 1936. Among the displays are a variety of artifacts from the archaeological digs at Lembah Bujang and a collection of early Chinese ceramics. Opening hours are from 10am to 6pm, closing between noon and 2pm on Fridays.

Outside Alor Setar, to the east, is the Royal Mausoleum at Langgar. Follow Jalan Langgar through town, under the expressway and out through the ricefields, and just after the "25km Kuala Nerang" milestone, about 9.6km (6mi) from Alor Setar, turn off for Makam Di Raja on the left. The narrow road winds past wooden kampung houses into the large walled compound, the final resting place of Kedah's royal family for generations and also the burial site of Malaysia's popular first prime minister, and Kedah prince—Tunku Abdul Rahman.

*Opposite: Prayer rugs cover the marble floors of the elegant Masjid Zahir, a landmark in downtown Alor Setar. **Above, left:** The facade of the early-20th century Masjid Zahir. **Above, right:** Thai influences are apparent in the architecture of the Balai Besar, "The Large Audience Hall".*

PERLIS

Touring the Smallest State

Perlis, Malaysia's smallest state, covering 795km² (307mi²) in the extreme northwest of the peninsula, shares more than two-thirds of its border with Thailand which has always exerted a powerful influence over the region. Although ruled by Malay chieftains subject to the Sultan of Kedah, the Thais raided Perlis for centuries.

Following an attack in 1821, the region came under Thai rule for 21 years, but when Kedah was handed back to the sultan, Perlis was given to Syed Hussain, the son of a former chief, who became the Raja of Perlis, although he still paid tribute to Bangkok.

In 1909, the Thais relinquished their Malay vassal states to Britain and an English Resident was installed at Arau, the royal capital. During the Japanese occupation during World War II, the Thais were handed back Perlis as a reward for becoming allies of Japan, but this brief annexation ended when the Japanese surrendered.

Perlis has no outstanding historical sites or glorious beaches, but is very picturesque and still looks much like the view a 1930s travel-writer glimpsed from his train window. "Marsh and jungle, rice-fields, rubber trees, undulating forest and distant hills were an endless panorama of delicious green..."

Driving north from Alor Setar there are two routes to Kangar, the nation's smallest regional capital. Travelers en route to Kuala Perlis for ferries to Pulau Langkawi can take the coastal road or the alternative route which heads north to Jitra, then to Kodiang, the border town 40km (25mi) from Alor Setar. Ricefields flank both sides of the road, and finger-shaped limestone massifs rear up from the plains. The distant blue hills denote the border between Malaysia and Thailand.

Arau, is the royal town and home to the Raja of Perlis, one of the world's longest-serving monarchs who ascended the throne in 1945. The red-roofed, Istana De Raja (Royal Palace) is a mixture of colonial and Moorish architectural styles. Opposite, crowned by golden domes is the Royal Mosque which can accomodate 7,000 worshippers. From Arau it is 14km (9mi) to Kangar, the quiet capital, where it is rare to meet another traveler. Just before the town, on the right, is Kangar's major attraction, the **Masjid Syed Alwi**, an attractive art deco style mosque built in the

R. MOHD NOH SALLEH

early 1930s. Black, onion-shaped domes crown the flat roof and the central dome has stained-glass windows in the shape of crescent moons.

Downtown Kangar is a mixture of old wooden and new cement shophouses. Food stalls abound around the busy bus and taxi station. On the outskirts, are an elegant 1930s State Secretariat and clocktower, and a lone high-rise office block. Take Jalan Tun Abdul Razak and turn off into Jalan Pengkalam Assam which has recently been renamed

after Dato' Wan Ahmad, a former royal secretary, and the late owner of Perlis' prettiest traditional Malay house. This whimsical, pastel-colored house built in the 1920s features tiled and hipped roofs, roof ridges of Chinese tiles, intricate wood carvings, decorated gables, stained-glass panels, and doors painted with flower-pot murals.

Follow the Alor Setar road and turn off for the port of Kuala Perlis, the state's second-largest town and the gateway to Pulau Langkawi. This is a real working-class fishing town and at low tide is hardly attractive—surrounded by acres of mudflats and a pervading aroma of dried fish.

There seems little point in lingering and most people only stay long enough to board the first ferry to the islands. But when the tide comes in and the sun sets behind Pulau Langkawi, the open-air seafood restaurants which cover the wharf front open for business, and the place comes alive.

From Kangar, take the north road which terminates at Padang Besar, the border town 34km (21mi) north. Turn right, just out of town for Sungai Batu Pahat, 10km (6mi) from Kangar, a popular picnic and swimming spot which also has a golf course and a Snake Farm where a large collection of venomous snakes are kept for serum research. It is open to the public from Sunday to Wednesday 10am to 4pm and on Thursday from 10am to noon. Further along the main northern road,

turn right, past villages of traditional wooden houses, to Tasik Melati, a small lake popular with local picnickers.

Back on the main road, detour to Bukit Keteri for a closer look at the curious, limestone "sugar-loaf" hills. Follow the left-hand road to Chuping which turns off just before the cement factory at Bukit Keteri. High up, in the limestone cliffs on the right, notice the ladders hanging from cave entrances which are used by daring guano collectors who scale the cliffsides and enter the caves to search for bat excreta which is used for fertiliser. Further on at Chuping, lime-green sugarcane fields stretch to the horizon.

When driving around these northern districts be on the lookout for turban-clad motorcyclists with pet monkeys riding tandem. These are *beruk*, the pig-tailed monkeys that clamber up palms to collect young coconuts. Further north, turn left for Kaki Bukit and nearby Gua Kelam "The Dark Cave," a 370-m (1,213ft) long limestone cave. A wooden walkway built over a subterranean stream winds through the floodlit cave and leads out to the Wan Tangga Valley. An Englishman in the 1930s enlarged the cave once used for transporting tin ore from a mine near the entrance.

At the end of the northern main road is the railhead of Padang Besar, a typical dusty border town of duty-free shops, restaurants, open-air markets, smugglers and border police. Malaysians flock across the border to Pekan Siam, a ramshackle bargain-hunters' market town on the Thai side of the border. Buses and taxis run from here to Hat Yai, the commercial and notorious nightlife center of Southern Thailand.

Opposite: Women harvest rice using small crescent-shaped knifes which do not offend the rice spirits. *Above, left:* Limestone hills are characteristic of the Chuping area. *Above, right:* Datuk Wan Ahmad's home in Kangar is the most elaborate traditional home in Perlis.

PULAU LANGKAWI

Archipelago of Legendary Islands

In the far northwest, where the Indian Ocean funnels into the Melaka Straits, are a group of 104 idyllic isles. Here, even in the late 80s, visitors could bicycle about on old crushed-marble roads, and it was a novelty to meet a car. Apart from one luxury hotel that was in danger of becoming a white elephant, accommodation was merely thatched huts on the beach.

But then it all changed, and Pulau Langkawi was discovered. An aggressive tourist promotion campaign and duty-free status may have been the main reason the islands rapidly appeared on the international scene, but many locals believe that it was something altogether more spiritual: that the seven-generation curse of Mahsuri had finally ended.

The curse

According to legend, in the late-18th century, when the beautiful Mahsuri lay dying, after being speared to death for a false accusation of adultery, she cursed Pulau Langkawi, saying that it would not prosper for seven generations. And indeed, the island, although blessed with great natural beauty, and formerly renowned for its abundant spices, did seem to suffer. The Thais and the Achehnese from Sumatra repeatedly invaded, the pepper crops failed, and historians even ponder why the strategically-sited islands were passed over by the British when they chose Penang for their base.

Now the seven generations have finally come to pass, and whether for psychological, spiritual, or economic reasons, the islanders' future now seems assured as hotel chains compete for the best real estate, and visitors arrive by the boat load. However, Pulau Langkawi still retains much of its former quietude and rural charm. Even in the peak Christmas season dozens of totally-deserted islands are a short boat ride away.

The predominantly Malay population of around 28,000 lives on the main island of Pulau Langkawi, where forest-covered marble and limestone mountains dominate the interior and far northwest. The best beaches and most of the accommodation is on the west coast, with other picturesque beaches in the far northeast. The rice-growing villages of the interior, away from the tourist centers, are still traditional. Kuah, the main port town is set in a bay overlooking a horizon of islands.

JILL GOCHER

Home to 3,000, it has most of the restaurants and shops.

Arriving

To get to Pulau Langkawi, travelers can fly or go by sea from Penang, but the most popular route is to take the high-speed ferry from either Kuala Kedah (1hr) or Kuala Perlis (40min) on the mainland. Once on board, the locals settle down to watch wrestling videos or re-runs of old Charlie Chaplin movies as the muddy mangrove coast is left behind.

The ferry charges through pale-green seas, and then enters the labyrinthine passages of the Langkawi islands—once the haunt of pirates, and still notorious for smugglers ferrying contraband from Thailand. Rocky islets with tiny, crescent-moon beaches pass by, then the first luxury hotel is sighted. The boat then swings around into Bass Harbour, where, framed by coconut palms beneath a mountainous backdrop, the island capital of Kuah sprawls along the foreshore, its onion-domed mosque reflected in the quiet glassy waters.

Taxis and minibuses ply from the bustling jetty into town and the duty-free shops where most domestic visitors head for. International travelers, however, usually head straight to the west coast beaches of Pantai Tengah and Pantai Cenang (22km/14mi), further northwest to Pantai Kok, or to Tanjung Rhu (23km/14.3mi) on the northern coast.

Bicycles are a slow, but relaxing way to enjoy and get around the island, and motorcycles and cars are also easy to rent. An excellent network of well-signposted, sealed roads extends throughout the 524km2 (202mi2) main island, and it's possible to bicycle around in one day.

Pungent odors and a beauty's grave

From the jetty, parklands fringe the harborside where sailboats lie at anchor, past the yellow-domed mosque to Kuah, named after the Malay word for "gravy" as the town featured in a legend known as "The Broken Cooking Pot." The once sleepy main street lined with wooden Chinese shophouses, has now extended into new blocks and word has it that the old shophouses are soon to be demolished.

Kuah has the cheapest and best variety of food on the island, there are numerous hawker stalls, an excellent food center—great for local seafood—next to the bridge, Chinese restaurants and an ever-increasing variety of seafood and western-style eateries scattered around the duty-free shops.

Heading west from Kuah, the town quick-

Opposite: A panoramic view of a horizon full of islands greets swimmers at this resort hotel near Kuah. **Below:** *Early morning reflections in a glassy sea at Pantai Chenang, Pulau Langkawi's favorite resort beach.*

JILL GOCHER

ly reverts to rural kampungs, and at the Langkawi Golf Club the left turning heads to Empangan Malut—a Chinese-run village renowned for its dried fish business, pungent odors and lack of tourists. The next road on the right goes to Makam Mahusri, the tomb of Langkawi's heroine. Along this road, traces can still be seen of the original crushed-marble road built in 1962 and only recently upgraded. There are not too many places in the world where the marble is so abundant that it has been used for roadbuilding.

Turn off for Mahsuri's Grave, at Kampung Mawai in Ulu Melaka, which has been recently restored using the same white marble. Although the site has been somewhat commercialized the restoration is aesthetically done. There is a well, apparently used by Mahsuri, and at the adjacent, traditional Kedah-style house, demonstrations of paddy-pounding and weaving are staged.

White sands and longboat tours

Back on the main road continue along for Pantai Cenang, a long stretch of white sands, flanked by coconut palms and lodgings ranging from simple A-frame huts to five-star luxury hotels. Commanding a prime position at the head of the beach, and also top of the price range is the **Pelangi Beach Resort**, which is constructed in traditional Malay style using jungle hardwoods. The beach is best for swimming at high tide, and the flat

firm sand makes for excellent jogging. Many of the chalets have sea views and it's very pleasant to stretch out with the sea breeze rustling the palms, watch the rainbow-coloured windsurfers slicing through the jade green waters and gaze out at the offshore islands, and the dragon-back mountains that provide a dramatic backdrop.

Wooden longboats, with shade-canopies to protect passengers from the fearsome midday sun visit a number of outlying islands. Popular three-hour tours generally stop at Pulau Singa Besar, where there's good beaches and a rather sad wildlife sanctuary. They then continue to Pulau Dayang Bunting, "The Isle of the Pregnant Maiden," where legend has it a woman who was childless for 19 years conceived after drinking the waters of the deliciously cool freshwater lake now named Tasek Dayang Bunting, "The Lake of the Pregnant Maiden." After World War II, when a Japanese soldier was apparently taken by a white crocodile here, no one dared enter the lake, but it is now a popular swimming spot, and infertile women still visit.

Boatmen will also point out the nearby 91-meter high (291 ft) Gua Langsir, "Cave of the Banshee," a bat-filled haunted cave, but few will venture near. Not because they fear the ghosts but because they want to avoid damaging their boats on the shallow, rocky shore.

Opposite Pantai Cenang is Pulau Bras

Basah, where there are overnight chalets and serene, uncrowded beaches. Nearby are numerous tiny islands, excellent for day trips to play at Robinson Crusoe. South from Pantai Cenang there are more resorts at Pantai Tengah. The larger ones offer boat trips for snorkeling near the outer islands, but the best diving—and the only decent scuba-diving in the Melaka Straits—is at the **Pulau Payar Marine Park**, a three-hour boat journey to the south of Langkawi. Here, there are still sizeable "live" coral reefs and the waters are clear with good visibility.

Rice riddle

Continue along the coastal road past the airport, and take a right for Padang Matsirat, a small inland town, renowned for its "Field of Burnt Rice." The site is a nondescript, fenced-off square of ground, where after heavy rain, burnt rice grains appear on the surface.

According to legend, villagers burnt their rice rather than leave it to the Thais who invaded Langkawi only months after Mahsuri's execution. Among those killed was the chieftain who had ordered her death. Proof, say believers, of the effectiveness of Mahsuri's curse.

Back on the coastal road is Kuala Teriang, a small village where a wooden footbridge crosses a stream to the fishermen's settlement on the point.

From Kuala Teriang the road follows the coast to picturesque Pantai Kok where the waters are clear and the sand a talcum-white. Small chalets cluster in the arc of the bay, and further around at Burau Bay are another two luxury resorts. Turn off just before here to Telaga Tujuh, "The Seven Wells." The walk through the rainforest is very pleasant, and the waterfalls are good if it's not the dry season when the 91-meter rock face all but dries up.

Northern beaches

From Pantai Kok take the main highway north and turn off to Teluk Datai where the road winds along the deserted western end of the north coast to a magnificent luxury resort with a private beach set amongst towering rainforest and a deafening insect chorus. The beaches along here are rocky, but there are good views across to Thailand's islands.

Return to the main road and continue northwest, past the over-rated Pasir Hitam, "The Beach of Black Sand," and turn right at Padang Lalang for Tanjung Rhu. This road runs along the coast, with pretty views of off-shore islands. Then a mangrove-fringed river

enters from the right and follows the road to Tanjung Rhu, so named because of the *rhu,* or casuarina trees that shade the beach.

It's a quiet place, despite the presence of two resorts, and some food and souvenir stalls. Rising from the waters, just offshore, are a collection of curious limestone outcrops, and in the distance are the mauve silhouettes of distant Thai islands. Children love this beach because of the shallow lagoon and the vast sand flats at low tide.

Back at Padang Lalang take the main road back to Kuah which passes Telaga Air Hangat, a hot springs on the right, then rural villages and rubber plantations. Watch out for the striated marble cliffs to the left, 6km (4mi) from Kuah, where they sell and display everything from marble bathrooms to chess sets and a miniature marble version of the Kuah Mosque.

An alternative route from Kuah heads up through the center of the island past Ulu Melaka and roads lead off to a Forest Recreation Park at the foot of Gunung Raya. Another leads to the mountain's summit at 881m (2,890ft) and a satelite base control station.
—Wendy Moore

Opposite: *Children love the clear tepid waters of Pulau Langkawi.*

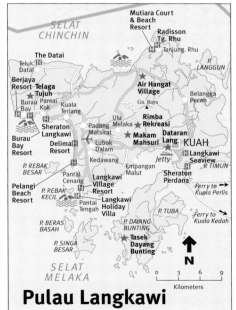

Pulau Langkawi

PART V

Introducing the East Coast

Golden beaches shaded by coconut palms which bend with the prevailing tradewinds stretch into the distance. Offshore, wooded isles shimmer in the South China Sea and rainbow-colored fishing boats ply the estuaries where villages perch on stilts.

This idyllic cameo regularly occurs along the east coast which comprises the states of Kelantan, Terengganu, and Pahang. There are no cosmopolitan cities, nor traffic jams. The beaches are deserted and unpolluted, traditional customs, arts and crafts still thrive, and the population is almost entirely Malay, in stark contrast to the ethnic diversity of the west coast.

The east coast maintained its original identity partly due to geographical factors: the mountainous interior deterred early road builders, and the annual monsoon closed river ports for up to six months a year. Although minerals were discovered, they were not present in the same quantities found in the west. The eastern mines also experienced transportation problems due to the vast distances involved. Consequently the east was spared the massive influx of tin mining and plantation workers.

The colonial British were keen to transplant the Union Jack to the east, but there were political problems. Both Kelantan and Terengganu were loosely under the suzerainty of the Thais, and although Malay sultans remained in control, they still had to make yearly tributes to the Thai court. In 1909 Kelantan and Terengganu were transferred from Thai to British rule against the wishes of the northern sultans, who preferred Bangkok's loose, more distant control to the pervasive influence of the western powers. However geographical isolation ensured that interference by the new overlords was kept to a minimum.

The sea has always been the lifeblood for east coasters and remains so today. Cowrie shells, used as pre-coin currency, were exported from the Malay coast 4,000 years ago, and early history records that tortoise-shell, corals and *trepang* (sea slugs), as well as inland products like camphor, incense, gold, and jungle exotica like bezoars—monkey gallstones used as talismans—were being traded for cloth, copper, ironwares, musical instruments, beads and pottery from at least the 5th century.

Arabs, Chinese, Indians, and traders from the vast Malay archipelago frequented the eastern sea lanes, and traded in ports like the legendary Langkasuka, and Marco Polo's Lokak—which some scholars suggest was in Kelantan. Construction of the inland railway from Gemas in Johor, to Tumpat in Kelantan during the 1930s, and the building of a road from Kuala Lipis to Kuantan in Pahang, effectively ended the east's isolation, but the vast coastline was still without roads until comparatively recently. In 1982, the East West Highway was completed, finally linking the northern coasts of the peninsula and reducing the road distance from Penang to Kota Bharu by over 600km (373mi).

Apart from Terengganu's recently-discovered oil and gas wealth, economically the east coast still lags behind the progressive west coast. But this works to the traveler's advantage as much of the east's traditions have been maintained. Kelantanese men still wear their original headgear, kite-flying and top-spinning are still popular, wood-carvers, gold and silversmiths, silk-weavers, and batik-painters still flourish, and in countless fishing villages life still follows the rhythms of the sea and the annual monsoon. Travelling the east coast is as much a journey through time as through space.

Overleaf: A Kelantanese with his kite, known as a wau bulan, or moon kite. Photo by R. Ian Lloyd. **Opposite:** Fisherman still wear turbans at Kampung Dasar Sabakon Kelantan's north coast. Photo by Radin Moh'd Noh Salleh

CRAFTS

Ancient Arts Perpetuated in the East

In the heyday of royal patronage when hundreds of palace ceremonies were practiced, Peninsular Malaysia had a great variety of arts and crafts. Their production was part of the daily routine of the *kampung* people. Preparations for the elaborate court ceremonies involved the whole community which worked within the palace grounds, and the mobilization of village experts brought about the creation of teams of highly-skilled and specialized craftsmen. Some of these traditional folk arts are still practiced today and flourish around Kota Bharu—the undisputed center of Malay arts and crafts.

Crafting a royal trousseau

In Kelantan, the silver and gold jewellery-making owed much to the patronage of the Sultan and his court. As these skills were always in regular demand, gold and silver-smiths normally lived on the perimeter of a royal palace. Most of their needs were supplied by their patrons and thus they were able to spend their time crafting painstakingly delicate and beautiful objects.

Long before a royal wedding there would be a period of intense activity when craftsmen produced ornaments and objects for the marriage ceremonies. Most were made of silver and included items such as trays, bowls, plates and ladles for the dining table, and kettles—often elaborately embellished—to hold the water for cleansing hands after eating.

The custom of betelnut chewing called for a whole array of utensils including containers for lime, tobacco, cloves, receptacles for *sireh* leaves, pounders and special cutters for the betel nuts, which were all contained in rectangular caskets. Formerly, betelnut chewing was such an integral part of Malay life that no expense was spared in fashioning the containers, and many of them fully reflect the splendor of those bygone days.

Every piece was the result of a painstaking process of hammering, etching and carving, and each bears the stamp of the ingenuity and skill of the craftsman. Goldsmiths fashioned pendants, chains, rings, anklets, armlets, and a particularly attractive elliptical-shaped cummerbund buckle called a *pending*, which was worn with ceremonial dress. Motifs were mostly drawn from the plant world, and the patterns of flowers, leaves and

intertwining stems have much in common with the best Kelantanese wood carving. Repoussé and filigree were the main decorative techniques employed.

Equally important at every ceremonial function was the royal wardrobe. Traditional costumes were made from a silk cloth known as *kain songket* which is renowned for the diversity of its designs and considered to be the pinnacle of the Malay weavers' art. It is characterized by intricate patterns worked in gold and silver threads, and is of exceptionally fine quality.

The background is silk, woven traditionally on a simple four-posted frame loom with treadle operated heddles for the pattern threads. Hand-thrown bamboo shuttles produce a "floating weft" of gold or silver threads which creates patterns of lozenges, chevrons, and repeated floral motifs according to a prescribed blueprint.

Kain songket is usually produced in standard sarong lengths and is still popular as a dress for special occasions such as weddings and palace functions; it also regularly appears in the fashion houses of Paris.

The art of batik

Batik is by far the most popular textile made in Kelantan. Earlier batik was produced by wood-block printing, but now the stamps are made with thin zinc strips bent into the desired patterns and soldered together to form a printing block with a handle.

The cloth is spread on moistened strips of banana tree stems which provide a cool surface underneath so that the wax used to mark the pattern will not run when applied. Traditionally, beeswax was used but nowadays micro wax and paraffin combined with resin achieves the same result. Only one side of the cloth is printed. For the first stage the printer dips his stamp into a pan of wax, flicks away the excess, and then applies the stamp to the material.

The cloth is then immersed in the dye bath where the parts untouched by wax take in the dye. The area which has been dyed is then covered with another application of wax, with the uncovered parts absorbing the next color. It is almost impossible to avoid cracking the wax in the course of handling, and veining inevitably appears, even in the best of batik. The wax is completely removed by boiling in water, and the cloth is then washed to remove excess dye, dried in the sun, and pressed ready for the market.

In Kelantan, as well as most of Malaysia,

R. MOH'D NOH SALLEH

batik is also produced by simply hand-painting the design onto the cloth with a *canting* or wax pen. Floral or geometric designs are applied to Chinese silk or rayon which are sold as sarong lengths or made into colorful ready-to-wear clothing.

Woodcarvers used motifs similar to those found in metalwork and textile design. For centuries the Malay woodcarver enjoyed royal patronage: in the past all palaces were made of wood and were decorated with intricately carved panels, windows, doors, arches, and pillars. Being a country rich in timber resources it was not difficult for craftsmen to find suitable materials.

Much of the woodcarvers' traditional knowledge and skills have been handed down through the generations, and their work can be seen in old palaces and houses in Kota Bharu, and in Terengganu. Beautiful carvings also adorn musical instruments, as well as objects like the *rehal*—a wooden Koran stand—betel boxes, cake moulds, coconut shredders, food and tool boxes, walking sticks, kris hilts, and even the prows of fishing vessels.

—*Mohd. Kassim Hj. Ali*

Opposite: *Curving leaf and floral designs are typical themes for Kelantanese wood-carvers.*
Above: *Batik hand painted witht the canting wax pen is a speciality of the cottage-craft workshops near Pantai Cinta Berahi.*

TRADITIONAL PASTIMES

Shadow Plays, Giant Drums, Tops and Kites

The traditional pastimes once practiced throughout the peninsula during the natural breaks in the agricultural calendar and other festivals have all but died out along the west coast, but the east still embraces the ancient arts and in Kelantan their popularity is actually on the increase.

Wayang Kulit—shadow puppet drama

Historians believe that the shadow play is as old as civilization itself. Among the theories regarding its origin, one school believes that it came from China while another attributes its home to India because in every Southeast Asian country the repertoire includes stories from the great Indian epics—the *Ramayana* and *Mahabharata*. Others are convinced that it originated in Java because of the ancient terminology used in the dialogue.

Most historians agree, however, that the

R. IAN LLOYD

shadow play was initially an animistic ritual, and traces of customary observances can still be witnessed in modern performances. The shadow play in Kelantan is particularly eclectic, combining Siamese, Javanese, Indian and Chinese influences. But the most conspicuous elements are of Javanese and Siamese origins. No one can say for sure when the shadow play was first introduced into Kelantan but it had gained a strong foothold by the start of the 19th century.

Performances were staged when offerings were made to the spirit of the rice-paddy, before and after a harvest, weddings, childbirth, circumcision, and during the Sultan's birthday and national holidays. It is still performed on a special wooden stage with an *atap* roof, usually located well away from dwellings to avoid accidentally "inviting" the spirits into homes when they are summoned by the puppeteer during the opening and closing ceremonies.

Behind the white screen onto which the shadows are projected are two banana stems into which the puppets are stuck. The good-natured characters are positioned on the right, while the forceful ones remain on the left. A lamp, suspended between the puppeteer and the screen, causes shadows to fall on the screen. The narration is accompanied by a small orchestra consisting mainly of percussion instruments.

The puppeteer, or *dalang*, has the enormous task of being director and manipulator of the puppets, actor, singer, narrator, and above all the musical conductor, all rolled into one. He also commands the power to contact the spirits whose blessing is sought before and after each performance. In the eyes of the audience he is both powerful and highly respected.

Wayang Kulit performances begin around 8pm and end at midnight. The number of puppets used for a performance ranges between 50 and 70 depending on the story being told. They are made from cowhide or goatskin and are hand-painted, although the colors never appear on screen. After the ritual and opening ceremony has been performed, there is a 30-minute prologue using the "tree of life" and a few characters from the main story to introduce the play to the audience. Then the main drama unfolds. At the end of each performance the puppeteer chants an incantation into the smoking incense to thank the spirits.

Into the air

Kite-flying, which dates back to the 16th cen-

R IAN LLOYD

tury, is also very popular. The kites, or *wau*, as they are known, come in a variety of shapes and sizes, the most popular being the moon kite, so named because its crescent-shaped tail. Most kites measure about 2.1m (7ft) from tip to tail and 1.8m (6ft) across the wings. The frame is made by tying thin strips of bamboo together. The wings are covered with three layers of paper; a plain background, the bold decoration and finally intricate cut-out-designs depicting flowers, leaves or small animals. Each kite also has a bow which makes a humming sound during flight. Kite flying competitions are held between the best groups from each state and participants are judged not only on how the kite flies, but also on the shape, color and ornamentation, as well as the grace with which the kite can be manoeuvred and the music it makes in flight.

In most parts of the world, top-spinning is considered a children's pastime, but in Malaysia it is an adult affair. In Kelantan, contests are held between pairs of men to time how long each competitor's top, known as a *gasing*, can spin. Two large tops of equal size and weight are matched against each other. After the initial throw, each is skillfully transferred to a small stand where it may spin for an hour or more before falling. Another game, using smaller tops, is played between teams of men who attempt to knock their opponents tops out of a circular area until

only one is left.

Top makers are very selective in choosing the correct type of wood. It must come from a certain species, and should be cut from the base of the tree, where the grain is most compact. After curing for three weeks, it is shaped on a homemade lathe. An iron or lead rim is then added, a steel spike inserted at the base, and a beautifully handcrafted ornamental silver cap is fitted on top. The finished article, shaped like a discus, measures 71cm (28in) in circumference and weighs between 5.4 to 7.2kg (12-16lb). Because of its size, children are discouraged from participating until they are sixteen.

The beating of *rebana besar*—the big harvest drum which measures 60cm (2ft) in height and 1m (3ft) in diameter is another popular activity. The skin is made of cowhide secured by a stout rattan hoop. Wooden wedges resembling the spokes of a wheel are beaten into the frame to give the skin to the required tension. The drums are usually played in pairs but on special occasions as many as six are used. The drum is placed on its side and struck using the palm of the hand. The sound is so penetrating that it can be heard a mile away.

Opposite: A Kelantanese villager makes ready to throw his top. **Above:** *Hidden behind the screen, the* Tok Dalang, *narrates the story and plays out the roles of his shadow-puppets.*

MAK YONG

Dance Drama in Honor of Mother Earth

The strains of the *rebab* coupled with the voice of the main performer reach a crescendo. The *Mak Yong's* hands and entire body sway while the chorus girls sing in harmony. The audience is lulled by the refined dance steps and soothing songs into a fantasy land of drama and intrique, and the musicians play a haunting tempo that seemed to reach to the inner depths of the onlookers' consciousness.

Mak Yong, as this performance is known, is a Malay dance drama which was acted out exclusively for the rajas and major chiefs until the turn of the century. For more than 300 years it was the favorite palace entertainment of the kingdom of Pattani in today's southern Thailand, and was then introduced to the rulers of Kelantan where it became equally prestigious and popular. Mak Yong reached the highest standard of refinement and artistic excellence in the courts of Pattani and

Kelantan. When royal patronage ceased, Mak Yong left the confines of the palace and became a popular folk entertainment among rural Malaysians, and performances still draw crowds today.

It is believed that Mak Yong originated as a ritual in honor of the spirit of Mother Earth, *Ma Hiang* or *Yong* (the term *Yong* means divinity), whose role was to watch over the rice crops. Thus, the main cast of Mak Yong is made up of women, consisting of four leading actresses who play the parts of the king (*Pakyong*), the hero, a young prince (*Pakyong Muda*), the queen (*Mak Yong*), and the heroine, a princess (*Puteri Mak Yong*).

The main characters wear elaborate traditional Malay costumes with headdresses, all sewn from *songket*—an exclusive silk-brocade fabric. Male actors only play supporting roles: comedians and court jesters known as *peran*, ogres, giants, jinns and others. There are also younger women in the cast who play chambermaids, known as *dayang*. A Mak Yong troupe also needs a male shaman, or *bomoh*, who plays a crucial role in ensuring the success of any performance.

Mak Yong are accompanied by musicians who play on an ensemble of *rebab,* a spiked fiddle, two *gendang* double-headed drums, and a pair of gongs known as *tetawak* which are hung facing one another. The *rebab* is a typical Malay chordophone that has three strings of metal wire played with a bow. The

body is hollow, wide at the top, and tapered towards the bottom. The *gendang* and *tetawak*, are used in most forms of Malay traditional music. Mak Yong's music consists mainly of solo singing, accompanied by the *rebab*. The songs are divided into themes such as love, sadness, travel and lullabyes.

The Mak Yong's repertoire of stories focuses mainly on palace intrigues and romances between princes and princesses. Among the most popular stories are *Anak Raja Gondang* (The Gondang Prince), *Dewa Indera* (The Royal Demi-god), *Dewa Muda* (The Young Demi-god), and *Dewa Pechil* (Pechil the Demi-god). The Mak Yong stories, music and songs were traditionally handed down the generations as part of the Malay oral tradition.

Epics in the open air

Performances take place on stage, or in a theatre called a *panggong*, built of *atap* and bamboo, which is open on all sides. In the past, due to the strong ritual connection with the earth spirits, the *panggong* was built on the ground so that during the Mak Yong performers would be sitting or moving about on the ground. Nowadays it is raised a few feet above ground to allow for maximum visibility for the large audiences which often attend.

A typical Mak Yong usually lasts between three and five evenings, but can go on for longer. The story is made up of three main parts: the *buka panggong*, the opening of the theatre ceremony; the *menghadap rebab*, salutation to the rebab; and the *pecah cerita*, the story proper. All performances begin with the placing of the musical instruments in their respective positions on stage. The *rebab* is set on the eastern side of the *panggung*, while other instruments are placed behind it, filling the back part of the stage for the *buka panggong*. This ritual is typical of many Malay traditional dance dramas.

The *buka panggong* ceremony is only carried out on the first night and its main function is to ensure a safe and smooth performance. During this ritual, the shaman, actors, and musicians pay respect to the powers of the universe—earth, air, fire and water—in order to assure the elements of their friendly intentions. The ceremony begins with the preparation of the ritual paraphernalia and proceeds with the shaman, or *bomoh*, reading the ritual mantra to appease the spirits. He continues to conduct the *buka alat-alat muzik* ceremony to appease the spirits of the musical instruments, and salutation songs are

sung, accompanied by the ensemble.

The performance proper is preceded by a musical prelude known as *lagu-lagu permulaan*, the entry and introduction of actors and actresses, and the *menghadap rebab*. The musical overture may continue for half an hour and ends when the actresses have made their way on to the stage. In *menghadap rebab*, the leading actress (Mak Yong) sings a long aria, interrupted by short choral passages from other actresses.

As well as for entertainment, Mak Yong is also performed for spiritual purposes. These performances are mainly concerned with propitiating the spirits, and include *semah angin*, to balance the basic elements of a human body; *sembah guru*, a ceremony for the salutation of a teacher; *memanggil semangat*, the recalling of a lost soul; and the shaministic *main puteri*. The basic function of all these ritual performances is to bring about some kind of healing process where illness is believed to be caused by the loss of the soul or from spirit possession. These performances can either be held on stage or in the house of the patient who requires the service.

—*Ku Zam Zam*

Opposite: *A Mak Yong in the 1950s. The male figure merely plays a supporting comedy role while the main parts are played by women.*
Above: *The leading actress, or Mak Yong, sings a solo in this performance, circa 1960.*

BANGAU BOATS

Talismans from the Days of Sail

They are carved in strange and fantastic forms, designed to ward off the forceful demons of the sea and to protect the crews of the small fishing boats: they are the *bangau* and remain a curious legacy from the days when sail reigned supreme on the South China Sea.

Essentially a sail guard, or spar holder, attached to the prow of the boats, *bangau*, Malay for the cattle egret, were not merely utilitarian objects but artistically decorated talismans carved into a variety of shapes ranging from sea horses and dragons to characters from the shadow puppet plays.

Although some *bangau* were carved in the likeness of birds, few resembled their namesake which at first seems an odd choice as egrets are rarely seen at sea. But according to Mubin Sheppard, the only historian to undertake a detailed study of these decorations, the

egret was probably chosen because of its well-known liking for fish. But there was formerly a deeper meaning behind the symbolism and decoration, for the *bangau* was where the *semangat*, or spirit, of the boat dwelt. Its presence helped the fishermen with their catch, kept fierce storms at bay and protected boatmen from sea demons which could cause freak winds, or throw a ship off course, never to be seen again.

From the 1950s onwards, as engines rapidly replacing sail the cumbersome spar-holders seemed fated to end up as mere historical ornaments on the museum shelf. But although the *bangau* fell out of favor on much of the east coast, it still survives in isolated fishing communities, particularly at Kampung Dasar Sabak, in the north of Kelantan, 10km (6mi) northeast of Kota Bharu, where a large fleet of 50 or more wooden boats, known as *perahu buatan barat* still proudly display these ancient figureheads.

Although now engine-driven, these boats retain the same basic design as their predecessors and the *bangau* is used to hold poles used for manoeuvering the boats to shore.

Myths of the oceans

The *perahu* boats are still painted and decorated in the elaborate Kelantanese style. Some *bangau* are carved to resemble mythological dragons, painted with realistic scale and glaring round eyes, which in Javanes

tradition show a propensity for violence. Were these originally made to warn off the *naga umbang*, a huge marine dragon that tradition has it lurks in the depths of the sea?

Some rakish prows are shaped like the *garuda*, a demonic birdman which is a remnant from pre-Islamic Hindu times. According to legend, the *garuda* lives in the top of a huge coconut palm, representing heaven, which grows in the center of the ocean known as *pusat tasek*, and beneath its roots is a whirlpool which is the boiling pot of hell.

Alexander the Great, known to the Malays as Raja Iskandar, figures in a Kelantanese legend along with the *garuda* which wrecks the Raja's boat and flings him into the infernal whirlpool. But he survives and goes on to further exploits. This story is still faithfully told in the shadow puppet plays of Kelantan.

A smaller version of the *bangau*, also a spar-holder, which shares the same horizontal beam, but on the opposite side of the boat, is known as an *ongkak*. On most east coast boats this is a mere 20cm (8in) peg, but on the decorative *dasar sabak* boats they too have become individual artists' fancies. The most popular representation is that of Raja Bota, a grotesque demon which appears as a villain in shadow puppet plays.

Dragons and long-knecked birds

On some of the more elaborate boats the entire front of the hull is painted with fire-breathing dragons, trident-wielding demons, and even the odd demure mermaid. All the boats are colored with rainbow stripes and beautifully maintained.

These days, engines have reduced the dangers of a fisherman's life, but it is still a hazardous business. The seamen are loathe to talk of the symbolism behind the *bangau*, for this is contrary to their Islamic teachings, but an old retired fisherman, mending nets on the beach, admitted that it "is better to keep the *bangau* newly-painted for one can

never be too sure of the fickle sea spirits."

Further down the east coast, the odd *bangau* is still to be found, and some of these actually resemble birds. At Penarik, in northern Terengganu, some *kolek*, crescent-shaped fishing boats with rakish sterns and prows, display *bangau* shaped like long-necked birds, but there the resemblance to the egret ends, for the heads are more like parrots. However, the small tuft of feathers carved on their heads could have been an attempt to imitate the bright orange feathers which the male egret sprouts during the mating season. But their origins remained obscure: the boat-builder was merely imitating a shape that his forefathers had copied before him.

The most elegant bangau of all, and the one that most resembles its ancient prototype, decorates a *kolek* boat at Beserah, just north of Kuantan. It depicts a snowy-white bird with a long neck and is very similar to the egret. It is possible the design originated from these more southern realms and then became more ornamented in Kelantan when it merged with other cultural symbolism.

Although most of today's east coast fishermen use stubby wooden diesel trawlers, there are still quite a few traditionalists who still put to sea each day in boats like the *perahu buatan barat*, the *kolek*, and the *sekochi*. And even though their matting sails have become obsolete, the *bangau* has defied modernity. These figureheads are still in pride of place on the bow—looking out in search of fish and protecting the fishermen from the wrath of the sea spirits, just as they have for centuries.

*Opposite: This Kelantanese fisherman renews the stripes on his traditional perahu buatan barat boat. **Above, left:** Fanciful designs adorn the prows of these boats at Kampung Dasar Sabak, Kelantan. **Above, right:** The bangau on the left is carved in the likeness of a shadow-puppet player. the smaller figure to its right is known as an ongkak.*

KELANTAN

Through the Land of Lightning

Kota Bharu, the capital of Kelantan, "the land of lightning," sprawls along the eastern bank of the flood-prone Kelantan River in the northern tip of the state. Hub of the fertile rice basin, and seat of the royal sultanate, the town is also the heartland of Malay arts, crafts and traditional pastimes.

The old royal center, north of Jalan Tengku Chik, is where most of the historical buildings are found. Between Jalan Hilir Kota and Jalan Hulu Kota, which translate as "the downstream and upstream roads of the fort," a high wooden wall, entered through elaborately-carved gates, leads to the **Istana Balai Besar**—the Royal Palace and Audience Hall—built in 1844. In the 1920s one of the few tourists to visit isolated Kelantan was invited here for Hari Raya breakfast with the sultan. He described the palace as "a wooden villa with windows of frosted glass." The building

is still in its original state, but only the grounds are open to the public these days and photography is not permitted.

On the northern side of the square is Istana Jahar, another royal palace built by Sultan Mohamad II for his prime minister in 1887. Carved panels and wooden fretwork decorate this palace which has recently been renovated into the Royal Custom Museum. Follow the lane around the back of the museum to the Muzium di Raja, the Royal Museum, which is housed in the blue-and-white Istana Batu (The Brick Palace).

Opposite here is Kampung Kraftangan (Handicraft Village) built in traditional Kelantanese style. Open from 10.30am to 6pm, the complex displays the state's renowned crafts and exhibitions are held on subjects such as Islamic architecture, ceramics, batik-painting, textiles and silk-weaving. Programs are available from the tourist information office on Jalan Sultan Ibrahim beside the Muzium Negeri (State Museum).

Return to the square, past Istana Jahar, and facing Jalan Sultanah Zainab is the Masjid Negeri (State Mosque), a rambling 80-year-old mosque which comes alive on Friday, the Muslim prayer day, when thousands of worshippers pack the halls, and the streets outside are buzzing with hawkers selling religious books, chanting beads, headgear and traditional medicines. To the left of the mosque is the Islamic Museum, another

attractive old wooden building with a Pattani-style tiled roof, and next door is Kelantan's oldest brick building, formerly a bank, which has been converted into a War Museum.

A marvellous market

Walk back to Jalan Tengku Chick, past the three-storey Bazaar Buluh Kubu where shops specialise in Kelantanese batiks and songket, to the **Pasar Besar** (Central Market), the undisputed hub of town, and the peninsula's most colorful market. Munshi Abdullah, a scribe to Sir Stamford Raffles, Singapore's founding father, traveled through Kelantan 150 years ago and remarked on the diligence of Kelantanese women. These days they are still considered just as hardworking, and throughout the state they are seen cooking sweet corn by the roadside, tilling the rice and tobacco fields, bartering fish on the beaches, weaving silk, and painting batik. But, nowhere is the female presence as pervading as in the Pasar Besar where women traders totally dominate.

Dressed in batik, with their heads delicately veiled and adorned with gold jewelery, the feminine merchants chew on betel nut and haggle over prices while sitting amidst piles of colorful fruit and vegetables. The entire scene is bathed in a filtered yellow light which streams through the translucent roof. Pink lotus shoots, feathery fern tips, prickly durians, scarlet chillies and a bewildering variety of other produce contributes to the sights and aromas of Kota Bharu's greatest attraction. Upstairs are food stalls specializing in Kelantanese-style rice and curries, *nasi dagang*—rice and tuna, *nasi kerapu*—rice with herbs; and there are countless more stalls dealing in spices, dry goods, local biscuits and cakes.

Although nothing beats watching a real village performance of the shadow puppet play *wayang kulit*, or catching a festival where traditional contests in *gasing* (top-spinning), *silat* (self-defense), and kite-flying are performed, travelers can see these enacted each week at the Gelanggang Seni, the cultural center. In a small lane off Jalan Mahmud, not far from the Hotel Perdana, the center is open from February to October, but closed during the fasting month and the annual monsoon. Performances of top-spinning, *silat*, kite-flying, and *rebana* (giant-drums) are held on Monday, Wednesday and Saturday afternoons, and traditional dances and *wayang kulit* are held at 9pm on Saturdays and Wednesdays respectively. Kelantan hosts an international kite festival every May, the rebana drum festival in July, a top-spinning festival every September, and many traditional pastimes can also be seen at the annual *puja umur*—the sultan of Kelantan's birthday on March 30th and 31st.

The beach of passionate love

Malay silversmiths, obsolete in most other states, still thrive in Kota Bharu, and they can be found hammering away on their repoussé work and creating fine filigree at shops along the southern end of Jalan Sultanah Zainab. Most of Kota Bharu's other arts and crafts are produced along the road to Pantai Cinta Berahi, the famous beach of passionate love.

Songket weaving is centered in workshops around Kampung Penambang, 3km (2mi) from town, where women weave silk threads into handsome brocades—once the prerogative of royalty. Bolts of the shimmering cloth are on display, but they are not for everyday wear. Most of the buyers are Malays purchasing lengths for wedding costumes, or royal and official functions. Even a simple 2m (6.5ft) sarong length can cost hundreds of dollars.

Opposite: As the shadows lengthen, food stalls take over the carpark opposite Kota Bharu's Central Market. Below: A wistful Kelantanese girl dressed in her lacy best for the Sultan's birthday celebrations.

R. MOH'D NOH SALLEH

From Kampung Badang, 8km (5mi) from Kota Bharu, to the beachfront at 10km (6mi), are dozens of workshops where girls paint tropical flowers on hand-painted batiks and youths stamp cloth with traditional Kelantanese patterns. At other cottage factories, kite-makers paste delicate designs onto their *wau bulan*—moon kites—which can have a wingspan of 2m (6.5ft). Most of the craft shops are a short distance from the nearby beach of passionate love and it is pleasant to stroll from the beachside chalets around the palm-shaded lanes where there is always some work in progress.

The tradewinds always seem to blow along Pantai Cinta Berahi. The South China Sea pounds the shore and clouds the air with a fine mist. The long golden sands are excellent for walks but avoid the weekends when Kelantan's favourite beach is packed with local sightseers.

East along the coast is Pantai Dasar Sabak, famous for its painted fishing boats and the World War II site where the Japanese first came ashore to conquer the Malay Peninsula in 1941. To get there, take Jalan Pengkalan Chepa to the airport then on to Pantai Dasar Sabak where a bunker marks the historical wartime spot. At the beachside *kampung*, 1km (0.6mi) further east, fishermen still take to sea in beautifully-decorated *perahus*. In the absence of a harbor the boats are hauled up the beach by their chanting crews.

Wats, rice and tobacco

Kota Bharu is a good base for exploring the fertile Kelantan Basin, bordered by Tumpat in the north, Pasir Puteh in the southeast and Tanah Merah in the southwest. To get to Tumpat, the old railhead town 15km (9mi) from Kota Bharu, take the bridge across the Sungai Kelantan to Wakaf Bharu, then head north through rice paddies which become tobacco fields in the dry season.

Outside of town is one of the region's many Thai *wat* temples for this border area is home to Kelantan's Thai Buddhist minority. A large, gold-tiled Buddha stands beside the temple approached via a gateway decorated with elephants. Time-warped Tumpat hasn't changed much in decades; the old wooden railway station dominates the town and original shophouses line the main road. On Jalan Dato is the elegant District Office built in the town's heyday in the 1930s.

Cross the railway line, and just out of town where a lagoon flanks the road, boat-builders on the opposite shore can be seen crafting large ocean-going fishing boats from jungle hardwoods. Further along is Pantai Seri Tujuh, a popular beach and boating lagoon and venue of the international kite festival. Mid-morning, along the beach, fishermen cast a huge net offshore, then teams of men haul both ends up the beach until the fish are trapped into a flapping, silvery semi-circle,

Kelantan Basin

THAILAND

Narathiwat

Pantai Sri Tujoh

Pantai Mek Mas

Pengkalan Kubur

K. Besar

Kg. Semut Api

Pantai Cahaya Bulan

Tumpat

Batik & Kite Workshops

Kg. S. Pinang

Kg. Badang

War Memorial

'Bangau' Boats

Songket Weaving

Pengkalan Chepa

Kg. Pantai Dasar Sabak

Kg. Penambang

Chabang Empat

Wat Phothivihan (Reclining Buddha)

Wakaf Baharu

KOTA BHARU

Kg. Peng. Datu

Kg. Jambu

Meranti

Kubang Kerian

Pantai Irama

Pohon Tanjong

Kg. Binjai

Perupok

Bachok

Wat Uttamaran

Pasir Mas

Kg. Mulong

Kilometers

Gyal Periok

Repek

Masjid Kampung Laut

Kg. K. Melawi

Nilam Puri

Pauh Lima

Rantau Panjang & Golok

East West Highway

Gua Musang

Kuala Terengganu

N

and then ladled into a waiting *perahu*. A few kilometers past Pantai Seri Tujuh is Pengkalan Kubur and the Thai border.

Southwest from here at Cabang Empat, turn right for Wat Phothivihan where swallows nest in the earlobes of Malaysia's largest Reclining Buddha housed in an ugly building which looks like a football-stand. Nearby, older and more aesthetic temples house Buddhist shrines. Follow this road to Repek where in the harvest season mechanical harvesters chomp their way through a golden sea of rice, and wooden threshing stalls dot the landscape.

At Repek, turn west for Kelantan's oldest and prettiest Thai temple—Wat Uttamaram. Monks in saffron-colored robes wander about the quiet, shaded grounds where cows graze, and wind chimes and temple bells tinkle in the breeze. This elaborately-decorated *wat* has fanciful flame-like, upturned roof ridges, an orange and green, multi-tiered roof, and fabulous dragons entwine the verandah columns. Continue along this rural road and turn left alongside the river to Rantau Panjang, a border town popular with Malaysian bargain hunters. On the Thai side is Golok, a seedy town renowned for its unabashed nightlife. Return from Rantau Panjang through Pasir Mas, an old riverine town and home to (it is generally contended) Malaysia's prettiest women. Kelantan's history abounds with tales of beautiful women including the legendary warrior queen Cik Siti Wan Kembang who ruled during the 14th century and whose pet deer is immortalized on the state's official crest.

On Highway 8, 10km (6mi) south of Kota Bharu is Masjid Kampung Laut, possibly Malaysia's oldest mosque which was removed here from its former floodprone site beside the Kelantan River. Built around 300 years ago by Javanese missionaries after a lucky escape from pirates.

Another fascinating region is the little-visited eastern beaches around Perupok, Bachok and Kampung Melawi. Along the road from Kota Bharu, women can be seen tilling tobacco fields and rice-paddies, and hawkers shoulder poles strung with conical food-covers woven from pandanus leaves. On the coast, the beaches stretch in an unbroken line from one horizon to the other. Bachok's Pantai Irama has a beachside park and a rest-house, but the beaches are usually deserted, except for the odd fisherman. South at Kampung Melawi, a very traditional village way off the tourist trail, crescent-shaped fishing boats known as *kolek* still put to sea and the shoreline is strewn with shells. The palm-fringed beach extends from here all the way to Besut on the Terengganu border.

Below: *At Pantai Sri Tujuh, near Tumpat in Kelantan's far-north, fishermen still haul their nets in by hand.*

R. MOH'D NOH SALLEH

PULAU PERHENTIAN

Palm-Fringed Islands of the North Coast

I plunged into the clear turquoise sea. A large rainbow cod, startled at the intrusion, sought refuge under a pink tabletop of coral. Unperturbed, a giant clam sat alone on the sandy seafloor, its striped lips ready to crush its unsuspecting prey. Psychedelic parrot fish nibbled away at a coral branch, and orange-and-white-striped clownfish hid from predators amongst the lilac-colored tentacles of reef anemones.

Out of breath I resurfaced, alone in the sea, the jungle chorus from behind the beach sounding deafening after the silence of the underwater world. After the dive I ran up the deserted beach, drew a freshwater bath from the well, and sat down under the coconut palms to admire the view from Pulau Perhentian Besar: Malaysia's most quintessential tropical island.

At the northernmost tip of Terengganu,

the Perhentian island group, are 21km (13mi) off the coast of Kuala Besut, a fishing town not far from the Kelantan border. Wooden fishing trawlers converted into passenger boats make the two-hour crossing across the South China Sea to the jetty on Pulau Perhentian Besar (literally big Perhentian) where there are chalets, a resort, talcum-white beaches and no villages.

Across the narrow strait which separates the two islands is Pulau Perhentian Kecil the "small" island, home to a fishing community, and has a couple of provision shops, coffee shops, and the islands' only mosque. The island is renowned for its clever musical villagers who are adept at *berdikir barat*, a rythmic rap-like repartee between two teams of singers who make up lyrics as they go along, accompanied by hypnotic drum beats.

Perhentian Besar is a perfect destination for travelers seeking solitude, and a chance to do as little as possible. The waters are clear and clean, the beaches dazzling white, the interior rainforest is still virginal, and there are several interesting small coral reefs close enough to shore that even the most inexperienced snorkelers can enjoy the tropical underwater world. Even when the island is booked solid at holiday weekends Perhentian Besar still seems half-deserted.

Modern travelers may have only been coming to Pulau Perhentian for less than a decade, but for centuries mariners have been

JILL GOCHER

using the islands (literally translated-"the stopping-place islands") as a refuge from bad weather and a port to stock up on fresh water. Mentioned on Chinese sailing charts from the 15th century, Pulau Perhentian was a port of call on the prosperous maritime trade route, known as the second silk road, which flourished between China, Southeast Asia, India and the Middle East.

Kuala Besut, the jump-off port, is 68km (42mi) south of Kota Bharu. Goats recline on wooden verandahs, and sun themselves in the middle of the road in this sleepy fishing town. Sometimes a street market enlivens the waterfront road, and people from outlying villages crowd the stalls which are stocked with cheap Thai clothes, dried squid, woven pandanus mats and fruits and vegetables. There is always action at the dock: Kuala Besut is the home port of one of Malaysia's largest deep-sea fishing fleet, and dozens of smaller local trawlers.

Island boats run more frequently in the mornings, and on weekends, which in Terengganu and Kelantan fall on Thursday and Friday, but if you are stuck in the town overnight there are good beaches to the north and south, and a peaceful resort overlooks the beachfront, a few kilometers south of Kuala Besut on the way to Kampung Raja. For travelers arriving by car there are many private car parks in town where vehicles can be left overnight for a small fee.

Ferries leave from the wooden town jetty, and as all travelers are only in town to go to the islands it is virtually impossible to miss the boat as the boatmen and townspeople direct everyone to the next departing boat. They rarely leave on time—casting off only when they are full. The journey out is usually through glassy seas where flying fish skip across the surface and dolphins are occasionally spotted.

During monsoon season, from November through March, seas can get very rough and few boats make the crossing. Even if you get out in fine weather the seas can quickly mount and sometimes it is difficult to find a boat for the return journey. The water is also murky during this season, visibility is poor, and many east coast resorts close down. Boats, when you can get them, land at either the jetty near the resthouse or at the new dock close to the low-key resort.

Trails wind along the coast linking both jetties, and a track continues around the beaches to the north to the popular backpackers' beach which faces Pulau Perhentian

Kecil across the strait. The accommodation here is cheap and basic wooden huts with rock-bottom amenities, but the views, the water, and the beach more than make up for it. For travelers who like to relax in more comfort there is a small, resort south of the jetties on an equally pretty beach.

Canoes and snorkeling equipment can be rented from the chalets and the resort. The reefs in front of the beach are shallow at low tide and the corals and marine life can be easily observed. Take care though, when the tides are running, particularly in the channel between the islands, as the current can become very strong. All Terengganu's offshore islands are protected under Marine Park status.

Thick rainforest grows right to the beaches and well-marked trails wind across the island to deserted beaches on the windward side. Starting from the last chalet to the south of the new jetty, a trail winds uphill and descends to a long bay. Midway along this beach another trail heads inland to the resort and at the end of the bay another track leads across the island. This enjoyable trek which offers a break from the beach takes around two hours.

Opposite: Children make the most of the crystal-clear waters at Pulau Perhentian Besar.
Above: A perfect day for beachcombing along Perhentian Besar's main beach

TERENGGANU

An Ancient Port and Endless Sand

Beautiful fishing boats, a stone palace and flag pole atop Bukit Puteri, religious schools, a bustling Chinatown, and a predominance of fishermen, were all remarked upon by Munshi Abdullah, a Malay writer who visited Kuala Terengganu in 1836. These days, the state capital has boomed with Terengganu's new oil wealth, but beneath this veneer much of Abdullah's 19th-century observations are still relevant.

Situated beside the estuary of the river which the state is named after, Kuala Terengganu, 168km (104mi) south of Kota Bharu, is probably the oldest port on the east coast. Some scholars believe that it was one of two ports marked on Ptolemy's second-century map of the Malay Peninsula—the earliest-known cartographic record of the region—which was apparently drawn from information supplied by Indian sailors.

Later, Chinese and Arab annals record that Kuala Terengganu was a major trading port, and Javanese records from the 1360s show that it was part of the vassal states of the Majapahit Empire. But the most famous historical evidence is the Terengganu Stone, inscribed with the oldest-known Malay text in the Arabic script which was discovered 24km (15mi) upriver at Kuala Berang. This stone fragment records Islamic rules proclaimed by Raja Mandulika in the mid-14th century and proves that Terengganu converted to Islam at least 25 years before Melaka. Ever since Sayid Hussin, an Arab tin-prospector, found the historical stone in 1897 it has been kept in the National Museum in Kuala Lumpur, but there are plans to bring the Terengganu Stone back to its home state.

Kuala Terengganu

Kuala Terengganu sprawls along the riverbank and around a promotory to the South China Sea. The oldest, and most colorful part of town is centered around the waterfront and extends back to Jalan Masjid, while the modern "petro-dollar" part of town is along Jalan Sultan Ismail. Start a morning tour at the bustling **Central Market**, pass through the entrance flanked by women vendors who sit haggling amongst piles of bananas and durians, then weave your way inside through the rows of stalls which sell everything from sausage-like *keropok likur*, a shrimp delicacy,

to traditional blue-and-white Terengganu batiks and locally-produced brasswares. **Chinatown** starts at the market corner and lines both sides of Jalan Bandar. Its old shophouses which have housed generations of family businesses, are built in the distinctive southern Chinese style with curved roof ridges, arched windows, carved signboards, and decorative tiles. The small frontages are deceiving for these townhouses are cavernous family dwellings, often with warehouses attached, that stretch 30m (98ft) from the road and extend out onto stilts above the river. Old shops here sell local brasswares, nautical equipment and conical trishaw drivers' hats made of palm leaves.

East of the market, next to the post office, a staircase ascends 200m (656ft) to the summit of Bukit Puteri (Princess Hill) where fortifications have stood for centuries. From the old fort, which played an important role in the early 19th-century Civil War, there are panoramic views across the estuary to the fishing village of Seberang Takir.

A large brass bell, called a *genta*, made by a 19th-century craftsman from neighboring Kampung Tanjung is still housed beside the fort and was used in the past for warning the population of fires, and of men running amok. It was also rung during Ramadan to signify the breaking of the fast. Also on the summit is a lighthouse, a flagpole, and some fine old cannon including the legendary Meriam Beranak, "the cannon that bears children," with its offspring—a tiny cannon—beside it.

At the base of Bukit Putri is the royal compound, once enclosed by a high stone wall, which houses the apricot-and-white Istana Maziah, built in French provincial style in 1894. This former royal palace is still used for official functions. Behind the palace on Jalan Kota, are remnants of the old stone wall, and an entrance leads to some 19th-century wooden houses that are still home to Terengganu royalty, although the sultan now resides in a new palace on Jalan Sultan Mahmud, south of town. On the corner of Jalan Kota and Jalan Masjid is the Masjid Abidin which was originally built of wood in 1793 but has been substantially renovated. Inside are some beautiful wood carvings.

The boat-builders' island

Across the river from Kuala Terengganu is Pulau Duyung, a 50-cent ferry ride from either the jetty east of the market or from the riverside end of Jalan Sultan Ismail. On the riverine island, traditional carpenters still

Opposite: *Trishaws are still a popular mode of transport along Jalan Bandar, a waterfront street lined with old Chinese shophouses.*
Below: *"Chick" blinds of split bamboo, painted with advertisements, shade the pavements and the shoppers from the fierce sun in the heart of Kuala Terengganu's Chinatown.*

carry on the art of building wooden boats, using the prized red cengal wood from Terengganu's interior rainforests. The *pinas*, Terengganu schooners 18 to 21m (60-70ft) long, which once sailed to Bangkok and Saigon, haven't been built for decades but the craftsmen still use the same boat-building techniques to make ocean-going trawlers and wooden yachts for an international clientele.

Pulau Duyung is connected by a new bridge to town, but it is much more pleasant to make the trip by water and view Kuala Terengganu across the river. Apart from the boat-builders, the island has interesting old *kampung* with traditional wooden houses, and on neighboring Pulau Duyung Kecil, connected by a path, is the ruins of a 19th-century mansion once owned by Tok Duyung, a famed Islamic religious teacher.

In the northeast of town in Kampung Tanjung and Kampung Ladang watch out for signs advertising Tembaga dan Batik workshops, usually in the ground floor of kampung houses, where traditional Terengganu-style batiks and brasswares are still made.

Other attractions further afield include the State Museum on the top of Bukit Kecil; Pantai Batu Buruk, a favorite tree-lined beach 1.5km (0.9mi) from town; Suterasemai, a silk-weaving center, 5km (3mi) south at Chendering; Masjid Hiliran, a historical 19th-century wooden mosque on Jalan Hiliran; further out from there, along Jalan Kuala Hiliran then Jalan Losong Ferry is the Komplex Budaya, 3km (1.9mi) upriver at Kampung Losong, where some 19th-century wooden palaces have been resited beside the river.

From Kuala Besut in the far north, to Cukai, 261km (162mi) south, the Terengganu coast is practically one long beach. Fringed by coconut palms and casuarinas, these cream-colored sands are occasionally broken by estuaries. The only flaw in this otherwise impeccable coastline is the 40km (25mi) stretch between Kertih and Chukai, close to the Pahang border, where Terengganu's vast petroleum and gas complexes cast an Orwellian shadow over the surroundings.

The lonely north coast

North of Kuala Terengganu, the main road to Kota Bharu heads inland, but there is a quiet coastal road which begins just north of the Jambatan Sultan Mahmud, Malaysia's second-longest bridge, and follows the beaches 42km (26mi) to Kampung Penarik.

The good beaches start at Batu Rakit, 14km (8.6mi) from the roundabout north of

the bridge and continue till Merang—not to be confused with Marang, the more popular fishing town south of Kuala Terengganu.

Follow the seaside road to Pantai Merang, a bay north of a small rocky headland where boats often shelter from the mid-year southwest winds. On a hill overlooking the beach is a resthouse and at the base are A-frame chalets. Food vendors set up beside the beach at weekends when the people from the surrounding kampung come here for picnics, and there's some basic, but traditional homestays operating just out of town for travelers who want a real kampung experience far from the other tourist haunts.

Offshore, to the northeast is Pulau Bidung Laut, which served for a decade as a United Nations shelter for thousands of Vietnamese boat people. Further north, the hazy-blue island in the distance is the divers' paradise of **Pulau Redang**, Terengganu's largest archipelago, 50km (31mi) from Kuala Terengganu, and the location of a billion-dollar resort development. Enviromental groups are keeping close tabs on the project as the reefs around these islands are Peninsular Malaysia's most pristine.

Boats run from Kuala Terengganu to Pulau Redang, but boat charters are expensive. A good way to visit is with an organized dive group or tours which include arrangements for accommodation and food. These groups often depart from Pantai

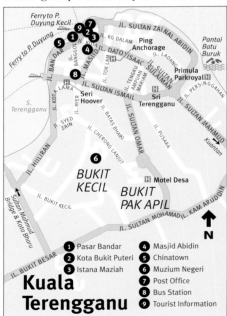

BUKIT
KECIL   BUKIT
        PAK APIL

Kuala Terengganu

1 Pasar Bandar
2 Kota Bukit Puteri
3 Istana Maziah
4 Masjid Abidin
5 Chinatown
6 Muzium Negeri
7 Post Office
8 Bus Station
9 Tourist Information

Merang which reduces the boat trip to around three hours. If you've got plenty of time you can always put up in a kampung house and take pot luck at scoring a boat back to the mainland.

Just north of Kampung Merang, turn off for Pantai Bari, another idyllic beach which is always deserted. From here the road runs along the coast to Kampung Penarik, with delightful beaches all the way, however don't make the mistake of thinking you can plunge in minus swimwear or topless: even if you think the beach is deserted someone's bound to show up, and conservative Terengganu is not the place to offend the locals.

Marang and Pulau Kapas

Heading south from Kuala Terengganu, follow Jalan Sultan Mahmud which turns into Route 3, the main East Coast Highway. At Rhusila, 10km (6mi) south, the heartland of the Parti Islam fundamentalists, some women wear *purdah* veils, and the men dress in turbans and the long Arabic *jubah*. Their seafront shops specializing in cheap basketwares and dried fish flank the highway and there is also a government-run Kraftangan shop with an excellent array of Terengganu fabrics and crafts.

Marang, 5km (3mi) further south, is the quintessential fishing town, with the prettiest harbor in Malaysia. Bird-like *kolek* boats, painted in pastel hues, and squat wooden fishing boats anchor in the bay and come and

go past the sand spit to the sea. Along the shoreline, racks of squid and salted fish dry in the sun, boats being repaired lie on the shore like beached whales, and in the distance behind the beach, Pulau Kapas, an offshore island, seems to hover in a midday mirage above the shimmering sea.

There are plenty of chalets and guesthouses in town. Across the bridge in Kampun Rhu Muda, there are good swimming beaches and cottage-craft workshops specializing in woodcarving and hand-painted batik.

In the north of town, budget-priced chalets face a lagoon which runs along the back of a picturesque beachside kampung, where houses stand high on stilts to protect against the wrath of the monsoon seas which often sweep over the village. A wooden footbridge spans the lagoon to the fishing village, and it's a short walk from here to the beach. Old wooden shophouses line the tiny main street of Marang, which is alongside the waterfront to the left of the highway.

Some of these have now become backpackers' lodgings, where Malay beach boys lounge on the verandah and strum their guitars. Others are small offices which cater for

Below: *Dressed in traditional outfits with silk brocade headgear and short sarongs known as samping, Terengganu boys are as resplendent as the girls at an annual festival in Kuala Terengganu.*

ALAIN EVRARD

trips to Pulau Kapas, a short half-hour boat ride from Marang jetty. As the island is only 6km (3.7mi) offshore it is ideal for travelers who don't have the time to spend on a lengthy boat trip to some of the more remote islands. The beaches are clean and powdery white, the water is clear and excellent for swimming, but for good snorkeling and diving it's better to organize a trip to neighboring Pulau Gemia. The chalets are grouped together on the main beach which gets quite crowded, but there are more deserted bays around the southern headland.

Much of inland Terengganu is either monotonous oil-palm plantations or inaccessible mountainous rainforest, but 20km (12mi) outside of Kuala Berang, located 25km (15.5mi) southwest from Marang, is Empangan Kenyir, reputedly the largest dam and man-made lake in Southeast Asia. The enormous dam wall supports a vast network of sunken valleys—the flooded headwaters of the Sungai Terengganu. A road spans the top of the wall with spectacular views across the vast lake to the forested mountains beyond.

On the lakeshore are boats for hire, and tour companies organize overnight stays on houseboats and longer fishing trips. The lake has many famous freshwater species and the angling is excellent. There are also a number of waterfalls which can only be viewed by boat. Just before Kuala Berang, another road turns off to the left to Air Terjun Sekayu, a seven-tiered waterfall and forest recreation park, 18km (11mi) from the turnoff. The park is well maintained and there are trails up through the rainforest to the head of the falls. It is very popular with the locals, who much prefer to hang out at freshwater waterfalls than by the sea, but through the week it's quite peaceful. There is a mini-zoo with some white gibbons, and a resthouse and chalets for overnight stays.

The giant leatherback turtles

Heading south from Marang along the East Coast Highway, the road hugs the coast 41km (25mi) to Rantau Abang, a 19km (12mi) stretch of beach where the giant leatherback turtles come ashore every year to lay their eggs. Measuring 1.5m (5ft) long and weighing over 350kg (772lb), the largest of all sea turtles return to nest between the months of June and September, although August is the peak season. Numbers have declined rapidly in recent years and the government has introduced heavy fines for egg-collecting, and is making a major effort to ensure that the turtles keep returning.

Not so long ago onlookers climbed on the turtles' backs, sat waiting with transistor radios blaring and took flashlight photos. Now all of these activities are banned. Fisheries department officers collect the eggs after they are laid and place them in hatcheries until they hatch, then the hatchlings are watched as they return to the sea.

This all may sound too organized, but the sight of these massive turtles lumbering up the beach by moonlight to lay their eggs, perhaps having swum from the Atlantic to return here, is an awe-inspiring experience and well worth being woken up in the middle of the night for. Don't expect to see them on your first night. You have to be lucky as even in the nesting season, numbers have declined to such alarming rates, it is rare to sight a landing. However, the smaller but no less fascinating green and hawksbill female turtles also come up to Rantau Abang to lay their eggs. These too are protected species, and are now offered as turtle-watching tourism fodder.

Concerted effort is being made to ensure the survival of the species, including research by the Fisheries Department, awareness and educational campaigns and intensive media coverage. Tourism has been identified as a threat to turtles, so make sure you read up all you can about interacting with turtles at the Turtle Information Center. Run by the Fisheries Department, it is open ..

Why they return to Rantau Abang every year is yet another one of nature's mysteries. Some villagers believe that they are lured in by a large black stone which looks like a turtle, but experts think that the steep incline of Rantau Abang beach, which can be dangerous for swimming, is perfect for turtle-landing, although this theory is not foolproof for there are other sites along the coast which also offer a sharp dropoff.

A **Turtle Information Center**, run by the Fisheries Department is open during the season and has film shows and displays. There is ample chalet accommodation, from budget A-frames to the more traditional Malay-style chalets, and most have a restaurant. Alternatively there is a small complex of simple restaurants serving local fare just south of the Information Center.

Tanjung Jara, 10km (6mi) past Rantau Abang, is a private resort, but the award-winning architecture—based on the original designs of Terengganu's old wooden palaces—is worth stopping off to see even if you don't stay over. The entire complex is made of wood, stained in the traditional manner and decorat-

ed with wood carvings. Set around a lagoon and along the beachfront, the resort blends in beautifully with the surroundings and is a great place to unwind in luxury. This resort is also kept informed of turtle-landings and visitors make the short trip north in a mini-van.

Dungun, just south of Tanjung Jara, was once a thriving port with an upstream ore mine, however, these days it's just another sleepy fishing port where salted-fish dry on racks in the sun, diesel-powered trawlers throb in and out through the estuary and housewives cycle to the riverside market. Kampung Seberang Pintasan, on the northern promontory, just down the road from Tanjung Jara, is the best place to watch the sun go down when the fishing boats are silhouetted in a river of molten gold.

Wooden boats crowd the riverbank at photogenic Paka, 20km (12.4mi) south of Dungun, a traditional east coast village which has changed little over the decades, unlike the next port south, Kerteh, which has been transformed by the state's vast offshore petroleum and gas deposits. Waste gas flames belch into the sky, and miles of serpentine pipelines dominate the road south past the huge gas-processing plant and refinery complex owned by Petronas, the national oil company. A safe distance from here, well-planned oil-workers' suburbs set in tree-lined streets border the highway to Kemasik where the scenery again reverts to Terengganu-style fishing villages.

Pantai Kemasik, just south of town, is a long, white-sand beach with a distinctive offshore rock formation which is popular with oilworkers' families on the weekends. The highway south follows the coast past Kijal, a sleepy seaside village which is well-known for its delicious *kuini*, a type of mango. When it's not fruit season, the enterprising women hawkers sell *lemang* rice cooked in bamboo, with *rendang* a spicy, dry beef dish.

Chukai and adjacent Kemaman, 18km (11mi) south of Kijal, is the last port on the Terengganu coast before the highway crosses into Pahang state. Tourists rarely stopover here as they are usually en route to the beach resorts, but the town has a bustling market place alongside the riverfront, banks, and good local restaurants. At the nearby seaside village of Kuala Kemaman where old wooden houses stand high on stilts above the sand, every vacant block is covered with shrimp crackers drying on mats in the sun. There are no tourists here, and everyone still ekes out a living from the sea. In the mid-afternoon heat—siesta time—the only sounds are the soft lapping of waves and the tradewinds rustling the palms along the long beach which runs all the way south to Pahang.

Above: *At Marang, fishing boats moor in the lagoon, and in the distance is the popular resort island of Pulau Kapas.*

KUANTAN & PAHANG

A Vast Region Ruled by the Ocean

A long coastline of golden beaches, mountainous offshore islands, cool hill resorts, tranquil fishing villages, lotus-covered lakes, and rainforests with West Malaysia's highest mountain and longest river, all contribute to make Pahang, Peninsular Malaysia's largest state covering 35,965km^2 (13,886mi^2), a highly popular tourist destination.

Because of the region's size many of these attractions are nearer and much more accessible from the west coast than the east. For this reason the Cameron Highlands are included in the Perak chapter, Fraser's Hill in Kuala Lumpur, and Taman Negara (the national park) and the Kenong Rimba Forest Park near Kuala Lipis in the Rainforests chapter.

Legendary kingdoms

Pahang is the Khmer word for "tin" and as the tin mines upstream from Kuantan at Sungai Lembing had been worked since prehistoric times some historians think that this is where the state's name derived from. Other interesting associations with the ancient Khmer from today's Kampuchea is that the indigenous Orang Asli, the Jakun, speak a Mon-Khmer dialect and there are legends suggesting that an ancient Khmer city lies buried in the silt under the waters of Tasek Cini. But archaeologists have yet to study the region seriously.

Settled since the Stone Age, Pahang was well known to early Chinese mariners who came for the sandalwood and elephant's tusks as Pong-fong, and later to Arabs and Europeans as the gold-rich kingdom of Pam, also known as Pan, Phaan, Paham, and Pahangh. But the state emerged as a separate entity only in the 15th century when it was captured by a son of the sultan of Melaka who started the Pahang dynasty at Pekan which is still the royal seat beside the Pahang River.

A riverside capital

Kuantan, situated about midway down the east coast, only took over from inland Kuala Lipis as the state capital in 1955, and although the town was mentioned as far back as the 12th-century when it was known as Tan-maling, probably after the nearby promontory of Tanjung Tembeling, nothing tangible remains from antiquity and there are few historical buildings. The further south one travels on

R. MOH'D NOH SALLEH

the east coast the more homogenized the society becomes, and Kuantan also lacks the wealth of cultural traditions found in Kota Bharu and Kuala Terengganu. However, the town is pleasant enough and is a good base to explore the neighboring beaches, fishing villages and other nearby attractions.

As the closest east coast center to Kuala Lumpur (259km/161mi), this fast-growing town ringed by surburban developments is the commercial and industrial hub of Pahang. There are some old black-and-white colonial administration buildings fronting the Padang opposite Jalan Mahkota, and on the northern side facing Jalan Masjid is the fantastic, new State Mosque with its huge arched entrance reminiscent of Mughal-India, which features intricate mosaic-tile work, and four soaring minarets.

Jalan Mahkota and parallel Jalan Besar have some interesting old Chinese shophouses and in this grid is where most of the banks, offices, downtown hotels and restaurants are located. The shaded walkway which extends along the riverbank is pleasant in the evening and there are lots of foodstalls overlooking the river.

Beaches and fishing villages

Teluk Chempedak, a sandy bay enclosed by rocky headlands 4km (2.5mi) from Kuantan along Jalan Teluk Sisek is the town's major attraction. At the north end of the bay there's a paved promenade with handicraft shops, seafood restaurants, and cheap eating stalls. Trails wind through the rainforest which grows right to the water's edge around to another shaded bay.

In the early morning the jungle is alive with birds and it is easy to spot monkeys swinging through the trees. To the south of the promenade are two international-class hotels, and a range of alternative accommodation. There are plenty of better beaches on the east coast, but Teluk Chempedak is lively, great for watching the local action, good for swimming, sunbaking, jogging, jungle-walks, and eating seafood, and if you are an early riser the apricot dawn over the South China Sea is a treat.

Beserah, 10km (6mi) north of Kuantan along Jalan Beserah (the main highway north), is one of the east coast's most fascinating fishing villages. Take the turnoff to the beach where the foreshore is covered with wooden racks raised high on stilts where salted fish dry in the sun. Dawn is the best time to arrive, for the sea is like glass and some-

times even dolphins and dugong can be seen at this hour. Men shoulder the heavy rattan baskets of fish down to the drying racks and then a group of sarong-clad girls and women, both Chinese and Malay, squat on the decks and begin covering the split bamboo floor with the silvery, salted fish.

When the tide comes in, the sands underneath the stilted racks are covered with water and boys leap about in the shallows spearing fish. Across the tidal lagoon, before the sand dunes slope down to the beach, woven mats are spread out and covered with *ikan bilis*, the dried, anchovy-type fish that are a basic ingredient in Malay cuisine. Under tin roofs near here are sheds where the *ikan bilis* are cooked in vats of salt water before drying. The entire village runs on the salted-fish business and the day's action all centers around the afternoon catch. When the boats return depends on the season, but the locals usually know—give or take an hour—and it is a sight worth waiting for.

Offshore, the tubby trawlers unload the catch into beamy open boats which ride the waves into the shallows, and there, amidst the

Opposite: At Beserah, a fishing village north of Kuantan, women spread salted fish to dry on split-bamboo platforms raised on stilts off the ground. *Below:* This Pahang fisherman spends his mornings at sea and his afternoons mending nets under the coconut palms.

R. MOH'D NOH SALLEH

R. MOH'D NOH SALLEH

foaming surf, the fishermen transfer the baskets of fish onto a waiting cart pulled by water buffalo. When the cart is full, the driver shouts and urges the buffalo out of the water and the carts thunder up the white sands to the *ikan bilis* sheds. Perhaps, in years gone by, other fishing villages also used buffalo to transport the fish from boat to shore, but this is the only east coast *kampung* which still uses this method.

A range of lodgings is available at the beachside village where traditional wooden houses are shaded by coconut palms, and travelers can make a stopover in this interesting *kampung*. South of the town, just over the bridge is a batik workshop, and close to the beach on this side, women make homemade *keropok*, dried prawn crackers.

Just north of Beserah, at Kampung Sungai Karang, the inland road goes to Pusat Cenderamata (1.8km/1mi), a craft center which has shellcrafts and jewelery made from local gemstones. About 5km (3mi) north at Balok, the long beach has fine white sands and is great for swimming. An international windsurfing contest is held here every December/January when the annual monsoon kicks up a good surf on the otherwise placid waters. There are resorts and some excellent seafood restaurants along the coast to Pantai Batu Hitam, where the beach is shaded by whispering casuarina trees.

North of here, the highway makes a detour around the Kuantan port, and then heads up the coast past the picturesque estuary at Sungai Ular. Here, wooden fishing boats with gaily-painted yellow cabins, and rainbow-colored sampans moor beside the river, and coconut palms tower above the seaside village. Fishermen sit in the shade mending their nets, and the womenfolk gather at the water's edge to buy fish fresh from the boats. Local boatmen can ferry you out to tiny Pulau Ular, a nearby island which derived its name "snake island" from a legend which tells that it was formed by a giant sea serpent. This quiet village has some very basic huts, but is totally unaffected by the tourism which thrives both to the south and north.

Laid-back Cherating

Cherating, 47km (29mi) north of Kuantan, looks like a typical Pahang village on the highway, but turn off to Kampung Cherating and every *kampung* house seems to have turned into a mini-resort. This is the backpackers' favorite hang-out on the east coast mainland, with a proliferation of chalets and restaurants. The beach stretches for miles to the south, and is great for swimming and windsurfing. Even in the peak season there's an uncrowded feel to the place.

If you're not interested in the beach there are plenty of other cultural activities including trying your hand at batik-painting. The Souvenir Center near the highway has good courses, and this is also a good place to learn the art of weaving *mengkuang*—pandanus leaves—which locals weave into mats and baskets. Travelers can also get to participate in Malaysian sports like *sepak-takraw*, a game similar to volley-ball where a rattan ball is kept aloft without using your hands. Resort owners also run river trips up the Sungai Cherating to out-of-the-way traditional *kampungs* and they also organize trips to other places of interest.

Around the headland north of Kampung Cherating is Asia's first Club Med with 4km (2.5mi) of private beaches and five-star luxuries amidst self-imposed isolation. About 5km (3mi) north is Pantai Chendor, where green turtles—known as *penyu agar*, a smaller turtle than the giant leatherbacks—come ashore to lay their eggs from May to September. Just north of here is the border between Pahang and Terengganu.

Inland from Kuantan

For an interesting excursion to a Buddhist cave temple, a waterfall and an old mining town, take Jalan Bukit Ubi from downtown Kuantan and continue west, past the Lencongan Kuantan (Kuantan By-Pass) to the turnoff to Sungai Pandan waterfall about 18km from town. Follow the signs another 12km to the forest park with its spectacular falls which cascade down a tiered rockface. These falls are also approachable from the main Kuala Lumpur highway to Kuantan. Turn north just before the Kuantan airport.

Back on the Sungai Lembing road, just past the turnoff to the falls is the small village of Panching. At the Police Station take the right-hand fork for 4km (2.5mi) through palm-oil plantations to the solitary limestone hill which contains Gua Charas (Charas Cave). Fifty years ago a visiting monk from Thailand came here to meditate and the caves have been visited by Buddhists ever since.

At the base of the hill is a small temple, and a steep 50m (164ft) staircase ascends the cliff-face to a cave containing a reclining Buddha sculpted from the natural limestone. It is best to visit early morning when the otherwise gloomy cavern is illuminated by sun-rays from an opening in the cave ceiling. Leading off from here, and higher up, are more caves, but torches are needed for exploration.

At the end of the road, 34km (21mi) from Kuantan, is Sungai Lembing, an old mining town which went to sleep when Malaysia's only major underground tin mine closed

down. There is little to do here, but the old town is interesting to wander around; nothing new has happened here in decades, since the bottom fell out of the world tin market.

The unpainted, old wooden shophouses, the magnificent, century-old raintrees draped with ferns, and the ruins of grand colonial mansions overlooking town are all memories of a grander past. Tours of the old mine can sometimes be organized in advance through the Tourist Information Centre at the LKNP Building near the Kuantan post office.

Just before Sungai Lembing, the right-hand road which crosses the river leads to Gunung Tapis, an isolated and mountainous rainforest region which is accessible only with a four-wheel-drive vehicle. The scenery is magnificent, and there are some beautiful waterfalls, but there are no facilities and potntial visitors must bring all their own food and camping equipment.

Opposite: *Fishing trawlers, painted in the characteristic Pahang colors (each state has its own color combination) crowd the estuary at Sungai Ular, an untouched fishing village.* **Below:** *Walking trails lead through the lush rainforest to the tops of these falls at Sungai Pandan, west of Kuantan.*

R. MOH'D NOH SALLEH

PEKAN

Polo and the Pahang Sultanate

Chickens scratch around the old wooden houses, and children cycle along the bucolic road. It looks like any other *kampung*, but then the quietude is shattered by an insistent throbbing. The children dismount, and peer through the high fence bars as a helicopter lands, and their sultan disembarks in front of his gold-domed palace. There is still a feudal air to Pekan, the royal capital of Pahang.

Located 44km (27mi) south of Kuantan, on the southern bank of the Sungai Pahang, West Malaysia's longest river, Pekan was described by 15th-century court annals as having "rivers running fresh to the sea, plentiful gold and jungles stocked with elephants." Conquered by Mansur Shah, the son of the Sultan of Melaka in 1458, Pekan has been the home of Pahang's dynasties ever since. The present sultanate trace their lineage to Bendahara (Prime Minister) Wan Ahmad who took

the title of Sultan in 1882 after a long civil war.

Pastel-colored, 19th-century shophouses along Pekan's main street face a riverbank shaded by ancient raintrees. Nearby, is the excellent **Sultan Abu Bakar Museum**, a 70-year-old brick mansion, once the British Resident's home and later the sultan's palace. Royal regalia, textiles, neolithic artifacts, and treasures from a recently-recovered Chinese junk are among the many collections on display.

Across the bridge is Masjid Abdullah, an art deco mosque built in 1929, and the multi-domed Abu Bakar Mosque built by Sultan Abu Bakar who ruled Pahang from 1932 to 1974. At the end of Jalan Istana Abu Bakar is the opulent royal palace, its marble entrance topped by huge replicas of arched elephant's tusks—the symbol of Pahang's royalty. The palace overlooks spacious polo grounds where international tournaments are held. Sultan Haji Ahmad Shah, Pahang's current sultan and his sons are all expert players and promising Pekan youths are sent to Argentina to learn the finer points of the "sport of kings."

Other interesting sights around Pekan include the old Istana Leban Tunggal, an original wooden palace, and the Silk Weaving Center at Pulau Keladi.

Below: Sultan Ahmad of Pahang (center), shaded by a yellow umbrella—a color reserved for royalty—is flanked by his personal staff outside his palace at Pekan in 1885

MUZIUM NEGARA

TASIK CHINI

Malaysia's Answer to Loch Ness

"It's head was a big as a tiger's and it had horns like a deer," exclaimed Pak Lasah, a centenarian of the Jakun people, while describing the legendary serpent-like creature he spied in Tasik Chini, a series of shallow lakes in central Pahang. Others, including a British engineer in the colonial days, also glimpsed the elusive *naga*, but like its Scottish kin, the "monster" of Lake Chini is still awaiting discovery.

Other legends about the lakes are equally intriguing. Stories persist that an ancient, walled Khmer city once existed here, but when threatened by attack, the inhabitants used a system of aquaducts to submerge the city, intending to drain it later. Aerial photographs showing unnatural straight lines indicate that a town may have existed near the lake, and linguists point to similarities in the language and culture of the Kampuchean Khmer and the local Jakun people, but tangible proof is lacking. The lakes have always been sacred to the local Malays as they are said to be the abode of Seri Pahang, a legendary white crocodile.

Tasik Chini can be reached by road from the town of Chini, off the Kuantan/Segamat Highway, but the more sedate way is by boat from Kampung Belimbing, a village on the northern bank of the Sungai Pahang, 83km (51.5mi) west of Kuantan. Once across the broad Pahang River, the boats wind their way 4km (2.5mi) along the winding Sungai Chini. Snaking lianas drape to the water's edge where the riverbanks are anchored by the buttress roots of giant trees. After the gloom of the jungle, the lakes dazzle with color. The waters are also home to many delicious freshwater fish, and from June to September, the lakes are covered with lotus flowers. Wreathed in cloud, 823-m (511ft) high Gunung Chini, said to be the breeding place of the legendary serpents, looms behind the lake.

The boats dock at a floating jetty beside a small resort hidden by rainforest—an ideal spot to stay overnight. Wooden longboats can be chartered for fishing, and to visit the nearby Orang Asli villages. Or you can cruise the lakes, hoping for a glimpse of the legendary serpent, or traces of the mysterious lost city.

Below: *The enigmatic Tasik Chini, a system of lakes in the backlands of Pahang.*

R. MOH'D NOH SALLEH

PART VI

Introducing the Rainforests

Smothering the central mountainous ridges, stretching the entire length of the Malay Peninsula, from the Thai border in the north to the southernmost state of Johor, are the great green heartlands: home to 14,500 species of plants and trees, 600 varieties of birds, over 200 different mammals as well as untold thousands of invertabrates and insects.

These fecund realms are among the most ancient of the world's rainforests, for when the last Ice Age brought havoc to the ecosystems of the Amazon and Central Africa, the Malayan jungles were scarcely touched and continued to thrive undisturbed.

"It is a world in which man seems an intruder," wrote Alfred Russel Wallace, the great biologist, when he viewed the virgin forests of the Malay Archipelago in the mid-19th century. "Where the weird gloom and solemn silence combine to produce a sense of the vast, the primeval, almost the infinite."

In Wallace's day, man had made scarcely a dent on this green mantle which in many places stretched from the shores of the Melaka Straits to the the South China Sea. Not that it's potential was unknown, for the Orang Asli, the indigenous dwellers of the interior, had for millennia been trading aromatic woods, rattans and resins with the coastal Malays who, in turn, bartered with merchants from China, India, Arabia and the Malay archipelago.

Prized products included rhinceros horn which was made into cups and ground into powder for use as a fever cure—the main reason for the decline of the one-horned rhino which Marco Polo took to be the mythical unicorn. And gallstones from honey bears which were worn as talismans.

Although these resources were utilized, the rainforests themselves remained inviolate until the British colonials discovered rubber, when immense acreages of West Malaysia's lowland rainforests were cleared for the new cash crop. The central forests remained rela-tively untouched until the last few decades, when land schemes transformed many forests into oil palm plantations, and logging made inroads into previously virgin tracts.

Recently, however, in the wake of growing domestic concern over the state of the environment, and mounting international criticism of over-logging, Peninsular Malaysia had become increasingly more ecologically conscious. No more rainforests are to be felled for land schemes, and logging has been scaled down in an effort to conserve valued forest resources.

Despite decades of punishment the West Malaysian rainforests are still vast, covering around 50% of the peninsula. There are large areas of undisturbed jungle throughout the central ranges, and some of the forests along the East West Highway are still in a virgin state, although access is difficult.

Taman Negara, Malaysia's original National Park, is only accessible by river, but it is still one of the best places to really experience the rainforest, for here there are large tracts of lowland dipterocarp forest. These rainforests which occur up to 304m (1000ft) above sea level are home to elephants, tigers, tapir, rhinoceros, deer, bear and wild boar, and are the richest and most dense tropical forests, where often over 240 species of trees grow in a single hectare.

Slightly higher up is the less dense hill dipterocarp which gives way at around 800m (2,624ft) to mist-shrouded montane forests. Other accessible rainforests include the Kenong Rimba Jungle Park outside Kuala Lipis in Pahang, and the newly-explored, but less accessible Endau-Rompin region shared between Pahang and Johor.

Overleaf: Many Orang Asli, like this Temiar hunter from Kuala Woh in Perak, still use blowpipes. **Opposite:** *Each rainforest tree species has its own season, flowering and fruiting independently. Photos by R. Ian Lloyd*

ORANG ASLI

Original Peoples of the Peninsula

Known collectively as the Orang Asli, or "original people"—a term introduced in the late 1950s—Peninsular Malaysia's aboriginal people consist of about 20 tribal populations, numbering more than 90,000.

Orang Asli languages fall into two major groups. First, there are those that are local dialects of Malay—a member of the Austronesian language family spread throughout island Southeast Asia and the Pacific. Second, there are "Aslian" languages, belonging to the Mon-Khmer division of the Austroasiatic family and therefore related to Vietnamese, Cambodian and many other languages in mainland Southeast Asia. These languages give a valuable clue to the question of the "origins" of the Orang Asli (*see Prehistory, page 24*).

The most popular classification divides the Orang Asli into three major sub-divisions; the Semang (or Negritos), the Senoi, and the

R. MOH'D NOH SALLEH

Aboriginal Malays (or Jakun). This system works neatly, however, only for about half of the Orang Asli groups.

The Semang live in the northern parts of the Peninsula and number around 2,400. Interestingly, this number has remained constant since the early 1800s, so they are not dying out, as has sometimes been claimed. They comprise a network of small populations who formerly lived mostly by nomadic hunting and gathering. Their physical appearance—darker skinned, more curly-haired and slightly shorter than other peninsular populations—has long been assumed to result from their biological kinship with other so-called Negrito peoples in the Philippines and Andaman Islands. But recent research suggests that they may be more related to their fellow Orang Asli, and that their appearance results from genetic change following millennia of close adaptation to living in the forest depths.

There are at least six named groups of Semang, differentiable by their linguistic, cultural and social features: the best known are the Kintaks, Kensius, Jahais, Mendriqs and Bateks. While some still retain the option of turning to a nomadic lifestyle, most now live in relatively settled circumstances, not far from the roads or larger rivers leading to small towns like Baling, Grik, or Kuala Krai. They operate largely within the cash economy, through selling collected or farmed produce, and by earning wages as laborers.

The Senoi—which means "human being"—number around 46,000, and occupy the upland, middle portions of Perak, Kelantan, and northern Pahang. The two main groups, the Semais and Temiars, lived until recently by slash-and-burn cultivation, supplemented by fishing, trapping and the trading of forest products. Nowadays, they cultivate fruit and rubber for sale, and have also taken up paid employment and even entrepreneurship.

The Aboriginal Malays of Johor, Negeri Sembilan and southern Pahang, who number around 35,000, differ from the other Orang Asli in speaking dialects of Malay as their own language. They are mostly the descendents of the same people from among whom the Malays also emerged centuries ago. The two main groups are the Temuans of Selangor, Negeri Sembilan and Melaka, and the Orang Hulu of Pahang and Johor.

They live largely by swidden agriculture, but they also specialize in the collection of forest products for trade with the outside world. Even now, they are major suppliers of wood oil, resins and cane. In holding on to this distinctive economic niche, they developed a pattern in which the members of each village maintain closer relations with their non-Orang Asli partners than with people in other Aboriginal Malay villages. They also differ from the more widely-connected and egalitarian Semang and Senoi societies in preferring to marry close relatives and maintaining ranked sets of local headmanships.

The slopes of Gunung Benom in central Pahang are home to a great variety of Orang Asli groups who do not fit neatly into Semang-Senoi-Malay classification. Significantly, the name Benom is not Malay, but an old Mon-Khmer world for "mountain." The sedentary and relatively accessible Jah Hut are famous for the high quality of their wood carvings. The secretive Che' Wong live deeper in the forest and they forage, farm, and collect for trade. On the northern slopes of Gunung Benom live the Batek Nong, the most southerly Semang group in the Peninsula. The Lanohs of the middle Perak river valley, between Lenggong and Grik, have been regarded as Negritos, but their language is related to Temiar and they have been more sedentary than nomadic.

Further south, the Semelais, Semaq Beri, Temoq and Mah Meri have similar lifestyles to Aboriginal Malays, but they speak Southern Aslian languages. Their residence patterns range from the sedentary (Mah Meri) to nomadic, from coastal (Mah Meri and occasional Semaq Beri) to interior (the rest), and from dry land (Temoqs, many Semelais, most Semaq Beri) to lakeside (Semelais living on Tasik Bera). Livelihoods vary from fishing, farming, hunting, gathering and collecting for trade. The Mah Meri also produce fine wood carvings for the art market, in a different style those of the Jah Hut.

In Johor there are Aboriginal Malay populations whose history and way of life links them more with the sea than the land. The Orang Kanaq on the west coast near Benut also live on the Indonesian side of the Straits of Melaka. Although Muslims, they regard themselves as Orang Asli, perhaps because their distinctive language is not a Malay dialect. The Orang Kanaq, who originate from Riau, have puzzled observers by maintaining their tiny population of 30-40 people for several generations. The Orang Seletar, who live in the mangroves along the narrow strait separating Johor from Singapore, are the descendants of the Orang Laut, or "sea people," who played a crucial role in the early

Orang Asli Groups of Peninsular Malaysia
(Approximate distribution)

THAILAND
PERLIS
KEDAH
Kensiu
Kentaq
Jehai
PENANG
Lanoh
KELANTAN
Temiar
Menriq
TERENGGANU
PERAK
Batek
Semai
Semaq Beri
Jah
Che Hut
PAHANG
SELANGOR
Wong
Temoq
Mah
Meri
Temuan
Semelar
Semelai
NEGERI
SEMBILAN
MELAKA
Orang Hulu
JOHOR
Orang
Kanaq
Orang
Kuala
Orang
Seletar
SINGAPORE

Legend
Languages
☐ Northern Aslian
☐ Central Aslian
☐ Southern Aslian
☐ Malay Dialects
Boundaries
— International
— State
- - - Ethnic groups

history of the region. A few Orang Seletar families who continue to live in boats make a living by catching fish and crustacea along the shorelines.

Usually, visitors wishing to see Orang Asli need to get off the beaten track. However, the road from Tapah to Cameron Highlands passes through Semai country, and some villages are beside the road. Temiars can frequently be seen in Grik and Gua Musang, and the East West Highway passes through Jahai and Temiar country. Taman Negara is within the territory of the Bateks, several of whom work as guides and porters.

Tourists should note, however, that Malaysian law entitles the Department of Orang Asli Affairs (JHEOA) and local police to limit the access of outsiders to Orang Asli settlements. To avoid problems, seek advice beforehand. When visiting settlements, try to do so in small numbers to avoid swamping the people's resources and invading their privacy. Small gifts are appreciated, as are offers to buy any of their handicrafts. However, these can be expensive, especially Jah Hut and Mah Meri wood carvings and "real" used blowpipes from the Temiars and Semais.

—*Geoffrey Benjamin*

Opposite: Necklaces of trade beads and a bark headband are the favored body ornaments of this Temiar tribesman from the Perak foothills.

TAMAN NEGARA

Forests from the Dawn of Time

From high up in the misty mountains, the serpentine river winds its way down through the overhanging jungle. Vines and creepers loop from tree to tree like the rigging on ghostly galleons, and where the sunlight penetrates along the riverbanks, flowering lianas with clusters of orange blossoms splash color through the evergreen rainforest. Up in the tree tops where the great trunks suddenly burst into branches are huge hanging fern gardens and equatorial orchids that bloom, as the Malays say, "for the eyes of God alone."

Inside the giant bamboo stands are luminescent fungi that glow in the dark and on the ridges grow pitcher plants that devour insects. White-faced monkeys rattle the treetops and, frightened by the boat's engine, flee chattering into the depths of Taman Negara, Malaysia's largest and oldest National Park, which sprawls 4,343km^2 (1,677mi^2) through the backlands of Pahang, Kelantan and Terengganu states.

In Malay, Taman Negara, means simply "The National Park," and within its boundaries are found every type of inland forest habitat ranging from dense lowland rainforests to the "cloud" forests of the montane regions. Crowning the mountainous range which bisects the park from east to west is Peninsular Malaysia's highest peak, the remote Gunung Tahan, 2,187-m (7,175ft) high. It is a difficult, but rewarding climb for travelers willing to undertake the 9-day trek to the summit.

Established as a sanctuary since 1937, the park's interior rivers run pure and unpolluted and century-old trees still endure, safe from the chainsaw and the bulldozer. There are spectacular waterfalls, towering limestone massifs, and within this green heartland live the vast majority of the country's highly diverse wildlife.

Seeking out the shadow-dwellers

Species native to the park include the shy and elusive elephant; the tiger—who the Orang Asli say causes those who sight it to not eat for a week; the *seledang*—the wild cattle which early hunters feared more than the tiger; and monkeys, deer, otters, leopards, squirrels, bats, rats, shrews, and a fantastic spectrum of birds and insects.

But travelers have to be aware that the

tropical rainforest is nothing like the African savannah and that most of the animals are nocturnal. Even experienced jungle bashers may spend a week in the dense jungle and see nothing more exciting than a mound of elephant dung, a flash of feathers and a legion of leeches. They may see you, but the shadow play in the gloom of the rainforest floor provides excellent camouflage and their superior sense of smell ensures that most of the larger creatures will always be well out of sight.

Wild pigs and deer often graze and root around the chalet areas, and birds can be easily sighted. Tapir, and *seladang* can sometimes be viewed at salt licks from the overnight hides. For travelers with patience, the ability to appreciate the rainforest and endure its discomforts, and a large measure of luck, Taman Negara can still provide an unforgettable reward—the sight of one of the rarer mammals.

The river approach

The only access to the park is by boat along the Sungai Tembeling which forms the southeastern boundary. The 59-km (37mi) boat journey from Kuala Tembeling, the closest road access to the park, is a unique experience. It take three to four hours along the river, and sometimes longer in the dry season when passengers have to disembark in particularly shallow sections.

Beyond the 35-km (22mi) marker, Taman Negara begins on the western riverbank while the eastern side is cultivated land and *kampungs* all the way to Kuala Tahan; the site of camp headquarters where the silt-colored Tembeling meets with the clear, tea-colored Sungai Tahan which originates in the untrammeled reaches of Gunung Tahan.

After the restful river journey, lulled by the hypnotic jungle chorus, Kuala Tahan, the administration and accommodation center, seems incredibly busy. Wooden longboats jostle for position at the wharf, coming and going with boatloads of tourists. At the reception, forms are filled out, fees paid, chalets, beds, boats, treks, guides and everything else is organized while throngs of visitors eat ice-cream sundaes at the restaurants. But only a few hundred meters inside the ever-present jungle, it is surprising how the crowds are quickly swallowed up by the sheer immensity of the park.

Most trails start from Kuala Tahan, and they range from easy one-hour strolls around the area near the headquarters to gruelling 9-day treks up Gunung Tahan. Always start out

as early as possible, for this is when the birds and animals are active and it is also the most pleasant time to walk. Even though the rainforest is considerably cooler than the cleared land, the lowland regions are still hot and humid and even the fittest traveler may find walking a struggle in the middle part of the day. If you are not used to trekking in equatorial jungles the best way to begin is to start out on shorter trails and get acclimatized before attempting longer walks.

Trails and hides

The trail to Bumbun Tabing (*bumbun* means "hide") takes around 90 minutes (3 hours there and back) and is excellent as a starter. For much of its length it meanders along the eastern bank of the Sungai Tahan where deep pools like Lubuk Simpon (15 minutes from base) are great for a refreshing dip. Nearby grow spectacular *tualang* trees, the highest "dominants" in the rainforest. These grey-barked giants, which often reach 76m (250ft) high, stand head and shoulders above the canopy.

At the junction of the Bukit Teresek trail, hikers can either follow the Bumbun Tabing

Opposite: During the dry season boats have to be hauled upstream in some shallow section of the Sungai Tahan. **Below:** *A baby monkey snuggles up to its mother on the forest floor in Taman Negara.*

trail or take a detour along the prettier Rentis Neram (*rentis* means trail) which follows the riverbank overhung with ancient *neram* trees, a type of myrtle with smooth trunks and ribbons of bark.

Bumbun Cegar Anjing, an overnight hide, is reached by fording the river along the Rentis Neram. Deer often browse here on a grassy old airstrip and sighting of *seladang* are not uncommon. At Bumbun Tabing, a hide overlooking a natural salt lick at the end of the trail, wild pigs and barking deer are often sighted and the unique tapir with its long trunk and black and white markings is sometimes spotted here. Just before Bumbun Tabing the Rentis Tahan-Trenggan begins.

About 1km (0.6mi) along, the left branch leads to Gunung Tahan, and the right-hand track meanders through lowland rainforest, where monkeys and gibbons are often sighted, to Bumbun Kumbang, a 13-km (6hr) walk from headquarters. This overnight hide is good for viewing tapir, sambar and barking deer, and can be alternatively reached by a 45-min boat journey and a 45-min walk from the river.

To maximize chances of spotting animals at all hides it is best to be inside a few hours before nightfall. For night viewing, it is advised to rotate watches and to shine a torch onto the clearing every 15 mins. Animals are apparently not disturbed by torchlight and hang around long enough to be observed.

Bukit Teresek, a hill lookout at the end of a short but steep trail from Kuala Tahan is an excellent place to view the rainforest from above. Along the trail in the early morning, the "wak wak" cries of gibbons and the piercing squeals of giant squirrels can often be heard and are sometimes glimpsed swinging through the canopy.

From the highest lookout, panoramic views stretch across the roof of the lowland rainforest and on clear days extend to Gunung Tahan, the table-topped mountain to the left of center. Viewed from above, the canopy crowns vary from vermilion to copper tones, and through the entire spectrum of greens. Nowhere is there a grouping of the same colors for in the tropical rainforests each species only appears sporadically and each has it own seasonal rhythms.

Other walks from headquarters include the interesting Rentis Belau, which starts on the opposite bank of the Sungai Tahan, climbs a couple of spurs and then traverses magnificent lowland rainforest. A detour leads off to Gua Telinga, a limestone cave, about an hour's stroll from base, where a rope walk leads through the dark cavern—home to thousands of bats and the non-poisonous cave-racer snake which crushes the bats and then swallows them. Further on are the hides at Bumbun Belau and Bumbun Yong where salt licks attract tapir, and sambar and barking deer.

Climbing the peninsula's highest peak

Gunung Tahan is of course the ultimate goal for the serious trekker, but preparations must be made well in advance as the entire trip takes around nine days and all supplies must be carried from headquarters. The 61km (38mi) trail traverses several river crossings, climbs up and down hills and mountains before the main peak is reached. The journey is both arduous and exhausting, but well worth the time, expense and effort if you are fit enough to enjoy it.

The first day to Sungai Melantai is a five-hour walk through reasonably easy terrain, but the second day to Kuala Puteh is a tough trek which covers 26 hills and takes a good eight hours. The third day's trek to the scenic campsite at Kuala Teku is spent fording the Tahan and in dry seasons six crossings are usual, whereas if the river is high the trail follows some high spurs to avoid danger.

The real climb starts on the fourth day and ascends to Wray's Camp—named after a co-leader of the 1905 botanical survey—at

MORTON STRANGE

1,100m (3,600ft). This region is montane oak forests where elephant tracks are common. From here, most climbers stay overnight at three higher camps in order to make the final push fo · the summit early in the morning. At this altitude, amongst the cloud forests, where trees seldom grow higher than six or seven meters (20ft), and orchids and pitcher plants thrive, the overnight temperature often plummets to four degrees Celsius.

From the highest Padang camp the trail climbs to the summit plateau, which rises from 1,400m (4,600ft) to 2,187m (7,174ft). In this peaty, rocky world stunted tea-trees only grow a meter high and mists can quickly swirl in and obscure the trail. After traversing a gully of bonsai trees, mosses, ferns and orchids, the path finally climbs to the summit where if the climber is lucky with the weather, spectacular birds'-eye views sweep across the world's oldest rainforests to the horizons.

Fishing and birdwatching

For travelers who are not keen on spending hours tramping through the rainforest, Taman Negara also offers some interesting boat trips and excellent fishing for these rivers are home to over 200 species of fish. The one-hour jaunt to the rapids and swimming holes at Lata Berkoh is a pleasant and relaxing excursion and there is a overnight fishing lodge 200m (656ft) downstream. Anglers often catch the famed *sebarau*

carp here in quiet pools near sunken logs and *toman* (snake-heads) are found in still, deep pools. The Malayan *mahseer* (*kelah*), popular with sports fishermen, prefers pools along the swifter river sections, and the best sporting fish of all, the *kelesa,* which often leaps high into the air when hooked, inhabits deep water pools.

Other popular river trips include the exciting, rapid-studded stretch between Kuala Tahan and Kuala Trenggan and then up this latter river to Kuala Kenyam. This is a favorite venue for birdwatchers as the prolific wild fruit trees here attract a fantastic array of species. Further upstream, the river trip continues past banks draped with huge *neram* trees, and traverses undisturbed rainforest up to Kuala Perkai which also offers excellent fishing and has an overnight lodge.

Some visitors may complain that there are few animals left, for no one is assured of a sighting, which should always be considered a bonus rather than a certainty. It is true that most of the larger mammals live in the far-off untrammeled and most inaccessible regions, but the park was originally proposed as a place where wildlife could live undisturbed by man, and during its half a century of existence Taman Negara has most certainly lived up to that purpose.

Opposite: The common palm civet is often seen from hides around Taman Negara.

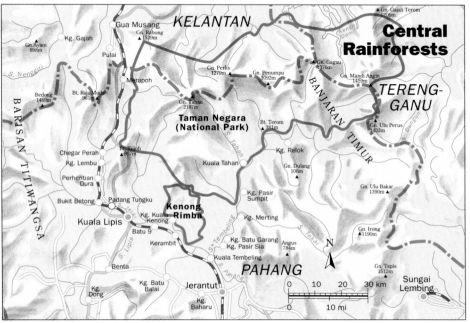

KENONG RIMBA

Deep in Elephant Country

It happened on a day pregnant with promise. We were about a mile into the jungle and the early morning mist still blanketed the canopy far above our heads. The previous night's rain dripped from giant leaves, an ultramarine butterfly colored the gloom and a sharp mosquito-like bite signalled my first leech encounter of the day. Then Ahmad, our guide, stopped abruptly, pointed to a large pile of hay-like dung in the middle of the muddy path, and calmly announced, *"tahi gajah"*—elephant droppings.

It was clear that this was no special event for Ahmad who was born and bred here, but I had often tramped along rainforest trails in the hope of spotting at least some small sign of these giant pachyderms. Finally, in the northwest region of Pahang state, at Kenong Rimba, which translates as "the primeval jungles of Kenong," I had seen and smelt tangi-

ble evidence that the Malayan elephant really does exist.

Further along we were rewarded with an even more conclusive proof: elephant footprints in the mud, three times the size of my palm print. But they were already a few days old and the rainy season had just finished; a signal for the elephants to move deeper into the forest.

Setting this region aside as a jungle reserve was the brainchild of Hassan Tuah, who now runs tours from his tiny office in Kuala Lipis, Pahang's old colonial capital. After a long battle with bureaucrats and timber tycoons he succeeded in seeing Kenong Rimba established as a state park. He is unerringly enthusiastic about the park: its virgin forests, its limestone caves, and its prolific wildlife. "Our northern borders meet Taman Negara," he explained, "and much of the larger wildlife lives in the undisturbed rear section of the park."

A town worth exploring

Kuala Lipis is the jump-off spot for Kenong Rimba, and is an interesting old town to spend time in while en route to the park. Located where the fast-flowing Sungai Lipis meets the Sungai Jelai (which laters turn into the Pahang, Peninsular Malaysia's longest river), Kuala Lipis was one of Pahang's earliest settlements, renowned as a trading center for gold and jungle products centuries before it became the colonial capital in 1898.

After Kuantan took over as the state capital in 1955, little happened in Kuala Lipis and the sleepy town still maintains many colonial buildings and a main street lined with picturesque old wooden shophouses. At the hilltop resthouse, formerly the British Resident's home, a museum houses Neolithic tools, pottery, brassware and fabrics. Other historic buildings include the Clifford School, built in 1913, and the Lipis District Offices constructed in 1919.

From Batu Sembilan to the forest

Next morning, in the pitch-dark long before dawn, we met Ahmad at the Kuala Lipis railway station, and take the local train to Batu Sembilan (Ninth Mile) where settlers, who hacked their farms from the jungle were smoking *kretek* (clove cigarettes) and drinking coffee, waiting for the mist to rise.

In a grey dawn, we walked to the jetty and boarded a longboat for the 20-minute run down the Jelai River and then into its tributary, the Kenong River which the park is named after. From the Kampung Dusun jetty, on the fringes of civilization, it is a half-hour walk to where we came across more evidence of the elusive giants.

The elephant caves

Limestone hills, pockmarked with caves and draped with vines, thrust upwards through the forest canopy. At Gua Batu Tangga, "the cave of rock steps," curious ledges line the rear of the cavern, and a little further on is Gua Batu Tangkup, where elephants shelter

during the torrential monsoon. The trail into the cave narrows between boulders which have been polished marble-smooth over the centuries by the mighty mammals squeezing past the entrance. Inside the cavern the earth has been beaten-down flat and there are more piles of elephant dung. Stalactites hang from the roof and it is easy to imagin those regal creatures sitting in this primeval shelter, dry as a bone, while the monsoonal rains pound the world outside.

Sweet potatoes, aloe and bat guano

As we pressed on through the forest the trees become higher and filtered sunlight flickered through the canopy high overhead. A strong aromatic scent filled the air. A tree was flowering on the roof of the jungle. Beside the track, the ground was dug up, for here, Ahmad explained is where the Batek, a sub-branch of the indigenous Negrito people, have been digging for sweet potatoes.

Further along the trail we met two couples, the men short and muscular, and the women with wooden combs stuck in their hair and their sarongs hiked up high to enable them to move freely through the jungle. They were out searching for *gaharu*, a fragrant aloe wood used to make joss-sticks, which constitutes a major source of their income. When they finally bounded off down the slippery track their barefoot tread was sure and certain, unlike ours as we stumbled

over tree roots in our so-called jungle footwear.

We stopped for lunch beside the virgin stream of the Sungei Kesong, under the limestone massif of Gunung Kesong. Fish darted about in the shallows of these clear waters far from the muddied streams polluted by loggers. Great mud slides on the banks indicated that we were not the only ones to have lingered here, for these marks were made by elephants crossing the shallow stream.

Upstream, we entered the aptly-titled Gua Hijau, or Green Cave, where the walls are stained bright green. Bat guano lay thick on the ground and inky black recesses lead into a labyrinthe of undiscovered passages.

Beyond the trail

Further afield there are other places worth seeing. A longer trek leads to the Seven Steps Waterfall in the far north of the park, or adventurous travelers can even climb the limestone ranges of the Kesong Valley to search for the elusive and rare desert goats, believed to be kept by dwarfs.

On the edge of the park, beside the river at Kampung Dusun, are a series of rapids where the village women wash clothes on a flat limestone shelf and a short trip downriver by dugout canoe leads to Gua Batu Tinggi, where the river flows through a cave.

Kenong Rimba harbors many a mystery, for these tropical rainforests contain plants which are still little known to scientists. Most importantly, however, it serves as a haven for wildlife amid a rapidly changing landscape.

*Opposite: The caves of Gunung Kesong reflected in the waters of the river of the same name, at this shallow crossing favored by elephants. **Above, left:** Figs sprout, not from the branches of this lowland rainforest tree, but from the base of its trunk. **Above, right:** Vines and ferns intertwine in the lush riverside foliage.*

ENDAU ROMPIN

Mysterious Denizens of the Forest

Home to Malaysia's largest population of the Sumatran rhinoceros, one of the world's rarest animals, Endau Rompin, a reserve covering an area of 93,000 hectares of tropical lowland forest, sits astride the boundaries of Johor and Pahang states. On the southeastern side of the peninsula, the park falls in a biogeographic area known as the Riouw Pocket with flora akin to that of western Borneo. However this phenomenon is not evident in Endau-Rompin's fauna which is representative of the mammals, birds, reptiles, amphibian and fishes found in the peninsula.

Hairy beasts and fairy tribes

The indigenous Orang Ulu who use these forests for hunting and gathering, live in Kampung Peta, just outside the park boundary on the Johor side, and at Kampung Mok, located on the Pahang side. The elders of Kampung Peta possess a rich heritage of legendary tales featuring hairy giants, fairies, spirits and dragons. For each strange rock formation there is a fairy tale to explain its shape. The uncannily quiet plateau at Padang Temambung, a shrubby grassland habitat covered with what appears as a criss-crossing of paths is a sacred place—the home of a Chinese fairy princess and the gateway to the Orang Ulu heaven. The landslips at Gunung Beremban have been attributed to the awakening of the earth dragon, which occured when a careless individual brought vinegar up to the peak and aroused the sleeping dragon with the pungent smell.

Endau-Rompin is also believed to be inhabited by the Malaysian version of the Bigfoot, known as Serjarang Gigi, "widely-separated teeth". The beast is a hairy giant, well over 3m (10ft) tall with arms as big as a normal person's thigh.

When things go missing in camps or the village, the incidents are attributed to fairy tribes known as the Orang Bunian, and visitors are advised not to bathe naked in the streams in case their behavior offends the fairy women.

Much of the beauty of Endau Rompin—its numerous waterfalls, rapids, pools and clear forest streams—is due to the geology of the park. At the Upeh Guling Waterfall there are a series of holes caused by the erosive swirling action of stones and pebbles in the

river current. A rock formation at Gunung Janing resembles a sailing ship, and at the source of the Sungai Endau is another formation which looks like a crouching man swallowing the river and letting the water pass through him which the Orang Ulu call The Old Man of Endau.

Considerable areas of the park consist of sedimentary successions overlying or capping more resistant volcanic or granite bedrocks. This provides the setting for the formation of plateaux and mesas and causes rapids and waterfalls at each interphase with a distinct drop in elevation along the rivers and streams which are full of deep pools.

Geology has also played a part in creating a mosaic of ecological habitats. Hikers who start from Kuala Jasin and then climb up Gunung Janing pass by riverine forest, lowland dipterocarp forest, up through hill dipterocarp and into a pure stand of fan palms. Further along is a patch of swamp forest with pitcher plants and monkey puzzle trees.

A rich array of fauna

The bird life in the riverine and lowland forests is rich with bulbuls, flycatchers, spider-hunters, sunbirds, drongos, magpie robins, flowerpeckers, orioles, pigeons, and the entire spectrum of the avian fauna of the peninsula. Encounters with tigers, deer, wild boar, gibbons, leaf monkeys, macaque, squirrels, tree-shrews, tapirs, civet cats, otters and even rhinoceros can also be had by the lucky few who have time to spend on extended trips into the forest.

Monitor lizards can often be seen basking in the sun by the old logging tracks or along riverbanks. Flying lizards and agamid lizards are often sighted playing among the branches of trees. Snakes are present but harder to see. Tortoises and terrapines can occasionally be sighted in the streams and in the forest. Crocodiles are reported in the main river but are rarely found in the park.

Frogs are abundant along the streams and rivers and their chorus and calls permeate the evening air. A popular riverside frog *rana blythi* from Sumatra appears in the Guinness Book of Records as one of the world's largest frogs. Here, the species can attain over a kilogramme in weight.

The rivers are good fishing grounds for the bony-tongued *arawana*, and the carp known locally as *sebarau*, both of which are good sport fish. Lurking in deep, river pools are the giant catfish and the fearsome giant snake-head which has been known to attack unsuspecting swimmers who venture into their territorial pools.

Looking for birds and animals in the forest is a challenging pastime for park visitors. Hikers can explore the forest, climb the often tough hill trails, and there are good rapids for white-water enthusiasts. Travelers can also visit Kampung Peta where the Orang Ulu produce mats woven from pandanus leaves, and other artifacts made from wood and rattan.

Hikers are advised to purchase leech socks, to at least deter these ever-present bloodsuckers. There is little to fear from snakes, but if a tiger is known to be around do not venture into the forest on your own, it is always much safer to go with a group. Ask and follow the advise of the rangers and inform them if you do decide to hike on your own. Hire a guide if you are uncertain of the way as it is better to be safe than sorry. By following these basic guidelines Endau Rompin will provide the travelers with an unforgettable nature experience.

—*Kiew Bong Heang*

Opposite: Early-morning mist still hovers above the rainforested hills of Endau-Rompin, an untouched and remote region, currently being set aside as a state park. *Below:* Wallowing in a salt lick, this rare Sumatran rhinoceros is one of a group of some 20 individuals—the Peninsula's largest group—which lives in the Endau-Rompin region.

WWF MALAYSIA

PART VII

Introducing Melaka

"Malacca fascinates me more and more daily. There is, among other things, a mediaevalism about it. The noise of the modern world reaches it only in the faintest echoes," wrote Isabella Bird, the intrepid Victorian traveler who visited Malacca, now Melaka, in 1879.

In the course of the last century, progress has of course caught up with the town, but remnants of its six centuries of history remain. Sailing *perahu* from Sumatra still dock at the riverside and their merchant sailors still barter charcoal for rice. The labyrinthine lanes of Chinatown still harbor age-old family businesses, and squeezed in between 18th-century shophouses are ancient temples, historic tombs, and elegant old mosques. At the centre of the old port town is the renowned Town Square with its terracotta-red Dutch buildings, and the Portuguese ruins on St. Paul's Hill.

Interwoven in the early history of this ancient trading capital is the story of Negeri Sembilan—formerly a series of nine territories to the north of Melaka—which was first settled by the matriarchal Minangkabau people from Sumatra in the early decades of the 15th-century. Although not as well-known as Melaka, Negri Sembilan is a scenic state which still maintains a strong Minangkabau identity in its characteristic architecture which features "buffalo-horn" roofs, its spicy *nasi padang* cuisine, and its cultural tradition of Adat Perpateh, a unique matrilineal system.

Queen of the spice trade

It seems that the older a city is the more fanciful are the legends that surround its birth, and Melaka is no exception. Around the last decade of the 14th century, Parameswara, a fugitive Sumatran prince, sailed up the Melaka Straits in search of a new kingdom and put ashore at an obscure fishing village where, according to legend, his royal hunting dogs were intimidated by a miniscule mousedeer. This auspicious sign (apparently Kandy

in Sri Lanka was founded after a similar occurrence) convinced Parameswara that this was to be the site of his capital and he called it Melaka after the tree that he was resting under.

There were other less whimsical reasons for the choice, for the port was sheltered and conveniently situated at the crossroads of the monsoons to enable merchants from Arabia and India to sail down on the southwest trades, and the traders from China and the Spice Islands to arrive with the northeast monsoon. With the young prince's royal pedigree and the port's favorable location Melaka soon became a bustling entrepot where spices, scented woods and jungle exotica were exchanged for Indian textiles, and porcelain, silks and metalware from China.

Melaka's rise to fame was meteoric and in less than a century the city became the paramount trading port of the vast Malay world. Dominant among the traders were the Muslim Indians, wealthy and respected merchants whose religion commanded considerable prestige in the region. Upon Parameswara's conversion to Islam, when he became the first sultan of Melaka, the port was thrust into the international class, for at this time Egypt controlled the Spice route to Renaissance Europe and allowed only Muslim shipping.

On the hill overlooking the harbor, the sultans and their court enjoyed a life of medieval opulence, residing in gilded palaces, borne aloft on silk-caparisoned elephants, seated on golden thrones and waited on by hundreds of slaves. Sultan Mansur

Overleaf: A Straits Chinese wedding group wear satin robes from China, but the bride's headdress is copied from Malay traditions. Photo circa 1900. Opposite: Malay children pose on the original terracotta paving and lean against the solid wooden doors of Melaka's Stadthuys. Photo by Radin Moh'd Noh Salleh

Shah's reign, from 1459 to 1477, considered as the Golden Age of Malay power and culture, was enlived by legendary happenings, intrigues, scandals, and the exploits of Hang Tuah, Hang Jebat and Hang Kasturi—the three musketeers of the Melakan Sultanate.

The Portuguese conquest

In the words of a Portuguese historian, by the end of the 15th century, Melaka was "the richest sea port with the greatest abundance of shipping that can be found in the whole world." Tales of the "wondrous Golden Chersonese" and the "city where the winds meet" were heard and heeded by the Portuguese who were lusting to overtake Arab domination of the spice trade.

After an abortive first attack on the city in 1509, the Portuguese were forced to retreat, but they returned in full force two years later under the command of Alfonso de Albuquerque, the Governor of Portuguese India (Goa). Their timing was perfect for there were palace squabbles and the sultanate had lost the support of the Orang Laut, the sea tribes, which were vital for a naval battle. Although the Malays fought furiously, led by Sultan Mahmud on his war elephant, they were overcome and the monarch and his court fled south to Johor.

The Portuguese, eager to make their mark on their new conquest, immediately started construction of A Famosa, an impos-

ing stone fort that encircled the base of St. Paul's Hill, and constructed churches, administrative buildings and churches using some of the stones from the sacked Malay palace and mosques. The fort dominated Melaka for centuries until the British destroyed it in 1806, and the Porta de Santiago is today the only surviving gate.

Trade initially flourished, but then slackened when the wealthy Muslim traders defected to the Islamic ports in Sumatra. Joao de Barros, a Portuguese traveler who visited Melaka in 1540 prophetically remarked that "the Portuguese arms and boundary marks placed in Africa and Asia (...) are material things and time may destroy them; but it will not destroy the religion customs and language which the Portuguese have left in those lands." His prediction still rings true: the Portuguese Eurasians of Melaka are still zealous Catholics, still speak Cristao, an archaic form of Portuguese, and maintain many ancient cultural traditions although the links with their mother country were broken over 350 years ago.

The Dutch burghers take over

Troubles, however, besieged the Portuguese Empire, the tiny homeland did not have the manpower or money necessary to ensure the survival of their far-flung dependencies, and corruption and greed undermined the crown's treasury. Throughout the Portuguese

occupation the Malays continued to wage war against Melaka from their new southern base in Johor.

When Dutch traders first contacted Johor at the start of the 17th century they were welcomed as possible allies against both Portugal and Aceh who had wrecked Johor's trade and repeatedly destroyed its capitals. After entering into treaties with Johor, which still controlled the Orang Laut as its personal navy, the Dutch gained control of the Melaka Straits, captured Portuguese vessels and were so sure of their succession as Melaka's overlords they even measured the ramparts of the A Famosa fortress by moonlight.

With the help of Johor it took the Dutch six months to win Melaka. In 1641, with most of the town decimated, the burgers of the Dutch East India Company took command. Unlike the Portuguese, they were only interested in commerce, not crusades, and Islamic traders returned to Melaka and many mosques, some of which still survive, were built. The Hollanders proceeded to rebuild Melaka in the image of a Dutch trading town. A Famosa was repaired and the date 1670, together with the United East India Company's coat of arms was engraved on the Porta de Santiago, and can still be seen today.

The rebellious Minangkabau

To the north, however, the fiercely independent Minangkabau settlers of today's Negri

Sembilan were not about to pay Dutch taxes and they rebelled under their charismatic leader Raja Ibrahim. Denounced by the Dutch as a presumptuous imposter, he claimed to be able to poison the wind, bewitch firearms and render himself invisible. Raja Ibrahim was the first to call on all fellow Muslims, regardless of race, to fight the infidel Dutch, but he failed to enlist the support of the Bugis who were settling neighboring Selangor, and who had always been suspicious of the Minangkabau.

In the 18th century, the Minangkabau of Negri Sembilan, who were no longer being protected by Johor and were at the mercy of the Selangor Bugis, turned to their Sumatran homelands and imported Raja Melewar, a prince from their traditional royal house, who could unite and defend them. He was proclaimed as the Yang di-Pertuan Besar of Negeri Sembilan in 1773 and his heirs have ruled the state from their royal capital, Sri Menanti, until the present.

Melaka passed out of Dutch hands in 1824 when under the terms of the Treaty of London, all the lands west of the Melaka Straits fell to the Dutch including the English territory of Bencoolen in Sumatra, and everything to the east including Melaka came under British rule.

Later, during the mid-19th century, Sungai Ujong, the largest of the nine territories of today's Negeri Semblian, was the center of a tin rush and continual disputes arose over who controlled the Linggi River, the major channel for the tin trade. This in turn disrupted the tin trade with the Straits Settlements of Melaka, Singapore and Penang, which were under English control, and the colonials, worried about declining profits, intervened and placed a British Resident in Negri Sembilan in 1874.

The warring territories gradually accepted the British status quo—they had little choice—and finally a treaty was signed between the Yang de Pertuan Besar Mohammad, the four major chiefs (known as Undang), and the British in 1895. When Malaya gained independence from the British, Mohammad's son Abdul Rahman became the first Yang di Pertuan Agong, the paramount ruler of independent Malaya.

Opposite: Porta de Santiago is the only surviving gateway of the great fort of A Famosa which once encompassed all of St. Paul's Hill. *Above:* Christ Church, built by the Dutch in the mid-18th century, faces Melaka's Town Square

BABAS & NONYAS

The Merging of Two Cultures

Along Melaka's seafront drive, the gentle tradewinds stir the sultry air and waft into palatial old homes which overlook the Melaka Straits. On one breezy verandah, a foursome of elderly women sit around a table playing *cherki*, a little-known card game similar to dominoes.

Their pastime is unusual—for mahjong is the popular game for women of their age—but their clothes are also odd, for instead of wearing the ubiquitous Chinese pantsuits they are dressed in the Malay fashion of batik sarongs and embroidered *kebaya* blouses, their hair swept back in chignons and secured with golden hairpins. And something else is different too, for their chatter is not any Chinese dialect, but Malay, the tongue of their adopted homeland.

These women comprise a veritable "who's who" of Melaka's most prominent families. They are members of the unique ethnic minority known as the Straits-born Chinese or *peranakan*, which means "born here" in Malay. Many families can trace their family tree back centuries, to the days when their adventurous ancestors sailed from China in junks laden with brocades and pearls to barter and trade at Melaka. Some of these merchants married local Malay women, and some families even claim royal descent.

Of noble beginnings

According to a 15th-century court history, when the Ming Emperor sent his daughter Princess Hang Li Poh to marry Sultan Mansur Shah "500 youths of noble birth" accompanied her. They settled at the foot of the hill known since then as Bukit Cina, "Chinese Hill," and took up local brides. From these early alliances the distinctive Malayanized culture of the Straits Chinese evolved which is totally different from that of later Chinese immigrants who came to Malaya during the British colonial days.

From the beginning, the *nonyas*, as the women are called, and the *babas*, their menfolk, were wily and clever at trade. Many became exceedingly wealthy and developed an opulent lifestyle—a combination of the Chinese talent for making money and the Malay love of enjoyment. In the 17th century, Dutch monopolies forced many *babas* to the British ports of Penang and Singapore, but Melaka has always remained their cultural heartland.

A life of leisure

Pampered by servants, the *nonyas* spent their leisure time visiting, gossiping, and chewing betel-nut: a Malay habit. Their abiding passion was beadwork which they picked up from the Minangkabau women and most of their trousseau, including wedding slippers, pillow ends, belts and bed decorations were intricately beaded, all for their most spectacular event—the *nonya* wedding.

The traditional wedding ceremony, rarely seen these days, ran for 12 consecutive nights and was a glorious mixture of Chinese and Malay tradition. The elaborately embroidered gowns were imported from China, but the bride's golden headdress, glittering with diamonds, was Malay.

A love for spicy and piquant food also sets the *peranakan* apart from other Chinese as their cuisine uses Malay ingredients like coconuts, *belacan* (dried shrimp paste), chillies and abundant spices. Delicate cakes and

pastries were laboriously prepared and today's nonya are still adept at cooking these traditional *kueh* (cakes). Following the Malay style, the *peranakan* eat with their fingers. Chopsticks—handed down through generations—were never actually used for eating, but merely for ceremonial purposes at the family's ancestral altar.

The Golden Age

Melaka's Heeren Street, now called Jalan Tun Tan Cheng Lock after a famous *baba* millionaire/politician, has long been their ancestral center, and is lined with Chinese-style town houses some of which date from 18th-century Dutch times. These cavernous homes, often 46m (150ft) long, incorporate Chinese, Malay, Portuguese, Dutch and English influences—a mosaic of Melaka's multi-cultural past.

Even their porcelain was different, for the wealthy *nonyas* ordered custom-made sets direct from China. Just over a decade ago no one wanted the bright enamelled wares decorated with peony flowers and phoenix birds—the *peranakans'* favorite symbols—but today, Nonyaware, as it is known, is highly prized by ceramics collectors. Their unique silverware, known as Straits Chinese Silver, is also sought after by antique dealers, and by *nonyas* whose families were forced to give up their heirlooms during the Great Depression of the 1930s.

Many *babas* had run rubber plantations during their "Golden Age" under British rule, but when rubber fell in value to five cents a pound—compared to 1912 when the same weight had raised five dollars—businesses were ruined overnight. Some *babas* found the sudden change too much to endure, for many of that generation were hedonists who had never worked a day in their lives preferring to live off the family fortunes. Opium smoking, gambling, womanizing and expensive cars had already eroded many a *peranakan* fortune. Some *babas*, however, were successful and prominent in their own right, and today their descendents are still wealthy.

Just over a decade ago, the *babas* and *nonyas* were in danger of dying out, but fortunately their culture has experienced a revival. Although many customs are no longer practised, Malaysians and Singaporeans of Straits-born descent have become more conscious of their heritage. *Nonya* food continues to be popular, there's been a spate of nostalgic books, and the new generations are paying top prices for Nonyware porcelain and Straits Chinese silver.

Opposite: Symbolic animals and flowers carved in teak decorate this gilded screen at William Chan's ancestral home in Melaka's Jalan Tun Tan Cheng Lock. Above: Wearing traditional sarong and kebaya, Mrs. Chua (center) and her nonya friends while away the hours playing a traditional card game called cherki.

MELAKA TOWN

A Stroll Through History

Situated on the west coast of the peninsula, beside the straits named after it, Melaka—the nation's oldest town—is unique in that it has directly experienced all of the major phases of Malaysia's history; from the establishment of the Malay Sultanate in 1396, through the Portuguese, Dutch, and English colonial eras, followed by the Japanese occupation and finally independence in 1957.

Located 147km (91mi) south of Kuala Lumpur, and 245km (152mi) north of Singapore, bustling, modern Melaka, capital of the state of the same name, now sprawls into the surrounding rice paddies and onto land reclaimed from the straits. But at its heart Melaka still retains much of the ancient aura of "the queen of the spice trade."

Walking is by far the best way to get about town—with trishaws as a good alternative. The old downtown layout is still much the same as it was centuries ago with the merchants' hub (Chinatown) on the northwest bank of the Melaka River, and the government and administrative area on the southeast side.

The best place to start a stroll is at the famous **Town Square**, sometimes known as the Red Square because of its distinctive terracotta-red buildings, or the Dutch Square, because most of the historical buildings around its edge date from the Dutch colonial era in the 17th to 18th centuries.

The **Stadthuys**, built in 1650, and recently restored to its former glory, is the square's most dominant structure. The former governor's residence, it is one of the oldest buildings in the East. The massive masonry walls, which now house a historical museum, were constructed on the foundations of the old Portuguese fort.

Early etchings show that the building was originally whitewashed—it wasn't always red—and during the Victorian era, the English used it to house visiting guests. A 19th-century traveler reported that "there must be more than forty rooms in this old place, besides great arched corridors, and all manner of queer staircases and corners."

To the left of the Stadthuys is the Christ Church, painted a brilliant post-box red, built in 1753 with bricks imported from Holland. Inside, the original hand-carved pews still serve for the multi-cultural Anglican congre-

R MOH'D NOH SALLEH

gation who come on Sunday to listen to any of three sermons in Mandarin, English and Tamil. Seventeen wooden beams, 15m (49ft) long, each hewn from a single rainforest tree, span the nave. Church records date back to 1641 and set in the floor are 16th-century Portuguese tombstones which predate the Dutch conquest.

Beside Christ Church, stands an attractive red building with an arched verandah, built in Dutch style in 1931. This was the town post office until recently, when it was converted into the Youth Museum.

In the center of the square, carved from English marble, is the Queen Victoria Fountain, which was constructed in 1904 to celebrate the monarch's 60-year-long reign. Beside the fountain is the Tan Beng Swee clocktower constructed by a rich Straits Chinese family in 1886.

Opposite, is the **tourist information office**, and to the right a bridge spans the Melaka River. It was built in the late 19th-century to replace an earlier one constructed in the 17th-century, which in turn had replaced the original Melaka Bridge which was slightly upriver from here. Historical accounts describe the first bridge as being built of stone, strong enough to support the sultan's elephants, and wide enough to house the town's main bazaar. In 1511 the Portugese successfully conquered Melaka by storming the bridge from the shelter of a junk which they had floated upriver on a spring tide.

From the Town Square, follow Jalan Kota, passing some more old Dutch houses on the left, until you reach Melaka's most enduring symbol, the old stone gateway of **Porta de Santiago**. This is all that survives of the original walls of the great Portuguese fortress of A Famosa which once encompassed all of St. Paul's Hill.

Contained within its massive, laterite walls were a castle, two palaces, government buildings, five churches and two hospitals some of which were built from the stones of the previous Melakan Sultanate's buildings. Above the archway of Porta de Santiago is the date 1670, and the coat of arms of the VOC (Dutch East India Company) which were added by the Dutch when they were repairing the fort after taking over from the Portuguese.

In 1807, A Famosa fort was blown up by the British who feared that when Melaka returned to Dutch rule after the Napoleonic wars that it would pose a trade threat to their recently-established port of Penang. Munshi Abdullah, in his *Hikayat Abdullah* tells of "pieces of the Fort as large as elephants, and

Opposite: *Calendars featuring Tamil screen idols and Hindu deities, chunks of rock sugar, altar offerings and sundry goods crowd onto the "five-foot-way" of this Indian store in Melaka's Jalan Bunga Raya.*

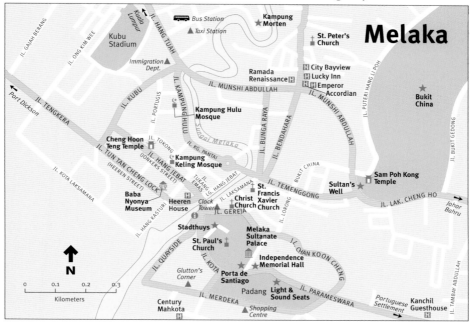

even some as large as houses, were blown into the air and cascaded into the sea." Sir Stamford Raffles, the founder of Singapore, stepped in and saved the last remaining gateway, Porta de Santiago. But it was too late, for in the words of Munshi Abdullah "the Fort was the pride of Malacca and after its destruction the place lost its glory..."

From the stairs behind the gateway, a path climbs to the summit of the hill crowned by the ruins of Sao Paulo (St.Paul's Church) which gave the hill its name. Built by the Portuguese in 1521, the Protestant Dutch later destroyed the roof and used the building as a fort. Leaning against the church walls are massive granite tombstones, dating from Dutch times, carved with poignant inscriptions—testimony to the Hollanders' short, difficult lives in the tropics.

A miraculous occurrence

The empty crypt was once used as a temporary burial site for St. Francis Xavier who had often visited the city he called "the Babylon of the East", in reference to its debauched inhabitants. The saint was attributed with miraculous powers, and many of these tales are still believed by Melaka's Portuguese Eurasians. Apparently, after the body had been sent to Goa from Melaka, the Pope requested the saint's arm to be sent to Rome. According to the tale, when the limb was severed, blood flowed from the wound even

though St.Francis Xavier had been dead for 62 years. By the church tower, the statue of the saint is also armless for the same limb was broken off, not long after its erection, by a falling branch. Proof, say superstitious Melakans, of the saint's unearthly powers.

Opposite Porta de Santiago, is the **Independence Memorial Hall**, with displays and videos chronicling the nation's fight for freedom. Crowned with onion domes this colonial building was once the Malacca Club, where planters came to drink and play cards. The novelist Somerset Maugham stayed here and was told the true murder story of a wife and her lover who conspired to kill her husband which inspired him to write his short story *Footprints in the Jungle*. The club features prominently in his tale, as does Melaka which he calls Tanah Merah.

Carry on around Jalan Kota for the **Melaka Sultanate Palace**, a multi-gabled, wooden reconstruction of the famed 15th-century palace of Sultan Mansur Shah. It houses a cultural museum with dioramas depicting court life in the Malay kingdom's "Golden Age" and historical and cultural displays. The palace features beautiful wood carvings, and was built at immense cost, but it still isn't as splendid as the original which according to the Sejarah Melayu, had gilded beams, and a roof of copper and zinc shingles.

Past the palace, on the next corner is an interesting old Dutch cemetery with tombstones dating from the 17th century. Follow Jalan Mahkamah along the side of the cemetery into Jalan Gereja, then take the lane to Jalan Laksamana to view the twin-spired Saint Francis Xavier Church which was built in Gothic style in 1849.

Continue up this street to the busy crossroads which lead into Jalan Bunga Raya and Jalan Bendahara, the two main shopping streets. On this the corner are some interesting Indian shops selling spices, incense and colorful Hindu calendars and posters.

Cross the bridge over the Melaka River, into the labyrinthine lanes of old Chinatown. Directly after the bridge, turn left into Lorong Hang Jebat, a narrow thoroughfare flanked with pastel-colored, antique shophouses. Turn right into the Jalan Kampung Kuli, past the silversmiths' shops to Makam Hang Jebat, where a white-walled archway leads to the ancient tomb of Hang Jebat, one of the famous warriors of the 14th-century Melakan Sultanate.

Backtrack to Lorong Hang Jebat, then turn right into Jalan Tukang Besi

(Blacksmiths' Street) where smiths still pound away at metal heated over charcoal forges, and where tinsmiths beat out objects ranging from the religious to the mundane, from lanterns and altars to watering cans and bathtubs. At the next block this road becomes Jalan Tukang Emas (Goldsmiths' Street) and although the jewelers themselves have now moved elsewhere, family businesses still continue their age-old trades. To the left is the Sri Poyyatha Vinayagar Moorthi Temple, one of Malaysia's oldest Indian temples, built in 1781.

On the next corner, dominated by a pagoda-style minaret, is the Masjid Kampung Keling. Built in 1748, the mosque features a three-tiered, pyramid-shaped roof, and a majestic Victorian chandelier hangs from the ceiling of the white-tiled prayer hall. Melaka's Indian Muslim community, formerly known as Keling, who originated from the Coromandel coast, still frequent this mosque built by their trading ancestors in Dutch times.

This same road now becomes Jalan Tokong, where colorful shops sell religious paraphenalia, and craftsmen make fake videos and Mercedes out of paper to be burnt at Chinese funerals. On the left, an elaborate archway leads to the main courtyard of the Cheng Hoon Teng, the oldest Chinese temple in Malaysia founded in 1646 by a Chinese refugee fleeing the Manchus. Translated as the Abode of Green Merciful Clouds, the temple is primarily dedicated to Kwan Yin, the goddess of mercy, whose bronze image imported from India in the 19th century bears more than a passing resemblance to Queen Victoria.

Devotees light bunches of joss sticks and toss I-Ching fortune sticks in front of the main altar, and before the lesser ones of Kwan Ti, the god of wealth (the patron saint of tradesmen) and Machoe Poh, the queen of heaven (guardian of fishermen and travelers). Behind the main building are halls devoted to Confucious and other deities, and one houses carved ancestral tablets. The temple's massive tiled roof is elaborately decorated with porcelain figures from Chinese mythology, and there are beautiful carvings and giltwork in the halls.

Take the next turn right into Jalan Portugis, then right into Jalan Masjid for Kampung Hulu Mosque built in 1728 which features the pagoda-style minaret and pyramid roof which are a hallmark of Melaka's 18th-century mosques. Follow Jalan Kampung Hulu, turn left into Jalan Kubu—a

curving street lined with pastel-colored Chinese shophouses—and continue along here to Jalan Hang Jebat, also known by its former name of Jonkers Street. This is one of Melaka's most famous thoroughfares and has been a center for merchants since the town's beginning. The first historical sight on the left is the mausoleum of Hang Kasturi, one of the renowned warriors attached to the 15th-century court of Sultan Mansur Shah. He attained notoriety by having an affair with one of the sultan's concubines, and as a result was killed by the legendary Hang Tuah. Opposite, is the Hui Kuan, the Hokkien merchants' guild, which has beautiful stone carvings beside the entrance.

Antiques street

Further along are the antique shops which Jonkers Street is renowned for. Melaka's Indian Muslims still dominate the antique trade, carrying on in the tradition of the late T.J. Kutty, whose descendants still run his original 1930s business. Gone are the days when old wares could be bought for a song, but Melaka is still Malaysia's best venue for buying antiques. Straits Chinese Silver is best

Opposite: Shop columns painted in Chinese calligraphy are a common sight in Melaka's old Chinatown. *Below:* The proprietress of Fatimah's, an antique shop on Jonkers Street, with rows of charcoal-burning irons.

R. IAN LLOYD

the 17th-century, although the most elaborate were built during the 19th and early-20th century. Once, only those lucky enough to know a *peranakan* family ever managed to visit one of these Melakan ancestral homes, but since William Chan opened his family residence, **The Baba Nonya Heritage** at No. 50, visitors can now enjoy an in depth tour of one of Melaka's most elaborate homes and get a unique insight into the *peranakan* lifestyle.

Built in what is known as Chinese Palladian style—a fusion of High Victorian,

at Tian Wah on neighboring Jalan Hang Kasturi. Klasik, an antique shop on the right, specializes in Nonyaware porcelain, reproduction blackwood chairs inlaid with mother-of-pearl, and red-and-gold Chinese furniture. Fatimah's, on the left, is good for old Dutch sideboards, gas lamps, blue-and-white ceramics and charcoal-burning irons. Wah Aik, a traditional cobbler, on the left, makes handmade shoes, including miniature replicas of those for Chinese bound feet.

After lunch, a well-known pork satay seller sets up beside the coffee shop on the corner of Jalan Hang Lekir, and down the bridge end at No.2 a tiny shop serves the most fragrant chicken rice in Melaka. One old *baba* townhouse on the right, has been converted into a restaurant, and although the prices are inflated, the interior decor is original, there are some beautiful gilded wood-carvings, and diners can lunch on marble-topped tables.

Just before the Melaka River bridge turn right into Jalan Tun Tan Cheng Lock, formerly Heeren Street, which means gentlemen's street in Dutch. However, before exploring this architecturally-renowned street make a detour down to the riverbank. Downstream, elegant Sumatran *perahus* still dock, and the far bank is lined with wooden barges that transport goods to the ships anchored offshore.

From the Heeren Street jetty, or from behind the tourist information center on the opposite bank, visitors can board boats for a 45-minute cruise of the Melaka River. The boats travel downstream past the *perahus* and the barges to the estuary, and then head upriver along the old canal flanked by hundred-year-old townhouses and warehouses to Kampung Morten, a picturesque Malay *kampung* where wooden boardwalks link the houses. A miniature lighthouse characterizes the beautiful old home of the late Haji Hashid which is now a private museum.

Heeren Street is where the rich *babas* built their townhouses, some of which date from

Chinese and tropical architecture—the 27-meter-long house (88ft) was built in 1896. A huge panelled screen, intricately carved and gilded in unusual two-tone gold leaf, separates the main hall from the *tiah gelap*, the room where unmarried maidens could peer out at male guests. Archways carved with dragons, phoenix birds, and flowers decorate the formal rooms where portraits of ancestors peer from their gilded frames at opulent marble tables, blackwood furniture inlaid with marble and mother of pearl, and priceless antiques. A magnificent teakwood staircase winds upstairs to the flamboyantly-decorated bedrooms and downstairs is an original 19th-century kitchen.

Further down Jalan Tun Tan Cheng Lock, set back from the road on the left, is the Chee Mansion crowned by a tower on the roof that for many years was the highest structure in Chinatown, and was also used as a navigational aid for sailors on the Melaka Straits. An eccentric blend of Dutch, Portuguese, Chinese and English styles, the house was built by a Eurasian architect in 1919 for the wealthy Chee family whose fortunes were made from rubber and banking, and whose descendants still live in the house today.

Walk back to the bridge, then follow Jalan Laksamana, past the Indian shops selling Javanese batiks and prayer rugs, and the bookshops selling English-language books. At the next intersection turn right into Jalan

Temenggong. Two blocks along here, past some excellent coffee shops which specialize in Indian *roti canai* and *murtabah*, is the Melaka Sikh Temple which has a prayer hall with an arched verandah and a decorative front entrance.

Continue to busy Jalan Munshi Abdullah and the hill directly in front is Bukit Cina, the huge Chinese graveyard hill, reputed to contain at least 12,500 tombs, some dating back to the 15th century. To the left, at the base of the hill beside Jalan Puteri Hang Lih Po, is the Chinese temple of Sam Po Kong. Set around a white-washed courtyard, the temple is dedicated to Cheng Ho, the famous Muslim Admiral of the Chinese Fleet who sailed to Melaka in the 15th century.

Adjacent to the temple is the Perigi Raja, the well of the Princess Hang Lih Po, who returned to Melaka with the famous admiral in 1459 to become one of the wives of Sultan Mansur Shah. Apparently, she and her 500 handmaidens lived near here at the base of Bukit Cina which is the largest and oldest Chinese graveyard outside of China.

Starting from just along Jalan Puteri Hang Lih Po, a good jogging trail winds up and around the hill for about 3km (1.9mi) and passes some ancient graves dating from the Ming Dynasty (14th to 17th century), and some huge horseshoe-shaped tombs of the Kapitan Cina who were the heads of the Chinese community during colonial times.

Two 15th-century Malay Chieftains are buried on Bukit Tempurong Plain, and some old *keramat*—sacred Muslim graves—are found on the northeast foot of the hill. From the top of the hill, the panorama sweeps from the green paddy fields beyond the town, past the hilltop St.John's Fort, out across the straits to Pulau Besar and other offshore isles, and then back to the patchwork of red-tiled roofs of old Chinatown and the highrises of Melaka's new commercial district.

Return to Jalan Munshi Abdullah, and turn right into Jalan Bendahara. Two blocks up on the right, with a distinctive Iberian facade, is St. Peter's Church, which was built in 1710. Malaysia's oldest-functioning Catholic church is the traditional place of worship for Melaka's Portuguese-Eurasians, who trace their roots back to the 16th-century Portuguese conquest. The first Augustinian fathers arrived in 1587 and their traditions are still upheld, especially at Easter when the mass culminates in a candlelit procession when a statue of Christ is borne aloft.

Opposite, left: Gilded "ancestor" tablets at the Cheng Hoon Teng Temple, Malaysia's oldest Chinese temple.*Opposite, right:* Wooden clogs known as terompah, *because of the sound they make when walking on hard surfaces, are a common sight in Chinatown's sundry shops.* **Below:** *Melaka's Portuguese Eurasians gather at St. Peter's for an Easter procession.*

R. IAN LLOYD

AROUND MELAKA

Warrior Tombs and other Straits Sights

On the outskirts of Melaka town and around the compact state are many historical sights, and some of Malaysia's oldest and most picturesque kampungs, with traditional wooden houses with their distinctive high-pitched roofs and tiled staircases.

Some attractions, like the Portuguese Settlement, St.John's Fort, Tranquerah Mosque, and the new State Mosque, are a short trishaw ride from downtown. While the sights further afield are accessible by both taxi and bus, it is best to rent a car for a day to explore the scenic countryside.

North along the straits

Heading west from the Melaka River bridge, follow Jalan Tun Tan Cheng Lock which becomes Jalan Tengkera, and continue along the seafront of the Melaka Straits to Masjid Tranquerah. This beautiful mosque built in 1728 features the distinctive Melaka-style, pagoda-shaped minaret and a Javanese-style tiered roof. In the grounds is the grave of Sultan Hussein Shah of Johor who ceded Singapore to Raffles in 1819.

After the mosque, this road becomes Jalan Klebang, where many rich *baba* families built mansions during the turn-of-the-century rubber boom. Set in spacious seaside lawns, some of these stuccoed residences with their shuttered windows and arched foyers, are still in pristine condition; others are dilapitated haunted houses, and a few have been revamped into restaurants and hotels.

At **Klebang Besar**, about 8km (5mi) from town, the Malay foodstalls perched on the sandy beachfront are a great place to watch the sunset and dine on satay and baked fish. Turn left at the Tanjung Kling Mosque with its unusual octagonal minaret, and just down this road on the right is the presumed tomb of Hang Tuah, the greatest warrior of the 15th-century Melakan Sultanate. Many historians dispute the State Government's claims that this is the legendary grave, but there is no doubt of its antiquity and many superstitious Chinese come here to get divine inspiration for lucky lottery numbers.

From the grave, follow the road around to **Pantai Kundor**, a traditional Malay fishing village overlooking a sandy beach. Further north, after Masjid Tanah, turn left for the best swimming on the coast at Tanjung

JILL GOCHER

Bidara—a long sandy beach where the calm waters are studded with granite boulders.

Heading southeast from Melaka town, follow Jalan Parameswara, turn left into Jalan Bukit Senjuang, and then take the sharp right turn up the hill to the 18th-century St. John's Fort, 3km (1.9mi) from town. From the white-walled Dutch fort there are panoramic views of the surrounding countryside. According to legend, an underground tunnel runs from here to Porta de Santiago at the foot of St. Paul's Hill. Apparently the entrance was bricked over centuries ago and its location remains a mystery to this day.

European heritage preserved

Return to Jalan Parameswara and turn off at Jalan d'Albuquerque for the **Portuguese Settlement**, home of the Eurasian descendants of the Portuguese who conquered Melaka in the 16th century. It looks similar to any Malay village, but the streets bear names like Texeira and Sequiera, and some of the population look decidedly Iberian. Cristao, an ancient Portuguese tongue, is still spoken here, and some old cultural dances and traditions are still carried on.

At the Portuguese Square visitors can watch cultural performances on Saturday nights, and the surrounding restaurants serve up spicy Portuguese-style cuisine. At Easter and Christmas, families celebrate in "open-house" style and visitors are welcome to join in. During the Feast of St. Peter's on the 29th June, fishermen decorate their boats which are blessed for the coming year.

Traditional kampungs flank the road south to Muar. At Umbai, 13km (8mi) from Melaka, turn right to the jetty at Pengkalan Pernu, where boats ply across the straits to **Pulau Besar**, "the big island," which has clean sandy beaches, good for swimming, and a luxury resort.

Further south, at Serkam, turn right to Makam Tun Teja, the mausoleum of the heroine Tun Teja, the beloved consort of Sultan Mahmud Shah, who died here in 1510 while fleeing the Portuguese invasion. The whitewashed mausoleum is surrounded by rice paddies where women still use traditional curved knives to harvest the rice.

A formidable dwelling

Just past Merlimau, 23km (14mi) from Melaka, turn right to the **Penghulu's House**, the prettiest traditional house in Malaysia. This beautifully-ornamented home was built by Malay carpenters in 1894, and

features a colorful staircase of art nouveau tiles, fine wood carvings, a central courtyard, a decorated pillar known as a *tiang seri*, and an original interior. The descendants of the Penghulu—the chieftain of Merlimau—still live in the house and visitors are welcome, as are donations which help with the upkeep.

Modern tourist attractions

For sights north of Melaka, follow the signs for Kuala Lumpur. At Peringgit, view the fantastic **State Mosque**, built in traditional Melakan style but in extremely grand porportion. Continue to Ayer Keroh, 10km (6mi) from town, where many attractions are close together. **Mini Malaysia** and **Mini Asean** has full-sized replicas of typical architecture of Malaysia's 13 states and Asean's member countries. Nearby is the Melaka Zoo; the Hutan Rekreasi, a forest recreation park with shaded jogging trails; a golf course and several resort-style hotels. Other attractions include a crocodile farm, butterfly and reptile sanctuary, and a fish park.

*Opposite: Skirts swirl at the Portuguese Square every Saturday night when the local residents hold a cultural show featuring Portuguese dances. **Above:** A descendant of the famous penghulu, or chieftain, who built this renowned home at Merlimau, rests on the art nouveau tiled steps which lead to the serambi or verandah.*

NEGERI SEMBILAN

Wooden Palaces and Living Stones

Settled since the 16th century by Minang-kabau settlers from the Sumatran highlands, the mountainous state of Negeri Sembilan located south of Selangor, north of Melaka, and east of Pahang, is often overlooked by travelers en route to either Melaka or Kuala Lumpur, especially since the construction of the North South expressway which bypasses all the state's major towns.

Seremban, the state capital, 64km (40mi) south of Kuala Lumpur, grew up around the same time as the latter, but always suffered by comparison. Just over a century ago it was a mainly Chinese town which served the local tin-mining industry, and was only accessible by boat up the tortuous, winding, Sungai Linggi river, an 18-hour journey from the coast. Towards the end of the century, however, it was linked by rail and road and consequently became the colonial capital. A num-

ber of important government buildings were constructed, some of which still survive today. The newer industrial areas, built in the last decade, have sprouted in satellite towns away from downtown, and as a result, the heart of old Seremban still retains much of its old charm.

The English always practised the "divide and rule" policy of keeping the Asian and European sections of town separate, and the layout of Seremban town still basically follows the old pattern. In the commercial end of town—the original Chinatown—in the grid of streets between Jalan Tuanku Munawar and Jalan Yam Tuan, many turn-of-the-century shophouses built in the Southern Chinese style still survive, jammed between newer concrete additions that sadly lack the architectural details of their predecessors.

All the government buildings—both old and new—are on the higher ground to the east of Chinatown. Beside the Gothic-inspired, Catholic Church (Gereja Katolik) on Jalan Yam Tuan, walk east to Jalan Dato' Abdul Kadir and to the concrete bunker-like State Secretariat on the corner of Jalan Bukit. In direct contrast is the adjoining State Legislature Building, also built in contemporary style but featuring elegant Minangkabau roofs with their sweeping curves and upturned eaves. Across the road is its predecessor built in 1912, a marvellous neo-classical building withcolumns and archways

R. MOH'D NOH SALLEH

which is now the State Library.

Follow Jalan Dato Hamzah, which over-looks the attractive Lake Gardens, or Taman Tasek. Shaded parklands, popular with pic-nickers and joggers surround around a man-made lake. At the park's pavilion, music and cultural shows are staged on the weekends. Opposite the Lake Gardens are more colonial buildings, built in the same style as the State Library, which now house the District Land Office. Further down the road is the Masjid Negeri, or State Mosque, which has an unusual scalloped roof supported on nine pil-lars, which represent the original nine territo-ries of Negeri Sembilan.

Minangkabau palaces

Rather inconveniently sited, but worth a visit nonetheless is the **State Museum** (Muzium Negeri) and Cultural Park (Taman Seni Budaya) located 2km (1.2mi) west of town along the link road to the North South Expressway. The Cultural Handicraft Center, built after the fashion of a wooden Minang-kabau palace, displays handicrafts and histori-cal artifacts, but the most interesting part of the complex are the Istana Ampang Tinggi and the Rumah Minangkabau, two original Minangkabau style houses.

Built in 1861, the former is now the State Museum. The superior, rainforest hardwood is stained with *damar minyak* which repels termites, and the roof is of thatched *atap*. The house was originally an upriver royal resi-dence and was moved to downtown Seremban in 1953 where it served as the museum. It was recently relocated to the Cultural Park.

Of the same style, but of more elegant pro-portions, the **Rumah Minangkabau** is a beautiful example of 19th-century Malay craftmanship and could well have been the palace which Victorian author Isabella Bird visited in 1879 at nearby Mambau. She "thor-oughly liked his house (...) There was a rich, dim light in the room, which was cool and wainscoted entirely with dark red wood."

The extremely low doors built into chiefs' houses are believed to have been designed that way so that the respectful visitor always has to bow when entering. Beautiful wood carvings of verses from the Koran adorn the interior panels, and the entrance stairs are also carved. The two-tiered roof with its curved ridge, characteristic of Minangkabau houses, is made from hand-cut wooden shin-gles. The Rumah Minangkabau was disman-tled from its original site at Mambau in 1924

and shipped to England where it was part of the Malaya display at the Royal Wembley Exhibition. Later it was relocated at its pre-sent site.

Sri Menanti, the royal capital, 33km (20mi) east of Seremban, is reached by fol-lowing Jalan Zaaba through town and then turning off on the road to Kuala Pilah. This route follows Malay kampungs and then winds up through the scenic Bukit Putus pass, site of an 1875 skirmish when the local Malays rebelled against the British and stock-aded the pass. However, a force comprising the Royal Artillery and the Ghurkas eventual-ly drove out the defenders.

Just over the crest of the hill is Hutan Rekreasi Ulu Bendol, a picturesque forest park where the Bendol River cascades over smooth granite boulders, and trails weave through the rainforest. From here the road winds down to the vale of Terachi. Shaded by fruit trees, and adorned with trailing bougainvilleas, traditional Minangkabau houses decorate this attractive kampung. Opposite the police station, is an unusual 70-year-old coconut palm with a corkscrew trunk

*Opposite: The colonial grandeur of Seremban's imposing State Library. **Below**: Minangkabau memorabilia like this antique gong, are on display at the Istana Ampang Tinggi, the 100-year-old wooden palace in the grounds of Seremban's cultural center.*

imported from China at the turn of the century.

Port Dickson, Negeri Sembilan's well-known beach region, is 29km (18mi) southwest of Seremban. Take Jalan Rasah out of town, past Rasah and Mambau to Lukut, where a 1km (0.6mi) detour around the back of town leads to Kota Lukut, a hilltop fort. Overlooking the Lukut River, it was built in 1847 by Raja Juma'at. Substantial stone walls made with laterite (a soft red stone which turns hard when exposed to the elements) still remain, and moats and the foundations of

which apparently bears extra-sweet fruit.

At Terachi, turn right for Sri Menanti and follow the road through picturesque kampung to the seat of the Negeri Sembilan royal family whose Sumatran ancestors first settled here four centuries ago. The opulent Istana Besar built in the 1930s, with an azure-colored tiled roof, is the home of the current Yang di-Pertuan Besar.

The nearby **Istana Lama**, the old palace, and the general appearance of Sri Menanti's sleepy town has changed little since it was described by Cuthbert Woodville Harrison in his *Illustrated Guide to the Federated Malay State* (1923). "The palace itself is built entirely of dark red wood in Malay style, the two ends raking skywards to flamboyant gables. Set against the background of dark green hills with a broad lawn in front it is the fitting culmination of the Sri Menanti valley and its dozens of little Malay houses, any one of which might serve as model for the Astana itself." The Istana Lama is beautifully decorated with wood carvings and apparently the 99 supporting pillars represent the 99 warriors of the different clans. There are plans to turn the old palace, built in 1902, into a museum.

East then south

Kuala Pilah, further east, the largest town in the region, is a good place to taste typical Minangkabau cuisine. Specialities include beef *rendang*, a dry, coriander-flavored curry, and chicken and vegetables cooked in coconut cream with firey *cili padi* (bird's eye chillies).

North of downtown on Jalan Bahau is an interesting old archway with a roof of Chinese design which was built by the local Chinese in 1905, in honor of Martin Lister, Kuala Pilah's first British Resident. Directly opposite is the old Sim Tong Temple which has an elaborately-decorated roof ridge, featuring dragons and other Chinese symbolism, and inside are some priceless wood carvings

buildings inside the fort complex can still be seen, remnants of those fighting days when the Bugis from Selangor and the local Minangkabau vied for control of the lucrative tin trade.

Port Dickson itself, 8km (5mi) south of Lukut, is a large port town with oil refineries which offers little of interest to visitors. Take the town bypass to the southern beaches which are extremely popular with both locals and citysiders from Kuala Lumpur who flock here every weekend and public holidays. Although not in the same class as east coast beaches, the 18km (11mi) stretch of sandy coastline offers a diversion from the inland and is good for windsurfing and canoeing.

Athough many local people swim here, the southern Melaka Straits are quite polluted and the hotel swimming pools are probably a safer bet. Along the popular beach fronts at Pantai Bagan Pinang and Teluk Kemang are hotels, resorts, and plenty of restaurants and foodstalls well-known for their inexpensive seafood.

At the southern end of the beach stretch, 16km (10mi) from Port Dickson, turn off for **Blue Lagoon**, a resort bay, and Tanjung Tuan (Cape Rachado) where an old colonial lighthouse overlooks a rainforested promontory with expansive views across the Straits of Melaka. On extra clear days, the swampy Sumatran coast can apparently be spied across the water. Visitors here are besieged by cheeky monkeys, who raid picnic baskets and crawl over cars. The promontory is also a popular stopover for migratory birds and during September/October and March/April there are large concentrations of hawks and eagles. Further south at Pasir Panjang there are camping and picnic grounds set in a forest recreation park which overlooks the Straits of Melaka.

A tomb and stones which grow

At **Pengkalan Kempas**, further west on the road to Linggi is the 15th-century tomb of Sheikh Ahmad Majnun Shah, a holy man who rebelled against Melaka's Sultan Mansur Shah. An inscribed pillar by the grave gives two contradictory descriptions of the Sheikh; the inscription in Jawi says he was a saintly religious man, while the other in Sumatran Kawi script claims he was a traitor. Legend has it that the circular hole, 11.5cm (4.5in) in diameter, below the inscriptions, was used to test oaths, and that it would apparently tighten around a victim's arm if he was lying.

Of much greater antiquity than the tomb, and even more mysterious, are the three adjacent carved megaliths which date to around the 2nd century, and stand about 2m (6.5ft) high. They are called "the spoon", "the sword" and the "the rudder" because of their respective shapes and the latter has curlicue floral carvings. No in-depth archaeological study has been undertaken on the stones which obviously date from the pre-Islamic era. The Sheikh's grave was obviously sited here because it was already considered a sacred place.

Megalithic stones, known locally as *batu hidup*, "living stones," are found in many sites around Negeri Sembilan and in northeast Melaka. Some villages believe that these stones grow—hence the name—while others maintain that they were merely gravestones. Though not as celebrated as the Pengkalan Kempas collection, other such stones are found at Tampin near the Melaka border.

Negeri Sembilan's other attractions on the main highway south, include the **hot springs** at Pedas, 20km (15mi) from Seremban on the main highway south, and the picturesque Minangkabau houses at the next towns of Rembau and Kota.

For travelers with their own transport there is delightful drive north along the Kuala Lumpur road to Setul, then turn off for Ulu Beranang and Broga, a picturesque kampung region with some old wooden mosques and scenic villages against a backdrop of the mighty hills of the main range.

Above, left: Curved roof ridges and long shuttered windows are features of rural Minangkabau houses like this one at Terachi.
Above, right: These mysterious carved megaliths are found beside an ancient grave at Pengkalan Kempas.

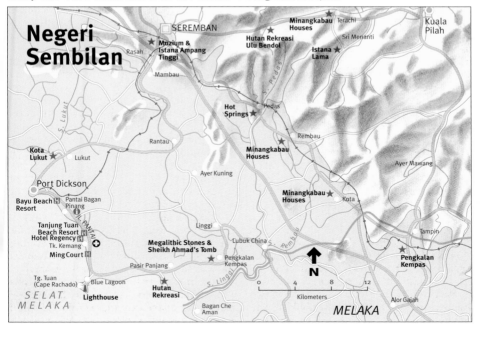

PART VIII

Introducing Johor

Johor, the most southerly state on the peninsula, is also one of the most developed, with vast oil-palm plantations and a fast-growing industrial sector. Nevertheless there are still picturesque kampungs from Muar to Pontian on the Melaka Straits, some beautiful forest reserves, offshore islands, historic ruins as well as the bustling capital of Johor Bahru with its royal palace brimming with antiques.

Chinese traders in the 9th century spoke of a legendary kingdom known as Lo Yueh "a place where traders passing back and forth meet." Historians speculate that it was located in Johor but there is no tangible evidence. Johor's history really begins when Sultan Mahmud Syah of Melaka fled from the Portuguese in 1511 and set up his court on Bintan Island in the Riau-Lingga archipelago.

Following his death, his son, Sultan Alauddin Riayat Syah, moved his royal base to Pekan Tua, close to today's Kota Tinggi, and established the kingdom of Johor which quickly became the dominant Malay power on the peninsula. The courtly traditions of Melaka were faithfully adhered to and the Johor royal court set the standards by which all other peninsular kingdoms were judged.

During the 16th century Johor suffered numerous raids by the Portuguese and the Acehnese from Sumatra, and when the Dutch first appeared in the early 17th century, Johor saw them as an ally. Consequently when the Dutch attacked Melaka the armies of Johor provided assistance. After the successful conquest, the Dutch governor of Batavia acknowledged that "without their help we would never have become master of that strong place."

Johor was still a power to be reckoned with in the late-17th century due mainly to the skills of the powerful Laksamana, who commanded the allegiance of the Orang Laut, or Sea People. But times were changing. After Sultan Ibrahim's suspiciously early death, the Laksamana family were driven out and the Orang Laut reverted to piracy, which threatened Johor's trade. In 1699, believing that Johor's decline was due to the weak rule and atrocities of the sadistic Sultan Mahmud, the nobles of the court had him murdered. This act changed the course of Malay history for according to tradition, only God could punish a ruler, especially those of "white blood" descended from the Melaka line. Sultan Mahmud had no heirs, and in the words of a Thai chronicle, "his lineage disappeared and was never heard of again."

The enormous scale of *derhaka*, or treason, within the palace worked to the advantage of the powerful Bugis. After fleeing civil wars in Sulawesi and setting up bases in Selangor they began infiltrating the Johor court, then being run by the unpopular Bendahara family that had conspired to kill Sultan Mahmud. They were so successful that Bugis underkings effectively ruled Johor for most of the 18th century.

In 1819, the factionalized court worked to Stamford Raffles' advantage, when, by playing one group off against the other, he acquired the island of Singapore. By the end of the 19th century, the Temenggung line finally ousted the Bendahara family and established the dynasty which still runs Johor today. Most notable was "the father of modern Johor" Temenggung Abu Bakar who later took the title of Sultan. He wisely introduced a constitution prohibiting his state from aligning with European powers, but his son Ibrahim ruled at the zenith of British power and was finally persuaded of their right to rule. Ironically Sultan Ibrahim remained in power long enough to see the situation reversed in 1957 when Malaya achieved independence.

Overleaf: Crystal furniture and priceless antiques on display at the Istana Besar, the royal palace in Johor Bahru. **Opposite:** Malay girls wearing the traditional long blouse, known as baju kurung Johor. Photos by R. Ian Lloyd

JOHOR BAHRU

Where Mainland Asia Ends

Just across the narrow straits which mark the border of Singapore and Malaysia, Johor Bahru has always suffered in comparison to its fast-paced and sophisticated neighbor in the south. Formerly used an entry and exit point, today Malaysia's most southerly capital is experiencing a boom. Attracted by the stable political situation and low wages, investors are pouring into the state and Singaporeans flock here on the weekends to take advantage of their stronger dollar, cheap markets, low-priced seafood, and the thriving, underground nightlife.

Despite, Johor Bahru's new image, the town still has a relaxed ambiance which is distinctly refreshing for visitors eager to escape the sterility and organization of Singapore. Local wags say that their more repressed southern neighbors come here to let loose—as soon as they cross the border,

smokers head for restaurants where they can puff away uninhibited, food freaks can enjoy the proliferation of cheap outdoor eating, and gum-chewers can chomp legally.

Once known as Tanjung Puteri, Johor Bahru means "New Johor," and was the creation of Sultan Abu Bakar, who moved his capital here in 1866. This southern gateway still bears his stamp: many of the town's historic buildings were built during Abu Bakar's reign. Most of Johor Bahru's 750,000 inhabitants live in sprawling outer suburbs but the town's commercial hub is in the grid of streets north of the causeway where quaint old shophouses are rapidly giving way to high-rises.

Most parts Johor Bahru worth visiting are along the road facing the straits. Address confusion can easily happen along here: the road changes names four times along its length. Although the town's sights are somewhat spread out it is a pleasant stroll from one to the other as a shaded promenade runs the entire length of the seashore road which begins as Jalan Ibrahim at the causeway which links the two nations.

Officially declared open in 1924, the causeway has always been a vital link to Singapore carrying road and rail traffic, gas and water. A section was blown up by the British during World War II in an attempt to stop the Japanese invading, but it proved a futile excercise. Less than a month later the

R IAN LLOYD

Japanese repaired it and took possession of Singapore Island.

At the general post office, take a detour up the steep road on the right to the imposing, Sultan Ibrahim Building, which houses the state government offices. Known as "the fort", because of its massive, 65m (213ft) granite tower, it is a dominant feature of Johor Bahru's skyline. Built in the early 1940s, the offices are a mixture of Saracenic and art deco styles, and display fine stone-carvings and mosaic work. Further along Jalan Ibrahim, past the 19th-century court-house, is the Istana Besar with a brilliant blue roof of glazed tiles.

The Royal Palace was built by Sultan Abu Bakar in 1866 and was recently renovated as the Muzium Di Raja (**Royal Museum**) housing the incredible antique and heirloom collection of the royal family of Johor which was mainly collected by the anglophile Sultan Abu Bakar and his son Ibrahim on their many European jaunts. Despite the fact that Abu Bakar was regarded as being a very "British" Malay—he played cricket and would quote Tennyson—he was a shrewd ruler, who although on intimate terms with the British royal family, staunchly resisted English intervention in Johor.

The opulent palace is still much the same as described by a grandchild of Queen Victoria: "The interior is lined with white marble,and arranged in a sort of Moorish fashion (...) everything combines to give an air of magnificence, and comfort." The Royal Museum is filled with priceless antiques and exceptional features include the crystal furniture in the Reception Room, the golden thrones in the Throne Room and the Hunting Room adorned with stuffed trophies of Johor's once prolific wildlife. Istana Besar is surrounded by beautifully-landscaped lawns and gardens which are open to the public. There's a children's playground, an orchid garden, and and a Japanese tea-house, presented to Sultan Ibrahim by the crown prince of Japan in 1939.

Further west, on a hill overlooking the seafront, is the Sultan Abu Bakar Mosque, built in 1900 at a cost of $400,000. Four octagonal minarets with fan-shaped stained-glass windows surmount the prayer hall of Johor's largest mosque. Around the circular driveway, hawkers lay out colorful prayer rugs from Turkey to tempt the devout, and tourists looking for souvenirs. Opposite, on Jalan Gertak Merah is the Johor Zoo, which is popular with children. Below the mosque is the

Islamic Center, built in Middle-Eastern style, and nearby is Tepian Tebrau, an open-air food center, renowned for its cheap seafood.

Past the hospital, turn right for MAWAR, a complex with a government-run Kraftangan (handicrafts) exhibition and sales center, it also has a restaurant and tea terrace. Opposite, is the JARO workshop, a rehabilitation center well-known for its leather bookbinding, basketware, and other crafts made by the handicapped.

Further around the seafront, overlooking the straits from its commanding hilltop situation is the Istana Bukit Serene, the home of the Sultan of Johor. Other places of note around town include the Arulmigu Rajamariamman Devassthanam Temple, Johor state's largest Hindu temple, which has a tiered entrance arch bedecked with statues of gods and goddesses. The temple is right in the heart of downtown, opposite the new Kota Raya Plaza hotel and shopping complex on Jalan Ungku Puan. Behind town on Jalan Mahmoodiah is the Royal Mausoleum in a beautifully-maintained Muslim graveyard shaded by fragrant frangipani trees.

Opposite: Crammed with Singaporeans returning from a weekend in Malaysia, the Causeway, which links Johor Bahru with the island republic also carries vital supplies of gas and water. Above: Different types of rice on sale at a Johor Bahru dry-goods store.

SOUTH OF MUAR

Through West Johor's Scenic Village

Stretching from the old port town of Muar in the northwest corner of Johor state, to the tip of mainland Asia at Tanjung Piai, the 200-km (124mi) coastal road traverses some of the prettiest rural villages in Malaysia. Muar, also called Bandar Maharani, sprawls along the banks of the Muar River. Sumatran *perahus* still dock at the town jetty and boatmen can often be seen hoisting their mighty canvas sails at the rivermouth.

Muar is mentioned in the 16th-century *Malay Annals*, as the founder of Melaka had considered the port for his capital, but later opted for Melaka as its prominent hill made for better defence. Muar is considered as the heartland of Johor culture, and the dialect is considered the purest Malay on the peninsula. Both men and women wear the distinctive, collarless Johor-style *baju* shirt and the region is famous for its *ghazal* music which

originated from Arabia.

Downtown Muar, dominated by 19th-century shophouses, is very much a Chinese town at its heart. Coffee shops still have marble-topped tables and bentwood chairs, and there are many interesting dry-goods shops and old-style businesses. South of the commercial center, overlooking the river, is Bangunan Sultan Abu Bakar, an elegant, neo-classical government building which dates from the turn of the century, when its royal namesake revitalized Muar's architecture. Nearby, the courthouse, police station, customs house and high school all date from this same era. South, along the riverbank parklands shaded by ancient raintrees, is the stylish Masjid Jamek built by Sultan Ibrahim. From here, a walkway leads to Tanjung, the riverside park which has picnic tables and food stalls selling local specialities.

Magical Mount Ophir

North of Muar, take a detour to the legendary Gunung Ledang, called Mount Ophir by the British. In the 15th century, Melaka's Sultan Mansur Shah wished to marry the beautiful Princess of Gunung Ledang. Her dowry list of trays of mosquito's hearts and a vat of tears didn't perturb him, but he withdrew his marital offer when she requested a cup of his son's blood.

The waterfalls of the 1,276m (4,186ft), the cloud-wreathed mountain make it a favorite

venue for weekend climbers and picnickers. It is also where local *bomoh* shamen are reputed to go for their esoteric training and to commune with the same fairy princess that had bewitched Sultan Mansur. To get to the mountain take the road from Muar to Tangkak and 11km (7mi) north of here, on the road to Segamat, turn off at Sagil for the waterfall and the start of the summit trail.

South of Muar, the road to Batu Pahat, 50km (31mi) south, winds through some delightful kampung regions, famous for their

tropical fruits such as *duku*, rambutan, and durian, and during the fruiting season the roadsides are flanked by fruit stalls. Traditional Muar-style wooden houses, with long shuttered windows and covered porticos, painted in pastel shades and surrounded by palms and fruit trees, line the sides of the road.

At Parit Pecah, 18km (11mi) south of Muar, there is a unique Bugis house with a high pitched roof of wooden shingles. This 100-year-old house is the only surviving one of its kind in Malaysia. The region, south of here to Batu Pahat, is famous for its numerous *bomoh*, and patients come from all over the country and Singapore to seek cures from these traditional medicine men.

Batu Pahat, surrounded by characterless suburbs crammed with electronics and textile factories, looks a thoroughly uninteresting town. But it's well-known for its cheap and excellent Chinese and Malay food, and the old downtown area is worth a visit. Sailing boats from Sumatra still dock along the riverfront, and the market area has many old shophouses decorated with plaster curlicues and circular columns displaying Chinese calligraphy, where blacksmiths, tin-smiths and basket-makers still work

Seafood at Asia's tip

Travelers enroute to Johor Bahru, can either turn here for Ayer Hitam and take the main highway south, or they can opt for the longer,

but more interesting Route 5 along the coast. Leaving Batu Pahat, this road winds through hilly country, past vegetable farms and market gardens down to the flat coastal plain criss-crossed by canals. Along this scenic road, villagers shell coconuts and dry cocoa on mats, and the tidal canals are filled with wooden fishing boats.

At Benut, 50km (31mi) south of Batu Pahat, there is an early 20th-century mosque, and 24km (15mi) further on at Pontian there is a tree-lined seafront drive with good food-stalls and a view of the wooded offshore isle of Pulau Pisang.

It is 59km (37mi) from Pontian to Johor Bahru, but the coastal road continues to Kukup, a renowned seafood haunt, 19km (12mi) south. The entire town is perched on stilts above the mangroves and the buildings are connected by boardwalks. Chilli crabs, baked fish, garlic prawns, and a variety of other culinary pleasures are served at any of a dozen seafood restaurants. Tour boats depart from the jetty for the floating fish farms and to Pulau Kukup, a nearby mangrove island.

To get to Tanjung Piai, the tip of mainland Asia, follow the road to Serkat, turn right at the mosque and then follow the signs to the end of the road. Two wooden jetties lead to a couple of small restaurants set high above the straits. Across the pearly waters is a horizon full of Singapore-bound shipping and in the distance are the jagged outlines of the island republic's towering downtown skyline. The menu board at Restoran Atan says it all: "Southernmost of Asia is at Our Feet."

*Opposite: Heading back to the depot through an avenue of rubber tress, a tapper shoulders buckets of latex collected from this estate near Batu Pahat. **Above, left:** Trees must be tapped in the cool early morning when the latex flows best. **Above, right:** Floral decorations adorn the minaret of the Benut Mosque.*

EAST JOHOR

Ancient Forts and Beach Resorts

The importance of rivers as the major transport arteries of the past can be seen by the number of peninsular states that were named after their principal rivers, Johor being one of them. The Sungai Johor, which begins in the hills west of Kota Tinggi, is not the state's biggest river but it has figured in Johor's history since the very beginning. Along its banks the early sultanate built capitals and forts, and some of the region's most historic events took place here.

Gruesome beginnings

Kota Tinggi, the gateway to East Johor, 40km (25mi) north of Johor Bahru was probably the location of Pekan Tua, the royal capital established by the Melakan sultanate after they were ousted by the Portuguese. A jumble of wooden and concrete shophouses, the town is typical of rural Johor.

In the surrounding kampungs, there are a number of famous graves including the mausoleum of Sultan Mahmud, the last "white blood" sultan of the Melaka line, who was murdered by his nobles in 1699.

According to Malay history, a nobleman, Megat Sri Rama delivered the fatal blow. He would seem to have had good reason: his pregnant wife had been disembowelled on the sultan's orders. But because this was an act of *derhaka*, or treason, he suffered for years from a wound made by the dying sultan's sword, and legend has it that his descendants never set foot in Kota Tinggi for fear of Sultan Mahmud's revengeful ghost.

Located at Kampung Makam, just north of town, this yellow-canopied tomb is still a pilgrimage site for many Malays. The regicide was a momentous event in Malay history: not only because only God can punish a sultan, but because he had no heir, and his ancient lineage died with him.

Back along the road are more historical tombs including that of Bendahara Tun Habib, whose descendants founded the current royal families of Johor, Terengganu and Pahang states.

A crowd-pulling cascade

Kota Tinggi's biggest attraction is the **Lombong Waterfall** (Air Terjun Lombong) which is located 14km (9mi) northwest. During the rainy season the 37-m (121 ft) high falls are thunderous and the surrounding rainforest is covered with misty spray. The swimming pools at the base are cool and refreshing and there's a restaurant and overnight chalets scattered amongst the rainforest. Throughout the week it is very peaceful, but on weekends it becomes inundated with local tourists.

North of Kota Tinggi, turn off to Desaru, a popular beach resort 54km (35mi) to the east along a highway through huge oil-palm plantations. About halfway along, turn off to Teluk Sengat, then follow the signs 8km (5mi) to Johor Lama, for the ruins of Kota Batu, or Stone Fort, that the Portuguese wrested from the Malays in 1587.

The national museum cleared away the undergrowth in 1960, and a rectangular area with earth ramparts and some original blocks of stone are still visible. Much of the fort, which commands a superb position overlooking the broad Johor river, is still covered in thick bamboo.

Built by Sultan Alauddin Riyat Shah in 1540, the fort was defended by 8,000 Malay

and Orang Laut (Sea Tribe) warriors who resisted the first Portuguese attacks. But, when the enemy gathered reinforcements and renewed their onslaught two weeks later, Johor Lama was overtaken.

Portuguese historians claim the conquistadores made off with a fortune in gold, hastily buried by the departing Malays, and spoils included 2,000 sailing boats and 2,500 guns and muskets. Boats often make the trip to the fort's jetty from the opposite bank of the Johor river at Kong Kong, 35km (22mi) east of Johor Bahru.

From the fort, continue past the durian trees, and the little wooden houses to sleepy Kampung Johor Lama on the riverside. Beneath a forest of coconut palms there's a mosque with a wooden minaret, some colorfully-painted houses, and a long jetty where fishermen spread their nets to dry and boys splash about in inflated inner tubes. Many of the inhabitants here are descendants of the Orang Laut, the original navy of the early Johor sultans.

Desaru, Johor's most popular beach resort, is 11km (7mi) east of the turnoff on Route 92. The golden-sand beach is flanked by trees, which give rise to its name "place of casuarinas." The clear, blue waters are excellent for swimming and windsurfing, and are by far the best beaches within a two hour drive from Singapore. There are a couple of big resort hotels, and an exclusive golf course which faces the South China Sea and has the rainforest behind.

The deep southeast

Continue south 28km (17mi) for the fishing villages at the southeastern tip of Johor. At the end of the road take the left fork for Teluk Ramunia, past the shipyards, to Sungai Musuh, where there are picturesque waterways crammed with wooden fishing boats. From the palm-fringed coastline are views of the busy shipping lanes to the metropolis of Singapore, and the violet hills on Pulau Bintan in Indonesia beyond.

Some enterprising villagers have built chalets, and although the beach is not as good as Desaru, the kampung atmosphere makes for a pleasant stay. Back along the coast is Sungai Rengit, a fishing village renowned for its seafood, and at Tanjung Pengelih there is an overgrown British observation post built during World War II. Across the straits, the geometric horizon of Singapore's housing blocks looks very near, but it is a world away from the calm of Johor's sleepy southeast.

Opposite: Freighters en route to Singapore harbor hover on the horizon while villagers search for shellfish in the shallows of the Johor Straits off Pengarang. **Above:** *Golfers enjoy the breezes from the South China Sea at Desaru's waterfront golf course.*

SOUTHERN ISLANDS

Jewels in the South China Sea

Swallows circle overhead and the trade winds murmur through the casuarinas along the seafront walkway at Mersing. Joggers hurry past, families stroll by, and couples relax in the cool of the evening and gaze out to a horizon studded with the silhouettes of more than 64 offshore islands. Some are mere rocks thrusting up from the seabed, others are isolated "Robinson Crusoe" hideways, and many more are well-known resort isles including the renowned Pulau Tioman.

Mersing, a bustling port town 124km (77mi) north of Johor Bahru, and 186km (115mi) south of Kuantan, is the gateway to all these islands. Passenger boats depart from the town's jetty, and many resorts have offices in town (*see Practicalities, page 266*).

Although Pulau Tioman is in Pahang, boats still depart from Mersing. Wooden trawlers, known as "slow boats" which have been converted to passenger ferries make the four to five hour journey, but there's also less-frequent faster boats which cut the journey to around two hours. There are also an island airport with flights from Kuala Lumpur and Singapore—the landing is tricky and spectacular—but the best way to appreciate the island (if you have the time) is to take the sea approach.

Spectacular Pulau Tioman

Manoeuvering their way through the fishing trawlers and the traffic of the Mersing River, the island-bound boats negotiate the shallow harbor and enter the sparkling waters of the South China Sea. Lulled by the heat and the diesel throb, passengers drowse as the wooden boat slices through the glassy sea. Faint islands appear like rocks in a Japanese garden, and flying fish scoot across the water.

Hours pass and the once-distant, mountainous massif of Pulau Tioman, the largest island along the east coast, now comes into focus. Dominating its skyline are the horn-like granite peaks of Batu Sirau and Nenek Si-Mukut, which rear 914m (3,000ft) above a wilderness of virgin rainforest. The forest creeps down to a coast ringed with bays of white-coral sand, and lapped by turquoise waters. No other island off the peninsula can match Tioman for sheer geographic splendor.

Located 32km (20mi) off Pahang's coast, the 113km^2 (44mi^2) island, has only become a

popular traveler's destination in the last decade, but it was known to the ancient mariners of the spice trade for at least a millenium before. The pinnacle peaks provided an unmistakable landmark, and the island offered sheltered ports all year round. Early Chinese sailors knew the island as Zhumashan, "the mountain of *rami*" because of the abundance of the nettle-like *rami* plants which they used to make rope.

Pottery finds which have been unearthed at Juara on the east coast, and Teluk Nipah in the southwest indicate that the island was an important port of call from the 11th to the 19th century. When motors replaced sails the island was no longer visited by traders and slumbered in obscurity until it was rediscovered by adventurous travelers in the 1960s.

Until recently, the bulk of Pulau Tioman's 1,500 inhabitants were dependent on fishing for a livelihood but this has been fast replaced by tourism as the island's major money earner. During the peak holiday periods the beaches and resorts become quite crowded, and visitors outnumber locals, otherwise the island reverts to its former quietude.

Except for isolated Juara, a village on the remote east coast, and Mukut, a fishing community on the south coast, most of the population lives along the protected northwest shores around the large village of Tekek where most of the resorts, and the island's main jetty is located. Tekek also has a mosque, a school, shops, a tiny museum, and lots of little restaurants, chalets, huts, and a delightful sandy beach.

The island's only road, 3km (1.9mi) long, runs from the airport just north of Tekek to the luxury Berjaya Tioman Beach Resort situated on a long, sandy beach. The swimming is excellent here and there is good snorkeling around the reefs which encircle Pulau Rengis, the small rocky islet just off the coast from the resort. A group of Hollywood movie makers set up camp near here over 30 years ago to shoot beach scenes for the Cinemascope musical "South Pacific." The location of their camp is now occupied by the resort's golf course.

The backpackers' mecca

A concrete path only wide enough for motorbikes runs north past chalets and patches of rainforest to the headland at Tanjung Musuh. Here, it reverts to a trail over a rocky promontory and down to Kampung Ayer Batang, the favorite travelers' beach and the location of some of the best and original

"thatched-hut" resorts like Nazeri's and ABC. Now dozens of other establishments have sprung up along the bay with these two pioneer resorts at either end.

Beaches north and south

The southern end of Ayer Batang beach is creamy-white sands and is excellent for swimming. Rainforest creeps to the back of the resorts, and *biawak*, iguana-like lizards up to 1.5m (5ft) long, can often be seen. The orange-billed mynah bird, known as the *tiong*, which some locals believe gave Tioman its name, is often heard mimicking other birds. Lesser flying foxes, *keluang kecil* (actually a type of bat) are only found on the offshore islands and make their home in the coconut palms along the foreshore. At dusk they noisily set out to forage in the jungle.

The beach at the northern end is rocky and not as good for swimming as the south end. A trail heads from the far end of the beach and climbs the headland to Penuba Bay where there are some chalets and a pretty beach. The trail continues past Monkey Bay, which has steep dropoffs good for scuba diving, although it is much easier accessed by boat. It is possible to walk all the way to Salang, a beautiful bay in the far northwest which is popular with dive groups, but the

Opposite: *A revamped junk serves as a cruise ship in the waters off Pulau Tioman.*

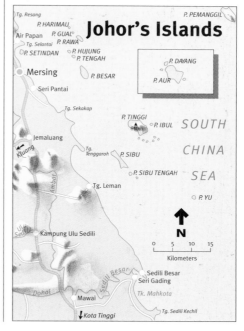

trail is rather unkept. If you don't like trekking go by boat.

The trail to Juara

Most of the 19-km (12mi) long by 12-km (7.4mi) wide island is still covered by virgin rainforest, and is home to an uncommonly-large mousedeer population. Sometimes these elusive creatures, which stand only 22cm (9in) at the shoulder, can be seen along the cross-island trail which connects Tekek to Juara on the east coast.

Take the turnoff to the mosque, and follow the footpath which climbs through thick rainforest to the top of the watershed. The waterfall here is good for a refreshing dip. The path then descends through jungle and through a rubber plantation and coconut palms to Juara.

Around 40 families live in this isolated community which now survives more on tourism than on rubber tapping or fishing. There are chalets and a couple of small restaurants. The seas are crystal clear and the beach is long and sandy. Deep-sea fishing trawlers and squid boats often shelter in the bay which has been used by sailors for centuries. Evidence of the port's antiquity came to light in 1976 when villagers digging the ground to make a football field, chanced upon ancient Chinese ceramics dating from the 12th century. More porcelains were discovered at Teluk Nipah, in the southwest, and ceramics from both sites are now on display at the Sultan Abu Bakar Museum in Pekan and the Muzium Sudut at Tekek.

The southeastern settlements of Teluk Nipah and Mukut are still quite traditional. Boat services are sporadic, so these places are only feasible if you have time on your hands. A round-the-island boat service goes to the waterfall which is a short walk from Kampung Asah, just east of Mukut. It's a pleasant spot to cool off amidst the rainforest, but the real charm in the south is the spectacular scenery and the untouristy atmosphere. Freshwater streams cascade down from the granite peaks which soar over the village, and the beaches to the west of Mukut are deserted even in the holiday season.

Good diving

A novice snorkeler can still find plenty of interest on Tioman's beach reefs, but the best diving is at Pulau Tulai, about 5km (8mi) off the coast from Salang, in the far northwest. The island is often nicknamed coral island, and chalet owners run boats there. The best corals are found off the rocky coast where snorkeling is best done from a boat. There are boulder-sized brain corals, gardens of staghorn coral, and in the deeper waters are candelabra-shaped sea whips. Marine life is plentiful and striped angelfish, butterfly fish and the darting clownfish contribute to the rainbow-colored underwater world.

Located 16km offshore from Mersing is Pulau Rawa. This quintessential tropical island with its dazzling white beach and turquoise waters is home to the region's pioneer resort run by a member of the Johor royal family. Apart from the sun and the sea, there is little to do here, as the island is small, but as it is only a 45-minute boatride, Rawa is a popular weekend jaunt and is ideal for travelers who want a short island hop.

The general's hat

Pulau Hujung, further south, is a small forested isle with beautiful beaches, also popular with day trippers. There are some private retreats here, but there is no overnight accommodation. Close by is Pulau Tengah, which looks bare compared to the others in this group as it was used as a temporary camp for Vietnamese boat people during the early 1980s and most of the jungle was cut down. A rusting metal ship grounded on the sandy shores provides a grim reminder of their hurried flight.

As its name says, Pulau Besar is the largest of the small archipelago comprising Pulau Hujung ("the end") and Pulau Tengah ("the middle"). Only a few years ago this hilly isle supported a small fishing village and tourists were rare, but now low-key resorts dominate the western shores where all the best beaches are found. During the week the island is still very peaceful. Cow trails lead through the copra plantations, past wooden kampung houses, and weave in and out of pretty bays with white sand and clear blue waters.

Known to the ancient Chinese mariners as "general's hat island" the conical silhouette of Pulau Tinggi, literally the "lofty island," looms to the south. Some locals say that it was used as the long-distance shot of Bali Hai in the movie *South Pacific*, which was partially filmed on Pulau Tioman.

The solitary, granite peak, over 609m (2,000ft) high, rears above the dense rainforest. The lower reaches are swathed by coconut plantations which descend to the pristine, white beaches. It has become a favorite getaway for local and foreign tourists although the villagers still rely principally on copra and fishing for their livelihood.

In contrast to mountainous Tinggi, Pulau Sibu the next island to the south (a short ride from Tanjung Leman) has only small hills and much of the island is easy to walk around. The first resort only opened a relatively short time ago, but now there are a range of places

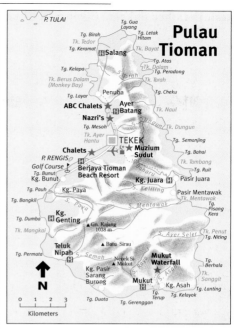

to stay at. This island still retains a pleasant kampung atmosphere. Solar electricity was introduced to Pulau Sibu as a government-assisted pilot scheme and the solar panels which stand outside each kampung house provide power without the thumping of generators.

Two untouched islands

Remote Pulau Aur, and Pulau Pemanggil, are at least six hours by boat from Mersing and are the most untouched of all the islands in the Johor archipelago. Far from the muddy effects of mainland rivers, the waters are crystal clear with abundant marine life and prolific corals.

Facilities are available on both islands but rooms are basic kampung-style and the boat service is highly irregular, but for travelers wanting to really get away from it all, these two islands are untouched and marvellously uncrowded.

Opposite: *This panorama from the promontory at Tanjung Mesoh, shows Pulau Tioman's mountainous interior, still covered in virgin rainforest, and its long, palm-shaded beaches.*

PART IX

Introducing Singapore

Nations are usually products of their history. While marveling at the sky-scraping, chrome-and-glass facade of Singapore, the visitor might be forgiven for thinking that this tropical island republic must surely be the exception to that rule.

The trick for understanding Singapore is to look beyond and beneath that facade. Do not be deceived by the glitzy, westernized sophistication of the cosmopolitan Singaporeans, for just below the surface they are unequivocally Asian.

Singapore's history has been determined as much by its geography as anything else: situated at a crucial crossroads for trade, shipping, and now communications, between the related twin cultures of Malaysia and Indonesia, and within reach of the former Khmer, Thai and Indian empires too.

In 1819, when Stamford Raffles of the East India Company arrived to sign treaties with the local Malay ruler, the Temenggong or Viceroy for the Sultan of Riau-Johor, his party found fragmentary remains of the 14th-century palace of the ancient kings of Temasek, as Singapore was once called, on the hill now called Fort Canning.

Standing at the mouth of the Singapore River was a huge boulder, mysteriously inscribed with a script that has never satisfactorily been deciphered, and in the first act of "urban renewal" vandalism in Singapore, this was blown to pieces by a British engineer in 1843, to make way for new construction.

A Singaporean playwright, Robert Yeo, wrote a play which centered on a dialogue between Raffles and Singapore's former Prime Minister Lee Kuan Yew, seeing them as kindred souls. It is true that Lee, the country's first elected prime minister of an independent Singaporean government in 1959, and regarded as the patriarch of the nation, occupies a place in Singapore's history as monumental as that of Raffles, that of the founder of modern Singapore. But significantly, there is a statue of Raffles in the city center, not of Lee, and old colonial street names have never been changed. Lee's Singapore has always striven to balance the mystique of the Oriental god-king with the rationality of the corporate technocrat.

Raffles—the founding father

In the 1820s, Raffles laid down the communally-based design of the city center—a design which persists even today. His blueprint survives in the Central Business District (essentially, the colonial British area) clustered around the commercial artery formed by the Singapore River, in Chinatown, south of the river, and Kampung Glam centered around Arab Street, the stronghold of Malays and other Muslims from the region.

Perhaps most importantly of all, it was Raffles who determined that Singapore would be a free port and would welcome all comers, provided they contributed to its economic development. These founding principles remain unchanged today.

Raffle's open-door policy stimulated the immigration of wealthy and entrepreneurial Chinese merchants from Malaya, Indian workers from the subcontinent, and a flood of poor but industrious southern Chinese escaping the turmoil of their homeland during the 19th and 20th centuries. Hence, Singapore's three-million population today roughly comprises 76% Chinese, 15% Malays, 6.5% Indians, and 2.5% "others" including Eurasians.

Back in the prosperous, and somewhat smug, colonial 1920s and '30s, Eurasians and Chinese were still not quite the thing at the Singapore Cricket Club, and even British soldiers below officer's rank were routinely

Overleaf: The Manhattan-like skyline of Singapore's central business district.
***Opposite:** Dressed in Chinese brocades, a Singaporean girl carries on her ancestors' cultural traditions.*

refused entry to that oasis of gentility, the Raffles Hotel.

World War II changed everything. Singaporeans passing the Padang shortly after the British surrender to the invading Japanese on February 15, 1942, were treated to the hitherto unimaginable spectacle of ragged Europeans lined up like cattle, preparing for internment in Changi Jail.

But on September 12, 1945, the Padang was again witness to historic events: on the steps of City Hall, Admiral Lord Louis Mountbatten received the Japanese surrender for the British.

The Japanese surrender notwithstanding, the mystique of colonial power had been shattered for ever by the British defeat. By 1959, Singapore had won internal self-government under its first fully-elected government, dominated by the People's Action Party (PAP), under the leadership of feisty Cambridge-educated lawyer, Lee Kuan Yew, Singapore's however was a singularly bloodless battle for independence, achieved largely through the political process.

Lee Kuan Yew rebuilds the nation

Lee and his colleagues proceeded to tackle Singapore's many ills: a burgeoning population ill-matched with growing unemployment, inadequate education and housing facilities, and a virtually empty treasury. Convinced that the PAP was a communist party, foreign investors at first shied away from the new Republic. As if this were not enough, the PAP had to deal with internal political rifts between its largely communist left and the moderate-socialist right—on which side Lee himself stood. These tensions were reflected in widespread social unrest during the early 1960s, focusing around the proposal to merge with Malaysia, which was supported by Lee Kuan Yew.

Merger did in fact come in 1963, but only after a huge security sweep rounded up and detained indefinitely trade unionists, students and other agitators. Detention without trial remains an option on the government's books today. Lee is credited with being possibly the only Third World leader to have ridden the communist tiger to power without being devoured by it.

The Malaysia experience did not work, culminating in the trauma of Singapore's virtual expulsion to full independence in 1966. A much-toughened government set about the taming of the trade union movement, as well as extensive industrialization and massive rehousing programmes, all of which were to prove highly successful strategies in terms of economic development.

Above all, a Raffles-style milestone decision was made to invite and encourage foreign capital and expertise, and to teach Western science, technology and languages in school. Herein lies the key to Singapore's

now unique character, in many ways quite alien to that of her Southeast Asian neighbors.

While it is true that the PAP put in place networks and structures, including measures to control the press, which fortified its power throughout society and made opposition extremely difficult, it was perhaps Lee's charisma and ability to keep the national "rice bowl" full that kept him and his party in power for so long. The PAP still runs Singapore today.

Lee remained in charge until November 1990, when he handed over to the current Prime Minister Goh Chok Tong. However, Lee still sits in Cabinet, as does his son, Brigadier-General Lee Hsien Loong, as Deputy Prime Minister.

Where East meets West

Singapore is a city that forces you into constant double-takes. Nothing is what it seems. The Asian gent in the western suit with a mobile phone and laptop computer is conveniently reversible into a Confucian sage lecturing you on the virtues of "filial piety," and the vices of the decadent West.

The Indian restauranteur still wears his traditional white *lungi* (wraparound skirt), hangs Hindu images in his shop, and eats with his fingers off a banana leaf, but uses a closed-circuit TV to check on empty tables upstairs.

The gorgeous young air hostess may seem a Suzie Wong lookalike, but actually she is most likely extremely chaste and living with her mother. This is not so much a schizophrenic nation as a multi-phrenic one. Asian television newsreaders speak old-style "BBC English," but local Chinese are returning from universities overseas with American accents, while baseball-capped kids tote skateboards along Orchard Road. On the streets, the dominance of the English language combined with Asian mother-tongues has produced a genuine Creole, jestingly referred to as "Singlish."

The dignified forms and gentlemanly foreplay of British justice are still here, yet the laws and their application seem at times somewhat severe: death for drug trafficking, hefty fines for littering, and so on. Underlying it all though is the ancient Chinese concern for the good of the collective, the community, rather than that of the individual. This is also a brash "money-faced" and food-obsessed place given to reminding itself that it is the best and the first. Local banks strive to build the tallest skyscrapers in the region, super-efficient Changi Airport is indisputably one of

the world's best, and the port is the world's busiest, to name but a few superlatives already achieved.

The biggest worries facing Singapore today are the problems of success. The Republic is already one of the richest nations in Asia, with huge foreign and cash reserves. Nobody wants, or needs, to be a servant in Singapore any more. Singaporeans import their maids from the Philippines, Sri Lanka and Indonesia.

Typically, having virtually won the race, Singapore is not resting on its laurels. Under the new, more velvet-gloved, regime of Goh Chock Tong, the concerns for gracious living, leisure and recreation, personal freedoms, literature and the arts, history, environmental and heritage conservation, all of which come naturally to affluent societies, have at last been given more room to breathe than in the past.

Singaporeans are urbane, well-traveled and well used to hosting the seven million tourists visiting their country each year. They will receive you warmly, providing only that you do not step on their toes by criticizing them or their country.

—Ilsa Sharp

Opposite: *The gardens overlooking Singapore's harbor: a favorite backdrop for wedding photographs.* **Below:** *Chinatown's streets becomes a bazaar during the Chinese New Year celebrations in January/February.*

PEOPLE

Island of Cultural Contrasts

When visitors touch down at Singapore's ultra-modern Changi Airport, their first impressions are fashioned by the high-tech buildings, and the orderliness of the beautifully-manicured gardens. These impressions are soon followed by the realization that this small island bustles with people of various races. How surprised they would be to learn that just 170 years ago, the land they are standing on was both hilly and swampy, devoid of any permanent buildings, and inhabited by a few hundred *orang laut,* or sea people, who made this tropical isle their home.

Today, Singapore and its surrounding islands has about 2.8 million inhabitants, but the number swells annually as some 7 million visitors pass through the island for business and leisure. Together, they contribute to making Singapore one of the most densely-populated countries in the world with a total of

over 5,200 people per square kilometer. Why was there such a phenomenal increase in population when most countries have increased their numbers no more than tenfold?

The early history of Singapore tells of its dominance by various sultans who at times settled in the nearby Riau Islands or in neighboring Johor. Singapore, with its low-lying hills and swampy shores was not a particularly attractive place to live, although a few enterprising Chinese had established small plantations of gambier and pepper. The seafaring *orang laut* who roamed the region, created shore settlements and came and went as the whim took them.

However, in 1819 when Stamford Raffles established a trading post on Singapore, records show that there were 30 Chinese, although this information was gleaned more by hearsay than an official count. It was not until 1860 that a census of population was made and by that time the handful of inhabitants had swelled to a grand total of 80,792.

A mecca for Asian migrants

This radical change in demographics occurred as under British rule Singapore prospered rapidly as a port and attracted waves of migrants from nearby territories and from mainland China. Malays from the peninsula were not slow to recognize the opportunities and moved southward with the wave of Chinese migration. Just three years after Raffles first landed, Malays comprised some 60% of the 10,683 inhabitants of Singapore but with the influx of Chinese from the mainland the proportions were soon to change.

By mid-century, migration was a well-organized affair that included women as well as men. By the 1860s the Chinese became the majority and that ratio has continued till today: they now comprise 76% of the population.

Arriving with Raffles in 1819 were 120 Indian soldiers and several Indian clerical assistants. Scope for work was wide and others soon followed from Malayan Penang, India and Ceylon. When Singapore became a penal station in 1823, the British transported a few hundred convicts who were put to work constructing buildings, and indentured laborers were shipped from southern India to work for the government. Entrepreneurs, too, moved from Bengal, Gujarat and Punjab, and so the mix of Indians from the subcontinent was established. Other major groups attracted to the burgeoning isle included the neighboring Javanese, Bugis, Balinese and peoples from Sumatra.

By the end of the century, Singapore had become a thriving entrepôt and a well established settlement, and its success continued to attract migrants. Because many of the settlers came to the island without families, it was inevitable that some intermarriage would occur. Single Chinese married Malay women and a new group of people, *peranakans*, was created. Individually referred to as either *nonya* for women, or *baba* for men, the *peranakans* have their own, characteristic style of dress, customs, and a delicious hybrid cuisine. Westerners married Asians and the offspring of these unions became the Eurasians.

A cosmopolitan society

Attracted by its cosmopolitan atmosphere and the opportunities for work, more and more foreigners have come on a strictly controlled, temporary basis to Singapore. The Asian faces one sees on the streets today may belong to the Japanese, Thai, Filipino or Korean communities, all of which live and work in the republic for a finite period of time. In addition, expatriate English, Australian, American, French, German and New Zealanders form small but strong communities here.

Thus the basis for the remarkable mix of people that make up the rich fabric of Singaporean society was established, each bringing to the island their own culture as well as customs, religion and mythology.

The Hokkien, Cantonese and Teochew ancestors of today's Singaporean Chinese came from southern China, bringing their Buddhist, Taoist and Confucian beliefs. Although the majority of Chinese follow these faiths, a large number are Christian.

Much has been done to integrate the different races to form a homogenous Singaporean identity, and the policies that have fashioned this have largely succeeded. Young people are proud to be Singaporean, irrespective of race, and now intermix freely. The days when the Chinese, the Malays and the Indians each lived in different districts are largely gone, as the same racial ratios that contribute to the total population are followed in allocations in housing estates and educational institutes. One interesting outcome of this melange of backgrounds is the emergence of a local English dialect, Singlish, which is peppered with Malay and Chinese words.

Because the dynamics that have created Singapore are still at work today, the country and its people, continue to change. Singapore does not stagnate, nor will its people.

—*Fiona Nichols*

Opposite: *This Malay leaves his shoes outside the door, a habit of all Asian Singaporeans.*
Above: *Indian women wear red sarees to signify their married status.*

FESTIVALS

Preservation of Age-Old Traditions

Although Singaporeans commemorate at least 20 festivals, only 10 of these are official holidays as one of the sacrifices in the strive for economic success was a reduction in the number of public holidays. But this has not affected the survival of many time-honored festivals and the nation's cultural diversity presents a fascinating showcase with celebrations happening every month.

As many festivals follow lunar calendars the dates change from year to year, so it is best to check at tourist information offices for dates and venues.

Starting from the beginning of the Roman calendar, New Year's Day, January 1, is celebrated at midnight with fireworks displays over the Esplanade. Thaiponggal, on January 14, is a South Indian thanksgiving celebration when devotees offer rice, vegetables, sugar cane and spices to their deities. In the tem-ples, particularly the Perumal Temple on Serangoon Road, they sing and chant prayers to the accompaniment of bells, clarinets, drums and conch shells.

Thaipusam, held during January or February, is the most colorful and dramatic Hindu festival. Held in honor of the deity Lord Subramaniam, it is a time of penance and rejoicing. On festival day, male devotees enter into a trance-like state, pierce their bodies with skewers and the hooks of the *kavadi*—a metal wheel decorated with peacock feathers—and then walk in procession from Serangoon Road's Perumal Temple to the Chettiar Temple on Tank Road.

Chinese New Year, also known as the Lunar New Year, held during January or February, is celebrated for 15 days until the final day known as Chap Goh Mei.

On Chinese New Year's Eve, Chinatown's streets are packed with hawkers and throngs of customers. During the holiday, the Chinese visit relatives and friends, don new clothes and shoes, and present money packets, or *ang pau*, to younger relatives. Traditional dishes are eaten, and lion and dragon dances are performed. The celebrations end with a Chingay Parade of colorful floats, stilt-walkers, dancers and acrobats along Orchard Road.

Hari Raya Puasa, the major Muslim festival which marks the end of the fasting month, or Ramadan, occurs in April or March. The

Malay areas of Geylang Serai, Bussorah Street and Arab Street are packed with food stalls selling special delicacies, and the shops are crammed with fabrics, carpets and clothing. Muslims celebrate with prayers, then after the traditional feast they don new clothes and visit relatives and friends.

Later in April, the Chinese celebrate Qing Ming when they visit graveyards, and offer food and burn joss sticks to honor their deceased ancestors. Good Friday is a public holiday when Christians attend special church services.

In May, Vesak Day commemorates Buddha's birth, enlightenment and death. At Buddhist temples, saffron-robed monks chant prayers and distribute food to the poor. Pigeons are set free and devotees bring donations to the temple.

In June, the Dragon Boat Races are held in honor of the poet Qu Yuan, who committed suicide by drowning. Dragon boat teams from all over the world converge here for the annual races. Also in this month, Muslims celebrate Hari Raya Haji, which commemorates the Haj or pilgrimage to Mecca. Muslims gather for prayers, and sheep and bullocks are ritually slaughtered and the meat is distributed to the poor.

July or August sees the Festival of the Hungry Ghosts, the seventh month of the lunar calendar, when Chinese believe that the restless souls of the dead roam the earth. To appease these unhappy spirits, bonfires of joss paper are burnt and grand street operas, known as *wayang*, are held.

Every August 9, National Day, Singapore's independence is celebrated with a grand parade and fireworks. Later, in August or September, the Mooncake Festival is held when the Chinese exchange mooncakes: sweet pastries stuffed with red bean or lotus-seed paste. This festival is also known as the Lantern Festival, and colorful lanterns are lit during the celebrations.

The Birthday of the Monkey God, is celebrated in October at the Monkey God Temple on Eng Hoon Street. A sedan chair, believed to be possessed by the deity, is carried in procession, flanked by mediums who slash their bodies with blades. Another Chinese celebration, the Festival of the Nine Emperor Gods, is held over nine days in September/October, when it is believed the gods visit the earth to grant good fortune.

Kusu, an offshore island, is the venue for a month-long pilgrimage in October/November, observed by both Malays and Chinese, which has its roots in two legends. In one, the island was once a turtle rescued by a Malay and a Chinese fisherman. The other legend concerns the deity Tua Pekong, who saved the lives of an epidemic-stricken crew.

From October through November, three Hindu festivals are celebrated. The first, Navarathiri, which means "nine nights", takes place at Tank Road's Chettiar Temple and devotees celebrate with traditional dances and a procession. The next, Thimithi, or Fire Walking Festival, is enacted at the Sri Mariamman Temple on South Bridge Road, where devotees, protected by prayers and faith, walk bare-footed across a four-meter pit of red-hot coals. The third, also a public holiday, is Deepavali, the Festival of Lights, when Hindus celebrate the victory of good over evil. Houses are gaily lit, and devotees throng the temples.

The year ends with Christmas, when Orchard Road becomes a sea of lights and colorful decorations, and Singaporeans celebrate with a shopping and partying spree which continues through to New Year's Eve.

—*Yeow Mei Sin*

Opposite: *A Chinese opera group known as "A Pair of Flying Swallows" performs in a Singapore street theater.*
Below: *His chest pierced by dozens of metal skewers, a Thaipusam penitent prepares to make his pilgrimage.*

SPIRIT MEDIUMS

Mediators Between God and Men

Midnight, on a narrow lane, people gather around a circle on the pavement, its circumference delineated by a white cord. Facing each other across the circle are a silent adolescent boy holding a black, triangular flag marked with eight trigrams of protection, and a white satin-clad medium wearing the tall, squared-off hat of Twa Ya Peh, the opium god.

Lit by candles, the circle is piled high with offerings: stacks of gold leafed rice paper charms; oranges, pears and limes; bowls of water and rice; five brown eggs painted with human features; a tiny wooden coffin with a needle-sharp spike fitted lengthwise through it.

The excorcist

Singapore's Chinese spirit mediums are intermediaries between gods and men, vehicles for the gods to act on earth. Sia Chai has been a medium for over 30 years. Recently a

BARBARA ANELLO

couple sought his advice as their son was possessed by a female ghost. He wouldn't eat, wouldn't speak, couldn't sleep. An exorcism was suggested to force the ghost out from the boy and return it to the spirit realm.

Assistants bustled about making preparations. One explained, "We begin with a chant to the Five Generals. We ask them to tell the opium god that we need his help. Only then will he come and enter the medium." Twa Yeh Peh prefers offerings of Guinness Stout and cigarettes. Some gods are vegetarian, some abstain from intoxicants. The opium god indulges.

While the assistants chant a deep, slow dirge, the medium enters trance. Slowly at first, he sways then he swings like a see-saw. The medium's dance is controlled fury. A trace of blood drips from his tongue, cut to inscribe characters on charm papers.

Trapping the ghost

Tenderly, he washes the boy's face with a blue cloth soaked in holy water. Drawing back, in a series of tai-chi-like moves, he proceeds to wrest the demon from the boy, pulling it forward with his outstretched hand, drawing it toward his own body. He crumples to the ground in a huddled heap with a gutteral animal snarl, a primeval, spine-tingling shriek. The boy sits motionless, perched on a stool, the crowd stunned into stillness for a frozen moment. The medium has impaled the unseen ghost onto the needle and shoved it into the tiny wooden coffin.

It is over. The medium wakes from trance and the boy and his family walk off to catch a taxi. Later, the temple assistants were asked about the boy. "Back to normal," they replied.

Gods for every occasion

Spirit mediums, known in Hokkien as *tangki's*, or "divining youth," are an intrinsic part of popular Chinese religion which encompasses Taoism, Shenism (*shen* means "deity"), ancestral veneration and Buddhism, with a sprinkling of Christian and Hindu elements. Popular Taoist gods represent nearly every facet of physical and psychological life: city god, kitchen god, god of walls, baby god, seven-year-old god, god of war and of poetry Beloved rulers and warriors were deified upon death, over generations, as history became myth and myth a history of the divine.

Rebels, renegades and criminals whose struggle against false, cruel authority touched the hearts of the people might also achieve godhood. Like the "Hanged Man" of

the Tarot, these were men who sacrificed themselves to bring about spiritual transformation in the world. The opium god is a "hanged god". So is Jesus.

In an elaborate iconographical system, each god, spirit or demon is identified by color, clothing, weapons and position in the multi-leveled hierarchies of heaven and hell. Gods and spirits can manifest in our world and exert an active influence for good or ill on the events of our lives.

It's not hard to find a medium. Some are associated with Buddhist and Taoist temples. Some operate from small roadside shrines, easily recognizable by the black triangular flags out front bearing the *pa kua*, the eight trigrams of the I Ching. On the front sidewalk shrine, the tiger stalks around an incense-filled urn. Yang counterpart to the Yin dragon, the tiger keeps the *kuei* (malicious spirits) from entering the temple. The open front door reveals an elaborate, tiered altar, crowded with hand-carved wooden images of the gods, bright with paint and gold leaf.

Trance and mortification

The Chinese lunar calendar marks full and new moon birthdays of the gods and other significant days when mediums perform in streets and temple courtyards. Some flail barbed-wire balls about their backs and shoulders, other wield blades as big as meat cleavers. Hot iron balls are kicked from medium to medium in a demonic soccer match. Although mortification is the most dramatic part of a spirit medium's activity, it's probably the least significant part.

Many mediums never practice any form of mortification at all. Most female mediums do not. Its purpose is to make visible the medium's state of trance, to give tangible proof that he is indeed inhabited by a deity. How else could he be master over fire, oblivious to physical pain? How could he insert hooks through flesh, pierce flesh without bleeding?

People have their own reasons for visiting a medium. They believe in the gods. They hear, through word of mouth, that the medium can heal illness or predict the future. Perhaps they have exhausted all other possible remedies for their problem before they decide to take it to the gods. Most usually try Western medicine before consulting a medium for a remedy, but if it doesn't work or is inappropriate, they may consult a medium.

The chosen ones

These vehicles for the gods may be plumbers, electricians, hawkers, housewives or mothers, but what sets these people apart from the ordinary is that they are chosen as vessels for the gods. While in trance, they are entered by one or more of the great pantheon of Taoist gods.

The god, acting through the medium, can advise, administer medicine, change *kuay oon* (bad luck) into good, subdue demons and deal with the whole range of problems that we mortals generate with such wild abandon on this karmic wheel of life.

—*Barbara Anello*

Opposite: *Brandishing a sword this youthful medium performs at a temple in Owen Road.*
Above, left: *The medium, dressed in green robes, gives advice while under trance.*
Below: *This medium performs a symbolic dance beside a bonfire of sacred papers.*

ARCHITECTURE

Pockets of Old Amid the Brand New

In the 1960s, before the demolisher's hammer put paid to much of Singapore's traditional architecture, the urban areas were dominated by highly-decorative, terrace-style shophouses and townhouses. This distinctive style known variously as Singapore Eclectic, Straits Chinese Baroque, or Palladian Chinese, combined rococo plasterwork, Malay wood carvings, European wall tiles, Chinese roof tiles, and Portuguese-style shutters.

Visitors may easily imagine that Singapore's architecture now consists only of high-rise apartments and shopping complexes, but surprisingly, there are still quite a few pockets of traditional streetscapes. These surviving architectural legacies are reminders of the not too distant past when Singapore was one of Asia's most exotic ports of call.

Stamford Raffles, Singapore's founder, started the trend back in the 1820s by decree-ing that shophouses must be constructed of masonry with tiled roofs—to guard against fire. His other public requirement which made such a lasting impression on the streetscape was the "five-foot-way", known in Malay as *kaki lima*, a continuous covered passage formed by the second floor overhanging the first, which afforded protection from the merciless equatorial sun and the torrential afternoon downpours.

Many early traders were wealthy Straits Chinese who had made their fortunes in the Straits Settlements of the Malay Peninsula. When they moved their businesses to Singapore, they imported the eclectic urban architecture that already existed in Melaka and Penang which utilized Chinese, Malay, Portuguese, Dutch and English influences. Elements shared by shophouses in all the Straits Settlements are five-foot ways, facades decorated with bas-relief plasterwork, jalousies—literally from the French for "jealousy"—slatted window shutters to provide ventilation and privacy, Chinese tiled-roofs, and ornate eaves, balustrades, pilasters and other baroque embellishments, and delightful combinations of pastel colorings.

Townhouses were built in the same fashion, but the ground-floor shopfront was taken over by the formal sitting room entered by the *pintu pagar*, literally "fence door," a heavily-carved half door which provided privacy when the *pintu besar*, or main door, was open.

Directly in front of the door was the family ancestral altar, usually a carved and gilded affair presided over by stern-faced ancestor portraits. Most houses have small frontages, but are surprisingly large inside.

Geomancy and symbolism

Chinese architectural traditions have always been involved with *feng sui*, or geomancy, and these townhouses were no exception. South was the preferred direction to face as this was the most harmonious situation. All houses

had at least one inner courtyard, known as air-wells, which apart from giving light and ventilation also facilitated the collection of rain water which brings good luck. Fish-shaped drainpipes, symbolizing "plenty", would channel the water towards the front of the house, believed to mean "wealth wisely spent," rather than to the back of the house where it would be "wasted wealth."

Symbolism was rampant in all decorative features as well as the coloring. Bats denote happiness, deer symbolize high status and wealth, cranes are for longevity and pheasants mean joy. Phoenix birds symbolizing "marital bliss" and peony blossoms for "eternal springtime" were the favorite symbols of the Straits Chinese. Colors were also very important, and both the Malays and the Straits Chinese loved pink—a sign of good fortune, and green—which symbolizes spring and peace.

If it hadn't been for tourism, most of these streets of remaining shophouses, and their residential equivalents, would have been history years ago. Singapore's town-planners only stopped their wholesale demolitions when they realized that travelers were bypassing their city for the more traditional towns of Melaka and Penang. When the first restored shophouses, known as Peranakan Place, opened on Orchard Road they were an overnight tourist success, and now many older buildings have preservation orders on them.

Colorful and attractive, the newly-restored shophouses of Tanjong Pagar, south of Chinatown, now house trendy boutiques, and are fashionable business addresses, but they are a trifle too sterile. However, there are still many traditional terrace houses and shops which still house their original inhabitants, and retain the character of old Singapore.

Emerald Hill Road, pronounced a preservation area in 1981, has 112 terrace houses built from 1902 to 1930. Despite being designed by 13 different architects, the streetscape is an aesthetic blend of richly detailed townhouses. To get there, walk up the side road through Peranakan Place on Orchard Road.

Chinatown, particularly in the old grid around Pagoda, and Terenganu Streets, has many fine examples of two- and three-storey shophouses with five-foot ways in an architectural style similar to the old Portuguese colonies of Macao and Melaka.

Along Desker Road, off Serangoon Road, are turn-of-the-century shophouses painted in delicate greens and blues, featuring fretwork eaves, decorative jalousies, and large arched windows bordered by neoclassical pilasters.

Some of the most ornate Singapore baroque shophouses still survive in the old Malay area of Geylang Road east of the city, and in the neighboring *lorongs* (lanes). The facades are covered with decorative tiles and an over-abundance of plaster bas-reliefs featuring Grecian urns, Chinese mythological characters and fruit and flowers. Also on the east coast are the picturesque terrace houses of Joo Chiat Road, dating from the 1920s, which feature Doric columns and beautiful windows.

Opposite: *Swing doors, known as* pintu pagar, *give privacy to townhouses when the main door is open.* **Above, left:** *Fanlights and slatted jalousies are features of Singapore's baroque-style shophouses.* **Above, right:** *Roses add an English touch to this tiled facade in Chinatown.*

FOOD

Feasts in Asia's Capital of Cuisine

As a tiny and unusually cosmopolitan island, Singapore has an extraordinary variety of food ranging from simple Asian peasant fare to the courtly cuisine of imperial China, and the exotic flavors of east-meets-west haute cuisine. If Singapore is not the culinary capital of Asia, then it certainly ought to be.

To understand the nation, one has to understand the Singaporean's passion for food—something akin to a national pastime. The average citizen eats between four and seven times a day—little but often. A typical day might start with a savoury rice porridge, noodles or a filling Indian *roti canai* and the day unfurls around the appetite. Soups for lunch. Take-away fried rice or tropical fruits for a small snack. Maybe a dessert of sickly sweet cakes or ice shavings topped with coconut milk. A curry, or seafood extravaganza could well be an evening meal and

there is always a late night nibble before heading home.

Singaporeans think nothing of driving across the island to sample their favorite dish at a popular cafe. More often than not they eat at local hawker centers, selecting an inexpensive meal from one of the stalls and sitting at communal round tables. Because of the cosmopolitan ethnic mix, there is a veritable potpourri of cuisines and what is called Singaporean food is the result of a felicitous blend of Indian, Malay and Chinese styles. The Chinese brought the wok, with rice and noodles (which Marco Polo borrowed and called "spaghetti"); Indians brought spices and thick sauces; and the Malays incorporated seafood and vegetables to form a style of cuisine that is hot and spicy, eaten in small quantities with rice.

Being an island nation, seafood is particularly important here: and this usually means the hot and fiery variety. Whilst these dishes can be eaten in a sophisticated city hotel, they are much more fun and easier to enjoy in a hands-on meal under the stars, down by the sea.

Along Singapore's east coast there are a number of seafood restaurants whose range of expertise extends much further than chilli and pepper crab, drunken prawns, deep-fried squid, Thai-style fish and steamed shrimp, whence the fish recently came. Here, there are no nouvelle cuisine decorations and minimalist portions. The food is wholesome and

fresh (it is still alive in a tank when you arrive at the restaurant and if you have the heart, you can select your own fish, crabs and prawns), and social etiquette encourages eating with the right hand.

Then there is satay, a dish favored originally by the island's Muslim neighbors. These fine kebabs of beef, chicken or nowadays pork, skewered, marinated and then cooked over a charcoal fire, are one of Singapore's finest delicacies. Dipped in a rich peanut sauce, and consumed with cubes of

fragrant steamed rice, they appeal to even the most jaded of palates.

And what the Chinese didn't bring to Singaporean cuisine, the Indians added. Originally it was the southern Indians who came, bringing their spicy tropical preferences, coconut and vegetarian curries served on banana leaves; then northern Indians and Punjabis arrived with recipies for their rich traditional cuisine that relied on baking and dry cooking. Fishhead curry is a tremendous favorite in Singapore and one finds that Sundays, the day when most locals eat out with family and friends, are inevitably popular days for this dish. The cheeks are the best part, and the eyes a delicacy!

Serangoon Road, the part of town known as little India, is the place for traditional, South Indian banana-leaf curries—some of the best value menus in town. Custom dictates you eat with your right hand, but restauranteurs will happily bring spoons and forks for the less adept diners.

While there are plenty of Chinese and Indian restaurants around Singapore, there are far fewer Malay restaurants even though the cuisine has immense merits. Much Malay food includes the usual Asian ingredients—chillis, ginger, tumeric, garlic and coconut—but features more stewed dishes than Chinese. Indonesian dishes offer many similarities to Malay. *Nasi campur*—rice with

a selection of meats, fish and vegetables—is common to both countries but the Indonesians tend to go easier on the chilli and heavier on the coconut flavor. The most popular style of cuisine is the very spicy Padang style from Sumatra. It is Indonesia's answer to *nasi campur*, and you pay according to the number of portions consumed. Large chilli-sauted prawns, rich beef *rendang* stew, spicy vegetables, eggs with chilli sauce, mouth-watering chicken curries and spiced or fried fish, all characterize *nasi padang*.

Smart Chinese dining is plentiful in Singapore. The decision lies with which style of cuisine. Cantonese, Shanghainese, Pekinese, Hainanese, Hunanese, Taiwanese, Teochew, or Sichuan—these are just for starters. There are also herbal restaurants where meals are quasi-medicinal with dishes cooked in healing herbs. Alternatively, Singaporeans in the know will head for restaurants where restorative health is promised from such culinary items as bear's paw, sea slugs, bull's penis and, in the pre-SPCA days, live monkey's brains and snake soup. Not for the faint hearted!

Singapore's dining options, however, extend far beyond the boundaries of Southeast Asia and Asia. Korean, Japanese, Vietnamese and Thai restaurants abound. Fine French, Italian, Swiss, Russian, German, Spanish, Lebanese and even Mexican restaurants can be found in the republic. But the best tip is to do as the locals do: eat Singaporean. *Selamat makan*: enjoy your meal.

—*Fiona Nichols*

Opposite: Chinese chicken rice, Malay satay sticks and an Indian curry. **Above, left:** Banana leaves serve as plates for curry and rice in this outdoor restaurant in Little India. **Above, right:** Noodles, eaten with spoon and chopsticks, are a favorite snack at any time of the day.

COLONIAL SIGHTS

A Tour of the Colonial Past

When Stamford Raffles stepped ashore in 1819 to plant the East India Company's flag—in effect, the British flag—he was presented with an imperial planner's dream, a virtually blank sheet of paper on which to design a do-it-yourself colonial city. There were scarcely any bothersome local buildings which had to be drawn around, or demolished, except for the Malay Temenggong or Viceroy's small village at the mouth of the Singapore River, which Raffles promptly moved to a less central location.

The impact of the empire

"Colonials" get a bad press nowadays. Yet men like Raffles were imbued with high and serious purpose. Of course, commerce and dominion motivated him and his ilk, yet there was far more to Raffles than mere money-grubbing. Steeped in Malay history, culture

and language, Raffles was familiar with the romantic mythology shrouding Singapore's early history. It was his extensive background reading that brought him to the tiny island in the first place. To underline his own, and Britain's, place in local history, he cannily chose to build his own bungalow, Singapore's first Government House, on "Bukit Larangan," or "Forbidden Hill," as Fort Canning was then called. Sacred and taboo to the Malays for centuries, the hill had been the preserve of their kings. Raffles no doubt hoped that British rule would acquire for itself some of the semi-magical kudos attached to this hill if he built his residence there.

Like all the finest British colonials, Raffles burned with missionary zeal to bring the light of civilization, education and justice, and to some extent, Christianity, to his native charges.

A surprising number of the men gathered around Raffles were Scots—St. Andrew's Cathedral was named after their patron saint. These were the men who shaped the city, particularly in that colonial heartland radiating from the Padang, the seafront cricket ground still at the city center today. But none more than George Drumgold Coleman, Superintendent of Public Works, who worked in Singapore from 1822-1844. Coleman Street, next to the City Hall, is named after him. He set much of the architectural tone of early Singapore, with his taste for classical Palladian style. Skilfully, he adapted this style to the tropics with features like wide verandahs for shade and rain-shelter, and louvred windows to filter the intense sunlight.

Initially, however, central Singapore was the creation of Raffles' own fertile brain. In typical British style, his town plan was premised on concepts of class, caste, creed and race. He allocated separate spaces to merchants, craftsmen, and cultivators, and to the Europeans, Chinese, Malays, Bugis (from Indonesia), Arabs and Chuliahs (South Indian Muslims).

Raffles' mark on the city is still visible today. For his own kind, Raffles reserved the Padang area. In those days, the sea ran at the very edge of the cricket ground. Reclamation first extended the land in 1890, and again in the 1980s. Besides cricket matches, many major events of national importance took place on the Padang—the rounding up of British civilians under Japanese occupation, the subsequent surrender of the Japanese, and the later political rallies for independence.

For the early British settlers, the Padang was a social magnet, and just before dinner, the pallid European wives and daughters, perspiring in crinolines, bonnets and gloves, would come here for their daily social ritual, the "Turn", when they would take their horse-drawn carriages along the Esplanade waterfront, salute and greet one another, stroll on the greens, and eye potential husbands exercising their mounts.

It is not easy for young Singaporeans today to admit or even to perceive it, but the tentacles of the British Empire still reach deep into their psyches—in their language, their legal system, in their sports, and in the way they run their social clubs. And not least, in the surviving grand old buildings that still encircle the Padang.

A Padang perambulation

Start your walk standing on Cavenagh Bridge. Ahead is the tower of the Victoria Memorial Hall in Empress Place, and behind, is Fullerton Building, housing the GPO, just as it did when it was first built in 1928. On the same site was Fort Fullerton, constructed in 1830 to defend the city. Beside the Fullerton Building, is Battery Road, named after the heavy gun battery arming Fort Fullerton. It leads into Raffles Place, first named Commercial Square when it was created by Raffles in 1823 by levelling a hill and filling in a swamp. This was the meeting place for the merchants of his day, and it is still a center of big business

today—the Stock Exchange is housed here.

When Raffles arrived, this section of the Singapore River was littered with skulls, the macabre remains of the victims of early pirate raiders. Cavenagh Bridge itself was assembled in 1869, from steel parts manufactured in Scotland—before that, one had to cross the river by ferry. By 1910, traffic across the bridge had swollen, with rickshaws and bullock-carts trundling alongside electric tramcars and the first motor cars. Hence the construction of the new Anderson Bridge right next door, reducing Cavenagh Bridge to a mere footbridge. You can still see the sign there announcing that cattle, horses and vehicles exceeding 3-cwts (hundredweight) are prohibited from crossing.

Cross the bridge into Empress Place, named after Queen Victoria of England, to view the Dalhousie Obelisk of 1850 to your left by the river, and the magnificently restored Empress Place Building, once known as the Government Buildings and originally built as the Court House in 1864. This grand old neoclassical building is now a museum

Opposite: A turbaned Sikh welcomes guests at Raffles Hotel, watering-hole for the rich and famous for over a hundred years. *Below:* On the banks of the Singapore River, against a backdrop of old and new architectural styles, the statue of Stamford Raffles surveys the city that he founded.

under renovation. It will reopen in 1998/99 as part of the Asian Civilisations Museum.

Ahead of you are the Victoria Memorial Hall and Theatre, complete with chiming clock tower. The theater, on the left side, dates from 1862 and was originally the Town Hall. The memorial hall, the right-hand half, is now the concert hall home of the Singapore Symphony Orchestra. It was built in 1905 as a tribute to Queen Victoria.

The 2.4-m (8ft) tall statue of Sir Stamford Raffles stands proudly outside the Victoria buildings. First erected in 1887, it bears a plaque praising Raffles, "to whose foresight and genius, Singapore owes its existence and prosperity."

Walking towards the back of the Victoria buildings, towards Parliament Lane, you come to Parliament House on your left, the oldest surviving government building in Singapore, on the site of the original Temenggong's camp in 1819. The core of the building is the house built for British merchant John Argyle Maxwell in 1827 by architect Coleman, fitted with a small lookout tower. Parliament now sits in an extended version of his home, which he first rented to government in 1841.

Behind the fence just past Parliament is a tall bronze Elephant Statue, a gift to Singapore from King Chulalongkorn (or Rama V) of Siam, now Thailand, in 1871. As you stand with the elephant on your left, you look straight ahead down High Street, Singapore's very first road, hacked out of the jungle by Raffles' officers in 1819.

Turning right up St. Andrew's Road, the domed Supreme Court on your left dates from 1939. Note the elegant murals above the grand entrance, by Italian artist Cavaliere Rudolfo Nolli. On the right, the Singapore Cricket Club building comprises a core dating from 1884, with additions in 1910 and 1921. It offers all sports—not just cricket—and is a favorite watering hole for local Indian lawyers, and Chinese and expatriate businessmen.

Next to the Supreme Court on the left is City Hall, once known as the Municipal Offices, completed in 1929. City Hall got its name only in 1952, when Britain first conferred the title of "city" on Singapore.

At the other end of the Padang is another sports club building that has its roots in the 19th century, the Singapore Recreation Club. This was where the all-white and largely British members of the Cricket Club allowed the "coloreds," the Eurasians, to have their own sports club. To this day, there is a strong Eurasian flavor to the "SRC".

Turn left from City Hall and walk up Coleman Street. On your right is the early English-style St. Andrew's Cathedral, completed in 1862 and built largely by Indian convicts. It is coated with a unique plaster made of shell lime, egg white, sugar and coconut

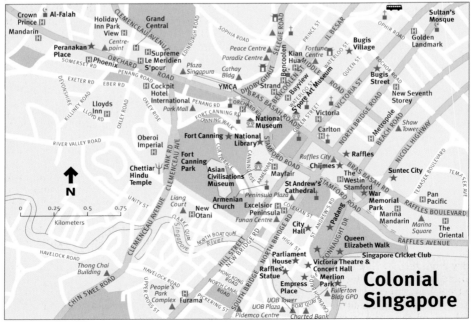

Colonial Singapore

water, hand polished with rock crystal. Cross North Bridge Road and walk up Coleman Street to Hill Street. On your right is Coleman's most exquisite creation, the Armenian Church, Singapore's first Christian church, built in 1835 for the small but prosperous Armenian community. To your left, is the fancifully turreted, red-brick Central Fire Station, built at the turn of the century. Further up Canning Rise is the Masonic Hall, headquarters for the Freemasons, dated 1879.

No. 39 Armenian Street houses the Asian Civilisations Museum. The first wing of the museum is dedicated to magnificent manifestations of Chinese art and culture.

A sacred hill

Walk up Canning Rise, past the Anglo-Chinese Primary School on your left (on this site since 1886), and climb the next staircase up the hillside parkland to your left which leads to Fort Canning, the once forbidden hill of the kings. On the hill, you can view the historic headstones of the colonial Christian Cemetery dating from 1823, including that of architect Coleman, besides the Malay shrine and grave of Iskandar Shah, the last king of Temasek, 14th-century Singapore. Note also the elegant Gothic Gateway designed in 1844 by Captain Charles Faber. Also on the hill are British army buildings from the 1930s, now a cultural center, and the original underground bunker used by the British General Percival during War War II to direct the unsuccessful defence of Singapore against the Japanese.

Retracing your steps down Canning Rise, take the staircase through the carpark of the distinctive red-brick National Library, built in the 1950s. You can walk through the library grounds onto Stamford Road. Next to the library is the elegant, silver-domed National Museum and Art Gallery complex, dating from 1887, and well worth a stopover.

Cross Stamford Road, then turn into Queen Street for the Cathedral of the Good Shepherd designed by Denis McSwiney, a pupil of Coleman, in the 1840s. Ahead, on Bras Basah Road, is the silvery dome of St. Joseph's Institution school of 1852, now the Singapore Art Museum. At Bras Basah Road, turn right. This road was named after the Malay for "wet rice"—traders used to bring the rice up the Stamford Canal on boats and dry it on the canal banks. The canal has been filled in only in recent times. On Victoria Street lies Chijmes with its five neo-Gothic styled buildings, including a chapel with beautiful stained-glass panels, and Caldwell House,

the oldest free-standing house in Singapore. This recently restored four-acre complex offers various restaurants as well as shops and boutiques and is an oasis of tranquility right in the heart of town.

Passing Raffles City on your right you encounter Raffles Hotel on your left. Time for a tea-break in the Tiffin Room or in one of the hotel's shady courtyards, there to dream of the days when the sea lapped the hotel's front steps, and the jazz-bands played for the naughty tea-dances of the 1920s.

Walk around the Beach Road side of Raffles City, cross the Padang and Connaught Drive road to the seafront Queen Elizabeth Walk, formerly the Esplanade.

Along Queen Elizabeth Walk is the Cenotaph monument to honor the dead from both World Wars, and at the end of the seafront walk is the Lim Bo Seng Memorial in honor of a Chinese resistance hero who was tortured to death by the Japanese in 1944. From here you can look across the mouth of the Singapore River to the (sometimes water-spouting) 8-m (26ft) tall statue of the Singapore Merlion, crafted by a local sculptor in 1972—a national symbol created by the Singapore Tourist Promotion Board.

—*Ilsa Sharp*

Above: *This sculpted family sits outside the recently-restored National Museum and Art Gallery built during the colonial era.*

CHINATOWN

A Step Back in Time to Old Singapore

Chinatown is located in the grid of streets running south from the Singapore River, where the early immigrants first came ashore off their cramped and miserable junks after the tortuous journey from China.

Despite ongoing modernization, the area still retains a noisy and colorful ambience of its own. Chinese Singaporeans still shop here for joss paper, lanterns, oil lamps, altar plaques, sweet meats, fresh fish and cheap vegetables. Chinatown's fortunetellers, temple mediums and medicine men still pursue their trade, and calligraphers and letter-writers can occasionally be found along the covered pavements generally known as "five-foot ways".

Chinatown is easily accessible from both Raffles Place and Outram Park MRT stations. From the latter, walk up Eu Tong Sen Street to People's Park Complex and Pearl's Hill

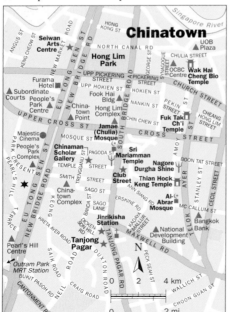

Centre, which is a favorite with locals for electronic goods. Opposite, on Smith Street beside the Chinatown complex, there are numerous shops selling a variety of things Chinese and Asian. They have replaced the clogmakers, maskmakers and artisans that still could be found here a couple of years ago. Walk down Smith Street, cross South Bridge Road and continue into Ann Siang Hill, where you can catch glimpses of the old Chinatown. In one of the first shophouses on the left there is a shop selling a collection of interesting antiques and curios.

Hindu and Chinese temples

North along South Bridge Road is the Sri Mariamman Temple with a staggering amount of Hindu religious figures all fighting to catch the eye on the tower over the entrance. This is Singapore's oldest Hindu temple, and is an important site for Hindu festivals, such as Thaipusam, Thimithi and Deepavali. Around the Sri Mariamman Temple are the streets of old shophouses which give Chinatown its traditionally rustic character.

Take a walk down Pagoda Street, Temple Street and Trengganu Street, and you'll see a side of Singapore fast disappearing. The fortuneteller, cobbler, vegetable seller and letter-writer can still be spotted here and there—even though souvenir shops seem to be taking over.

A good place in which to immerse oneself into the Chinese culture of days gone by is the Chinaman Scholar Gallery at 14B, Terengannu Street. Go up the stairs to the second floor, and you might think you just walked through a time warp. Collector and antique dealer Vincent Tan has recreated the ambience of a Chinese scholar's home from the '30s. Visitors are offered tea as he patiently explains the paraphenalia and old photographs. Open daily from 9 am to 4 pm.

Walk down Cross Street with its flea market, where old men sell all sorts of curios, and turn right into historic Telok Ayer Street. On the right is the Nagore Durgha Shrine, where Palladian doors and Doric columns blend harmoniously with Moorish architecture to give this mosque its characteristic design.

Close by is the Thian Hock Keng Temple, or "Temple of Heavenly Happiness." Among Hokkien Chinese, this is the premier place of worship, and presents a splendid example of Chinese rococo architecture. Hokkien immigrants, disembarking off their junks, made this temple their first destination on Singapore soil where they would light joss sticks to give thanks to the gods for their safe passage.

In 1821, a joss house was built, and today's temple was erected on the same site in 1840. To the left of the Thian Hock Keng Temple are the minarets of the Abrar Mosque. The Tamils used to call this the "Koochoo Pally," which means "small mosque", because its original structure was but a mere thatched hut built in 1827. In 1850, the hut was replaced by the present building.

Preserving the past

In the southern part of Chinatown lies the Tanjong Pagar conservation area—"yuppie Chinatown"—where old shophouses have been revamped into pastel brilliance. Craig Road, Tanjong Pagar Road and Duxton Road all hold a good number of pubs and restaurants done up to the nines. The rows of shops sell handicrafts, artworks, souvenirs and even furniture. Restaurants serve anything from Thai, Chinese, and French to Italian food. In Tanjong Pagar the visitor can still see local craftsmen at work—making clogs, kites and traditional seals.

The picturesque Jinrikisha Station at the corner of Tanjong Pagar Road and Neil Road can be rather misleading, for it now houses a restaurant. Jinrikishas—hand-pulled rickshaws—were a popular mode of transport before World War II, but were then replaced by the bicycle trishaw.

In the center of the commercial district east of Chinatown, between Robinson Road and Shenton Way, is the Lau Pa Sat Festival Market, a classical wrought-iron building dating back to 1894, Singapore's first municipal fish market. Since it's recent restoration it now houses a 24-hour food center.

Chinatown used to have dozens of coffeeshops, and you can still find some, although it is getting harder to be able to sit down on a bentwood chair and sip a cup of potent local coffee placed on a marble table top. These days much of the food is to be found in hawker centers where numerous stalls sell an amazing variety, from fried noodles to pig's intestines. Try the one near the intersection of South Bridge and Maxwell roads. The Kreta Ayer Complex, opposite People's Park Complex, has a hawker center on the second floor, where specialities include *yong tau fu*, beancurd, chicken rice, or *wan ton* noodles. Also worth a look are the various Chinese medicine shops and herbalists that sell an assortment of mind-boggling and exotic remedies.

—Shane Callahan

Below: *Streetside calligraphers are busiest at Chinese New Year, when homes and businesses are decorated with good-luck and long-life messages.*

LITTLE INDIA

Serangoon Road and Arab Street

Indian immigrants first settled around the region of Serangoon Road during early 19th-century British times when they were brought in to construct some of Singapore's most famous landmarks like the Istana—now the President's home, the City Hall and Saint Andrew's Cathedral. Today, this road, and its little side-lanes are still dominated by the Indian community.

There are spice grinders, fortune tellers, goldsmiths, flower-garland vendors, vegetable sellers, tailors, and Indian music-tape vendors. You can pick up hand-crafted bangles or anklets, leather sandals, saris, cooking pots of all shapes and sizes and ornate brass and gold jewellery.

To get to Little India take an MRT train to Dhoby Ghaut, then wander past the Cathay Cinema and up Selegie Road to Serangoon Road. You know you're there once you see

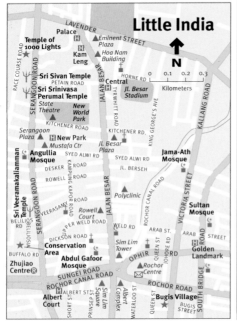

crowded Zhujiao Centre, just past Bukit Timah Road, where people from all over the island come for good deals in groceries and food. It's a great place to see how the customers haggle and also to taste what true local cuisine has to offer.

"Banana-leaf" restaurants

Food is a major preoccupation here. On every street corner hawkers set up shop. Look at the prata seller as he skilfully flips his sheet of dough over and over. The result is bound to be a treat. In most of the Indian restaurants, banana leaves serve as plates. Usually there is no cutlery for one is expected to eat using the fingers of the right hand (the left is considered unclean). Rice is scooped onto your leaf until you call out to stop and various spicy accompaniments of meat, fish or vegetable dishes can be chosen. The ever-popular Komala Vilas' on Serangoon Road is strictly vegetarian, and as well as "banana-leaf" curries they serve delicious Dhosai, a lighter form of fried bread, served with coconut chutney and curry.

Signs of religion are everywhere. Not just in the area's abundant temples, but also in restaurants and shops which all have prominently-displayed portraits of Shiva the destroyer, Hanuman the monkey god, Ganesh the elephant god and Krishna as a baby. Vendors in their tiny corners can also be found selling religious garlands made from jasmine and orchids.

Serangoon Road's Indian temples are colorful, adorned with statues of deities, and bustling with worshippers. The Sri Srinivasa Perumal Temple has broad red and white stripes while the nearby Sri Sivan Temple is gaily decorated with brightly-colored figures. The Sri Rama Temple also has a splendid entrance guarded by giant Hindu gods.

The most noticeable temple on Serangoon Road must be the Sri Veeramakaliamman Temple with its splendid entrance. Around late October, when Deepavali, the Festival of Lights, is celebrated, Serangoon Road is aglow with oil lamps, temples are adorned with floral decorations, and devotees carry the shrines of their deities in procession.

Two blocks north on Race Course Lane stands the Mahatma Gandhi Memorial Hall which had its foundation stone laid by Jawarharlal Nehru, the late Indian prime minister. A solid grey structure stands at the corner of Serangoon Road and Towner Road. The main place of worship for the 18,000 or so Sikhs in Singapore, the Central Sikh

Gurdwara, is also a gathering place for activities with its clinic and library. A prayer hall with a 13-meter-wide dome has enshrined in it the Ganth Sahib, or holy book.

The Chinese have also made their mark in Little India. On Race Course Road is the Leong San See, or Dragon Mountain Temple. Dedicated to Kuan Yin, the Chinese goddess of mercy, the temple has an impressive altar, decorated with birds, flowers and a phoenix. Nearby, the Buddhist Temple of 1,000 Lights houses a 15-meter seated Buddha. The temple is so named because the Buddha is framed by a string of lights.

Unlike much of Singapore, slick shopping malls are not so plentiful here. Old-style shophouses still dominate the streets where the pervading aroma is of exotic spices, where the women are draped in elegant sarees, and men are dressed in the distinctive white *dhoti*. Textiles, in every imaginable hue crowd the shops, and Indian pop-music blasts from the shopfronts.

A good place for electronics, perfumes, and traditional Indian costumes is Serangoon Plaza. On Buffalo Road, a tiny alley leads into a courtyard housing a hawker center and a series of renovated shophouses—another government conservation project. Most of the local residents, however, shy away from the modern-look eatery preferring their old tried-and-tested coffee shops and restaurants.

Arab Street

Turn down Dunlop Street for Abdul Gafoor Mosque, built in 1910, and noted for its framed family tree which traces the line of Muslim prophets. East of here is another interesting ethnic enclave centered around Arab Street, which is famous for traditional Muslim businesses dealing in textiles. rattan goods, perfumes, leatherwares, spices, prayer mats and Indonesian batik.

The area's most prominent landmark is the golden-domed Sultan Mosque on North Bridge Road, named after Sultan Hussein of Singapore, which was constructed in 1924 to replace an earlier mosque funded by Raffles. The little lanes around Arab Street are also worth walking through, especially Jalan Bussorah, which has interesting old houses.

Famous Bugis Street of yore is now an MRT station, but its successor, a recreated version, stands opposite on Cheng Yan Square. The gaudy transvestites have gone, and the new version is a tamer attraction where you can still dine under the stars, and shop for copy watches and souvenirs. The shopping complex Bugis Junction offers streets with a glass roof and air-conditioned comfort.

—*Shane Callahan*

Below: *A Brahmin priest strikes a lookalike pose beside this Hindu deity at a Serangoon Road temple.*

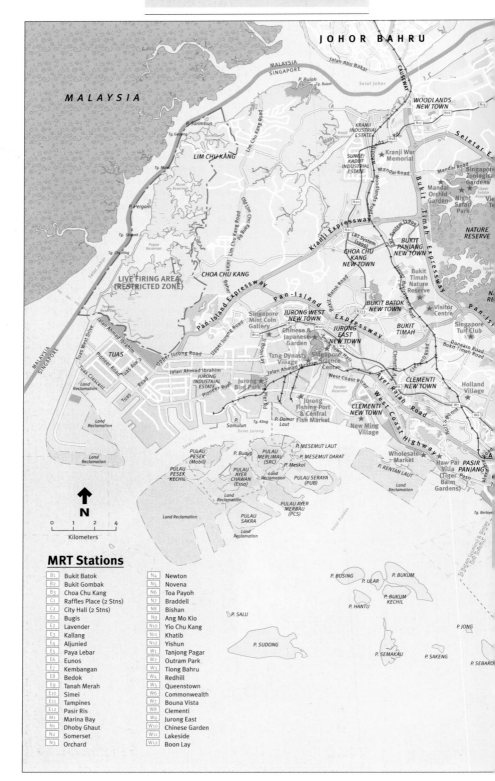

MRT Stations

B1	Bukit Batok
B2	Bukit Gombak
B3	Choa Chu Kang
C1	Raffles Place (2 Stns)
C2	City Hall (2 Stns)
E1	Bugis
E2	Lavender
E3	Kallang
E4	Aljunied
E5	Paya Lebar
E6	Eunos
E7	Kembangan
E8	Bedok
E9	Tanah Merah
E10	Simei
E11	Tampines
E12	Pasir Ris
M1	Marina Bay
N1	Dhoby Ghaut
N2	Somerset
N3	Orchard

N4	Newton
N5	Novena
N6	Toa Payoh
N7	Braddell
N8	Bishan
N9	Ang Mo Kio
N10	Yio Chu Kang
N11	Khatib
N12	Yishun
W1	Tanjong Pagar
W2	Outram Park
W3	Tiong Bahru
W4	Redhill
W5	Queenstown
W6	Commonwealth
W7	Bouna Vista
W8	Clementi
W9	Jurong East
W10	Chinese Garden
W11	Lakeside
W12	Boon Lay

SINGAPORE ISLAND
MALAYSIA

MALAYSIA
SINGAPORE

Selat Johor

MALAYSIA
SINGAPORE

EMBAWANG

YISHUN
NEW TOWN

PULAU
PUGGOL
BARAT

PULAU
PUNGGOL
TIMOR

Tg. Punggol   Tg. Tajam

Tg. Batu Kekek   Tg. Balai

Tg. Chek Jawa

JALAN KAYU

Punggol
Holiday
Camp

PUNGGOL

PULAU
SERANGOON
(Coney Island)

PULAU UBIN   Pulau Ubin

Selat Johor

YO CHU KANG

Punggol
Fishing
Port &
Wholesaler
Fish Market

PULAU
KETAM

Tg. Jelutong

Serangoon Harbour

ANG MO KIO
NEW TOWN

HOUGANG
NEW TOWN

Ang Mo Kio Ave. 3 Hougang Ave 4

Tampines Expressway

PASIR RIS
NEW TOWN

Resort,
Chalets   LOYANG

Batu Puteh
Fairy Point

Changi
Village

CHANGI

Fishing

SERANGOON
NEW TOWN

Tampines Road

Changi
Prison

Reclaimed
Land

THOMSON

Fishing

Crocodile
Farm

Upper Serangoon Road

PAYA
LEBAR

DEFU
INDUSTRIAL
ESTATE

TAMPINES
NEW TOWN

Singapore
Changi Airport

BISHAN
NEW TOWN

Hougang Ave 3

Airport Road

Bedok
Reservoir

SIMEI
NEW TOWN

TOA PAYOH
NEW TOWN

Pan-Island Expressway

BEDOK
NEW TOWN

KIM
CHUAN

BEDOK
NEW TOWN

Siong Lim
Sian Si
Buddhist
Temple

Paya Lebar Way

JALAN
EUNOS
ESTATE

Upper East Coast Road

East Coast Parkway

Malay
Village

Ehang Road

KATONG

East Coast Road

National
Stadium

GEYLANG

OLD KALLANG
AIRPORT
ESTATE

Still Road

East Coast Road

East Coast
Sailing
Club &
Lagoon

Nicoll Highway

Singapore
Indoor
Stadium

TANJONG
RHU

East Coast Parkway

East Coast
Recreation
Centre

UDMC
Holidays
Chalets

Reclaimed Land

Singapore
Crocodilarium

Tg. Rhu

PULAU BRANI
ntre

Buran
Darat

SEE SENTOSA ISLAND INSET

TEKUKOR

P. SERINGAT
(P. RENGET)

P. TEMBAKUL
(KUSU
ISLAND)

P. KEPPEL

Keppel
Shipyard

Cable Car
Towers

Exhibition
Halls

Keppel Channel

East Lagoon

Keppel Channel

World
Trade
Centre

Brani
Terminal
Building

P. BRANI

Singapore
Cruise Centre

Cruise Bay

P. SAKIJANG
PELEPAH
(LAZARUS
ISLAND)

P. SAKIJANG
BENDERA
(ST. JOHN'S ISLAND)

Underwater
World

P. RENGGIS

Fort
Siloso

Siloso
Beach

Ruined City &
Lost Civilization

Asian
Village

Musical
Fountain

CAUSEWAY
BRIDGE

Fountain
Gardens

Rasa Sentosa
Pasar Malam

Fantasy Island

Skating Rink

Maritime Museum

Selat Sengkir

Lake

BURAN
DARAT

Nature Walk
Dragon Trail

Butterfly Park &
World Insectarium

Rare Stone
Museum

Art
Centre

Plant
Nursery

Serapong
Golf Course

SENTOSA

Serapong
Golf Course

Images of
Singapore

Campsite

Playground

Food Village

Central Lagoon

Canoe Center

Sentosa
Golf Club

Tanjong
Golf
Course

Coralarium &
Nature Ramble

Telok
Durian

Tanjong
Beach

| 0 | 0.25 | 0.5 | 0.75 |

Kilometers

N

Sentosa Island

AROUND THE ISLAND

Theme Parks and Offshore Islands

In order to attract tourists to linger longer, Singapore is rapidly developing new attractions, preserving historical ones and introducing new forms of activities. Amid the concrete symbols of progress are nature reserves, beaches, theme parks, offshore islands, and a host of recreation spots. The compact size of the island, a mere 646 km^2 (404 mi^2), together with its excellent public transport system makes getting around an easy affair.

West of the city

A good place to start an island tour is at Mount Faber, off Telok Blangah Road. To get there take the MRT to Tanjong Pagar, then take a taxi. The scenic alternative is to ride up on the cable car from the Jardine Steps Station next to the World Trade Centre. From the summit there are panoramic views of Singapore and its offshore islands. Focus on the port area—you will see why Singapore is ranked as the world's busiest. Take a stroll, rest at the tea house, or take the cable car to Sentosa Island.

From Mount Faber, catch a taxi to Alkaf Mansion, in Telok Blangah Green. Formerly the 19th-century home of the wealthy Alkaff family, it has now been restored into a charming restaurant. The architecture is not purely colonial, but is blended with Asian and Arabic styles. Here, you can lunch or dine in the same rooms which were set for grand dinners and parties during the colonial heydays.

Further west at Pasir Panjang is **Haw Par Villa**, formerly known as Tiger Balm Gardens. Singapore's first theme park was built by the Aw brothers with the profits from their immensely popular Tiger Balm—a medicinal ointment. Open daily from 9 am to 6 pm, the park charges $S16.50 for adults, and $S10.50 for children under 12. Take an SBS bus No 10 or the MRT to Buona Vista, then SBS bus 200. This Chinese mythological theme park presents multi-media shows, boat rides, and animated presentations which bring to life the statues of Chinese gods, goddesses, legends, beasts and demons.

Tang Dynasty Village, Singapore's latest theme park, is further west in Jurong, the huge industrial complex. Open daily from 10 am to 6.30 pm, admission is $S15.45 for adults and $S10.30 for children under 12. To

et there, take the MRT to Lakeside Station, hen board bus No 154 or 240. In this largest Chinese historical and cultural theme park in Asia, architecture, street scenes and activities re recreated from Chang-An, China's Tang ynasty capital (618 to 907 AD).

Nearby are the **Chinese and Japanese Gardens**, open from 9 am to 6 pm. Admission for adults is $S4.50, children nder 12 pay $S2. The Chinese garden, which s Sung Dynasty influenced, is linked by a ridge to the Japanese garden. On the

Chinese side are courtyards, pagodas, fountains, bridges and a river on which visitors an paddle or row boats. At the Penjing Garden are bonzai plants from all over the world. The Japanese Garden features stone anterns, shrubs, hillocks and a tea-house.

Further south, at Jurong Hill is the **Jurong BirdPark**, the largest birdpark in Asia and one of the world's best. Open weekdays from 9 am to 6 pm and 8 am to 6 pm on weekends and public holidays, the park charges $S10.30 for adults, and $S4.12 for children under 12. To get there take the MRT o Boon Lay Station, then take SBS bus Nos 94 or 251 from the interchange. Over 8,000 birds of 600 species are housed here and attractions include the penguin parade, the world's largest collection of Southeast Asian hornbills and a variety of bird shows. Opposite the BirdPark is Jurong Crocodile Paradise, home to 2,500 crocodiles, where visitors can watch crocodile-wrestling shows daily at 10.45 am, 11.45 am, 2 pm, 3 pm and pm. Admission is S$6 for adults and S$3 for children under 12.

Singapore's oldest and most scenic parklands, the **Botanic Gardens**, on the corner of Napier and Cluny Roads, are open daily from 5 am to 12 midnight. To get there take the MRT to Orchard Station, then hail a taxi, walk, or take an SBS bus (Nos 7, 105, 106, 123 or 174) from Orchard Boulevard. Fifty-two hectares of tropical jungle, manicured lawns and beautifully landscaped gardens make the Botanic Gardens a favorite spot for picnics, strolls, workouts or simply a good rest. Over 2,000 plant species grow here, including Brazilian rubber trees, which were introduced to Singapore by Sir Henry Ridley. Once, monkeys roamed the grounds, but they have since been relocated. The orchid pavilion has some 60,000 orchid plants including Singapore's national flower, the Vanda Miss Joaquim.

Northwest of here, more or less in the center of the island, is the **Bukit Timah Nature Reserve**, which covers a 163-m-high hill—Singapore's highest point. On its slopes is a nature reserve of tropical rain forest where monkeys, birds, butterflies, and snakes make their home. Hiking up Bukit Timah Hill is an exhilarating experience, aided by well marked tracks along its slopes. Beneath the canopy of trees, admire the wild orchids, ferns, mosses, vines and creepers that flourish in this 81-hectare forest. From the summit, is a panoramic and unrivalled view of Singapore. To get there take a bus up Bukit Timah Road (No 171 from Scotts Road or Newton MRT) to Eward Circus, then walk up Hindhede Rd. (20 mins) to the reserve.

In the far north is **Mandai Orchid Gardens**. Take the MRT to Ang Mo Kio station, then SBS bus No 138. The Mandai Orchid Gardens are next to the Zoological Gardens, so you should really try to combine the two in one trip. This is Singapore's largest orchid garden, and a huge variety of blooms now grow in this lush tropical garden. Open from 8.30 am to 5.30 pm daily.

Opposite: A manta ray hovers over head at Underwater World at Sentosa Island.
Above, left: A sculpted nymph amongst the hothouse greenery of the Botanic Gardens.
Above, right: Waterside pagodas and an arched bridge are among the attractions of the Chinese Garden at Jurong.

The **Singapore Zoo**, open daily from 8.30 am to 6 pm, charges $S10.30 for adults and $S4.60 for children under 12. To get there, take the MRT to Ang Mo Kio station, then SBS bus 138, or take the MRT to Choa Chu Kang station, then TIBS bus 927. Singapore's zoo is rated one of the best in the world. Mapped on the open plan concept (as in the San Diego Zoo), it sprawls over 28 hectares and houses more than 2,000 animals.

If you do not want to walk it, then take the tram. There are various theme areas: Primate Kingdom for the apes, Antartica for the sealions and penguins, and Children's World, where visitors can touch the animals. One of the attractions of the zoo is having breakfast or tea with an orangutan (9 am and 4 pm, except on Sundays and public holidays). Other notable animals are the Bawean hog deer, the Komodo dragon and Sumatran tiger—which are all on the list of endangered species. Animal shows and animal feeding are highlights of a visit to the zoo.

Due north from the city is the **Kong Meng San Phor Kark See Temple**, a huge Chinese temple sited on Bright Hill Drive. To get there, take a taxi from Bishan MRT. The temple complex includes a crematorium, where thousands of urns of ashes are stored, and a lage turtle pool. This temple is particularly busy during the Qing Ming festival, when the Chinese honor their dead.

Throughout the complex are beautiful examples of Chinese architecture and sculpture. Occasionally, Chinese operas are staged here.

In the same direction, but closer to the city, is the Siong Lim Temple, on Jalan Toa Payoh. To get there, ride the MRT to Toa Payoh, then take a taxi or bus. Visible from the Pan Island Expressway, this temple is a majestic piece of architecture, complete with decorated gateways, courtyards and beautifully-carved Buddha statues imported from Thailand. Dating back to 1908, its construction was financed by wealthy Hokkien businessmen.

The East Coast

Massive land reclamation projects have reshaped Singapore's shoreline and many of the East Coast's attractions are on land that not so long ago was part of the Singapore Straits.

The **East Coast Park** runs alongside a 5 km-long beach which features shaded beaches, cycling and walking paths, food centers and many recreational attractions. To get there, catch a taxi (access by public transport is difficult).

At the East Coast Sailing Club, wind surfboards and lasers can be hired by the hour, and they also offer lessons. Canoes are rented at the Lagoon Food Center and bicycles can be hired from a booth near the Rendezvous Food Center next to the club.

The **Singapore Crocodilarium** at 730 East Coast Parkway, open daily from 9 am to 5 pm, puts on wrestling shows, twice daily.

Further east, and north of Changi Airport, is the **Changi Prison Chapel and Museum** located at Changi Prison. It is a memorial to the 85,000 prisoners held captive during the Japanese Occupation in World War II. The museum displays sketches, watercolors and photographs collected from that time. Notable are the collection of vivid photographs by George Aspinall. There are also rail spikes from the Thai-Burma railway where many POWs died. The chapel is a replica of that constructed by the POWs. Open from 9.30 am to 4.40 pm daily, but closed on Sundays and public holidays. Sunday services are held at 5.30 pm. For further information telephone 7437885 or 5430893. To get there, take the MRT to Tanah Merah, then board SBS bus No 2.

Offshore Islands

Off the coast of Singapore are around 58 smaller islands. About 24 of these are inhabited, some are in restricted zones and are inac cessible, while others range from deserted isles to popular tourist resorts.

Sentosa is an offshore island totally dedicated to fun and recreation. Museums feature Singapore's history and maritime developments. There are nature trails and cycle paths through secondary forests, a pristine beach with powder-fine sand, roller skating rinks, a butterfly park, restaurants, a hawker center and a luxury hotel.

At the popular **Underwater World**, visitors can experience the feeling of being in the ocean depths without actually being there. When you walk through its submerged acrylic walkway, you will be surrounded by more than 6,000 marine creatures.

Fantasy Island is Sentosa's water theme park that offers 13 different water rides, 31 water slides, three "activity" pools as well as an Entertainment Mall. Other attractions include **Volcano Land**, a "multisensory" experience with fossils, archeological digs and a "pit cage" that transports visitors to the heart of the "world's most active volcano", where half-hourly eruptions take place. **Asian Village** showcases ethnic architecture, arts, crafts and food, while **WonderGolf Park** is the first golf theme park in the region.

Sentosa can be reached by air, sea or via a bridge. Ferry services to the island operate from the World Trade Centre from 9.30 am to 9 pm on weekdays and from 8.30 am to 9 pm on weekends and public holidays. Visitors

can also take the cable car from Mount Faber. Various Sentosa buses are available, i.e. Sentosa Bus Service E from Orchard Road.

To get to the smaller southern islands of Kusu and St. John's, take the regular ferry services from the World Trade Centre. Return fares are $S6.20 for adults and $S3.10 for children under 12. Check schedules beforehand. From Kusu there's a 25-minute boat ride with fantastic views of Singapore's skyline. The island has a couple of small beaches and the famed Tuah Peh Kong Temple, crowded with pilgrims at the annual celebrations in October. Steps lead to the summit of the island where there are some sacred *keramat*—Muslim shrines. The shaded beaches at St. John's Island are excellent for swimming and picnicking.

Pulau Ubin offers a rural lifestyle that has hardly changed in 30 years. Traditional fishing huts *(kelongs)* sit on stilts over the sea, and there is an abundance of orchard trees and greenery. Activities on the island include camping, hiking and bicycling. Bumboats leave for Pulau Ubin from Changi Jetty, which can be reached by SBS bus No 2 from Tanah Merah MRT.

—*Yeow Mei Sin*

Opposite: *Dressing up for the camera is a popular pursuit at Singapore's Chinese mythological theme parks.* **Below:** *Breakfast with Ah Meng, the celebrated orangutan.*

PERIPLUS TRAVEL MAPS
Detailed maps of the Asia Pacific region

This five-year program was launched in 1993 with the goal of producing accurate and up-to-date maps of every major city and country in the Asia Pacific region. About 12 new titles are published each year, along with numerous revised editions. Titles in **BOLDFACE** are already available (32 titles in mid-1996). Titles in *ITALICS* are scheduled for publication in 1997/1998

INDIVIDUAL COUNTRY TITLES
Australia	ISBN 962-593-150-3
Burma	ISBN 962-593-070-1
Cambodia	ISBN 0-945971-87-7
China	ISBN 962-593-107-4
Indonesia	ISBN 962-593-042-6
Japan	ISBN 962-593-108-2
Malaysia	ISBN 962-593-043-4
Nepal	ISBN 962-593-062-0
New Zealand	ISBN 962-593-092-2
Singapore	ISBN 0-945971-41-9
Thailand	ISBN 962-593-044-2
Vietnam	ISBN 0-945971-72-9

AUSTRALIA REGIONAL MAPS
Brisbane	ISBN 962-593-049-3
Cairns	ISBN 962-593-048-5
Darwin	ISBN 962-593-089-2
Melbourne	ISBN 962-593-050-7
Perth	ISBN 962-593-088-4
Sydney	ISBN 962-593-087-6

CHINA REGIONAL MAPS
Beijing	ISBN 962-593-031-0
Hong Kong	ISBN 0-945971-74-5
Shanghai	ISBN 962-593-032-9

INDONESIA REGIONAL MAPS
Bali	ISBN 0-945971-49-4
Bandung	ISBN 0-945971-43-5
Batam	ISBN 962-593-144-9
Bintan	ISBN 962-593-139-2
Jakarta	ISBN 0-945971-62-1
Java	ISBN 962-593-040-X
Lake Toba	ISBN 0-945971-71-0
Lombok	ISBN 0-945971-46-X
Medan	ISBN 0-945971-70-2
Sulawesi	ISBN 962-593-162-7
Sumatra	ISBN 0-945971-47-8
Surabaya	ISBN 0-945971-48-6

Tana Toraja	ISBN 0-945971-44-3
Ujung Pandang	ISBN 962-593-138-4
Yogyakarta	ISBN 0-945971-42-7

JAPAN REGIONAL MAPS
Kyoto	ISBN 962-593-143-0
Osaka	ISBN 962-593-110-4
Tokyo	ISBN 962-593-109-0

MALAYSIA REGIONAL MAPS
Kuala Lumpur	ISBN 0-945971-75-3
Malacca	ISBN 0-945971-77-X
Johor Bahru	ISBN 0-945971-98-2
Penang	ISBN 0-945971-76-1
West Malaysia	ISBN 962-593-129-5
Sabah	ISBN 0-945971-78-8
Sarawak	ISBN 0-945971-79-6

NEPAL REGIONAL MAP
Kathmandu	ISBN 962-593-063-9

THAILAND REGIONAL MAPS
Bangkok	ISBN 0-945971-81-8
Chiang Mai	ISBN 0-945971-88-5
Phuket	ISBN 0-945971-82-6
Ko Samui	ISBN 962-593-036-1

Distributed by:

Berkeley Books Pte. Ltd.
(Singapore & Malaysia)
5 Little Road, #08-01, Singapore 536983
Tel: (65) 280 3320 Fax: (65) 280 6290

PT. Wira Mandala Pustaka
(Java Books - Indonesia)
Jl. Kelapa Gading Kirana
Blok A-14 No. 17, Jakarta 14240
Tel: (62-21) 451 5351 Fax: (62-21) 453 4987

PERIPLUS
LANGUAGE
GUIDES

These handy pocket dictionaries are a must for travelers
to Indonesia and Malaysia. Each book contains the 2,000 most
commonly used words and is bidirectional, giving definitions from
the language to English and vice versa.

Indonesian-English / English-Indonesian
Pocket Dictionary

**Indonesian Pocket
Dictionary *is available in
English, French, German
and Dutch editions***

Malay-English / English-Malay
Pocket Dictionary

Distributed by:
**Berkeley Books Pte. Ltd.
(Singapore & Malaysia)**
5 Little Road, #08-01, Singapore 536983
Tel: (65) 280 1330 Fax: (65) 280 6290

PT. Wira Mandala Pustaka (Java Books - Indonesia)
Jl. Gading Kirana Timur Blok A13 No. 23, Jakarta 14240
Tel: (021) 453 4988 Fax: (021) 453 4987

Periplus **Action Guides**

Our Action Guides illustrate that armchair travel is a thing of the past. The first book in the series, *Diving Indonesia*, was acclaimed by BBC World Magazine as "the most fascinating travel book" published in 1992 and has been a bestseller ever since. There are now five titles available in this exciting series, and forthcoming titles include *Bushwalking New Zealand*, and more surfing, birding and diving guides.

Surfing Indonesia

Another "first" from Periplus—the first surf guide to the world's largest archipelago. Author Leonard Lueras and his team of gonzo board-riders take you along thousands of miles of deserted shorelines, stopping at some of the best surf spots in the world. This book is very detailed, with maps, action-pumped photos and travels tips to get you there and back.

Birding Indonesia

The first guide to bird-watching in Indonesia, this book is written by the world's leading authorities on Indonesian birds. It directs you to sites as varied as downtown Jakarta to Irian Jaya's Arfak Mountains. Packed with travel information, a complete checklist of Indonesian birds, along with over 130 colour photos and 28 maps (some with habitats marked in colour), the book is a "must" for the serious birder.

Diving Southeast Asia

A truly unique book written by expert divers which tells where all the top dive spots in Asia can be found. Each site is mapped, photographed and described in minute detail. Details of dive facilities, prices, accommodation, transportation and the best times to visit are all given.

Distributed by:

PT. Wira Mandala Pustaka (Java Books - Indonesia)
Jl. Kelapa Gading Kirana, Blok A-14 No. 17, Jakarta 14240 Tel: (62-21) 451 5351 Fax: (62-21) 453 4987

Berkeley Books Pte. Ltd. (Singapore & Malaysia)
5 Little Road, #08-01, Singapore 536983 Tel: (65) 280 3320 Fax: (65) 280 6290

Bookwise International (Australia)
54 Crittenden Rd, Findon S.A. 5023 Tel: (08) 8268 8222 Fax: (08) 8268 8704

Periplus
Adventure Guides

The Most Complete Guidebook Series Ever Produced on INDONESIA

The spirit of adventure is alive and well in Asia – if you know where to find it! Unlike other guides which only describe the usual tourist sights, our Adventure Guides take you to all sorts of unusual places – from the jungles of upriver Borneo to the remote highland villages of New Guinea. Along the way, these books provide you with stimulating reading, detailed maps and stunning photography.

Practicalities

TRAVEL ADVISORY, TRANSPORTATION, AREA PRACTICALITIES

The following Practicalities sections contain all the practical information you need for your journey. The **Travel Advisory** provides non-transport facts about Peninsular Malaysia and Singapore—from information on the economy to health precautions and bathroom etiquette. It is followed by a handy language primer. **Transportation** deals exclusively with getting to, and traveling around Peninsular Malaysia and Singapore. The **Area Practicalities** sections focus on each destination and contain details on transport, accommodations, dining, the arts, trekking, shopping and services. Most of these sections include local street maps.

Sidebar tabs:
1 Kuala Lumpur
2 Perak
3 Penang
4 Kedah-Perlis
5 Terengganu
6 Kelantan
7 Pahang
8 Rainforest
9 Melaka
10 Johor
11 Singapore

CONTENTS

Kuala Lumpur 1 / Perak 2 / Penang 3 / Kedah-Perlis 4 / Terengganu 5 / Kelantan 6 / Pahang 7 / Rainforest 8 / Melaka 9 / Johor 10 / Singapore 11

1 Kuala Lumpur
2 Perak
3 Penang
4 Kedah-Perlis
5 Terengganu
6 Kelantan
7 Pahang
8 Rainforest
9 Melaka
10 Johor
11 Singapore

Travel Advisory

PLANNING YOUR ITINERARY

Peninsular Malaysia's extensive road and rail network make it an easy country to travel around —it is quite possible to circumnavigate the entire peninsular in two weeks. However, for travelers with less time, or for those who like to stop and really appreciate a place, it makes sense to limit your travels to a smaller area and opt to either visit the West Coast or the East Coast.

The west is more multicultural, has most of the major towns and cities, and some of the peninsula's most famous destinations like Penang, Kuala Lumpur and Melaka. The east, on the other hand is laid-back, mainly Malay culture, and has beautiful beaches and tropical islands. The interior regions like Taman Negara, the National Park, are a totally different experience, and travelers wishing to spend time here should allow for at least a week to really make the most of their visit.

If the hothouse atmosphere gets you down while on the West Coast, you can always head up to the hill stations such as Cameron Highlands to relax in the cooler weather and do some jungle trekking. Except for these hilly regions, the rest of the peninsula is hot and humid, and it is advisable to get an early start when sight-seeing. For travelers interested in Malay culture, the East Coast, particularly around Kota Bharu, Kelantan, is the most traditional. Many people still produce handicrafts and fish for a living, and many of the leisure activities like kite-flying and top-spinning are very traditional.

For history buffs, Melaka with its many historical sites and original Chinatown, is the obvious destination, closely followed by Georgetown, Penang, which is great for exploring on foot. For beach lovers, the west coast's top spot is Pulau Langkawi, followed by the northern beaches of Penang, while the east coast is really one long beach excellent for swimming. The most pristine beaches are found on the offshore islands including Terengganu's Pulau Perhentian, Pulau Redang; Pahang's Pulau Tioman; and the islands of Johor.

CLIMATE

Peninsular Malaysia lies in the tropical equatorial zone. The temperature is therefore constant throughout the year, averaging 26 degrees Celcius, and humidity is a high 80%. The temperature drops the higher you go—at Fraser's Hill, it's a cool 18 degrees Celcius. Land and sea breezes modify the temperature on the coast. Peninsula Malaysia is governed by the northeast and southwest monsoons. The former blows from Nov-Mar, and the latter, from May-Sept. The inter-monsoon periods are wet and are usually marked by afternoon thunderstorms. The East Coast in particular, is prone to floods at the end of the year.

TIME ZONES

Peninsular Malaysia is eight hours ahead of Greenwich Mean Time. Sunset is about 7pm and sunrise around 7am.

MONEY AND BANKING

All prices quoted in this book are in US dollars and at the time of writing, the rate was around U.S.$2.50 to the Malaysian ringgit. Government policy is to keep the ringgit low in value to make exports competitive, but the ringgit has been strengthening on its own due to the country's fantastic economic growth. Notes come in RM5, RM10, RM20 RM50, RM100, RM500, and RM1000. 100 sen make 1 ringgit, which is a coin. Other coin denominations are 1, 5, 10, 20, and 50 sen.

Carry change when you travel in taxis, coins for local buses, and don't expect small shops to have change for large bills. All major credit cards are accepted at large hotels, restaurants, department stores, handicraft shops, and airline ticketing agencies. They are also extremely useful when hiring cars. In the large towns and cities, there are many licensed money changers and numerous banks which change money and travelers' checks. Banks have a small commission, but money-changers have no charges although their rates are often better. Department stores and major hotels also change money, but this should be done only as a last resort as their exchange rates assure that they make a hefty profit.

Banking hours differ from state to state. Melaka, Negeri Sembilan, Pahang, Perak, Penang, Selangor, and the Federal Territory (Kuala Lumpur) follow the standard Western working week with banks closed on Saturday afternoon and all day Sunday. Kedah, Perlis, Kelantan, Terengganu and Johor follow the Islamic week and banks are closed on Thursday afternoons and all day Friday. Banks open at 9.30 –10am and close at 3pm through the week and on the half-day, they open at 9.30am and close at 11.30am.

TAX, SERVICE AND TIPPING

As all major hotels and restaurants add a 10% service charge, tipping is not necessary, unlike some countries where the service will drop if you don't tip big. Of course, like anywhere else, tips are appreciated, but don't feel obligated. In smaller restaurants, it is enough to leave the small change.

BUSINESS HOURS

Kelantan, Terengganu, Kedah, Perlis, and Johor observe Friday as a day of rest. Saturday is half day throughout Malaysia. Government office hours are 8am–4.15pm, except for Saturday, which is 8am–12.45pm. On Fridays, offices are closed from 12.15–2.45pm for Muslim prayers. Shops generally operate from 9am–9pm, although the bigger departmental stores open from 10am–10pm. In smaller towns, shops close by 5.30pm and on Sundays.

COMMUNICATIONS

Mail

Malaysia's postal services are fairly reliable and offer a full range of postal services. Post offices (*Pejabat Pos*) liberally sprinkle the country, and opening hours are 8am–5pm. Some facilities, mainly in large housing areas, open till 10pm. For express service, *Poslaju* gets the job done. Hotels and some bookshops sell stamps too.

Telephone and Fax

Domestic and long-distance phone calls can be made from any telephone in Malaysia. There are several public pay phones operators, and they accept coins, phone-card, and credit card. Telekom Malaysia public pay phones are most widespread throughout the country. Phone cards in various denominations can be bought from bookshops and some grocery stores as well as telecommunications outlets. A local call costs RM0.10 per three minutes.

IDD calls are preceded by 00. The Home Country Direct service is available as collect calls or by telephone cards (For information, call 102). Faxes can be sent and received at Kedai Telekom Bureafax centers and Pos 2020 post office centers in major towns.

Telephone Codes

From outside Malaysia, dial 60 (Malaysia's country code), followed by the city code, then the number. Within Malaysia and from Singapore, dial 0 before the city code.

Alor Setar	4
Batu Pahat	7
Cameron Highlands	5
Desaru	7
Fraser's Hill	3
Genting Highlands	3
Gunung Jerai	4
Ipoh	5
Johor Bahru	7
Kenyir	9
Kota Bharu	9
Kota Tinggi	7
Kuala Kangsar	5
Kuala Lipis	9
Kuala Lumpur	3
Kuala Perlis	4
Kuala Pilah	6
Kuala Selangor	3
Kuala Terengannu	9
Kuantan	9
Marang	9
Melaka	6
Mersing	7
Muar	6
Pangkor	5
Penang	4
Port Dickson	6
Pulau Besar	7
Pulau Kapas	9
Pulau Langkawi	4
Pulau Perhentian	9
Pulau Sibu	7
Pulau Tengah	7
Pulau Tinggi	7
Pulau Tioman	7
Rantau Abang	9
Seremban	6
Sungai Petani	4
Taiping	5
Taman Negara	9
Tasik Cini	9
Teluk Chempedak	9
Teluk Intan	5

ELECTRICITY

As Malaysia runs on 220 volts, 50 cycles, it is not possible to use American-made appliances without an adapter. These are easily bought in electrical shops throughout the country.

LANGUAGE

The national language is Bahasa Malaysia, or Malay, which is spoken not only throughout Malaysia but is the mother tongue of the vast Indonesian archipelago, southern Thailand, and the southern Philippines. For any traveler interested in spending time in this region, a basic knowledge of the language goes a long way to making travel more insightful, economical and much easier. Even if you only know a few words, Malays will be delighted to hear you speak their language and will be much more responsive to you.

Classical Malay attained its heyday during the 15th Century Melakan Sultanate, but this fine form of the language suffered during the colonial British era when Malay took second place to English. However, after Independence, Bahasa Malaysia or BM, which is based on Classical Malay, took over as the national language. Basic BM is easy to learn although the formal language which is used in newspapers and books requires more serious study. The language has taken on different words from the various cultural influences which have altered the Malay way of life. Arabic loan words are many, mostly arriving with Islam, and include the prayer times like *maghrib* – the evening prayer or the Arabic word for "west". Most Malay names like Mohammad, Mahmud, Azizah, Fatimah, etc., originate from Arabic, as all Muslims, even those with nicknames, must have an Arabic name which God will use to call them on the Day of Judgment. Sanskrit arrived even earlier when Hinduism was introduced by Indian traders and loan words include titles like Raja, Megat, Indera, and words like *maya* – illusion, and *guru* – teacher. The Portuguese, after their conquest of Melaka, introduced furniture, and words like *meja* – table, and *almari* – wardrobe are still used today. Other minor influences include Hindustani, Persian, Chinese languages, Turkish, Thai and Tamil. English loan words are many and are usually easily recognisable; among them, *polis* – police, *bas* – bus, *klinik* – clinic, and *teksi* – taxi. Malay varies however, from region to region, and there are quite different variations spoken in Kelantan and Terengganu on the East Coast. Isolated communities also have their own distinctive dialect like on Pulau Tioman where the old remaining families still speak a version which only occurs on that island.

Apart from the national language, English is widely spoken in the cities, major towns and tourist destinations. It is the language of commerce and can be understood at all banks, post offices, and large hotels. Even in small towns there is usually someone that can speak English, although don't expect to find English-speakers in isolated kampungs. Chinese languages are widely spoken amongst the Chinese, some of whom still know very little Malay even after generations of living here. Hokkien and Cantonese are two of the biggest dialect groups. Tamil is spoken by the Indian minority who originated from South India, and Hindi and northern Indian dialects are spoken by many Muslim traders who immigrated from these regions.

ETIQUETTE

Malaysians are hospitable and friendly people, and readily forgive visitors all kinds of faux pas. However, it helps to know a few basic rules. Dress modestly, especially outside the cities and when visiting religious buildings. This means covering arms and legs. Before entering a house, mosque, and Indian and Buddhist temples, take off your shoes at the door. Nudism is strictly out even in the most trendy of beach resorts. If you are offered food it is impolite to refuse it; a sip or a nibble is sufficient not to offend. Never help yourself to food before you are invited to eat. When offered food you should accept with your right hand, as the left is considered unclean. Politeness, humbleness, and patience are held in esteem as great virtues, and it is considered quite low class to argue, show affection, or raise your voice in public. Don't worry unnecessarily though about what is the correct behavior, as Malaysians know that you are a foreigner. Just relax, be courteous, smile a lot and you will be totally accepted.

SECURITY

Malaysia is relatively safe for traveling, but be careful of pick-pockets at all times, especially in crowded city bus stations and *pasar malams*. Carry your travel documents with you at all times. A waist pouch or money belt worn inside your clothes is best. Carry enough money in small denominations in a separate wallet for the day's activities. Lock your door and windows at night and whenever you are not in your hotel room. Make use of safe deposit boxes for valuables.

HEALTH

Hygiene

Although it is generally safe to drink Malaysian

water from the tap, most locals boil their water to be extra safe. Hotels always provide boiled drinking water, and bottled mineral water is available everywhere.

Hawker stalls, while offering some of Malaysia's best food, also unfortunately carry the risk of Hepatitis B, cholera and diarrhea. Although the government is strict on hygiene at stalls, avoid eating at places whose level of cleanliness you are not comfortable with. Ice is often made from unboiled water. Avoid peeled fruit.

You could fortify yourself with Hepatitis B vaccinations before leaving your country if you are in for a long stay. Always wash your hands before eating, and rinse eating utensils in the bowl of boiling water that is provided when you order a pot of Chinese tea. Imodium and activated carbon tablets can help ease diarrhea attacks.

Except for hotels and expensive restaurants, clean public toilets are virtually non-existent. Eating places and interstate bus stop-overs are arguably the worst. Many toilets require you to squat and toilet paper is unknown so carry your own. Nonetheless, you still have to sometimes pay 10 or 20 sen to use this utility.

Make sure though that you drink lots of liquid. Otherwise, you are opening yourself up to dehydration and exhaustion in the hot, humid climate.

Diseases

Dengue is a mosquito-borne disease that strikes at the beginning of the rainy season. Symptoms are headaches, body aches and high fever. Avoid getting bitten. In non-air-conditioned rooms, use mosquito nets, insect repellant, or mosquito-repelling coils (ubat nyamuk), easily available from the hotel reception counter or in any sundry shop.

Malaria is a possibility in rainforest areas. Also spread by mosquitoes, symptoms appear after a week or even several weeks. The early symptoms are similar to a common cold or dengue. After about seven days, the classic symptoms include a feeling of intense cold, very high fever, heavy sweating and a drop in body temperature. Seek medical help immediately. Again, prevention involves avoiding getting bitten by mosquitoes. Malaria tablets can be taken as a precaution, and the course usually runs a week or two before and after your trip. The tablets usually containing quinine; check if you are allergic to it. Tablets are available on prescription at most pharmacists.

AIDS is as prevalent here as anywhere else, so safe sex is the way to go. Contraceptives are widely available, so there really is no excuse.

Medical Treatment

There are clinics (klinik) in all towns. These are efficient with western-trained doctors who all speak English. There are government-run hospitals and private specialist hospitals in all major towns. Pharmacies are generally well-stocked, especially the big chains such as Guardian and Georgetown. For those who have bought this insurance, International SOS Assistance is contactable at ☏ (03) 7777377.

WHAT TO BRING ALONG

You could travel to Malaysia and leave everything but your passport and money at home and get by very nicely. Light cotton clothing is worn all year round, and is cheap and easily available. The only problem with buying clothes here is that larger Western sizes are sometimes difficult to buy outside of Kuala Lumpur, so if you are on the large side, it's better to at least bring along your own pants. T-shirts and cotton shirts are cheap and readily available, and many famous brands names are made in Malaysia and then sent overseas.

For excellent "safari" type clothing, the boutiques in Metro Jaya Department stores in the main towns stock a great array of cotton pants with lots of pockets, shirts, folding hats, and skirts and long shorts – all made of real cotton and are excellent for traveling or trekking in the rainforest. Although hiking boots and jogging shoes are available here, it is best to bring your own as they will be nicely worn in. Reeboks and other brands are cheaper here than in Australia and Europe, but are no bargain for visitors from the USA. Leave all your mini-skirts, backless dresses and sexy clothes at home. For even though many Chinese and Eurasians dress like this in the city, they don't get the stares that mat salleh (Westerners) do when dressed the same way. Even when dressed modestly you will still get plenty of looks, so unless you want a lot of unasked for attention it's best to go for loose-fitting comfortable clothes. They are also much nicer to wear in the hot, humid climate.

If you intend to go to the highlands like Fraser's, bring along a light sweater or sweatshirt as the nights can get chilly. If you wear glasses, bring your prescription along as spectacles are very cheap – even brand names – and there are opticians in every town in Malaysia. If you are on medication, bring your prescriptions along and ask your doctor for generic names for your medicine as these are often sold under different names in Malaysia.

Toiletries are readily available, both locally-made and imported, and visitors shouldn't have any trouble buying their favorite brand of toothpaste or deodorant. For the best choice, stock up in Kuala Lumpur's big supermarkets before heading off into the countryside. If you are traveling on the cheap, other sensible accessories include a small torch, water canteen, a day pack, pocket knife, and a money pouch. Rubber slip-ons, known as "slippers" in Malaysia, "thongs" in Australia and "flip-flops" in Britain, can be bought cheaply and are very useful for walking over hot beaches, and wearing when having a shower in shared bathrooms. Malaysians are not big on presents, and a huge smile to accompany your "*terima kasih*" (thank you) is all that is needed. If you feel like giving a small gift, coins from your own country or stamps are often appreciated.

ACCOMMODATIONS

In all the major cities and towns, travelers have a good choice of accommodations from luxury hotels in the major destinations to thatched huts on the beach. All hotels above budget class charge 10% service charge and 5% government tax on top of the bill, although this is sometimes included in the listed price. During the off-season, which is the monsoon (Oct-Feb) on the east coast, and June to September in Penang and Pulau Langkawi, prices drop considerably. Except for peak periods such as public and school holidays, you can safely ask for "discount" prices. Hotels often have "promotional rates" going as well, so it's wise to enquire first as these can often save you up to 30% on the listed rate.

The **luxury lodgings** are world-class and the regular hotel chains such as the Hilton, Sheraton and Holiday Inn provide the same service as their sister hotels elsewhere. Some of the luxury hotels that stand out, mainly because of their beautiful Malay-style wooden architecture, are the Pelangi Beach Resort at Pulau Langkawi and the Tanjung Jara Resort at Dungun (East Coast). Not all the main towns have luxury hotels, but most have comfortable first-class to intermediate standard hotels. These are always fully air-con, have hot water in the private bathrooms, and provide TV, IDD phones, and often room service.

There are cheap and basic **old Chinese-run hotels** in every major and minor town on the peninsula. Some are clean and neat and a great bargain, and others are hot, noisy and dirty. Some of these hotels have air-con and private bathrooms, but most have overhead fans and shared bathrooms. Some of these establishments double as brothels, especially in Ipoh, but this is only a problem if you are a single woman. Check out the room before you register. In many of the beach destinations, there are **chalets** (small huts usually containing twin beds) which vary from very cheap and basic to air-con ones with attached bathrooms. The cheapest accommodations are usually **"A" frame thatched-roof huts** with a mattress. One sheet and a pillow with a pillow-slip is usu-

ally provided, but if you are roughing it, it's a good idea to have a sarong you can use as a spare sheet, and another as a towel as some of the cheaper places don't provide towels. Make sure you've always got some mosquito coils as this will ensure a good night's sleep. Many of the more outlying island resorts don't have electricity but they provide a kerosene lamp. In some of the older-style resorts there are no showers, but merely a *mandi* – a tub of water which you douse yourself with using a plaster dipper. Bring your own toilet paper with you as this is often not supplied.

Peninsular Malaysia's best bargain accommodation is a left-over from the colonial days, the *Rumah Rehat*, or **Resthouses**. These are usually in the outskirts of town, and are sometimes a little hard to get to if you don't have your own transport. Originally, resthouses were constructed to look after the needs of the colonial civil servants, planters, and merchants when they journeyed "out-station", and basically they serve the same purpose today. Some resthouses, for example, in Pekan (Pahang) and The Gap (Fraser's Hill), still survive in their original colonial form. Others like in Mersing (Johor), and Taiping and Kuala Kangsar (Perak) have been rebuilt, but still offer the same services at very low prices. As resthouses are such a bargain, they are often booked out by Malaysians, so it is a good idea to always phone ahead to make a reservation. Rooms are huge and can often sleep an entire family; they usually have private bathrooms; and often their own verandahs. Some have air-con rooms as well as ones with overhead fans. Practically all resthouses have restaurants attached and as the proprietors don't make much money on the rooms, they usually offer a good array of tasty food as this is what they make their profit from. In smaller towns, sometimes the resthouse is "the" place to eat, and the food is usually excellent.

TOURIST INFORMATION

Tourism Malaysia offices and tourist information centers supply information, maps and brochures. The head office in Kuala Lumpur is at the Putra World Trade Center, Jl. Tun Ismail, ☎ (03) 2935188, fax: (03) 2935884, e-mail: tourism@tourism.gov.my, http://tourism.gov.my. Many tour and travel agencies and big hotels are also on the Internet, so log on to get the latest on prices and special offers.

Overseas, contact the Malaysian High Commission or Tourism Malaysia overseas offices: **Australia** ☎ (09) 4810400; fax: (09) 3211421 / ☎ (02) 9299 4441; fax: (02) 9262 2026. **Canada** ☎ (604) 6898899; fax: (604) 6898804. **France** ☎ (33101) 42974171; fax: (33101) 42974169. **Germany** ☎ (069) 283782; fax:

(069) 285215. **Italy** ☎ (02) 796702; fax: (02) 796806. **Japan** ☎ (06) 4441220; fax: (06) 4441380 / ☎ (03) 35018691; fax: (03) 35018692. **Singapore** ☎ (02) 5326321; fax: (02) 535665. **South Africa** ☎ (2711) 3270400; fax: (2711) 3270205. **South Korea** ☎ (02) 7794422; fax: (02) 7794254. **Sweden** ☎ (468) 249900; fax: (458) 242324. **Thailand** ☎ (662) 6311994; fax: (662) 6311998. **United Kingdom** ☎ (071) 93079; fax: (071) 9309015. **USA** ☎ (213) 6899702; fax:(213) 6891530 / ☎ (212) 7541113; fax: (212) 7541116.

TOUR AND TRAVEL AGENCIES

Tours are only useful if you have limited time, or you are the type who can't be bothered finding out how to get somewhere on your own. Ask at visitor information centers for city, country, and night tours. Also the tourist information office in Kota Bharu, Kelantan, does interesting cultural and historical tours (see Area Practicalities). Look in the "Tours and Travel" section of the Malay Mail, Kuala Lumpur's afternoon tabloid, if you are interested in getting cheap local tours to Pulau Tioman, Cameron Highlands, Pulau Langkawi and other favorite destinations. These tours are very popular with Malaysians and it is a good way to meet the locals. Other contacts are the big travel companies in the cities and major towns, who also handle city tours, accommodation bookings, car hire, and ticketing.

Reputable companies in KL (area code 03) include **Mayflower Acme Tours** ☎ 6221888, fax: 6270416 – they also have a fly-drive program which includes accommodations and sometimes breakfast; **MAS Golden Holidays** ☎ 7463000; **Great Value Holidays** ☎ 2483257, fax: 2613630; **SA Tours** ☎ 2429155, fax: 2429420; **Asian Overland Services** ☎ 45291100, fax: 4529800; **Reliance SMAS Tours** ☎ 2486022, fax: 2486190; **World Express Malaysia** ☎ 2489601, fax 2421129. **KTM Berhad**, ☎ 2757267/9, fax: 2757331, offers packages with rail travel.

Nature Tours

Ecotourism is a much-maligned term, but there are small, quality companies offering a range of tours that go through Malaysia's rich and varied ecosystems. From informative gentle nature walks to hardcore adventure and the catering to of esoteric interests, these companies tailor itineraries for individuals or groups, according to needs and budgets. They also offer standard tours. Prices vary immensely, but a half day/full day tour could average $100–160.

Catering to varied niche markets – **Kingfisher Tours**, ☎ (03) 2421454; fax: (03) 2429827. This specialized nature tour operator offers birdwatching, botanical, wildlife and general nature tours. Staffed by naturalists, standard tours include a 3D/2N tour to Taman Negara, 5D/4N tour to Fraser's Hill and Kuala Selangor, and a 21-day tour through the Peninsular and Sabah and Sarawak.

Meranti Nature Tours Tel/fax: (03) 4056492 focuses on birdwatching, wildlife, rainforest ecology, and nature photography and documentaries. The standard menu includes day trips to Kuala Selangor, Fraser's Hill, Gombak Forest Reserve and Ulu Kali Mountain. Longer trips can also be arranged. Meranti is managed by an experienced ornithologist/naturalist.

Wilderness Experience ☎ (03) 7822377, Fax: (03) 7822387 packages itineraries for the adventure-seeker. Run by a bunch of hard-core, knowledgeable jungle experts, their standard Endau-Rompin itinerary runs from 3D/2N to 12D/11N from a starting price of $200 per head. They also organize whitewater rafting tours in Selangor and Pahang for $62-360 per head.

Cruises

Cruises are slowly gaining popularity in Malaysia. Cruising in the Straits of Melaka is very stable, and there is no danger of storms or even choppy waves. While international liners do stop over, shorter local and regional cruise packages are offered by four local companies. Except for MAS's yachts, the other ships are small regional cruise ships.

Cruise packages include accommodation (various classes from quad share to suites), meals (international buffet), use of facilities (casino, karaoke, disco, movie theatre) and sometimes return transfers to Kuala Lumpur. Activities on board range from telematches to karaoke singing competitions and cha-cha-cha lessons. City/island tours at ports of call can be arranged but are optional. Cruises roughly work out at $60 per person per day for a standard quad cabin and suites are roughly $100–200. Peak periods are weekends and local school holidays.

On the top end are **Malaysia Airlines'** luxury megayacht cruises (see *Langkawi Practicalities*). The largest operator is **Star Cruises**. Its two ships are currently based in Singapore and the Malaysian embarkation point is Port Klang. The more luxurious ship is the 20,000 tonne **Gemini**, which carries 800 passengers, is decked out with a swimming pool and spa, and offers six meals a day. Star's packages include: 3D/2N trip to Langkawi/Singapore; 4D/3N trip to Langkawi/ Phuket in Thailand; 5D/4N trip to Singapore/ Melaka; 8D/7N trip to Langkawi/ Phuket/Singapore/Melaka.

The Empress is a 8,000-tonne beauty that accommodates 450 passengers. Its facilities include a swimming pool, clinic, conference room, and photo developing services. A highlight is its cabaret-style theatre. The ship plies between Port Klang and Penang, and this is covered in a 2D/1N trip. There are also 2D/1N mini cruises from either Port Klang or Penang, which basically take you out to sea. The 3D/2N cruises ply between Penang and Phuket, and on long holidays, especially Christmas and National Day, the ship does Port Klang/Langkawi and Penang/Langkawi trips.

The 11,000 tonne **Coral Princess** operates out of Port Klang. Facilities on this 399 passenger-capacity ship include a live band and amusement centre. Packages are: 2D/1N Port Klang/International Sea trip that goes out to sea; 3D/2N trips to either Singapore; Langkawi; or Pulau Pangkor; 4D/3N trips to Phuket; or Penang/Songkhla/Hat Yai (Thailand), travelling overland from Penang, and an overnight stay at Hat Yai: basically a shopping trip.

Book at travel agencies, who usually offer better rates than the cruise companies themselves. Mansfield Travels, Kuala Lumpur, ☎ (03)-2428980; fax: (03)-2428992 / Penang (04) 2621233; fax: (04) 2621835, handles packages for all three companies as well as the international liners.

Scuba Diving

Malaysia is becoming a major international dive tourism destination, thanks to its colorful and marine life-rich, world-class sites. The Peninsula's most spectacular reefs are on the islands off the east coast. Dive facilities are excellent and dive tour packages plentiful. There are two main categories of operators: those who organize scheduled trips, and those who handle walk-in tourists. The latter are generally sited at the dive destinations.

Unfortunately, as with elsewhere in the world, Malaysia's reefs are constantly under threat by mainland development, destructive fishing techniques, and tourists themselves. There is hence every need on the part of dive tourists to ensure their skills are up to mark, and to adopt a conservation-oriented approach at all times on land and in the water.

Besides tours, dive instruction packages are also available. Check with companies regarding liveaboards. Equipment can usually be hired, including wetsuits. Most trips average 4D/3N and you have to make your own way to the jump-off points on the mainland. For scheduled trips, contact: **Borneo Divers** ☎ (03) 7173066; fax: (03) 7184303 (they do underwater photography tours too); **Pro Dive** ☎ (03) 2737317, fax: (03) 2738317 (resorts in Langkawi and Merang; **Scuba Point** (resort in Pulau Tioman) ☎ (03) 7747288; fax: (03) 7754288; **Global Scuba Adventures** ☎ (03) 7355167; fax: (03) 7350823.

FESTIVALS

With such a multicultural population there is hardly a week in the annual calendar when a festival is not going on. Some national holidays and festivals occur on the same day every year, except for the major holidays based on the Chinese, Muslim or Hindu calendars which are lunar. The following monthly guide of major festivals is approximate except for specified dates. Check with the tourist information centers for the latest dates of lunar festivals. In addition to these important events there are many smaller festivals, like the International Kite Festival in Kelantan (July), Fraser's Hill International Bird Race (June), Kelantan International Drum Festival (July), Melaka's Festa San Pedro (June), and dozens more including Sultans' birthdays. **January**: Thaipusam. Hindu festival and procession when tranced penitents pierce themselves with metal hooks and spikes and shoulder elaborately-decorated yokes. Best at Kuala Lumpur's Batu Caves, and in Penang. **February**: Chinese New Year. Celebrated for 15 days when Chinese visit relatives, decorate their homes and shops with red banners, and celebrate with lion dances and firecrackers. **February**: Chap Goh Meh. End of Chinese New Year when temples are packed with worshippers and huge joss sticks are burnt. **April**: Hari Raya Puasa. The start of the fasting month of Ramadan, known in Malay as puasa, when Muslims refrain from eating and drinking from sunrise to sunset. Special food is available during this time and the fast culminates with Hari Raya when all Malays have open house and treat relatives and friends with festive culinary preparations. **May**: Wesak Day. To celebrate Buddha's birth, enlightenment and nirvana, special prayers are done at all Buddhist temples. **June**: Hari Raya Haji. To celebrate the annual haj or pilgrimage to Mecca, special prayers are held at mosques, and sheep or cattle are sacrificed for the needy. **July**: Maal Hijrah. The New Year of the Muslim calendar is celebrated with religious discussions and Koran recitals. **July/August**: Dragon Boat Festival. Celebrated wit the eating of rice dumplings and exciting dragon boat races in Penang. **August** 31st: Merdeka Day. Celebrated with parades, processions, and fireworks to commemorate independence from British rule. **September**: Prophet Muhammad's Birthday. Special prayers and Koran recitals are held at mosques to celebrate this spiritual event. **September**: Moon Cake Festival. Chinese festival to mark the victory of the peasants over their Mongolian warlords in ancient times. Special lotus-flavored moon cakes are eaten and colorful lanterns are displayed. **October**: Deepavali. Hindu festival of lights to celebrate the triumph of good over evil. Indian families offer prayers and hold "open-house" when relatives and friends visit. **December**: Christmas. Celebrated by Christians who pack the churches for midnight mass and hold "open-house" with special food treats.

SHOPPING

From bustling night markets to air-conditioned shopping malls, Peninsular Malaysia is a great place to shop. The only places where bargaining is not the done thing is in department stores where "fixed-price" means what it says, and in government-run handicraft stores. Anywhere else – bargain, especially in "touristy" areas. A good word to learn in Malay, even before the numbers, is *mahal* – "expensive" – as this is an essential part of bargaining. If you are not into bargaining, and even some Malaysians do this, ask for their "best price". This is usually at least 10 to 20% off their first quoted price. Always bargain when buying electrical goods, cameras, cassette-players and even when buying film in bulk. Don't expect to get much off the quoted prices of handicrafts, especially when you are at the source, like the batik workshops in Kelantan. They may drop the price by a few ringgit, but their mark-up is not much, and they are selling at half the price of what you would pay for a similar item in the city boutiques.

Remember to get international guarantee cards for electrical goods. Kuala Lumpur is the best for buying these, and for designer clothes (*see KL Practicalities*). If a tout accosts you and offers you "copy watches," these are fake designer watches which sell from upwards of $12. Real brands, however, are reasonably-priced. Kuala Lumpur's government-run handicrafts shops have a good variety, but prices are much lower at the source. Kota Bharu is the place to shop for *songket* (silk brocade), traditional silverware, hand-painted silk batiks, traditional stamped batiks, wood-carving and interesting souvenirs like kites and baskets. Melaka and Penang are good for antiques, the latter is best for antique furniture, and porcelain. Penang is good for curios (*see Penang Practicalities*). The Mah Meri, from Pulau Carey (*see p. 69*) produce beautiful "spirit" carvings out of a reddish wood. Those interested in primitive art can go to their village and see them working. The Jah Hut, from Central Pahang also make wood carvings. Enquire at the tourist information centers in Kuala Lumpur.

PHOTOGRAPHY

A large range of slide and print film is available, especially in the cities. Same-day processing of prints is available and many photo shops offer one or two-hour processing as well. Fewer outlets do slide processing, and it generally takes several days.

EMBASSIES AND CONSULATES

All numbers refer to offices in Kuala Lumpur, dialing code (03). **Australia** 6 Jl. Yap Kwan Seng, ☎ 2423122. **Belgium** 12 Lorong Yap Kwan Seng, ☎ 2485733. **Britain** 185 Jl. Ampang, ☎ 2482122. **Brunei** Wisma Sin Heap Lee, Jl. Tun Razak, ☎ 2612800. **Canada** Plaza MBF, Jl. Ampang, ☎ 2612000. **China** 229 Jl. Ampang, ☎ 2428495. **Denmark** Wisma Denmark, Jl. Ampang, ☎ 2022001. **France** 192 Jl. Ampang, ☎ 2484122. **Germany** 3 Jl. U Thant, ☎ 2429666. **India** 2 Jl. Taman Duta, ☎ 2533504. **Indonesia** 233 Jl. Tun Razak, ☎ 9841151. **Italy** 99 Jl. U Thant, ☎ 4565122. **Japan** 11 Persiaran Stonor, ☎ 2427044. **Netherlands** 4 Jl. Mesra, ☎ 2485151. **New Zealand** Menara IMC, Jl. Sultan Ismail, ☎ 2382533. **Norway** Bangunan Ankasa Raya, Jl. Ampang, ☎ 2420144. **Singapore** 209 Jl. Tun Razak, ☎ 2350111. **Spain** 200 Jl. Ampang, ☎ 2484868. **Sweden** Bangunan Angkasa Raya, Jl. Ampang, ☎ 2485433. **Switzerland** 16 Persiaran Madge, ☎ 2480622. **Thailand** 206 Jl. Ampang, ☎ 2488222. **United States** 376 Jl. Tun Razak, ☎ 2489011.

Bahasa Malaysia Primer

Bahasa Malaysia is not a tonal language and is therefore less difficult to learn than Thai or Chinese. There are no articles; *kampung* means "the village", or "a village". Plurals are indicated by doubling the noun; *katil-katil* means "beds" or has a qualifier, e.g. *banyak katil* (many beds). Tense is usually indicated by adverbs, the most popular ones being *sudah* which means "already", and *belum* which means not yet". Adjectives always follow the noun, as in *baju* (shirt) *merah* (red) – *baju merah*. Even a smattering of BM, including numbers, can be extremely useful, especially when bargaining. Knowing basic phrases like *berapa harga*, "how much," will sometimes be enough to lower the price.

Personal pronouns
I *saya*
we *kita* (inclusive), *kami* (exclusive)
you *anda* (formal), *saudara* (polite), *kamu* (friends and children)
he/she *dia*
they *mereka*

Forms of address
Man *Encik* (formal)
Man, father's age *Pakcik*
Man, older brother's age *Abang* ("*Bang*")
Woman, older, married *Puan* (formal), *Makcik*
Woman, young, single *Cik* (formal)
Woman, older sister's age *Kakak* ("*Kak*")
Younger brother/sister *Adik* ("*Dik*")

Basic questions
How? *Bagaimana?*
How much/many *Berapa?*
What? *Apa?*
What's this? *Apa ini?*
Who? *Siapa?*
Who's that? *Siapa itu?*
What is your name? *Siapa namamu?*

When? *Bila?*
Where? *Mana?*
Which? *Yang mana?*
Why? *Kenapa?*

Useful words
yes *ya*
no, not *tidak, bukan*
(NB: *Tidak* is used with verbs or adverbs; *bukan* with nouns)
and *dan*
with *dengan*
for *untuk*
good *bagus*
fine *baik*
more *lebih*
less *kurang*
better *lebih baik*
worse *kurang baik*
this/these *ini*
that/those *itu*
same *sama*
different *lain*
here *di sini*
there *di sana*

Pronunciation and Grammar

Vowels

a	As in father
e	Three forms:
	1) Schwa, like the
	2) Like é in touché
	3) Short è; as in bet
i	Usually like long e (as in Bali); when bounded by consonants, like short i (hit).
o	Long o, like go
u	Long u, like you
ai	Long i, like crime
au	Like ow in owl

Consonants

c	Always like ch in church
g	Always hard, like guard
h	Usually soft, almost unpronounced. It is hard between like vowels, e.g. *mahal* (expensive).
k	Like k in kind; at end of word, unvoiced stop.
kh	Like kind, but harder
r	Rolled, like Spanish r
ng	Soft, like fling
ngg	Hard, like tingle
ny	Like ny in Sonya

Grammar

Grammatically, Indonesian is in many ways far simpler than English. There are no articles (a, an, the). The verb form "to be" is usually not used. There is no ending for plurals; sometimes the word is doubled, but often number comes from context. And Indonesian verbs are not conjugated. Tense is communicated by context or with specific words for time.

Civilities

Welcome *Selamat datang*
Good morning (7am – noon) *Selamat pagi*
Good afternoon (12 – 4pm) *Selamat tengahari*
Good evening (4 – 7pm) *Selamat petang*
Good evening (after dark) *Selamat malam* (usually to say goodbye at night)
Goodbye (to one leaving) *Selamat jalan*
Goodbye (to one staying) *Selamat tinggal*
How are you? *Apa khabar?*
I am fine. *Khabar baik.*
Thank you. *Terima kasih.*
You're welcome. *Sama-sama.*
Pardon me / Excuse me *Maaf*

Numbers

1	*satu*	6	*enam*
2	*dua*	7	*tujuh*
3	*tiga*	8	*lapan*
4	*empat*	9	*sembilan*
5	*lima*	10	*sepuluh*
11	*sebelas*	100	*seratus*
12	*dua belas*	600	*enam ratus*
13	*tiga belas*	1,000	*seribu*
20	*dua puluh*	3,000	*tiga ribu*
50	*lima puluh*	10,000	*sepuluh ribu*
73	*tujuh puluh tiga*		

1,000,000 *satu juta*
2,000,000 *dua juta*
half *setengah*

first *pertama*   third *ketiga*
second *kedua*   fourth *ke-empat*

Time

minute *minit*
hour *jam* (also clock/watch)
day *hari*   week *minggu*
month *bulan*   year *tahun*
today *hari ini*   later *nanti*
tomorrow *esok*   yesterday *kelmarin*
What time is it? *Jam berapa?*
(It is) nine thirty. *Sembilan setengah* (Literally: "nine half")
How many hours /How long? *Berapa jam?*
When did you arrive? *Bila sampai?*
Four days ago. *Empat hari yang lalu.*
When are you leaving? *Bila berangkat?*
In a short while *Sebentar lagi.*
Sunday *Ahad*   Monday *Isnin*
Tuesday *Selasa*   Wednesday *Rabu*
Thursday *Khamis*   Friday *Jumaat*
Saturday *Sabtu*

Basic vocabulary

to be, have *ada*   to be able, can *boleh*
to buy *beli*   to know *tahu*
to get *dapat*   to need *perlu*
to want *mahu* (pronounced "mao")
to go *pergi*   to wait *tunggu*
at *di*   to *ke*
if *kalau*   near *dekat*
far *jauh*   empty *kosong*
full *penuh*
already, done, completed *sudah*
correct *betul*   wrong *salah*

big *besar*   small *kecil*
person, people *orang*
pretty, nice *cantik*   slow *perlahan*
fast *cepat*   stop *berhenti*
old *tua* (people), *lama* (things)
new, just *baru*   then *tadi, kemudian*
only *hanya, saja*   crowded *ramai orang*
Westerner *mat salleh*
bus *bas* (same pronounciation)
taxi *teksi* (same pronounciation)
train station *stesen keretapi*
toilet *tandas*   sleep *tidur*
bathe *mandi*   pain/ill *sakit*

Food

hot *panas*   cold *sejuk*
ice *ais* (same pronounciation)
bread *roti*   water *air*
milk *susu*   sugar *gula*
salt *garam*   butter *mentega*
tea *teh*   coffee *kopi*
soup *sup* (same pronounciation)
chicken *ayam* (ah-yarm)
beef *lembu*   fish *ikan* (ee-karn)
vegetables *sayur*

Smalltalk

Where are you from? *Dari mana?*
I'm from the US. *Saya dari Amerika.*
How old are you? *Umur berapa?*
I'm 31 years old. *Umur saya tiga pulu satu tahun.*
Are you married? *Sudah khawin belum?*
Yes, I am. *Ya, sudah.*
Not yet. *Belum.*
Do you have children? *Sudah ada anak?*
What is your religion? *Agama apa?*
Where are you going? *Nak ke mana?*

Pronunciation and Grammar

Vowels

a as in f**a**ther
e Three forms
1) Schwa, like th**e**
2) Like **e** in touch**e**
3) Short **e**, as in b**e**t
i Usually like long **e** (as in Bali); when bounded by consonants, like short **i** (hit)
o Long **o**, like h**o**pe
u Long **u**, like y**ou**
ai Long **i**, like cr**i**me
au Long **ow**, like **owl**

Consonants

c Always like **ch** in **ch**urch
g Always hard like **g**uard
h Usually soft, almost un-pronounced. It is hard between like vowels, e.g. *mahal* (expensive)
k Like **k** in **k**ind; at end of word, unvoiced stop.
kh Like **k**ind, but harder
r Rolled like Spanish **r**
ng Soft like fli**ng**
ngg Hard, like ti**ngle**
ny Like **ny** in So**ny**a

Transportation

This section gives you an overview of the wide range of travel options available during your stay in Peninsular Malaysia. A comprehensive run-down of travel services enables you to plan your way around according to time and budget. More specific details for each area you will be visiting can be found in the relevant Area Practicalities sections.

Prices are in US dollars, unless otherwise stated. Prices and schedules are given as an indication only as they change frequently according to the season. Check with a travel agent prior to departure for the most up-to-date information.

GETTING TO PENINSULAR MALAYSIA

By Air

Besides the national carrier Malaysia Airlines (MAS), 45 international airlines fly in and out of Kuala Lumpur's Sultan Abdul Aziz Shah International Airport. Other international airports are at Penang, Langkawi, and Johor Bahru. MAS fly to/from 78 cities around the world. MAS also have shuttle flights to/from Singapore, and daily flights to/from the other Malaysian international airports in Kuching (Sarawak) and Kota Kinabalu (Sabah). You could try cheap airlines like Aeroflot via Moscow from London, or Air Lanka, and Air India, via Colombo and Delhi or Bombay. MAS fly direct from London. Discount fares from the US are via the West Coast. Book ahead when the school year ends as this is a busy time with Malaysian overseas students arriving home for the holidays, and during winter in the northern hemisphere, the prime time for Malaysian resorts. Make sure you've got return bookings on the cheaper airlines as these are often overbooked. International flight departures are taxed RM40, domestic flights RM5.

By Train

The train line runs all the way from Bangkok in the north, through Peninsular Malaysia, to Singapore in the south. It is a marvelous journey, and a great way to see three countries at once. Tickets can be bought at either end, or from Kuala Lumpur which is cheaper than Singapore. KTM Berhad runs services every day and night. The West Coast route goes from Singapore to Butterworth from where the International Express travels daily to Bangkok. Alternatively, train up to KL and change for a train that goes to Haadyai. The East Coast route from Singapore ends in Tumpat, Kelantan.

By Road

Peninsular Malaysia shares a land border with Thailand and is connected to Singapore by two causeways. Share taxis run from South Haadyai, across the border at Bukit Kayu Hitam to either Alor Setar in Kedah or to Penang. Local buses also run from Haadyai to Sadao, then change buses for the border at Padang Besar in Perlis.

VISAS

All visitors must possess a passport valid for at least six months, or an internationally-recognized travel document endorsed for travel in Malaysia. No visas are required for nationals of all British Commonwealth countries (except Bangladesh, India, Pakistan, and Sri Lanka) and Republic of Ireland, Switzerland, Netherlands, and Liechtenstein. Nationals of the following countries are granted visa-free entry for three months: Austria, Belgium, Czech and Slovak, Denmark, Finland, Germany, Hungary, Iceland, Italy, Japan, Norway, South Korea, Sweden, Tunisia, and the United States. Visa-free entries for up to one month are granted to: ASEAN (except Singapore and Brunei), Argentina, Brazil, France, Greece, Poland, and South Africa. Extensions can be made at immigration offices, but proof of onward journey (airline tickets) and sufficient funds is usually required. Employment is forbidden on a tourist visa. Visitors must fill a disembarkation card to be handed over to Immigration with your passport upon arrival.

Customs

Visitors can bring in one liter of liquor, one carton of cigarettes, and personal possessions such as cameras, watches, cassette-players, laptop computers, cosmetics and so on. Narcotics, pornography (includes *Playboy*) and firearms are prohibited. Malaysia's drug laws are infamous with death penalties for trafficking in even small amounts of

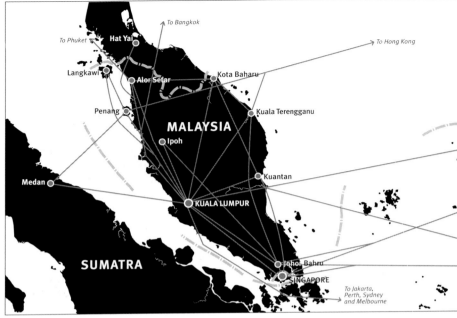

marijuana. The export of antiques must be accompanied by a license from the Director General of Museums. There is no limit to the amount of currency allowed into or out of the country. Customs will assess the value of any dutiable item and you will have to pay 50% of this amount as a deposit which is refundable when you leave the country.

TRAVELING IN MALAYSIA

Malaysia is an extremely easy country to get around with minimum fuss and bother. There are various options such as air, train, bus and the excellent system of "share" taxis (see below). To see the countryside at its best nothing beats hiring a car but this can be costly over the long term. Trains are slow, but pleasant, and often follow more scenic routes than the roads. Express buses are faster than trains and quite comfortable, but are not advisable for the faint-hearted as the drivers often blatantly disregard road rules. Long-distance air-con taxis are double the bus fare, but more enjoyable. Hitch-hiking is highly unadvisable, especially for women, as there is a very real possibility of being picked up by men who imagine that women who get into strangers' cars have loose morals.

By Air

Malaysian Airlines (MAS) has reasonably-priced domestic flights from Kuala Lumpur to Johor Bahru ($37), Ipoh ($26), Alor Setar ($45), Pulau Langkawi ($54), Kuantan ($30), and Penang, Kuala Tereng-

ganu and Kota Bharu ($42). There are other services which connect some of these major towns, like Kuala Terengganu to Penang, and Johor Bahru to Kuantan, for example. Air travel is quick but offers little in the way of scenery, although the patterns of oil-palm plantations creeping into the rainforest, and the incredible greenness of the landscape is spectacular from above.

MAS also has special night flights and advance purchase or excursion fares on some sectors which are cheaper than the regular flights. Families, or couples without children can also get a 25% reduction on return fares within Malaysia. There are also discounts for groups of three or more, but you must pay at least a week in advance. For travelers arriving from Sarawak or Sabah, it is much cheaper to fly to Johor Bahru than to take flights to Singapore. For prices and times contact a local travel agent or MAS, Bangunan MAS, Jl. Sultan Ismail, ☎ 50250, Kuala Lumpur, ☎ (03) 2610555; for 24-hour reservations, reconfirmation, and flight information, ☎ (03) 7463000.

There are also two smaller services. Pelangi Air's Fokker 50s service capital cities, Pulau Tioman and Kerteh as well as Sumatra in Indonesia. There are special fares for families, senior citizens, and group fares for a minimum of three passengers. For reservations, ☎ (03) 2524446, MAS, or travel agents.

Flights are only booked out during public and school holidays, when extra flights are put on to handle the crowds, but at all other times there should be no problems getting a seat.

Malaysia Airlines Domestic Routes

To Taipei, Seoul, Tokyo, Manila, Cebu and Davao

To Hong Kong

Kudat

Kota Kinabalu

Pamal

Sandakan

Labuan

Tomanggong

BRUNEI

SABAH

Lahad Datu

Bandar Seri Begawan

Sahabat

Lawas

Limbang

Long Sukang

Miri

Long Pasia

Tawau

Mulu

Long Semado

Semporna

Marudi

Bakelalan

Long Seridan

Bario

Long Lellang

Tarakan

Bintulu

Mukah

Belaga

Sibu

SARAWAK

Kapit

Kuching

KALIMANTAN

Pontianak

By Train

Peninsular Malaysia's train system was built by the British during the colonial era and still retains many of its elegant old railway stations from that period, including the fantastic terminal at Kuala Lumpur. It is a comfortable, relaxing and extremely reasonably-priced way to view the country, and often the rail goes through countryside which is otherwise only observable by private cars as buses take the main routes which are the most uninteresting.

There are two main rail lines; the West Coast line which runs from Singapore through Kuala Lumpur and Butterworth to Bangkok; and the East Coast line which branches off at Gemas in Johor and runs to Tumpat in Kelantan. KTM Berhad's daily services include Ekspres Rakyat (Singapore-Butterworth) and Ekspres Sinaran (KL-Butterworth), with stops at major stations. The night service sleepers are Senandung Malam (KL-Singapore, KL-Butterworth), and Ekspres Langkawi (KL-Arau-Haadyai). The International Express travels daily between Butterworth and Bangkok. Travelers can also travel via the East Coast to Tumpat, Kelantan from Singapore on the Ekspres Timuran and from Kuala Lumpur on the Ekspres Wau.

There is a choice of 1st Class AC, 2nd Class AC, and 3rd Class AC. 1st Class is almost double the price of 2nd but is hardly worth it if you want to save money. Both these classes can be booked a month in advance and have in-house videos and sub-Arctic airconditioning. Third Class is basic, cheap and sometimes very hot, but is a great way to meet the locals. A Railpass, available only to foreigners, can be purchased at the railway stations in Kuala Lumpur, Johor Bahru, Butterworth, Port Klang, Padang Besar, Wakaf Baru and Singapore. This gives unlimited travel in any class, for 30 days for $120, or 10 days for $55; berth charges on night trains are extra. However, it is often cheaper, especially if you want to travel 2nd or 3rd Class, to just buy the tickets when you need them. As an example, a 2nd Class air-con fare from Kuala Lumpur to Butterworth costs only around $14, so if you want to make the Railpass economical it means a lot of time spent traveling in trains. On overnight trains, sleeping berths are extra and must be booked and paid for when you buy your ticket. Children between the ages of four and 12 are charged half the adult fare, and children under four travel free. There are buffet cars on all express trains where snacks and light meals can be purchased. Ask about the seven-day Eurotrain Explorer Pass-Malaysia for students and YHA Card-holders, and other concessions. KTMB also offers holiday packages. Contact: ☎ (03)-2757265 / fax: (03)-2757331.

An elaborately revamped **Eastern and Orient Express** caters for the well-heeled who like to travel in colonial splendor. The "Raj"-type train services Singapore, Kuala Lumpur, Butterworth, and, in Thailand, Bangkok, Sukhotai and Chiang Mai. All meals are provided and a Penang island city tour on the Kuala Lumpur/Singapore to Bangkok sectors. There are three classes of accommodation; the Singapore-Bangkok sector starts at $1,500. Contact Skyzone Tours and Travel in KL, ☎ 2429288; fax: 2426228.

By Road

Express, air-con buses run between all of the peninsula's main towns. These are fast, generally leave and arrive on time, and are reasonably comfortable with padded seats and air-con although the seats are often placed a little too close for Westerners' long legs. They usually travel fast and the drivers have a penchant for overtaking on blind hills and generally disregarding road rules, although this is not as bad as in the past due to the use of the dual-carriageway highways, and undercover spot checks by police. Probably the worst thing about the buses is where they stop for food breaks, usually in the drab outskirts of towns at "truckers stops" where the food is awful, compared to the marvelous cuisine that can be found the length and breath of the peninsula. However, they are still an extremely popular and convenient way to get around the countryside, especially to towns that are not serviced by the railway.

All **inter-state buses** (except for the East Coast and interior Pahang) run from the crowded Puduraya Bus Station in the center of Kuala Lumpur. Touts selling tickets for "pirate" (unlicensed) buses will accost you on the overpass to the bus station telling you how the bus you want is full and how they have cheaper fares, but ignore them as they are not offering discounts, and continue on to the bus company booths inside the terminal. The times and prices are listed on the front windows of the booths. Different companies run south and north, but just walk along until you find the destination you want, it's easy enough. If the next bus, say to Ipoh, is full, then there is usually another bus-company booth close by that which also runs to the same destination. Prices are reasonable; for example, the route from Kuala Lumpur to Butterworth, costs $6 and takes around 6 hours.

Some companies have so-called VIP buses which are more comfortable and have seats that incline. These cost several ringgit more but are worth it for longer journeys. For about twice the price, you could opt for the more luxurious Mara Holdings (☎ 03-2985122) buses, which service only the major towns. The coaches are equipped with comfortable airplane seats, food is served on board and a blanket is supplied to hold off the freezing air-con temperatures.

All **East Coast buses** run from the Hentian Putra, opposite The Mall (shopping complex) on Jl. Putra in the northern section of Kuala Lumpur. There is another station, Hentian Pekeliling, on the ring road, Jl. Tun Razak, not far from Hentian Putra, which services Kuala Lipis and other inland Pahang towns. Local buses run between all the minor towns in Malaysia and are slow, but are reasonably comfortable and extremely cheap. The drivers are also not quite as maniacal, and although the buses are not airconditioned, everyone keeps their windows open and the wind keeps the buses from getting oven-like.

The quickest and best way to travel, though, is by **"share" taxis** which ply between all the peninsula's major towns. These are sometimes air-con Mercedes with comfortable seats, and even cassette-players which invariably play Malay love songs or Chinese pop. There are **long-distance taxi** stations, usually near the express bus stations at all the main towns. In Kuala Lumpur, the taxi terminal is upstairs from the Puduraya Bus Station. You must make it clear that you want to share the taxi, otherwise sharp-talking cabbies will try to talk you into chartering the whole cab, which costs four times as much. However, there is a quota for the number of taxis plying certain routes, and if that is filled, usually on public and school holidays, you might be asked to pay more for non-quota taxis as they will have to return immediately. Rates are also higher if traffic is heavy, especially traveling in the afternoon on the Karak Highway between the East and West Coast, so check with the driver if the fee is flat.

When you approach popular taxi stations the drivers will all be calling out their destinations, like "Melaka" etc., and you just head for that taxi. Sometimes you are the last passenger and they take off immediately; other times you have to wait until the taxi fills. This may be only 10 to 30 minutes if it's in the morning. However, if it's late afternoon, the wait may extend to one hour. But don't worry as the taxi driver has to return, and sometimes if no one else shows up he takes off half empty and then just looks for fares along the way. Prices are about double the bus fare, but are worth the extra as the drivers often take you straight to your hotel and they sometimes do pickups for free too if you are close to the station. (*See Practicalities for prices*).

The best way to see Malaysia is to drive. Dual-carriageway highways provide fast inter-city links throughout the Peninsula, and a **car** gives you the flexibility to turn off into rustic kampungs, fern-framed waterfalls, and other slices of Malaysian life. Road maps are plentiful, but road signs can be frustrating, so don't hesitate to pull up and ask for directions. Be warned, though, that directions might not always be accurate and you might have to stop several times, but hey, it's a great way to interact with locals.

The important thing is to maintain both patience and a sense of humor. This also applies when dealing with public transport that keeps "Malaysian time" (unpunctual) or slow-moving counter staff, who would rather gossip with her colleague than serve you, or queue jumpers. Don't expect things to be systematic although a system might appear to be in place.

Be persistent but polite at all times, and keep to the Do-as-the-Romans-do rule of thumb. Again, seek help or information from those around you, and you might just be pleasantly surprised to see someone go out of their way to help you.

Car Rentals

Malaysia is one of the easiest countries in Asia to hire and drive your own car. Drivers need a valid license from your own country. Companies prefer to deal with people paying with credit cards, although you can pay by cash, but they usually ask for a hefty deposit. All the big car rental firms are in Malaysia and rates start around $60 per day for the cheapest vehicles, although if you look in the Malay Mail (Kuala Lumpur's afternoon tabloid) you can sometimes find them for quite a bit less. Driving is on the left-hand side of the road, and rules are much the same as in any other country. Wearing seatbelts is compulsory in the front seats.

On highways and expressways the speed limit is 110kph and 80kph on trunk roads. In built-up areas and towns the speed limit is usually 50kph. As well as sometimes suicidal drivers, especially truckers, motorists must be constantly aware in the kampung areas of bicycles and stray animals, especially at night. There is an excellent system of roads across the entire peninsula, but some stretches of the main west coast highway can get very crowded with lorries. The North-South Expressway (Lebuhraya Utara-Selatan) makes long-distance driving a relaxed affair although the road by-passes all the towns. Although Malaysia has its own oil, petrol is not cheap at 45c a liter.

Malaysian Motorhomes, 10 Persiaran Stonor, Kuala Lumpur, ☎ (03) 2418541, rent out their fully-equipped motor homes which sleep four, are airconditioned and have built-in bathrooms. At $102 a day (with 1 free day per week's rent) this is a great way to see the country, particularly the inland and off-the-beaten track places.

INTERNATIONAL AIRLINES

These numbers refer to offices in Kuala Lumpur, dialing code (03). Aeroflot, Wisma Tong Ah, Jl. P. Ramlee ☎ (2610231). Air France, Plaza See Hoy Chan, Jl. Raja Chulan ☎ (2326952). Air NZ, Wisma Golden City, Jl. Bukit Bintang ☎ (2425577). Air Lanka, MUI Plaza, Jl. P Ramlee ☎ (2323633). American, Bang. Angkasa Raya, Jl. Ampang ☎ (2480644). Ansett Australia, UBN Tower, Jl. P. Ramlee ☎ (2019211). British, Plaza See Hoy Chan, Jl. Raja Chulan ☎ (2325797). Canadian, Wisma Golden City, Jl. Bukit Bintang ☎ (2425533). Cathay Pacific, UBN Tower, Jl. P. Ramlee ☎ (2383377). China, Bang. Amoda, Jl. Imbi ☎ (2427344). JAL, Menara Lion, Jl. Ampang ☎ (2611722). KLM, Parkroyal Hotel, Jl. Bukit Bintang ☎ (2427011). Lufthansa, Pernas International, Jl. Sultan Ismail ☎ (261 4666). MAS, Bang. MAS, Jl. Sultan Ismail ☎ (7463000). Qantas, UBN Tower, Jl. P. Ramlee ☎ (2389133). Royal Brunei, UBN Tower, Jl. P. Ramlee ☎ (2307166). Singapore, 2 Jl. Dang Wangi ☎ (2923122). Swissair, Wisma Singapore Airlines, Jl. Dang Wangi ☎ (2913254). Thai, Wisma Goldhill, Jl. Raja Chulan (2012900). United, Bang. MAS, Jl. Sultan Ismail (2611433).

1 **Kuala Lumpur** PRACTICALITIES

Most of Kuala Lumpur's best-known sights are within easy walking distance from each other in the heart of downtown, and the attractions on the fringes of the city can easily be visited by taxi. Plan your day so that you are walking in the early morning or late afternoon and spend the hot part of the day either relaxing in your hotel or shopping at one of the many air-conditioned shopping malls. The out-of-town trips are best done by car, but for those with plenty of time, they are also accessible by public transport.

Prices in US dollars. S=single; D=double; AC=airconditioning. Telephone code 03, except Fraser's Hill 09.

GETTING THERE

Kuala Lumpur, fondly known as KL, is the main international gateway to Malaysia and the hub of the domestic air, train and bus services.

By Air

Pending the completion of the multi-million dollar Kuala Lumpur International Airport in Sepang, all flights into KL come through the Sultan Abdul Aziz International Airport in the neighboring Selangor state, 22km from the city center. The airport, popularly referred to by its old name of Subang Airport, is served by the national carrier, Malaysia Airlines, and by 35 other international airlines. Terminal 1 (☎ 7464318) handles international and mixed domestic/international flights; Terminal 2 (☎ 7464555), the Singapore sector; and Terminal 3 (☎ 746 072), domestic flights. Taxis from the airport operate on a coupon system; coupons can be bought at a booth by the main entrance. Hand the coupon to the driver when you get into the taxi. A trip downtown costs around $7. **Buses** run hourly; off peak the journey takes about 45 minutes, but the traffic jams on the Federal Highway access road are legendary: avoid the morning and evening rush hours. Bus No. 47 services the route from the Klang bus terminal in downtown KL. The MAS head office is in Bangunan MAS, Jl. Sultan Ismail, ☎ 2610555. Other offices are in Complex Daya Bumi, Jl. Sultan Hishamuddin, ☎ 2748734, and the Mall, Jl. Putra, ☎ 4437573; or call 7436000 (24 hrs).

By Bus

Modern AC express buses to Kuala Lumpur run from Singapore's Lavender Street terminal, and from the Ban San terminal at the corner of Arab and Queen Streets. The 8hr journey costs $10, and most buses leave in the morning. Buy bus tickets in Singapore from Masmara, ☎ 02-7326555, from the bus station or at 05-53 Far East Plaza, 14 Scotts Rd, or from Kuala Lumpur-Singapore Express, ☎ 02-2928254. Express buses also go to Kuala Lumpur from all major West Malaysian towns. The long-distance bus terminal is the Puduraya Bus Station on Jl. Pudu, except for East Coast buses which use the Hentian Putra station on Jl. Putra, and the Pekeliling Bus Station on Jl. Tun Razak (for West Pahang).

By Train

Kuala Lumpur is connected by rail from Bangkok in the north to Singapore in the south. The Singapore train station is on Keppel Road, ☎ 02-2225165, and six daily trains run to Kuala Lumpur. Ekspres Rakyat departs at 7.50am and arrives 1.30pm; Ekspres Sinaran departs at 2.15pm and arrives at 7.44pm; and the Senandung Malam departs at 10.30pm and arrives 5.50am. 1st class AC $27, 2nd class AC $13.60, 3rd Class non-AC $8; sleepers are an additional $12 (1st class) and $6 (2nd class). The cheaper mail trains stop everywhere and are much slower. For travelers arriving from the north, tickets can be purchased in Bangkok for the entire trip to Kuala Lumpur; however, you must change trains in Butterworth.

ACCOMMODATIONS

Kuala Lumpur has a great variety of accommodations – from the most luxurious to the sleaziest – and is reasonably priced by international standards. Most of the luxury hotels are in the "Golden Triangle" centered around Jl. Ampang, Jl. Sultan Ismail and Jl. Bukit Bintang, about 1.6km east of downtown, while most of the cheaper accommodations is just north of downtown near Jl. Tunku Abdul Rahman.

Luxury

Kuala Lumpur Hilton, Jl. Sultan Ismail, ☎ 2422222, fax: 2493338. 589 rms. Luxurious, comfortable rooms in the heart of the business district. Popular discotheque. $164 S, $204 D, suites $224 S, $252 S/D.

Pan Pacific, Jl. Putra, ☎ 4425555, fax: 4417236. 571 rms. North of town center away from the main hotel area, but close to the Putra World Trade Centre and the Mall. Beautiful rooms and coffee shop well-known for its buffet and western snacks. $156 S, $168 D.

Regent of Kuala Lumpur, 160 Jl. Bukit Bintang, ☎ 2418000, fax: 2421441. 469 rms. Renowned for its service and opulent decor, the city's most luxurious and expensive hotel is located in the heart of KL's best shopping and nightlife. $200 S, $208 D, suites from $260.

Renaissance Hotel, cnr. Jl. Sultan Ismail/Jl. Ampang, ☎ 2622233, fax: 2631122. 399 rms. Black marble and crystal chandeliers are hallmarks of this hotel's graceful European style. Rooms are spacious, with good views of the city. $192 S/D, suites from $368.

Shangri-La Hotel, 11 Jl. Sultan Ismail, ☎ 2322388, fax: 2301514. 721 rms. Consistent award-winner for its cuisine, and well-known for its tropical gardens which give the hotel a cool shady ambiance although it's deep in the commercial district. $206 S/D, suites from $212.

Crown Princess, City Square Centre, Jl. Tun Razak, ☎ 2625522, 8003886 (toll-free), fax: 2624492. 576 rms. Within shopping center, city views, gym, swimming pool, Indo-Chinese, Chinese, and award-winning North Indian restaurants. $175 S/D, suites from $200.

Carcosa Seri Negara, Lake Gardens, ☎ 2821888, fax: 2826868. 13-suite hotel on 40 acres of private landscaped gardens, five minutes from the city centre. Former Governor's residence, two colonial mansions with large terrace, jacuzzi, and separate dining and living room. Curry tiffin and afternoon tea on the terrace. From $380.

High Intermediate

Concorde Hotel, 2 Jl. Sultan Ismail, ☎ 2442200, fax: 2441628. Centrally located. Attracts young travelers mainly because of its adjacent Hard Rock Cafe and trendy boutiques and eateries. $124 S/D, suites from $172.

Federal Hotel, 35 Jl. Bukit Bintang, ☎ 8003535 (toll-free), fax: 2489166. 450 rms. Older-style hotel with comfortable rooms in the heart of the shopping and nightclub district, revolving restaurant with western food. $104 S, $112 D.

Hotel Istana, 73 Jl. Raja Chulan, ☎ 2419988, fax: 2440111. 516 rms. Opulent "palace-like" decor, boasts a massive pillarless ballroom. Prices are reasonable, since amenities are as good as the luxury class hotels. $176 S, $188 D, suites from $260.

Hotel Nikko, 165 Jl. Ampang. ☎ 2611111, fax: 2611122. 470 rms. New, luxurious, spacious and very Japanese; boasts a popular Benkay Japanese Restaurant (book ahead). Ask about promotions. $164 S, $172 D, suites from $352.

Legend Hotel, Jl. Putra, ☎ 4429888; fax: 4430700. 450 rms. North of KL near the Putra World Trade Centre, and the Mall shopping center. Elegant decor and excellent dining at the Museum Chinese Restaurant. $136 S, $144 D, suites from $260.

New World Hotel, 128 Jl. Ampang, ☎ 2636888; fax: 2631888. 521 rms. Contemporary Asian design, Olympic size swimming pool and health club. Shares facilities with the adjoining Renaissance Hotel. $98 S/D, suites from $164, executive floor $204.

Hotel Capitol, Jl. Bulan, ☎ 2437000, fax: 2430000. 240 rms. New hotel in business and shopping center, one stop service to answer guests' needs at the push of one button, cafe with designer sandwiches and gourmet coffees. $92 S, $98 D, suites from $220.

Low Intermediate

Asia Hotel, 69 Jl. Haji Hussein, off Jl. Tunku Abdul Rahman, ☎ 2926077, fax: 2937734. 203 rms. Long-established mid-range hotel has good rooms with TV, hot showers AC, but is in the interesting, but fairly notorious Chow Kit market area. $56 S/D.

Champagne Hotel, Jl. Bunus, off Jl. Masjid India, ☎ 2986333, fax: 2932422. 37 rms. Great location in the fascinating "Little India" area. Surrounded by bargain shops, cheap Muslim Indian and Malay restaurants, and excellent-value lunch and night-time food centers. Rooms are comfortable and clean with own hot-water showers, AC, $30 S/D, $42 family.

Heritage Station Hotel, Main Railway Station, ☎2735588, fax:2732842. 160 rms. Right in the city center, renovations have retained the colonial feel, but rooms are now of standard size. Rates include breakfast. $52 S/D, suites from $105.

Hotel Malaya, Jl. Hang Lekir, ☎ 2327722, fax: 2300980. 238 rms. Located in the heart of old Chinatown and within easy walking distance of all the major downtown sights, bus station and GPO. Restaurant serves Western and Chinese food. $50 S, $76 D.

Hotel Pudu Raya, Puduraya Bus Station, ☎ 2321000, fax: 2305567. 175 rms. A great place if you're traveling by bus or share taxi as KL's main stations are downstairs. Take the lift to the 4th floor. All rooms AC with own bathroom. $ 41 S, $46 D, superior (with fridge) $49.

The Lodge, 2 Jl. Tengah, off Jl. Sultan Ismail, ☎ 2420122, fax: 2416819. 46 rms. The cheapest hotel in KL's most expensive junction, opposite the Hilton and Istana Hotels. Older, motel-style rooms with AC and hot showers, swimming pool, and excellent outdoor pavement restaurant. $46 S/D, superior $55 S/D.

Swiss Inn, 62, Jl. Sultan, ☎ 2323333, fax: 2017799. 110 rms. In the heart of Chinatown and easy access to great dim sum and hawker fare. Excellent people-watching sidewalk cafe. $45 S, $53 D.

Budget

Coliseum Hotel, 100 Jl. Tunku Abdul Rahman, ☎ 2926270. 10 rms. A historical landmark, this hotel is basic and pretty seedy, but the restaurant and bar, once frequented by Somerset Maugham and other notable novelists, is extremely popular and serves famous steaks. All rooms share baths, $11 S non-AC, $14 D AC.

KL International Youth Hostel, 21 Jl. Kampung Attap, ☎/fax: 2306870. 14 rms. Close to Railway Station, clean and comfortable. Dorm beds in AC rooms are $5 for first night, and $3.20 after that. Meridien International Youth Hostel, 36 Jl. Hang Kasturi, ☎ 2321428. In Chinatown and close to Central Market and all the major sights. Dorm beds (members) $3, rms. $10, all with common bath.

Sunrise Travellers Lodge, 89B Jl. Pudu Lama, ☎ 2308878. Popular with backpackers because of its closeness to the bus and taxi station at Puduraya. Prices are much the same as the Travellers' Moon.

Travellers' Moon Lodge, 36 Jl. Silang (the street south of Jl. Tun Perak), ☎ 2306601. 12 rms. Very friendly and centrally-located close to Chinatown and the bus station. Popular with backpackers. Dorm beds $3, S/D $10 with fan and shared bathroom. Breakfast is RM2.

Travellers Station, Main Railway Station, ☎ 2735588 (ext. 3070). New, comfortable and friendly backpackers, with kitchen, laundry, hot showers, notebooks on latest travelers' experiences, and Internet access. AC dorms and private rms from $5.

YWCA, 12 Jl. Hang Jebat, ☎ 2383225. 12 rms. Located just east of Chinatown. Clean, comfortable rooms only for women, couples and families. $12 S, $20 D, $32 family.

LOCAL TRANSPORTATION

Walking. It is best to walk around the downtown area as the traffic is often horrendous, and even though taxi drivers know where jams occur they still get stuck.

Taxis. The best way to get around town if the distances are too great to walk or if the weather – always hot and humid – has taken its toll. All the major hotels and shopping complexes have taxi stands, or alternatively you can just hail them from the side of the road. Avoid taking taxis from outside the Puduraya Bus Station as this is a notorious place for rip-offs; instead walk about a block away and hail one. Taxis should always use their meters, and usually do, except when going on long trips like the airport when they will usually quote a fare. Fares are very reasonable by international standards.

Buses. Another alternative, but some drivers have outrageous driving techniques, and blatant disregard of traffic rules, so a ride in one is a unique KL experience, but not for the faint-hearted. Have spare change ready, as Intrakota has a much-criticized policy of not providing change for their 90 sen flat fare rate. However, you can break notes at various main bus stations. To get to Petaling Jaya, the Airport, Shah Alam and Klang, take buses from the Klang Bus Station on Jl. Sultan Mohammed (just south of Central Market).

Light Rail Transport (LRT). Once this is completed, it will provide a comprehensive and convenient means of getting around KL and the Klang Valley. Although integration with other public transport routes has yet to be worked out, the finished sectors are already providing a welcome alternative to being stuck in a traffic jam. Buy tickets at stations.

KTM Komuter. Speedy, comfortable AC train service within the Klang Valley that is great for traveling into the outer areas, including Seremban in the south and Rawang in the north. To be integrated with the LRT and bus services. Buy tickets at stations. Ask at the Main Railway Station about day and weekly passes.

Car Hire. Most leading international car-hire firms have offices at the airport and in Kuala Lumpur, including Avis, Jl. Sultan Ismail, ☎ 2417144; Budget, 29 Jl. Yap Kwan Seng (off Jl. Ampang), ☎ 2625116; Hertz, Kompleks Antarabangsa, Jl. Sultan Ismail, ☎ 2421014. Other local firms include National, Parkroyal, ☎ 2480522; Orix Car Rentals, Jl. Sultan Ismail, ☎ 2423009; STT, 19 Jl. Dang Wangi (opposite Singapore Airlines), ☎ 2982064; SMAS, UBN Tower, Jl. P. Ramlee, ☎ 2307788, Mayflower, Jl. Segambut Pusat ☎ 6221888. Expect to pay around $42 per day. Also check the classifieds in the Malay Mail (afternoon tabloid) for cheaper rates.

DINING

Penang may be more well-known for its local cuisine, but KL has the most variety, for not only are the different regional cooking styles served up, but there is also a great range of international restaurants. Eating out is a passion with Malaysians, and most will frequent the outdoor food stalls anytime of the day or night which dish up a fantastic array of economically-priced meals. The majority of families buy *bungkus* (wrapped to take-away) meals at least once a week. Restaurants are also extremely popular, especially on special occasions. Malaysia has reasonably strict food and hygiene controls, particularly in KL, and it is safe to eat at outdoor eating stalls.

Hawker food

Popular food centers are the "Hilton" food stalls, behind the Hilton Hotel on Jl. Sultan Ismail, which are open for *nasi campur* (rice and curry lunch) where diners select what they like, buffet-fashion from a fantastic array of meat, vegetable, seafood and local Malay salad dishes known as *ulam*. Another good spot for this style of lunch is the outdoor food stalls in the center of Jl. Masjid India. At the northern end of this road, beside Semua House, the hawkers open from dusk till dawn and sell great satay, *nasi lemak* – rice in coconut cream, and heaps of other Malay specialties. There are also food centers in the basement of Lot 10 on Jl. Bukit Bintang; the ground floor of Ampang Park on the corner of Jl. Tun Razak and Jl. Ampang; and on countless sidewalks and corners throughout the city and its suburbs.

Malay

Because of the proliferation of excellent Malay stall food there are not as many restaurants as you would expect featuring the local cuisine. **Spices** in Concorde Hotel, Jl. Sultan Ismail, ☎ 2442200 has a good selection of well-cooked Malay dishes. Good for northern **Penang and Kedah**-style food is **Rasa Utara**, 34-35 Lower Ground Floor, Bukit Bintang Plaza, Jl. Bukit Bintang, ☎ 2488369. Try the *roti jala* – a delicate lacy pancake – with beef *rendang*, a dry curry, and their local iced drinks including sugar cane juice and fresh coconut. Prices are reasonable, around $10 for two. For **seafood** in a pleasant lakeside setting head for the **Nelayan Floating Restaurant** at Taman Tasek Titiwangsa, 3km north of downtown off Jl. Tun Razak. The path around the huge lake is a pleasant place for a walk if you feel like working up an appetite. Along Jl. Tuanku Abdul Rahman and Jl. Masjid India are a number of working-class, **economically-priced Malay** eateries which open from very early breakfast to late at night.

Chinese

Petaling Street, in the center of Chinatown, closes to vehicular traffic at night and becomes a **night market** where you can dine amongst the lively din of hawkers' shouts and competing cassette shops. Jl. Bukit Bintang and the lanes that run off it are also Chinese areas that offer a great choice of stall food. In Chinatown, try the *bah kut teh*, believed to have originated in Malaysia, a spicy pork soup always served with Chinese tea, and popular around mid-morning. *Yong tau foo* – deep-fried bean curd, fish balls and vegetables – another renowned snack is best opposite the Indian temple on Jl. Ulu Klang on the way to the zoo. The Chinese, although economical with most other things, love to splurge on a meal, and will pay exorbitant prices for the privilege of eating abalone, sharks' fins, or birds' nest soups. A favorite **up-market restaurant** is the **Golden Phoenix** at the Hotel Equatorial on Jl. Sultan Ismail, ☎ 2617777, which specializes in exotic seafood and venison dishes. Two good places for expensive dim sum – steamed and deep-fried tidbits – are the **Shang Palace** in the Shangri-La Hotel on Jl. Sultan Ismail, ☎ 2322388, and the **Teochew Restaurant**, 272 Jl. Pudu, ☎ 2416572. Other pop-

ular but pricey restaurants include the Hai-Tien-Lo in the Pan Pacific Hotel on Jl. Putra, ☎ 2935555, which has one of KL's most impressive menus; the **Ming Palace** at the Ming Court Hotel on Jl. Ampang, ☎ 2618888, which specializes in spicy **Szechuan** cuisine; and the **Hakka Restaurant** at 231 Jl. Bukit Bintang, ☎ 9858492, which does home-style Hakka cuisine and live seafood.

Indian

The best place to find cheap and tasty **North Indian food** is around the Jl. Tuanku Abdul Rahman/Jl. Masjid India area, especially for economical *roti canai* – Indian pancake with lentil curry – breakfasts, and afternoon snacks of murtabak – pancakes stuffed with spicy meat or sardines. Award-winning restaurant **The Taj** has outlets in both the Federal, Jl. Bukit Bintang, ☎ 2489166, and Crown Princess Hotels, Jl. Ampang, ☎ 2625522. Renowned for its *naan* – oven-baked flat breads, and chicken tandoori, as well as its excellent yoghurt drinks, *lassi*. For **South Indian banana leaf meals** and **vegetarian food** there are a number of small restaurants in the downtown area of Lebuh Ampang and Jl. Tun H.S.Lee just north of Jl. Tun Perak. These places are very cheap and do good *thosai* – thin crepes stuffed with potato curry and other South Indian specialties. South Indian food is also plentiful in the Brickfields area, just south of the Railway Station. For upmarket vegetarian food served on traditional stainless steel trays, try **Anna Lakshmi Restaurant**, at 94 Jl. Maarof, Bangsar, 3km from the city center.

Western

Fast food is easy to get in KL. There are at least a dozen **McDonalds** in KL. **Kentucky Fried Chicken** are at Plaza Yow Chuan, Jl. Ampang, and along Jl. Tuanku Abdul Rahman. **Pizza Hut** are in the basement of The Weld, Jl. Raja Chulan, and the basement of Yow Chuan Plaza on Jl. Ampang. **Delifrance**, for pastries, rolls and coffee has a popular cafe in Lot 10, Jl. Bukit Bintang, and on the ground floor of The Mall on Jl. Putra. The best American-style food is at the **Hard Rock Cafe** in Concorde Hotel on Jl. Sultan Ismail, and the virtually identical **Jump** on Jl. Tun Razak. Pricey, but the meals are huge, the coffee's great, and the music's loud. **The Lodge** outdoor restaurant on the corner of Jl. Raja Chulan and Jl. Sultan Ismail serves medium-priced and tasty steaks and grilled fish and is a good spot to people watch. Secreted behind the trendy pubs at Jl. Kia Peng is **Bon Ton**, ☎ 2413614, a charming colonial bungalow which has a wonderful menu of Eastern and Western dishes. Ring to book a table. A truly international (and expensive) selection of eateries is found in the upper-class **Bangsar** area, about 20 min from downtown KL, where you'll get everything from Mediterranean to Thai and American grills.

Japanese and other Asian

There are a number of expensive Japanese restaurants around KL including the **Keyaki** in the Pan Pacific Hotel on Jl. Putra; the **Chikuyo-tei** at Plaza See Hoy Chan, Jl. Raja Chulan; and **Kampachi** in the Pan Pacific. More moderately-priced and excellent value are the **Hoshigaoka Restaurants** at The Mall and at Lot 10 where a plate of sushi costs around $6, and there are a number of cheaper set meals. **Korean cuisine** is also popular – try the **Koryo-Won Restaurant** in Kompleks Antarabangsa, next to the KL Hilton, and **Nol Bol** in the Life Centre, near Concorde, where you get value-for-money Korean BBQ. For good **Thai food** head for **Cili Padi** in The Mall, the **Barn Thai Jazzaraunt** off Jl. Tun Razak near the Crown Princess, and **Barn Thai Vistana**, off Jl. Ipoh.

SERVICES

Banks

The major banks are all located in the downtown central business district and open from 9.30–10am to 4pm Mon–Fri, and 9am to 12.30pm on Saturday. Money changers have slightly better rates and are prolific around Jl. Masjid India, Jl. Tuanku Abdul Rahman, and at all major shopping complexes. Department stores change currency as do all large hotels but their rates are not as good.

Information

The best place for information is MATIC (Malaysia Tourist Information Complex), in a restored historical villa at 109 Jl. Ampang, ☎ 2943929, fax: 2621149. To get there, take the bus from Lebuh Ampang (Nos. 176, 177). Traditional dances and dramas are performed there in their theatre. Tourism Malaysia is in the northside of town at the Putra World Trade Centre (beside the Pan Pacific Hotel and opposite The Mall), on Jl. Tun Ismail, ☎ 2935188, fax: 2935884. Information centers can be found at Terminal 1, Sultan Abdul Aziz Shah International Airport, the Main Railway Station, ☎ 2746063. The Kuala Lumpur Tourist Information Centre is at the corner of Jl. Parlimen and Jl. Raja (opposite the Padang), ☎ 2936664.

Publications

Local English language dailies are the *Star, New Straits Times*, and the *Malay Mail*. For the latest sights and happenings in town, check out *Vision KL* or *Day & Night*, available in most bookshops.

TOURS

A KL city tour takes about three hours and runs in the morning and afternoon. It includes Chinatown, Railway Station, colonial buildings, Muzium Negara, Parliament House, National Mosque, Istana Negara, and Masjid Jamek. A "country" tour takes in "Embassy Row," a batik factory, Batu Caves, a Malay village and rubber-tapping. Selangor Pewter Tours cost about $10 per person. A nightlife tour includes dinner and a cultural show at a Malay restaurant and a tour of Chinatown by night, for around $22. For bookings, call: **Great Value Holidays**, MATIC, ☎ 2483257, **World Express Malaysia**, Bangunan Angkasaraya, Jl. Ampang, ☎ 2489601.

NIGHTLIFE

The favorite after-dark occupation for sedentary KL'ites is the *pasar malam* or night markets. Chow Kit area heading south into Jl. Tuanku Abdul Rahman is a maze of stalls and markets. Down the back lanes you will find the sleaze center of town. Each suburb hosts a *pasar malam* once a week. **Cultural shows** of traditional dance and drama are often staged at the MATIC tourist information complex in Jl. Ampang and sometimes at Central Market. Information offices have brochures that list what's happening each month. For **theatre**, check out the dailies, *Vision KL* or *Day & Night* or ring: Actor's Studio, Plaza Putra (underneath Dataran Merdeka) ☎ 2945400 for everything from music to drama and dance, or Theatre Upstairs, near the KL Tower, ☎ 2308122 for great comedy and revues. **Pubs** and **Nightclubs** cater variously to KL's trendy types or Chinese businessmen unwinding after work. The latter are especially fond of karaoke bars in the Bukit Bintang area; if you want this unique experience check out the huge **ATT KTV Musical City** on Jl. Imbi. A large mix of pubs has sprung up to cater to KL's increasingly cosmopolitan and overseas-cultured people. So you have a selection that includes the bar at **Coliseum Hotel** on Jl. Tuanku Abdul Rahman, noisy and popular with Indian lawyers, and **Hard Rock Cafe** in the Concorde Hotel, where Harley Davidsons line up, and which play good and loud recorded rock and sometimes have live bands. Besides the ones in the hotels, KL's nightspots come and go, and what's popular one month can well be closed the next. A popular venue is now around the back of the luxury hotel strip on Jl. Sultan Ismail, where some old colonial mansions have been revamped into nightclubs. **Modesto's** is a popular dance place and is chock-a-bloc on weekends, as is the adjacent **Brannigan's**. **Wall Street**, Jl. P. Ramlee, features jazz, and the prices of drinks rather than stocks rise and fall as the night goes by. Another jazz place with excellent Thai food is the **Barn Thai Jazzaurant** off Jl. Tun Razak, and opposite, **Tapas** in Micasa serves great margaritas. The very American **Jump** is a popular dance place, and bartenders' antics steal the show. Outside the city, the **Bangsar** suburb boasts neck-to-neck trendy, international joints, which come and go even faster than in KL, but guarantee a good night's fun.

MUSEUMS AND ART GALLERIES

Muzium Negara (National Museum), Jl. Damansara, ☎ 2825255. Open 9am to 6pm daily. Cultural dioramas and special theme exhibitions.

National Art Gallery, 1 Jl. Sultan Hishamuddin, ☎ 2300157. Open 10am to 6pm daily, closed on Friday from 12–2.45pm. Permanent exhibitions of local and foreign artists.

P. Ramlee Memorial, 22 Jl. Dedap, Setapak. ☎ 4231131. Former house and now museum dedicated to P. Ramlee, Malaysia's late, great film-maker/song-writer/actor and singer. Has videos of his movies and memorabilia from the 50s and 60s – great for film buffs.

Maybank Numismatic Museum, 1st floor, Menara Maybank. ☎ 2308833. Open 10am to 6pm. Notes and coins of early Malaya to the present.

Forest Research Institute Malaysia (FRIM) Museum, Kepong. ☎ 6342633. Open 8am to 4.15pm daily except Friday lunch and Saturday afternoons. Old colonial forestry museum set amongst beautiful forested grounds. Good for short jungle walks.

Gedung Raja Abdullah – Tin Museum, Jl. Raja Abdullah, Klang. ☎ 3327383. Open 10am to 6pm, closed on Fridays. This historical warehouse has displays on Selangor's early history and the growth of the tin industry.

Orang Asli Museum, km 24 Jl. Pahang, Gombak. ☎ 6892122. Open 9am to 5.30pm, closed on Fridays. Excellent displays of handicrafts and culture of Peninsular Malaysia's aboriginal peoples.

SHOPPING AND SOUVENIRS

Kuala Lumpur has recently become an attractive shopping destination rivaling Singapore because of the ringgit's more favorable rates. The cheapest shopping – for clothing, shoes, cassettes, and fabrics is at the Chow Kit market area, Petaling Street night market, most *pasar malams*, and along Jl. Tuanku Abdul Rahman. Globe Silk, Mun Loong, are both small department stores on the latter street which are popular with local bargain hunters although it's sometimes difficult to get western sizes. Pertama Complex and Campbell Complex are great for shoes and electronics. Jl. Bukit Bintang is a shopper's mecca comprising Bukit Bintang Plaza, the adjoining Sungai Wang Plaza (clothing, shoes, cameras, and electrical goods), and the more upmarket Lot 10, Kuala Lumpur Plaza and Star Hill. Across a lane from these adjacent plazas is Imbi Plaza which caters almost exclusively to computer shops where both hardware and software are on sale. Central Market has a large range of good souvenir T-shirts, batik clothes, cheap but well done local watercolors, and cheap curios. Batik cloth and clothing is also good at Batik Malaysia on Jl. Tun Perak. Royal Selangor, the world-famous pewter manufacturer has outlets all over the city and its factory in Sentul, 3km northeast of downtown is well worth a visit to see pewter being made.

AROUND THE NORTHEAST

To get to **Batu Caves**, the limestone massif renowned for its temple cave 13km northeast, catch a taxi, for a No. 11 minibus from Jl. Pudu or Nos.69/70 Len Seng bus from Jl. Ampang. For **Templer Park** and **Kanching Forest Reserve** take either bus Nos 66, 72, 78 or 83 from Puduraya.

Fraser's Hill
(Bukit Fraser)

GETTING THERE

To get to this colonial hill station, 101km north of KL, charter a taxi from Puduraya ($25), or a cheaper method is to get a share taxi to Kuala Kubu Bharu ($2.50) then catch the 8am or noon buses to Fraser's Hill, a 2-hour bus journey. Or you can charter a taxi from Kuala Kubu Bharu to the hill station for $12. Motorists, take heed that due to the narrowness of the road, it's open to traffic going up at odd hours, from 7am and traffic going down from 6am. The road is open to two-way traffic between 7.41pm and 5.59am.

ACCOMMODATIONS AND DINING

The top place to stay is the attractive but overpriced, **Smokehouse Hotel**, which caters to a small but wealthy clientele. Located 1.5km from the village, rooms cost around $150. In the center of the village overlooking the golf course is **Quest Resort**, ☎ (09) 382300. Its 88 rooms are comfortable and have a good view. $83 S/D on weekends and $67 on weekdays; prices include American breakfast. The Nuri bar, which doubles as a karaoke outlet, is probably the only nightspot in Fraser's, one of the few places open till midnight. **Fraser's Pine Resort**, a complex of holiday apartments, ☎ (09) 382122, on Jl. Quarry, 1.5km from the village center, overlooks jungle-clad hills. It has tennis and squash courts, a sauna, and kitchens and lounges in all apartments although only the expensive ones provide cooking facilities. One-bedroom suites $96, 3-bedroom suites $156.

The old stone **bungalows** run by the **Fraser's Hill Development Corp.**, which can be booked at the information center beside the clock tower, ☎ 09-3622044, fax (09) 3622273, are a good deal. Most are charming old houses with pretty flower gardens and great views. Some have housekeepers that provide good Malay-style meals. Rooms with attached bathroom cost around $32 S/D. The very central, but characterless **Puncak Inn**, above the shops, charges around $22. **Termerloh chalets** (12 rooms) are $20 per room. Probably the best deal of all is **The Gap Resthouse**, a marvelous colonial-style building with elegant old rooms, marvelous views, and a reasonably-priced dining room, but it's 6km from Fraser's Hill at the start of the one-way road. Good place to stay if you miss the last bus to Kuala Kubu Bahru. Rooms cost around $8 S/D with attached bathroom. All the pricey hotels have restaurants. The Merak Coffee House at the Quest Resort serves steam boat lunch and dinner at $8 for a minimum of two persons. For cheap eats, there are small outdoor Malay restaurants beside the shops. The restaurant at the Golf Club is reasonably priced for snacks, but the Malay food stalls about half a km from here, beside the children's playground, are the best deal in town. The Gap Resthouse does good strong black coffee and fried noodles, as well as western breakfasts.

SERVICES

Treks

Trails named after the pioneers of Fraser's Hill, such as Bishop, Hemmant, Kindersley and Maxwell, meander through rainforest. The latest to open and most difficult is the 6km Pine Hill trail.

Bird-watching

One of Malaysia's most popular bird-watching centers. (See Nature Tours in Travel Advisory)

TOURS

White water rafting. The Selangor River which gushes down from Fraser's provides some nice white water, mainly Class 1-2 from about 0.5km from the Pertak recreational area, and a Class 2-3 further up. **Nomad Adventures** Tel/fax: (03) 7047585, (017) 8889020, use two-person kayaks and single-person canoes; they throw in photos of you in action too. Only day trips. **Wilderness Experience** ☎ (03) 7822377, fax: (03) 7822387, offer rafting experiences, and do either day runs or a 2D/1N trip on weekends.

Genting Highlands

GETTING THERE

To get to Malaysia's most kitsch hill resort of high-rise hotels, casino and theme parks, well-heeled gamblers who can't afford to waste time catch a helicopter from Subang Airport. Buses and share taxis run from Puduraya. Buses stop at the Genting Skyway Station at Awana Hotel, and a cable car goes to the top.

ACCOMMODATIONS AND DINING

Everyone comes here to gamble and it's not a budget traveler's scene at all. Like all casino hotels, the luxury **Genting Hotel** makes most of its money on the take and the rooms are reasonable at around $52 (low season). There is also cabaret-style dinner theatre. The four-star **Highlands Hotel** costs the same, while the **Resort Hotel** and **Theme Park Hotel** are cheaper at $38. **Awana** is a golf resort, and is more pleasant, being midway up the hill. All the hotels have restaurants. For tours and prices, which includes gambling chips, ☎ 800-8228 (toll-free).

West of Kuala Lumpur

To get to Petaling Jaya, Shah Alam, or Klang, catch buses from the station in Jl. Sultan Mohamed, just south of Central Market or you can catch the KTM Komuter from the railway station. The KL-Klang bus No. 222 stops at Section 8 in Shah Alam and you can walk to the State Mosque and the Agricultural Park from there. Alternatively, charter a taxi from either Puduraya or from Shah Alam itself. From Klang buses go north to Kuala Selangor and south to Banting and Morib. It is easy to get to Jugra, the old royal capital, with your own transport, but quite difficult and slow by public transport. Carey Island, where the Mah Meri woodcarvers live is even more difficult without your own car, and before visiting you must get permission from the Department of Orang Asli Affairs in KL, ☎ 5590375. At Teluk Panglima Garang, 17km south of Klang, turn right to Carey Island, then right again across the river to the Golden Hope plantation. Sungai Bumbun village is up the first left fork, 20 mins down a dirt road.

2

Perak PRACTICALITIES

Perak's attractions are spread out, so the best way to see them is by road, which will take you through magnificent limestone scenery. There are few fancy hotels, except for Pangkor and Cameron Highlands, but there is always a rustic resthouse or clean Chinese hotel in which to spend the night. Cameron Highlands, Pulau Pangkor are heavily touristed by locals and Singaporeans, especially during public holidays.

Prices in US dollars. S=single; D=double; AC=airconditioned. Telephone code 05.

Ipoh and Kinta Valley

GETTING THERE

By Air

Malaysia Airlines fly daily to Ipoh from Kuala Lumpur ($26). Pelangi Airways flies once a week from Johor Bahru ($64) and Medan in Indonesia ($82). The airport is 5 km from the city. Taxis cost $5 to town. MAS office: Bangunan Seri Kinta, Jl. Sultan Idris Shah, ☎ 2414155. Airport ☎ 3122459.

By Road

From Kuala Lumpur's Puduraya taxi stand, share taxis cost $9 for the 3-hr journey. Express buses run hourly to Ipoh through the day, less frequently at night. Costs $3.80.

By Train

Traveling this way, you alight at the old Moorish Railway Station close to most hotels. KTM Bhd run regular express services from the north and south. The fare from KL is $16 1st class, $9 2nd class.

LOCAL TRANSPORTATION

Walking is the best way to get around Ipoh's old center where most of the historic sights and best eating are. To go further afield, taxis are inexpensive if shared. Ipoh's main taxi stand is on Jl. Raja Muda. **Taxis** can be chartered for trips to the cave temples ($2 to Perak Tong & Sam Po Tong), Papan, Batu Gajah and Kellie's Castle. The **local bus** system is slow and cheap, but everywhere is serviced by bus and it's an interesting way to meet the locals. **Cars** can be hired from the airport and from the major hotels from around $32 per day.

ACCOMMODATIONS

Rooms range from spacious luxury to basic lodgings that often double as Chinese-run brothels. The latter are okay for single males and couples, but single women are advised to go for medium-priced hotels which are a better bargain all round.

High Intermediate

Casuarina Parkroyal Hotel,18 Jl. Gopeng. ☎ 2555555, fax: 2558177. 198 rms. Luxurious, well-landscaped, swimming pool, shopping arcade, car-rental, disco, cocktail lounge and good buffet breakfasts. Outside of town. $88 S/D, suites from $180.

Heritage Hotel, Jl. Raja Dihilir, ☎ 2428888, fax: 2415299. 270 rms. Spacious, pleasant, overlooking the Turf Club, Continental grill, Japanese restaurant, Chinese restaurant, health club. $72 S/D, suites from $160.

The Syuen, 88, Jl. Sultan Abdul Jalil. ☎ 2641105, fax: 2640580. 290 rms. City center, rather garish decor, Cantonese restaurant, spa and Shiatsu massage, fun pub, disco, poolside bar. $92 S/D, suites from $200.

Intermediate

Hotel Excelsior, 43 Jl. Clarke. ☎ 2536666, fax: 2536912. 181 rms. Close to town, popular with Chinese businessmen because of its Chinese restaurant, disco, steambath/sauna and gym. $43 S, $47 D, suites from $67.

Hotel Lotte 97 Jl. Dato' Onn Jaafar. ☎ 2542215, fax: 2551160. 30 rms. Good central location, close to restaurants and fast food centers (Kentucky, A&W), value for money, clean rooms with TV, hot-water, phones, fridge. AC $28 S/D, suites $47.

Majestic Ipoh Station Hotel (100 rms). Ipoh Railway Station. ☎ 2555605, fax: 2553393. Definitely a nostalgia trip. Renowned old colonial hotel with huge verandah, original lights, old-style restaurant, and marvelous city views. $48 S/D, family rooms $72.

RegaLodge, 131 Jl. Raja Ekram. ☎ 2425555, fax: 2411555. 93 rms. New, close to town yet quiet location, restaurant/pub serving local and Italian food, rooms with AC, attached baths, TV, hairdryer. $31S/D, suites from $70.

Ritz Garden Hotel, 79, Jl. C.M. Yussuff, ☎ 2547777, fax: 2545222. Central, close to express bus station, good restaurant on top floor with buffet meals. $39 S/D, suites from $44.

Budget

The best budget accommodation is the **YMCA**, 211 Jl. Raja Musa Aziz, ☎ 2540809, fax: 2412093. Fairly close to town, next to park, basic canteen, clean, AC with attached baths, hot showers and telephones are $16 S, $20 D, dorms $6. Slightly pricier, but with large clean renovated rooms is the **Dragon & Phoenix Hotel,** Jl. Toh Puan Chah ☎ 2534661, fax: 2535096. In town close to shops. All with AC and attached baths. $28-$64 S/D but ask for discounts. There are dozens of cheap Chinese hotels close to the bus and railway stations. Most offer basic facilities, fans and shared bathrms, and are usually on busy streets, so try for a rear room. Singles around $6, doubles $8. **Embassy Hotel**, 35 Jl. C.M. Yussuff. 15 rms. ☎ 2549496. Clean rooms with attached bath and fan are $6 non-AC, $7-$15 AC.

DINING

Ipoh is famous throughout Malaysia for its Chinese food, notably *kway teow* – flat rice noodles fried with prawns, chicken and greens, and *popiah* – beansprouts shredded radish, and pork or prawns in a spring roll. Another local treat is the pomelo, *buah limau bali*, a pendulous-shaped citrus fruit with pink flesh rather like a sweet grapefruit. The fruit thrives in Ipoh's limestone soil especially around Tambun and dozens of fruit stalls line the main road south just past the Sam Po Tong cave temple. The really large variety is sought-after as Chinese altar offerings and although expensive are not as juicy as the smaller ones.

Chinese

There are so many good hawker stalls, often set up in the front of coffee shops, notably around Jl. Leech, and Jl. Sultan Yusof, that diners have merely to look at where the biggest crowds are gathering to ascertain the quality of the food. The Chinese are very fussy eaters and would never patronize a place unless the food is up to their exacting standards. A plate of noodles is rarely over $1. Jl. Leech (Jl. Bandar Timah) is the gourmet center. **Kedai Kopi Nam Heong** is good for mid-morning curry mee–mee in a moderate curry sauce, and their specialty, Ipoh Chicken Kway Teow. **Kedai Kopi Kong Meng**, another old-style coffee house is good for *kway teow, popiah,* satay, and roast chicken and rice. **Hall of Mirrors**, former barber shop with wall of mirrors, hence its name, specializes in the regular Ipoh mee dishes and a creamy caramel custard. **Sin Yoon Loong** is the original famous Ipoh "white coffee" shop where there is excellent home-made coconut jam (kaya) and toast for breakfast and a variety of local cakes. **Ming Court** near Excelsior Hotel is packed for dim sum breakfast. **Wooley Food Centre** in the outer suburb of Ipoh Garden and the **Stadium** are other local favorites with stalls specializing in a wide range of Chinese food. A $1 taxi ride from the town center.

Malay

Pusat Penjaja Padang Kanak Kanak, Jln. Raja Musa Aziz (formerly Jl. Anderson). This food center is set around a small park and is open to the wee hours serving a wide variety of Malay specialties including; satay, chicken-rice, nasi goreng, mee goreng, and local deserts like the shaved-ice treat ABC. For excellent fresh soyabean drinks and *chendol*, the coconut-milk and jelly drink, try the stall up the road from the Pusat Penjaja, two blocks from Jl. Sultan Iskandar Shah.

Restoran Perwira, 156 Jl. Gopeng, Medan Gopeng. Out of town on the main road south to Ipoh, this restaurant is a good place to dine when returning from Sam Po Tong cave temple. Serves the regular Malay standbys as well as sweet and sour fish, beef with soya sauce. Good for nasi campur at lunch.

Railway Station food stalls, to the left and right of the station. Not as good a selection as the Pusat Penjaja, but a good place to hang out while waiting for a train and listen to Malaysian rock on the juke-boxes. Stalls at the **Stadium** also dish up a variety of goodies.

Indian Muslim

Restoran Kader, 71 Jl. Sultan Yusof, in the Indian section of Chinatown, specializes in nasi kandar (a Penang-style curries and rice) and murtabak (spicy meat pancakes).

Behind City Hall next to the Clock tower is a food center specializing in nasi kandar and also good for murtabak, roti canai, kaya or toast. Cheap and centrally-located.

Western

FMS Bar, Jl. Sultan Yusof, overlooking the Padang, an original colonial restaurant serves western-style meals and is a good place for drinks in a bar little changed since the day when it was frequented by rubber planters and tin-mining bosses.

Royal Casuarina Coffee House, at the luxury hotel serves local and western coffeehouse fare, and is good for those craving a good steak and desserts. Prices to match the decor: expensive. **Cafe le Rendezvous** at Eastern Hotel, serves set lunches and dinners for cheap rates. MacDonalds is at Jl. Clare, A&W near Eastern Hotel.

SERVICES

Information

Perak Tourist Information Center, Jl. Tun Sambanthan (behind City Hall), ☎ 2412958.

Banks

Bank Bumiputra, Maybank, Jl. Sultan Idris Shah; Hongkong & Shanghai Bank, Jl. Sultan Yusof.

NIGHTLIFE

Ipoh's after-dark entertainment centers around a profusion of karaoke lounges and dimly-lit "lounges" known as pubs with resident bands, that often double as pickups for good time girls. Definitely not your English variety of pub where single women are scarcely noticed, for here it's unusual for unaccompanied women to enter. There are quiet discos at the big hotels.

Cameron Highlands

GETTING THERE

The **train** only goes to Tapah, but there are plenty of buses and shared taxis from there to the highlands as this is main reason most people get off here. Fares from Kuala Lumpur are $8 1st class AC, $3.50 2nd class AC, $2.50. **Buses** from Puduraya take 4 hrs and cost $7, to Tapah, $3. From Tapah buses leave from the bus station every hour from 8am to 5pm (excellent Indian Muslim restaurants opposite). The 2-hour journey costs $1.80. From Kuala Lumpur's Puduraya taxi stand, **share taxis** cost $51 per taxi all the way to the highlands. From Ipoh a seat costs $9 and from Tapah $5.

LOCAL TRANSPORTATION

Getting to the Cameron Highlands is no problem between the two towns of Tanah Rata and Brinchang because local buses ply this route frequently. Buses also run to Kampung Raja at the far end of the highlands road. Taxis can be hired by the hour ($6) for trips to Gunung Brinchang, Boh and the Sungai Palas Tea Estates.

Or fit travelers can get the bus to the Sungai Palas turn off and walk in past Robertson's Rose Gardens to the tea estate (4 km). There are great walking trails around Tanah Rata, ranging from easy to difficult. Maps with numbered trails are easy to obtain from the shops in Tanah Rata, but these are only a rough guide. Bring along some food and water and warm clothes on the less-frequented trails.

ACCOMMODATIONS

Prices to match the topography—much higher than the coast. During school holidays (in both Malaysia and Singapore) prices increase and popular places can be booked out for weeks ahead. However, even at peak periods you can still find a room, especially at the more expensive places.

High Intermediate

The Concorde Lakehouse, Lubok Taman, 30th mile, Ringlet. 18 rms. ☎ 4956152, fax: 4956213. Overlooking a lake (actually a man-made lake) this Tudor-style hotel is good for peace and quiet, but difficult to get around if you have no car as it's far from the towns. Formerly owned by the eccentric Captain Forster who used to display a "Full House" sign even if the hotel was empty. Full of memories, antique furniture, stone fireplaces, vast bathrooms. $88 S, $100 D, suites from $132.

Equatorial Hill Resort, Brinchang. ☎ 4961777, fax: 4961333. New, further up from Brinchang town, great views, Chinese restaurant, food court, heated swimming pool, tennis, squash. 1, 2 and 3 bedroom apartments with kitchenette from $79, hotel rooms $67 D.

Heritage Hotel, Jl. Gereja, Tanah Rata. ☎ 4913888, fax: 4915666. 170 rms. Hilltop, great views from balconies, Cantonese restaurant, BBQ & steamboat, bar, health center, traditional massage, squash, tennis, tours. $84 S/D, suites from $152.

Merlin Inn Resort, Jl. Tanah Rata, Tanah Rata. ☎ 4911211, fax: 4911178. 63 rms. Modern facilities and rms with views of the golf course, Chinese restaurant, bar, karaoke, pool tables. S/D $112, suites $184.

Strawberry Park Resort, Jl. Kemunting, Tanah Rata. 172 rms. ☎ 4911166, (03) 2626166, fax: 49114919. Refurbished garish mock-Tudor resort popular with Singaporeans and package tours, with all mod-cons, good views, squash, tennis, swimming pool, horse-riding. S/D $88, apartments from $124.

Ye Olde Smokehouse Hotel, by the Golf Course, Tanah Rata. 19 rms. ☎/fax: 4911214. Tudor-style retreat with English gardens, ivy-covered walls, overstuffed "chintz" lounges by the bar, wood-fires in the evenings, roast-beef and Devonshire teas. Definitely the best place in Malaysia to have a taste of the colonial life. From $140 S/D, $200 family rooms.

Intermediate

Kowloon Hotel, Main Road, Brinchang, ☎ 4911366, fax: 4911803. 24 rms. Overlooks the square at Brinchang, warm cosy rooms, carpeted, TV, IDD telephones, attached baths, and downstairs Chinese restaurant. $23 S/D, family $43.

New Garden Inn, Tanah Rata (opp. site playground). ☎ 4915170, fax: 4915169. 47 rms. Nice situation, quiet rooms with wooden floors, attached bathroom with hot water, Malaysian restaurant, karaoke. $66 S/D, $140 family room for 7 people with adjoining bath.

Budget (under $20)

Bala's Holiday Chalets, Jl. Tanah Rata, Tanah Rata. ☎ 4911660. 26 rms. Take the marked turnoff 2 km north of Tanah Rata, or just follow the back-packers. Run by the extroverted Bala, who organizes cheap tours and bus tickets, this rabbit-warren of rooms is for travelers who love to be around other travelers. Western-type snacks, good views and garden and notice board. Dorms $3, rooms with attached baths, hot water $26-$48 S/D. On the main road at Tanah Rata overlooking the main square, and close to food are **Seah Meng Hotel**, No. 39, ☎ 4911907, and **Sri Sentosa Hotel**, No. 38, ☎ 4911618. 11 rms each. Basic hotel with clean rooms, shared baths $10-$14, attached baths, hot water, about $20 S/D.

DINING

Malay foodstalls in the center of Tanah Rata's Main Road have a good variety of rice and curries – nasi campur, fried rice, noodle soups, and western-style meals including sizzling steaks and lamb chops. Cheap and tasty. Indian-Muslim food is good at **Restoran Kumar**, Main Rd, Tanah Rata. They serve roti canai, murtabak and briyani – rice cooked in ghee with spices served with mutton – good for cool evenings. Reasonably priced. Chinese food-lovers head for **Parkland Hotel**, Main Rd, Brinchang. Serves good steamboat, but best for more than two as the portions are large. $10 for two. **Jasmine Restaurant**, Main Rd, Tanah Rata has good value 4-course set meals for $4. **Ye Old Smokehouse Hotel**, serves excellent but pricey English meals including roast beef and dumplings in the cosy dining room. Less pricey but a treat is their Devonshire teas: scones, strawberry jam and cream (tinned) on the flagstone terrace. **Lakehouse Hotel** at Ringlet has expensive but excellent leg-of-lamb with mint sauce topped off with a cream caramel dessert. **Chop and Steak House**, Main Road, Tanah Rata has good western food at reasonable prices and large helpings of apple pie. Bala's provides backpackers fare with a set menu at night. Good for those staying there but hardly worth the journey out from town.

SERVICES

Banks Both Maybank and Hong Kong & Shanghai have branches in Tanah Rata's Main Road, Standard Chartered is on Jl. Station (near the clock tower).

Pulau Pangkor

GETTING THERE

Pelangi Air fly to Sitiawan (12 km from Lumut) from KL ($25) and Singapore ($78) four times weekly. Taxis meet all flights. Shared taxis from Ipoh to Lumut (83 km) cost $3 and leave from the bus station at Medan Kidd. From Kuala Lumpur, several daily airconditioned buses run from Puduraya bus station to Lumut; the 6-hour journey costs $5. From Ipoh, buses run at hourly intervals ($1.20), and there's also a daily bus from Cameron Highlands ($3.20). Cars are left at Lumut overnight at the council car-park west of the jetty, but for longer stays the private carparks which provide watchmen are safer. From the main town jetties, ferries ply the half-hour journey from Lumut to Pangkor every 15 minutes between 6.45am to 7.30pm for $1 return. Ferries also service the Pan Pacific Resort and the Pansea Pangkor Laut from special jetties at Lumut. On Pulau Pangkor, taxis run from Pangkor to Pasir Bogak (2 km) for $4 and can be chartered for around island and other smaller trips. Check the fare before you get in. Buses also run from Pangkor to the end of Pasir Bogak Beach at hourly intervals. Bicycles and motorcycles are a much better mode of transport for exploring the island. These can be hired at both Pangkor and Pasir Bogak for $2 a day (bicycle), $12 (motorcycle).

ACCOMMODATIONS

Pangkor's prettiest beach is the private domain of the luxurious **Pan Pacific Resort Pangkor**, 163 rms. Golden Sands, Pulau Pangkor. ☎ 6851399, fax: 68522390. Day trippers can use it however, with lunch thrown in for $16. Golf course, 5 restaurants, large swimming pool, tennis-courts, aquasports center (snorkeling, windsurfing, waterskiing), and a disco. Prices start from $128 S/D, house on the rocks $200, suites $240; discounts in off-season. **Pangkor Laut Resort**, Pulau Pangkor Laut. 137 rms. ☎ 6991100, 800-6400 (toll-free), fax: 6991200. Private island resort boasts the scenic Emerald Bay, AC cottages with bathrooms and verandahs, swimming pool, tennis courts, sauna, jacuzzi, gym and squash courts. $207 S/D, suites $500. In the north-east, the Malay village concept **Teluk Dalam Resort**, 119 rms. Has one-room chalets from $92 S/D, and two-room bungalows for $128; the island's first landscaped children's pool, cafe by beach, water sports; promotions include island tour and breakfast. ☎ 6855000, (03) 2626166, fax: 6854000. **Sri Bayu Beach Resort**, at Pasir Bogak, ☎ 6851951, fax: 6851050 which offers local cabaret-type entertainment with drinks, BBQ at its restaurant, disco, karaoke, swimming pool. $147 S/D, suites $200. **Sea View Hotel**, Pasir Bogak, 60 rms. ☎ 6851605, fax: 6851970. Old-style hotel facing the beach with seaside restaurant. Good value and location—great for sunsets. With bath and AC $46 S/D, AC chalets for $83, all with breakfast and tea included. The rest of Pasir Bogak and Teluk Nipah have a huge range of budget accommodation to choose from, including campsites. Walk along the beach till something catches your fancy. At Pasir Bogak, **Pangkor Anchor**, ☎ 6851363, is very clean, 34 mosquito-proof, A-frame huts for $7 in immaculately-kept grounds. The school-mistress proprietor, Mrs. Wong, shows a list of rules before you book in, but it is the cleanest and by far the quietest of all the neighboring establishments. **Khoo Holiday Resort**, 107 rms, ☎ 6852190, fax: 6851164, is popular with locals. AC, attached baths, rates include breakfast and dinner. $38 S/D; sea-facing, triple-share rooms $50.

DINING

All the hotels and "camps" have their own restaurants serving Malaysian food and some basic western fares, but Pangkor is best-known for its Chinese seafood meals – crabs with chili, baked fish, tiger-prawns in garlic, and lots of other succulent dishes – are best in Pangkor town at the kedai kopi (coffee shops) in the main street. Meal for two (fish, prawns, veges, and rice) costs around $16.

Along the Perak River

GETTING THERE

This region is best explored by car, rented from either Ipoh or Kuala Lumpur, or it is ideal for bicycling with flat terrain and tiny tarred roads with little traffic. However, travelers can catch local buses for the trip between Teluk Intan and Parit, or alternatively as the locals do, just hail share taxis anywhere along the route. Both express buses and share taxis run from Kuala Lumpur's Puduraya Station and Ipoh's Bus Station to Teluk Intan.

ACCOMMODATIONS

Rumah Rehat (Resthouse), 858 Jl. Rumah Rehat, Teluk Intan. Out of town in a quiet location. Rooms with attached bathrooms and overhead fans cost $14 S, $25 D. **Anson Hotel**, Jl. Sekolah, Teluk Intan. ☎ 6226166. 51 rms. Centrally located, and probably the best of the Chinese-run hotels in Teluk Intan. AC rooms around $18, deluxe $40. **Rumah Rehat Cempaka Sari (Resthouse)**, Jl. Kelab, Parit. ☎ 3772679. 12 rms. Wooden traditional-style kampung house and newer stone houses overlooking the Perak River. Marvelous setting and good value. New rooms. $30 S/D, wooden house, $14 AC S, $22 family.

DINING

Restoran Yussofia, Jl. Pasar, Teluk Intan. Turn-of-the-century shophouse with plaster relief of Arabic writing and a crescent moon and stars. Their *murtabak* and roti canai are as memorable as the decor. Malay food stalls in the square in front of the clock tower serve up cheap local specialties like gado-gado – bean curd and sprouts in a peanut sauce – and the old standbys fried rice, and lots of noodle dishes.

Kuala Kangsar

GETTING THERE

Trains depart several times a day from Ipoh and taxis can be chartered for $10 or less if you can find passengers to share the cost.

ACCOMMODATIONS

Rumah Rehat, Bukit Candan. ☎ 7763872. 17 rms. Great value, rooms have high ceilings and big windows, great river views from the dining room. Book ahead as it is usually full of civil servants. AC, hot water, $28 D, suite $46. **Mei Lai Hotel**, 7F Jl. Raja Chulan. ☎ 7761729. 6 rms. Basic Chinese hotel. OK if the resthouse is full. AC, attached bath $14.

DINING

Malay food stalls are down near the Sayong ferry jetty on Jl. Tambang (good for popiah). Ask around for char koay teow and chinese steak. On Jl. Raja Chulan, there are Chinese coffee shops and Restoran Sri Rahmaniah serves good Muslim Indian curries, *murtabak* and rojak. There's a KFC on Jl. Kangsar and on the corner of Jl. Sultan Iskandar is the Soon Fatt Bakery good for hot bread and cakes. Evening meals are best at the Resthouse, which serves Chinese food – try the steamed fish salad for something light. Meals for two with iced lime-juice costs $12.

Taiping

GETTING THERE

Express trains service Taiping daily from Ipoh/KL and Butterworth as do express buses. Share taxis from Ipoh's main bus/taxi station cost $3 per person. Walking is the best way to get around town, and the Lake Gardens is only 1 km from downtown. Land Rovers run from the base of Bukit Larut to the hill station every hour on the hour from 8am–5pm. The 40-min winding route costs $1.20. For tourist information, call the Municipal Council, ☎ 8080777.

ACCOMMODATIONS

Rumah Rehat Baru (New Resthouse), Jl. Sultan Mansor, Taman Tasik Taiping, ☎ 8072044. 27 rooms. Overlooking the Lake Gardens, quiet location with big rooms and balconies. Popular and often booked out. Phone before making the 1km trip from downtown. Rooms with fans $13 D.
Legend Inn, 2 Jl. Long Jaafar, ☎ 8060000, fax: 8066666. 88 rms. Classiest hotel in town, near express buses, spacious lobby and cosy cafe, view of Bukit Larut, big rms. $63 S/D, suite $88.
Hotel Panorama, 61–79 Jl. Kota. ☎ 834111. 70 rms. Centrally located next to a large supermarket. Rooms have no views, but great bathrooms, huge comfortable beds, Arctic-like AC so the blankets come in handy. $30 S/D, suite $56.
Meridien Hotel, 2, Jl. Simpang. ☎ 8081133, fax: 8075251. Decent, Chinese restaurant, room service, laundry, central AC, attached baths. $22 S/D, deluxe $27 S/D.
Bukit Larut Resthouses, ☎ 8077241. Bookings can be made in advance, or organized from the Land Rover station. Colonial-style rooms are $6-$20 each.

DINING

Taiping is a food freak's dream town and with so few international tourists the food is gen-uine local cuisine at uninflated prices. Every street corner has a coffee-shop with its own specialty – won ton mee, chicken rice, curry mee, to name a few. There are two big hawker centers in town – the Malay dominated Pusat Penjaja, and the multi-ethnic food center under the Fajar Supermarket, both on Jl. Panggung Wayang. At the latter, there is popiah, satay, rojak sotong – squid salad with peanut sauce – and fresh ginger tea. There's always Mc-Donald's for those who must. Bismillah Restoran opposite the town market has roti canai breakfast; the lunch-time *briyani istimewa* (special) is $1.50. The Resthouse has also a good restaurant for those who can't be bothered to walk downtown. On Jl. Kota towards the lake are Chinese restaurants. Seafood is fresh here.

Perak Museums

Muzium Perak, Jl. Taming Sari, Taiping. ☎ 8072057. Open daily 9.30am–5pm. Closed 12-2.45pm on Friday and on public holidays. Ethnography and natural history.
Muzium Di Raja, Bukit Chandan, Kuala Kangsar. ☎ 7765500. Open daily 9.30am–5pm. Closed Thursday afternoon, Friday, and public holidays. Royal heirlooms and artifacts.
Geological Survey Museum, Scrivenor Rd (off Jl. Sultan Azlan Shah), Ipoh. ☎ 557644. Open Tuesday–Friday, 8am–4pm; closed 12–2.45pm on Thursday and Friday.

Penang PRACTICALITIES

3

The state of Pulau Pinang, or Penang, consists of the island of Penang and Seberang Prai (Province Wellesley) a strip of land opposite on the mainland. They are linked by the 13.5km Penang Bridge and by ferry from Butterworth, the railhead to Kuala Lumpur and Singapore in the south and Bangkok in the north. Georgetown, the capital, in the northeast of the island, has a population of around half a million and that of the entire state is close to one million. Penang has long been the commercial and tourism hub of the northwest and as a result is well set up for travelers with a wide range of accommodations. Visitors either stay in Georgetown or along the northern beaches strip centered around Batu Ferringhi. The island's cuisine is famous throughout the region and is the main reason why many domestic tourists flock there throughout the year. Prices in US dollars. S=single; D=double; AC=airconditioned. Telephone code 04.

GETTING THERE

By Air

Frequent daily flights operate from Singapore (MAS, SIA) ($98); daily flights from Bangkok, Haadyai and Phuket (MAS, Thai); regular flights from Medan (Sumatra) and Madras (India) with MAS. Cathay Pacific also have a direct flight from Hong Kong. Malaysia Airlines' daily domestic flights are from Kuala Lumpur ($42), Johor Bahru ($71) and Langkawi ($20). Pelangi Airways fly there daily from Kota Bahru ($35) and thrice a week from Kuala Lumpur. Local Offices: Malaysia Airlines, Komtar, Jl. Penang, ☎ 620011. Singapore Airlines, Wisma Penang Gardens, Jl. Sultan Ahmad Shah, ☎ 363201. Thai Airways International, Wisma Central, 202 Jl. Macalister, ☎ 2268000. Cathay Pacific, Wisma Hai Tong, 28 Jl. Penang. Airport ☎ 2260917. Most agencies are situated along Jl. Penang and Lebuh Chulia. Taxis run on a fixed-price coupon system from Bayan Lepas International Airport to Georgetown hotels ($7–8.50) and Batu Ferringhi's seaside hotels ($8.50–11). Buses run from the airport to Pengkalan Weld, Georgetown.

By Sea

Passenger and vehicular **ferries** operate a 24-hour shuttle service between Butterworth on the mainland and Pengkalan Weld, Georgetown, every 20 minutes and hourly after midnight. The ferry jetty is next to the Butterworth bus and railway stations. A five-hour **hydrofoil** service links Penang with Medan (Sumatra). Office is next to the Tourism Malaysia Office opposite the clock tower in Georgetown. High-speed ferries also operate from Langkawi.

By Train

From Butterworth the International Express departs daily to Bangkok, fares are $40 1st class, $18 2nd class. Express trains from Kuala Lumpur cost $27 1st, $14 2nd. There are additional charges for overnight berths. Reservations can be made at Butterworth station, ☎ 3312796 or at the Railway Booking Station at the ferry terminal in Georgetown, ☎ 2610290.

By Road

Taxis operate from the railway station at Butterworth and take the long, but interesting route across the Penang Bridge. Fares around $20 to Batu Ferringhi, less to Georgetown. Long-distance, airconditioned **buses** operate to and from the bus station beside the railway at Butterworth. However, some companies in Georgetown also offer bargains on bus tickets around Malaysia and these buses operate from Georgetown itself. From Butterworth, bus fares (and taxi fares) are as follows; KL $8 ($17), Taiping $1.60 ($5), Ipoh $3.60 ($9), Alor Setar $2. Bus services also run from here to Hat Yai, Thailand $11, Phuket $19, Bangkok $28. Taxis take you all the way up too, but you have to change cabs at Bukit Kayu Hitam.

LOCAL TRANSPORTATION

Walking is the best way to get around the old center of Georgetown, but **trishaws** make a good alternative during the hottest part of the day and at night. Negotiate before you get in, but expect to pay RM2 per mile. If you arrive late at night the trishaw operators can always find you an empty room. Expect to pay $1.50 from the ferry jetty to the cheap hotel area around Lebuh Chulia. Penang's **taxi**-drivers are notorious for never using their meters, even with local customers, so bargain before the ride. From Georgetown to Batu Ferringhi the fare is around $8.

Bicycles can be rented from booths along the main road at Batu Ferringhi, or in Georgetown at the Eng Aun Hotel, 380 Lebuh Chulia for $2. Motorcycles are hired at Batu Ferringhi for around $10 per day – shop around for the best price as this is negotiable during off season. **Cars** can be hired from all the big hotels. Besides the airport, Avis are at 388, Batu Feringghi, ☎ 8811522; Hertz, Farquhar St, ☎ 2635914; National, Weld Quay, ☎ 2629404, but there are cheaper car-rental shops at Batu Ferringhi – try Ruhanmas Rent-A-Car, opposite the Golden Sand Hotel, ☎ 8811023. They charge $28 per day for a Nissan Sunny or $32, Suzuki Jeep.

Buses are the cheapest way to get about the island and the main bus terminus is at Lebuh Victoria, where city buses operate. No.7 goes to the Botanical Gardens. The other terminal is at Jl. Dr. Lim Chwee Leong. Terminal Blue buses (Hin Bus Co.) operate from Georgetown, passing Pulau Tikus, and along the northern beaches to Batu Ferringhi and Teluk Bahang; the Penang Yellow Bus Co., runs south of the city to the Snake Temple, on to Balik Pulau and west through the hills to Teluk Bahang; and the green (Lim Seng Seng Bus Co.) ply the Air Hitam route to the Kek Lok Si Temple and the Penang Hill railhead. It's possible to go all around the island in a day for around $2.50, but get an early start as the last bus from Balik Pulau to Teluk Bahang leaves mid-afternoon.

SERVICES

Information

Tourist Information Center, Level 3 Komtar, ☎ 2614461. Open 9.30am to 6.30pm. Tourism Malaysia is at the airport, and 10 Jl. Tun Syed Sheh Barakbah (opp. the clock tower), ☎ 2619067. Open office hours. Penang Tourist Association, close to Tourism Malaysia, ☎ 366665, open 8am to 4.15pm.

TOURS AND SIGHTS

Check with any travel agency for local tours. Saber Holidays at the airport charge $48 per car (4 passengers) per 4 hours to your tailor-made itinerary. They also do set tours. Georgetown is easy and fun to explore on foot by yourself with a Heritage Trail map (3 hours maximum). Ask at Tourist Information. The Pinang Cultural Center at Teluk Bahang, ☎ 8851175, offers cultural tours and performances at its village ($14), and dinner theatre ($36). There are also day trips to Langkawi ($44) and Paya Marine park off Langkawi ($32). Office, ☎ 2625630, next to Tourism Malaysia. **SA Tours**, ☎ (03) 2429155,

fax: (03) 2429420, has a 3D/2N fly/cruise package from KL, including 1 night on the Empress, 1 night in a Penang beach resort, and Penang city tour.

Consulates

Britain, Royal Norwegian, Sweden, Standard Chartered Bank chambers, ☎ 2625333. Royal Danish, Hongkong Bank chambers, ☎ 2624886. France, 82 Lebuh Bishop, ☎ 2629707. Indonesia, 467 Jl. Burma, ☎ 2274686. Japan, 2 Jl. Biggs, ☎ 2268222. Royal Thai, 1 Jl. Tunku Abdul Rahman, ☎ 2268029.

Communications

The GPO is at Lebuh Downing, one block along Lebuh Pantai from the clock tower, open Monday to Saturday 8.30am to 4.30pm. Another PO is on the ground floor of Komtar. Telekom, the center for international calls and faxes, is on Jl. Burma, open 24 hours a day. Calls can be made direct to your home-country operator.

Changing Money

Major banks are on Lebuh Pantai near the GPO, however they charge stamp duty and a commission on travellers' checks, making it a better proposition to visit the licensed money changers along Jl. Penang, Lebuh Chulia, Lebuh Pitt and Lebuh Pantai.

ACCOMMODATIONS

Penang is a popular tourist destination all year round but there is an off-season from May to August, when the sea gets choppy and dirty from the southwest monsoon, and some hotels, especially at Batu Ferringhi, give discount rates. Never accept the first rate quoted; always ask if they have a "discount" price. During the peak times around Christmas it may be difficult to get a room at the popular budget hotels, but Penang has an enormous amount of hotels in all price ranges and there are always empty rooms. Most beach hotels offer free shuttle services to town, but taxis are exorbitantly expensive to and from Batu Feringghi.

Luxury

Rasa Sayang Hotel, Batu Ferringhi Beach. ☎ 8811811, fax: 8811984. 316 rms. The original luxury hotel along the beachfront. Malay-inspired architecture, beautifully-landscaped lawns with mature tropical trees and coconut palms, huge swimming pool, health club, massage, squash, tennis, watersports, disco and excellent restaurants. $140 S, $156 D.

Golden Sands Resort, Batu Ferringhi. ☎ 8811911, fax: 8811880. 401 rms. Beachfront resort boasts the usual facilities, watersports center, swimming pools, 24-hr room service, lawns, beachfront bar and four restaurants including Italian. $102 S/D, suites from $260.

Penang Mutiara, Teluk Bahang. ☎ 8852828, fax: 8852829. 438 rms. Only five-star resort at Teluk Bahang, wau bulan chandeliers, songket decor. Peaceful, quiet and the beach is cleaner than at Batu Ferringhi. $140 S/D, suites from $280.

Penang Parkroyal, Batu Ferringhi. ☎ 8811133, 800 8268 (toll-free), fax: 8812233. 333 rms. Features local, Asian, Japanese and Continental cuisine, Art-Deco inspired disco, water sports, gym, flood-lit tennis courts. $120 S/D, suites from $300.

Shangri-La Inn Jl. Magazine, Georgetown. ☎ 2622622, fax: 2626526. 442 rms. Centrally located high-rise has great views across a sea of red-tiled shophouses to the harbor. Swimming pool, health club, Western and Chinese restaurants. From $144 S/D.

Beachcomber Paradise Hotel, 33A, Jl. Tanjung Bungah. ☎ 8908808, fax: 8908333. 198 rms. First hotel along the beach tourist belt that gives you easy access to town. Reasonable room rates and great food. $96 S/D, suites from $200.

Casuarina Beach Hotel, Jl. Batu Feringghi. ☎ 8811711, fax: 8812155. 180 rms. Renovated, all rooms face the sea, excellent Italian restaurant Il Ritrovo. $104 S/D, suites from $230.

Equatorial Penang, 1 Jl. Bukit Gambol. ☎ 6438111, fax: 6448000. 413 rms. Really a luxury hotel but rates are low because it is 15km from the beaches and Georgetown. Next to the Bukit Jambul Golf Course. Spectacular 41m-high lobby, gym, business center, Chinese, Japanese and Western restaurants. $115 S, $125 D, suites $240.

Sheraton Penang, 3 Jl. Larut. ☎ 2267888, fax: 2266615. 279 rms. Right in the town centre, minutes to shopping district, and food stores. $126 S/D, suites from $160.

High Intermediate

City Bayview, 25-A Farquhar St. ☎ 2633161, fax: 2634124. Central, good Malay restaurant with excellent views, revolving restaurant also with views of Penang, swimming pool, fairly standard rooms. $68 S, $77 D, suites from $111.

Feringghi Beach Hotel, Jl. Low Yat, Batu Feringghi. ☎ 8905999, 8008299 (toll-free), fax: 8905100. 350 rms. On the opposite side of the road with a bridge linking to a secluded, nice beach. All rooms face the sea. $40S/D, suites from $140.

Palm Beach Resort, Batu Ferringhi. ☎ 8811621, fax: 8811051. 142 rms. Nestled between the luxury hotels, this reasonably-priced hotel offers good off-season discounts. All rooms have IDD phone, TV, in-house video and refrigerator. Nice shaded beachside restaurant. From $80 S/D.

Lone Pine Hotel, Batu Ferringhi. ☎ 8811511, fax: 8811282. 54 rms. Best bargain along the beachfront. The rooms are nothing fancy but have TV, IDD telephone, fridge and pool. The old-style beachfront restaurant and gardens shaded by casuarina trees give it a laid-back feeling. Management is great with children. $35 S/D, huge family rooms $46.

Bellevue Hotel, Penang Hill. ☎ 892256. Only hotel on Penang Hill has bird's eye views of Georgetown. Breakfast amongst the clouds on the garden terrace. Quiet, cool and comfortable rooms are tastefully decorated. Has an aviary of exotic birds—the private collection of the owner, one of Malaysia's foremost architects. AC $72 S/D.

Low Intermediate

The Merchant Hotel, 55 Jl. Penang, Georgetown. ☎ 2632828, fax: 2625511. One of the many hotels in this price category on Jl. Penang. Competitive prices here mean that rooms in Penang are consistently cheaper than most other Malaysian cities. All rooms with TV, IDD phone, air-con, and there's a 24-hr Coffee House which offers buffet supper for $2.60 from 11pm till the wee hours – great for late-arrivals. $46 S/D, suites from $104.

Cathay Hotel, 15 Lebuh Leith. ☎ 2626271, fax: 2639300. 37 rms. Close to historical and downtown sites, this 70-year-old hotel is in itself an attraction with its tiled arched foyer, spacious verandahs, and immense lobby. Rooms are massive and spotless. AC rooms have large baths with hot water. Guests can also order meals from the restaurant at the back which doubles as a "massage" health club at night. Staff also organize onward travel and are very helpful. Rooms with fans $18 S, $20 D; AC $23 S, $26 D.

Waldorf Hotel, 13 Lebuh Leith, Georgetown. ☎ 2626141. 57 rms. Just down from the Cathay Hotel, and in a great location for touring the downtown sights – Cheong Fatt Tze Mansion is just opposite. Rather colorless compared to the Cathay, but good value since the rooms have attached hot-water baths and AC for $20 S, $24 D.

Budget

Ali's Guest House & Restaurant, 53 Batu Ferringhi. ☎ 8811316. One of the last surviving cheap spots along the beachfront. Turn down the lane to the beach just past the Hotel Parkroyal. The little restaurant in the garden is a favorite hang-out for budget travelers, and the staff are easy-going and helpful. Rooms with fan and shared bathroom are $8 S, $12 D, and rooms with AC and attached bath cost $24 D.

Shalini's Guest House, 56 Batu Ferringhi. ☎ 8811859. Just down the road from Ali's, Shalini's is a plain, two-storey house, but has a real Malay family atmosphere. Shalini's Penang/Malay cooking, breakfast and evening meal, is what regulars return for. Shared bath and fan $12 S/D; AC and attached bath $20; and AC and hot-water bath $28.

Swiss Hotel, 431F Lebuh Chulia, Georgetown. ☎ 2620133. 34 rms. A favorite backpacker's hotel for at least a decade, this old-style Chinese hotel is set back from the noisy street, is in the center of old Georgetown, and is adjacent to cheap travel agencies. $7 S, $9 D for rooms with fan and shared bath.

Eng Aun Hotel, 380 Lebuh Chulia, Georgetown.

☎ 2612333. 40 rms. Directly opposite from the Swiss Hotel and just as popular. $7 S, $10 D for large fan-cooled rooms with shared bath.

Tye Ann Hotel, 282 Lebuh Chulia, Georgetown. ☎ 2614871. 10 rms. Old-style hotel with basic facilities fan and shared bath. Popular with budget travelers for its ground floor restaurant serving authentic English breakfasts. $6.50 S/D, $2.50 for a dorm bed.

Wan Hai Hotel, 35 Lorong Cinta, Georgetown. ☎ 2616853. 13 rms. This historic lane of attractive old shophouses is quieter than Lebuh Chulia around the corner. Popular with budget travelers, also has a small roof terrace. All rooms have shared baths and fans for $6.50 S/D, $2.50 for a dorm bed.

Hang Chow Hotel, 511 Lebuh Chulia, Georgetown. ☎ 610810. Close to Jl. Penang's Indian-Muslim restaurants and shopping bazaars. Moneychanger and restaurant on the ground floor. Fan-cooled, shared-bathrooms are $5.75 S, $6.50 D.

Youth Hostel (Asrama Belia), 8 Lebuh Farquhar. Go around the back and up to the second floor for the reception office. Must have valid YHA cards and there is a midnight curfew. $4 for a dorm bed with shared facilities.

YMCA, 211 Jl. Macalister, Georgetown. ☎ 2288211, fax: 2295869. 75 rms. Open to both men and women. About 2km from downtown, but within walking distance of the Thai Embassy on Jl. Tunku Abdul Rahman, and reasonably close to Pulau Tikus. $M2 is added for non-members but is waived for holders of student or YHA cards. All rooms have attached baths. $14 S, $15 D for rooms with fans, and $16 S, $17 D, for AC.

DINING

Penang is regionally famous for its food and many Malaysians, Singaporeans and Thais come here just for the cuisine. Eating is by far the major leisure occupation of all Penangites and the proliferation of eating stalls, hawker centers and restaurants is testimony to their passion. "*Sudah makan*" – have you eaten? is a popular greeting throughout Malaysia, but in Penang it is universal. Everyone frequents the lowliest of food stalls In a hawker center, if in doubt, just look for the crowded stalls and the food is bound to be good. When Penangites splurge – usually on big family dinners – they go the full hog and flock to the high-priced resort restaurants along Batu Ferringhi. Mention Penang to most Malaysians and they instantly think of *laksa* – a fish-based soup with flat rice noodles seasoned with lotus flowers and herbs; and *nasi kandar* – a lunch speciality of various curried meats with rice which was originally carried by hawkers in containers which hung off a *kandar* – a pole supported on their shoulders.

Nyonya

The traditional cuisine of the *babas* (Straits-born Chinese), which combines Malay and Southern Chinese cooking styles, is widely available in Penang and specialties include *otak-otak* – spicy fish paste steamed in banana-leaf packets, *Curry Kapitan* – rich chicken curry in coconut cream, and *chendol* – coconut milk with palm sugar and green noodles colored with pandanas leaves. Hawker stalls in the Pulau Tikus area between Jl. Burma and Jl. Kelawei sell *nonya* food as do the following: **Sa Chew Restaurant**, 37B Jl. Cantonment, Pulau Tikus, good for *otak-otak* and *laksa*, but only open for lunch. **Nyonya Corner**, Jl. Pahang, authentic Peranakan dishes carefully prepared, check out their kerabu dishes (salads). **Dragon King Restaurant**, 99 Lebuh Bishop, Georgetown, all *nonya* specialities, open for lunch and dinner.

Malay

Some of the best Malay food in Penang is at tiny food stalls for these are often run by housewives, and home-cooked food is superior to restaurant fare. Persiaran Gurney (Gurney Drive) foodstalls get into gear after sunset and operate until the wee hours. The first Malay laksa stall from the roundabout (western end) is excellent. Take your plate and sit on the nearby seawall. There's a good soyabean drink stall next door, and a little further up a sweet corn seller. Malay roadside foodstalls, built onto kampung houses overlooking the seafront at Jl. Tanjung Tokong, serve cheap breakfasts – *nasi lemak* (rice cooked in coconut milk), and *roti canai* with an onion and meat sauce. Further along, in front of the high-rise flat at Tanjung Tokong are stalls selling take-away *nasi campur* (rice and curries). For kampung cuisine buffet style, check out the City Bayview Hotel's **Eliza Malay Restaurant**, Farquhar St. ☎ 2633161.

Indian and Indian Muslim

Meat and seafood curries in rich sauces dominate this cuisine which lacks the variety of vegetable dishes found in Malay restaurants. Most establishments also serve *roti canai* (pronounced *chahnigh*) – a griddle-fried, wheat-flour "pancake" served with *dhall* (lentil curry), and its sister dish *murtabak* which is stuffed with a mixture of spicy ground meat and vegetables. One of the best-known is **Dawood Restoran**, 63 Lebuh Queen, ☎ 2611633, opposite the Sri Mariamman Temple which serves excellent *nasi kandar*. **Hameediyah Restaurant** at 164A Lebuh Campbell, and the original **Craven Cafe** on Jl. Penang have good *nasi kandar* and *murtabak*. The lunch-time stall in the **Toon Leong Coffee Shop** at the corner of Jl. Transfer and Jl. Argyll, and late-night stalls around the **Chowrasta Bazaar** are also good. The tiny lane beside the Kapitan Kling Mosque on Lebuh Pitt is also well recommended for *nasi kandar*. They start early and by 7.30am diners are tucking into massive piles of rice and curries. Tables are set up on the sidewalk and in early morning the space is shared with old Chinese women practising tai chi. Another Penang Indian speciality is rojak with deep-fried seafood smothered with peanut sauce. Hawker stalls along Persiaran Gurney are renowned for this dish. Further out of town is the excellent **Restoran Ibrahim** on the main road at Teluk Bahang which is a popular lunch-time stopover for *nasi kandar*, light and delicate *roti canai*, and *murtabak*.

Indian vegetarian restaurants are centered around the "Little India" section roughly bordered by Lebuh Bishop, Lebuh Penang, Lebuh Chulia and Lebuh Pitt. **B.M. Sagars Restaurant** on Lebuh Bishop specializes in North Indian vegetarian, while the best and cheapest place for southern Indian cooking including *masala thosai* – fine, rice-flour pancake filled with potatoes and vegetables – is **Krishna Vilas** on Lorong Pasar, in the block between Lebuh Queen and Lebuh King. **Kaliaman Restaurant** on Lebuh Penang is renowned for its slightly more up-market food. They do "banana-leaf" lunches – a great mound of rice with curry sauce, meat, vegies, chutney and yoghurt – for around $3.20 per person.

Chinese

A book could easily be written on the Chinese hawker stalls of Penang, so the following is merely the tip of the iceberg. Breakfast is quick and cheap at the outdoor stalls along Lebuh Carnarvon near the Lebuh Chulia end. Good for Hokkien mee – spicy noodles with bean sprouts and prawns, *wan tan mee* – egg noodles with sliced pork and dumplings, and o chien, fried oyster omelette. Other good breakfast spots include the coffee shops along Jl. Penang, Pengkalan Weld, Jl. Burma – up the Pulau Tikus end. For lunch, Sin Kuan Hwa Cafe on the corner of Lebuh Cintra and Lebuh Chulia sells good Hainanese Chicken Rice – rice cooked in chicken stock with sliced chicken. Many coffee-shops offer a selection of rice with meat and vegetable dishes, for around $2. Try the coffee shops along Jl. Penang. Towards evening an entirely different selection of food stalls springs up. Good spots include Lebuh Cintra, the Esplanade, Jl. Macalister (near Jl. Penang), and further west at the all-time favorite Persiaran Gurney. Service starts about 6pm and goes till well after midnight. *Bah kut teh*, a spicy pork soup served with traditional tea, is popular.

Some Chinese restaurants offer no menu (usually the best) and others that do often make the choice confusing by the sheer volume of dishes available – often up to 100. Try some Penang favorites like "claypot" dishes which are cooked over a charcoal fire, *padi* chicken – frogs legs with chillies, *kai lan* – greens with oyster sauce, *pai kuat wong* – spicy pork ribs, and *ha lok* – deep-fried tiger prawns. Up-market restaurants always specialize in China's regional cuisines. Hokkien cooking is good at **Chuan Lock Hooi Restaurant**, 1E-F Jl. Macalister. Although Georgetown has good seafood restaurants, it always seems fresher by the sea, and some of the best establishments are along the seaboard at Tanjung Tokong. Try **Hai Chu Hooi**, secluded at 338 Jl. Tanjung Tokong, where you can dine on fresh prawns and chilli crabs and watch the sun set over the sea. At **Ferringhi Village Restoran**, 157B

Batu Ferringhi, where a baked grouper with spicy sauce costs $6 and barbecued tiger prawns $4.50. For a meal where you cook raw ingredients in a soup in a metal container, try **Coca Steamboat**, Level 3, Island Plaza, Jl. Tanjung Tokong. **Dragon Inn** on Gottlieb Road, dishes up authentic Chinese dishes minus the monosodium glutamate (MSG).

Western

Many of the Chinese coffee shops around Lebuh Chulia and Lorong Cinta serve westernised snacks and breakfasts, a wise sales technique developed over the years in response to the backpackers who can't stomach Malaysian food early in the morning. Congregated around the cheap hotel area, popular Lebuh Chulia hangouts include: **Tye Ann Hotel** at 282, which serves porridge and toast with marmalade, and similar menus can be found at the **Rainforest Restaurant**, 294A, **Eng Thai Cafe**, 417, the **Sin Hin Cafe**, 402, and **Tai Wah Coffee Shop** at 487. At Komtar in Jl. Penang fast food outlets include **McDonalds, Kentucky Fried Chicken** and **Pizza Hut**. Many of the hawker centers also do "western" meals with a colonial Malaysian flavor, including lamb chops, steaks, and "chicken chop" – a deboned, deep-fried chicken steak. A popular spot out of town is the **Medan Selera Mutiara**, a hawker's center off Jl. Tanjung Bungah, next door to the Mutiara shopping center which also has a great bakery and serves home-made pizza. All these are very popular with expatriates living on the northern beaches. All the Batu Ferringhi luxury hotels serve western snacks and meals. **Il Ritrovo** at Casuarina Beach Hotel, ☎ 8811711, is one of Penang's few Italian restaurants. The cheesecake at the **Rasa Sayang's** coffee garden is creamy and delicious and almost too big. **Beach Blanket Babylon**, Lebuh Bishop, ☎ 2638101, is better known as BBB, the ultimate place for yuppies to dine and hang out; serves Continental cuisine and gourmet coffee.

NIGHTLIFE

Eating outdoors with a few beers is perhaps the most popular way to enjoy a Penang evening. Interesting spots to meet the locals for a beer are the **Tiger Bar** at 108 Lebuh Muntri, **Sumi's Bar and Restaurant** at 22 Lebuh Pantai, and the **Hong Kong Bar** at 371 Lebuh Chulia. Pubs are usually not your English variety but dark and rather sleazy spots where businessmen usually bring their girlfriends not their wives. A notable exception is **20 Leith Street**, the pub with the same name as its address, opposite the Cathay Hotel. Housed in an old colonial-style mansion, its walls adorned with scenes by Penang artists and antique clocks, the pub features a beer garden and a cosy bar with dart board. For sports enthusiasts, **Beers**, at the Parkroyal Hotel in Batu Ferringhi, is a sports bar that has styrofoam figures, boutique beers, a genuine Wurlitzer jukebox, and a ceiling of personalised currency notes. All the big hotels have nightclubs or discos. Try **Juliana's** at the Shangri-La Inn and the yuppie Cinta Disco at the Rasa Sayang. Italian styled **Modesto's** has made its way from Kuala Lumpur to the Sandy Bay Paradise. Novotel's **Shock!** is a Videotheque with a large dance floor, live bands and energetic deejays. **Babylon Boom Boom** in China Street Ghaut is a cabaret supper club, stand-up comedy. **Sol Fun Disco** at Weld Quay is a warehouse-turned-techno disco with live cabaret shows.

MUSEUMS AND ART GALLERIES

Penang Museum and Art Gallery, Lebuh Farquhar, Georgetown. ☎ 2613144 Displays of historical documents and paintings, Nonya porcelain, Malay kris and handwritten Korans, contemporary paintings, and outside is an old Penang Hill train and a statue of Penang's founder Francis Light. Open 9am–5pm daily. **Museum and Gallery, Universiti Sains Malaysia**, Minden (opposite Penang Bridge), ☎ 6577888. Contemporary art, traditional shadow-puppet theater, textiles, jewelery and crafts. Open 10am–5pm, Monday to Friday. Closed Saturday and Sunday pm. **Forestry Museum**, Teluk Bahang, ☎ 8851280, arboretum and displays. Open 9am to 5pm daily. **Yahong Art Gallery**, Batu Ferringhi, ☎ 8811251. Arts and handicrafts on display and for sale including batik paintings by the Father of Malaysian batik, Chuah Thean Teng and his talented family.

LIBRARIES AND BOOKSHOPS

Penang Public Library, 1st floor, Dewan Sri Pinang, Lebuh Duke, ☎ 6577888. Open 9 am–5pm Monday–Friday and on Saturday mornings. Other libraries are at the **Universiti Sains Malaysia**, ☎ 870230; **British Council Library**, 43 Green Hall, ☎ 2630330, open Tuesday and Wednesday from 10am–8pm, and Thursday to Friday 10am–6pm and Saturday 10am–4pm; **Alliance Francaise**, 8 Jl. Yeoh Guan Seok, ☎ 366008, open 9.30am–noon and 3.30–7.30pm weekdays only. **MPH Bookshop** in Island Plaza, Tanjung Tokong has a good range of local interest books as does Times Bookshop in Penang Plaza on Jl. Burma. **Second-hand books** are available in small shops along Lebuh Chulia.

SHOPPING

Penang offers plenty of bargains for the traveler who like ferreting around markets and bargaining hard. Department stores are fixed price, but everywhere else haggling for a lower price is very much the done thing.

Antiques and Curios. Lebuh Leith has many interesting and musty old shops selling antique clocks, old bronze and brassware, chinaware, Dutch ceiling lamps, old phonographs, and Chinese embroideries and porcelain. Saw Joo Aun,

139 Jl. Pintal Tali, specializes in antique furniture as do a few dealers on Lebuh Bishop. Chop Hong Seng, 41 Lebuh Carnavon deals in antique porcelain. Other knick-knacks are also found in the markets along Jl. Penang.

Arts and Crafts. Seals carved in wood or marble, known as cap (pronounced chop), can be made with your own name translated into calligraphy. Some have Chinese lions, or even your own Chinese astrology animal, carved on the tops. Available at Yee Chai Art Gallery, 255 Lebuh Victoria; Tong Bee Trading Company, 319 Lebuh Chulia; and Yahong Gallery, 47 Lebuh Leith and also at Batu Ferringhi. Chinese religious paraphernalia is sold along Lebuh Kimberley and Lebuh Carnavon.

Cassettes and Videos. Copyright laws have slowed down sales in pirate cassettes and videos, not to mention computer software, but some are still available under the counter. These are often poorly-produced, and the legal variety are of much better quality. Cassettes cost around $4.80 and a CD $16. The larger shopping complexes like Komtar in Jl. Penang, and Penang Plaza in Jl. Burma have shops stocking a wide variety of music.

Clothing. At Batu Ferringhi, brightly-colored, hand-painted, batik sarongs and T-shirts are popular souvenirs and in the evenings, sidewalk stalls sell fake, but quite good quality, designer T-shirts like Gucci and Benetton. Other good buys are pantsuits and dresses in rayon with printed "batik" designs imported from Indonesia. Tailors make up clothes to your own specifications. It's wise to make a drawing beforehand. Chowrasta Market on Jl. Penang, and Piccadilly Bazaar behind Jl. Kuala Kangsar specialize in all kinds of cotton, silk, and manmade fibre cloths. "Little India" near Lebuh Queen and King sell brilliant-colored saris, Indian kurtas, and Punjabi-style pantsuits.

Gold. Chinese goldsmiths are found along Lebuh Campbell, between Jl. Pintal Tali and Lebuh Carnavon, and Indian Muslim gold dealers are found along Lebuh Pitt, opposite the Kapitan Kling Mosque. Gold jewellery is an excellent buy in Malaysia as the gold is 22-24 carat and the cost of workmanship is low. Indian shops around Lebuh Queen and King offer ankle bracelets, nose and toe rings in silver and gold.

Leatherware. Cheap leather sandals and bags are sold in stalls along Jl. Penang particularly around the Chowrasta area, and also in the night market stalls at Batu Ferringhi. Handmade sandals are also available from Medan Capal, 6 Jl. Dato Keramat.

Photographic supplies. There is a host of camera and photographic shops in Penang specializing in quick prints and print film, however for good quality slide film go to the dealers in Jl. Penang, just down from Komtar.

⁴Kedah & Perlis PRACTICALITIES

INCLUDES PULAU LANGKAWI

Most tourists skip the rest of the northern states and head for the holiday isle of Langkawi, but if you have time on your hands and your own transport, the peaceful rustic north of verdant fields and smiling faces is enchanting. Accommodations are basic, but with industrialization, fancier hotels are emerging. Gourmets must not miss out on northern specialties like laksa (spicy noodles) and ikan panggang (grilled fish).
Prices in US dollars. S=single; D=double; AC=airconditioned. Telephone code 04.

Alor Setar

GETTING THERE

By Air

Malaysia Airlines flies daily to Alor Setar from Kuala Lumpur ($45). Pelangi Airways flies there once a week from Kota Bharu ($28). MAS office, Kompleks Alor Setar, ☎ 7311106. Airport ☎ 7144021. The airport is 20 min north of town. Taxis charge $1 per person to Alor Setar.

By Train

KTM Berhad run the Ekspres Langkawi which leaves Kuala Lumpur daily at 8.45pm and arrives in Alor Setar at 6am. The return service departs Alor Setar at 8pm and arrives in Kuala Lumpur at 5.10am. Single fares: 1st class AC $28, 2nd class AC $12 (berths cost marginally more).

By Road

Express buses depart from Puduraya bus station in Kuala Lumpur throughout the day and night. Fares from KL are $11, from Butterworth $1.50. The express bus station is off Lebuhraya Darulaman. The service from Alor Setar to Hat Yai in southern Thailand for around $5. Taxis also go to Alor Setar from Butterworth, Bukit Kayu Hitam (Kedah's border town with Thailand), and from Kuala Lumpur's Puduraya taxi station. Cars can be easily rented from Penang's main hotels or from car hire companies (see Penang Practicalities, p.245). This is a great way to see the state, especially the southern "Rice Bowl" and Lembah Bujang.

LOCAL TRANSPORTATION

As most of the downtown sights are within a block

or two, walking is the best way to get around. For the Royal Mausoleum at Langgar, and the State Museum take a taxi or a local bus. Both the main taxi stand and the local bus station are on Jl. Langgar in the middle of downtown. Cars can be rented at the airport or ask at Hotel Royale and Hotel Grand Continental.

SERVICES

Information

Brochures and information can be obtained from the State Tourism Department, State Secretariat Office, Wisma Darulaman (behind Balai Besar), ☎ 7301957.

Banking And Business Hours

Kedah follows the east coast states and observes the Islamic weekend. Businesses close on Thursday afternoons and all day Friday. Banks open from 10am to 3pm, Saturday to Wednesday, and 9.30am to 11.30am on Thursday. Major banks in Alor Setar include: Bank Bumiputra, Jl. Tunku Ibrahim; Maybank, Jl. Sultan Badlishah; Chartered Bank, Jl. Raja.

ACCOMMODATIONS

Intermediate

Hotel Grand Continental, 134 Jl. Sultan Badlishah, ☎ 7335917, fax: 7335161. 122 rms. Alor Setar's fanciest hotel is conveniently situated in the center of the commercial district. All rooms AC with private bath, TV, IDD phone, coffee house. $48 S, $52 D, suites $100 D.
Hotel Samila, 27 Jl. Kanchut (Jl. Pekan Melayu), ☎ 7318888, fax: 7339934. 52 rooms. Overlooks downtown historical sights. All rooms have TV and in-house videos, hot-water bathrooms. Coffee

house serves Chinese, Malaysian and Western meals. Has a noisy night club on weekends. Otherwise good value. AC $32 S/D.

Hotel Royale, Jl. Putera, ☎ 7330922, fax: 7330925. 40 rms. Spacious rooms with hot-water bathrms and TV. Laundry and rent-a-car services. Their outdoor seafood restaurant overlooking the river is popular and very good. All AC $18.50 S, $23 D, $24 Triple, $3 20 for extra bed.

Hotel Grand Crystal, 40 Jl. Kampung Perak, ☎ 7313333, fax: 7316368. Good-value with hot-water baths, swimming pool, sauna and coffee house. Easy walking distance to downtown and sights. AC $22 S/D, deluxe $27.

Budget

Hotel Miramar, 246 Jl. Putra, ☎ 7338144, fax: 7311668. Three blocks from the clock tower. All rooms AC with bathrooms and baths with hot water, extra for TV. $18 S/D. **Flora Inn**, 8 Kompleks Medan Raja, ☎ 7324235, fax: 7337846. 20 rms. No frills lodgings near shops and walking distance to town. Non-AC, shared baths from $10 D; AC, attached bath, TV and telephone $26 D. There are many old Chinese-style hotels with basic accommodations around the bus and railway station which all offer much the same in terms of value. **The Resthouse**, 75 Pumpong, ☎ 7322422, is 2km out of town on the Lebuhraya Darulaman. Set beside the Royal Golf Club it is quiet and peaceful, but is inconvenient without your own transport. AC $7-$9, non-AC $4.80.

DINING

The regional favorite is *laksa* – a spicy fish and noodle soup – which is found at dozens of hawker stalls throughout the city, but is best at the two roadside restaurants, Zakariah Laksa, and Din Laksa, 4km from Kuala Kedah. Here diners can enjoy real homemade laksa and a panorama of the rice-fields. Further on at Kuala Kedah there are a number of excellent Chinese seafood restaurants on stilts over the river.

The **Seafood Garden** at Hotel Royale is popular with seafood enthusiasts, but avoid the weekends when it is often booked solid. One of the town's busiest eating spots is **Hajjah Restoran** Jl. Pegawai on the way to Kuala Kedah. It also has outlets in Sg. Petani and Langkawi. In line with its Thai-style decor are Thai-style noodle and rice dishes and a very hot and tasty *tom yam* – chili and prawn soup. **Restoran Yasmeen** and **Restoran Rose**, within the block just up from Jl. Tunku Ibrahim on Jl. Sultan Badlishah both serve Indian Muslim specialties including *murtabak, roti canai, nasi kandar* and *rojak*. For dinner, take a bus to **Medan Selera Darul Aman** on Jl. Tun Razak, which has stalls selling goodies such as *laksa, satay, tom yam*. For western dishes the coffee shops at the **Hotel Grand Continental** and the **Samila Hotel** serve sizzling

steaks, lamb chops and soups and salads, but these dishes are not as tasty as the local fare. For bread, cakes and sandwich fillings, the **City Point** shopping center on Jl. Tunku Ibrahim has a supermarket and an adjoining bakery with tasty sardine rolls, wholewheat bread and a large variety of cakes and pastries.

Lembah Bujang

Bordered by Gunung Jerai to the north and the Sungai Muda to the south, Malaysia's richest archaeological area, in the southwest of Kedah state, has dozens of pre-Islamic remains of Buddhist and Hindu temple mounts scattered around the valley floor which date from the 5th to the 14th century. However, many are yet to be excavated and are far off the beaten track. Best and easiest to get to are the four restored temples within walking distance of the excellent Muzium Arkeologi (Archaeological Museum) at the foot of Bukit Batu Pahat. To get there, turn off from the North-South Highway at Sungai Petani (U) and head north towards Bedong, turning off at Merbok. Buses run from both Bedong and Sungai Petani to Merbok, but from there visitors must walk as there is still no alternative transport, although it's a pleasant rural stroll up to the museum and the historical park. Taxis can be chartered from Sungai Petani 26km away, but of course nothing beats your own transport as there is no accommodation

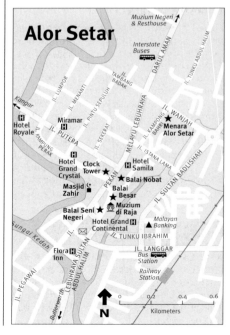

here. The museum is open daily from 8am to 4.15pm, and closed on Fridays from 12.15–2.45pm, and on the two major Muslim holidays Hari Raya Puasa and Hari Raya Haji. Entry is free. Guides are available but these should be organized beforehand by phoning the museum on 4572005, fax: 4574185.

Gunung Jerai

Kedah's only hill station is on the peak of Gunung Jerai, a massive limestone outcrop, 1200m high in the southwest of Kedah state. Located 59km from Penang and 34km south of Alor Setar, access to the mountain is from Gua Chempedak on the main trunk road. Jeeps ferry visitors up the winding 13km road to the top. Private cars are allowed access at their own risk. The **Peranginan Gunung Jerai** (30 rms) ☎ 4234345, fax: 7329788 has great views, idyllic setting, rooms with fans and attached baths for $37 per night and 3-room chalets for $80. Close by, the **Swiss Inn Sungai Petani** (100 rms) 1 Jl. Pahlawan, ☎ 4223333, fax: 4233423, is an elegant hotel with a beautifully-landscaped pool, tennis, squash, restaurant, pub. $37 S/D, suites from $120.

Pedu Lake

Peace by a man-made lake in kampung type lodgings is what Lake Pedu offers. To get there from Alor Setar, head towards Langgar, Pokok Sena and Kuala Nerang and follow the signboards from there. The road goes through rural towns and pretty scenery. The two resorts there offer pretty much the same facilities, restaurant, swimming pool, watersports, boats for hire, jungle-trekking. **Desa Utara Pedu Lake**, ☎ 7328888, fax: 7324999, is a village of 2- and 3-room chalets on 300 acres of forest. $100 S/D, suites from $140. **Holiday Inn Pedu**, ☎ 7304061, fax: 7304488, has 200 Kedah-Thai style chalets on 2 islands. $80 S/D, $180 suites.

TOURS

KTM Berhad, ☎ (03) 2757267/9, fax: (03) 2736527 runs a 4D/3N rail package at Gunung Jerai, which includes travel (sleepers), meals, accommodation at the resort, transfers, and tours to Lembah Bujang, Tanjung Dawai and Alor Setar, from $82 per person.

Pulau Langkawi

GETTING THERE

By Air

Malaysia Airlines flies daily into Langkawi from Kuala Lumpur ($54), Penang ($20), and Singapore ($117). Singapore Airlines also have a flight from Singapore. MAS office, Bangunan Tabung Haji, ☎ 9666622. Airport ☎ 9551322. Langkawi Airport is at Padang Mat Sirat, 20km from Kuah, and 14km from Pantai Cenang's beach resorts. Taxi fares are fixed price and paid with coupons bought at the airport's taxi counter. Charges are approximately $4 to Kuah and Pantai Cenang, and $5 to Tanjung Rhu and Pantai Kok.

By Sea

High-speed ferries operate from Kuala Perlis hourly to the main jetty about 1km from Kuah. Ring Kuala Perlis Langkawi Ferry Service: ☎ 9666950, LADA Langkawi Holdings: ☎ 9669923, Samavest: ☎ 9666087. Seven services operate between 8am and 6pm, and all offer AC, comfortable seats, and videos with the ubiquitous wrestling matches or blood and gore movies. The 40-min journey costs $6 first class, $4.80 economy one way. A similar ferry service plies from Kuala Kedah, a one-hour journey from Pulau Langkawi between 8am and 6.30pm. A high-speed catamaran operates daily from Penang – the offices are opposite the Clock Tower near the jetty. It leaves Penang at 8am and Langkawi at 6.5pm. During the west coast monsoon season, July to September, seas can be rough and services might be canceled. One-way 1st class $18, $14 economy class. Ferries also go to Satun in South Thailand. Four services run between 8.30am and 5pm for $7.20 one-way. The sea route from Phuket via Langkawi to Penang is popular with cruising yachts and some companies run cruises out of Phuket and Penang. For information inquire at the Penang TDC office near the clock tower on Pengkalan Weld in Georgetown.

By Train

KTM Berhad's Ekspres Langkawi leaves from Kuala Lumpur daily. They also offer holiday packages. Taxis and buses meet the trains at both Alor Setar and Arau and connect with the port towns.

LOCAL TRANSPORTATION

At Kuah jetty there are no problems getting a taxi – either a mini-bus or sedan car – to anywhere on the island. As Langkawi is duty-free, vehicles are much cheaper here than on the mainland. At peak holiday times there may be a wait but at other times there is no end of taxis to choose from. A **charter taxi** costs $5 to the beach resorts at Pantai Cenang, cheaper if you share. Returning from Pantai Cenang to Kuah it is easy to wander along the main road and hail a taxi or they can also be booked from most hotels. Some luxury hotels run a shuttle service between the airport and Kuah town.

Local buses service the main towns, and leave from the bus station in the center of Kuah opposite the hospital. Fares are cheap, but the service is often infrequent and buses don't go to many of the more popular smaller beach resorts. Services run from 8am to 4.30pm or 6pm.

The best way to get around is to hire your own transport. The roads are all paved and many are newly built to cater for the booming tourist trade. **Bikes** can be rented cheaply from bicycle workshops on the main street in Kuah, or more expensively from the larger hotels. Expect to pay around $5 per day for a mountain bike and much less for the standard type. **Motorcycles** are an excellent way to see the island and are hired from shops in Kuah, Pantai Cenang, or organized through hotels. Rates are around $14 per day and often no one bothers to check whether you have a license or not. **Car rental** is easily organized at the range of car hire places at the jetty in Kuah, or from locals who hire out their own cars. Rates are around $30 per day, for a newish air-conditioned Nissan sedan, and no one worries about licenses; insurance is extra and you have to fill up the car before returning it. Rates are much higher if you rent from the major hotels, but bargain during off-season for a 50% discount.

Boat trips around the islands can be organized from the beach resorts or ask the boatmen at Pantai Cenang. A 4-hr round trip including Pulau Dayang Bunting, Pulau Beras Basah and Pulau Singa Besar costs $72-$120 per boat (seats 8-12). Special itineraries which could include a BBQ and snorkeling can be arranged.

ACCOMMODATIONS

Room rates vary according to the season and soar during the high season from October to February, especially in December with the LIMA when rooms are often booked out months ahead. At all other times, except for major Malaysian public holidays, the island offers ample accommodation. During the southwest monsoon off-peak time between May and September, the beaches are tranquil and crowd-free.

Luxury

Berjaya Langkawi Beach & Spa Resort, Teluk Burau. ☎ 95955888, fax 95955886. 400 rooms. At the end of Burau Bay, Malay architecture with balcony or terrace, beach bar and restaurant, pool and bar, Jacuzzi sports and recreational facilities, tennis and disco. $100 S/D, suites from $200.

The Datai, Jl. Teluk Datai. ☎ 9592500, fax 9552600. 108 rms. Beautifully blended with the rainforest, secluded private beach, exquisite wooden architecture and fittings, swimming pool, limousine service, restaurants, library. $244 S/D, suites from $400.

Pelangi Beach Resort (350 rms), Pantai Cenang, ☎ 9551001, fax: 9551122. Traditional Malay style, palm-shaded complex includes restaurants, bars, pools, watersports center, tennis and squash, gym. $158 S, $171 D suites from $230.

Radisson Tanjung Rhu Resort, Tanjung Rhu, ☎ 9591033, 8005164 (toll-free), fax 9591899. 125 rms. North of the island on a 2.5km private beach. Beautifully landscaped surroundings, pool and restaurants, harmonious Balinese concept of spaciousness, luxury cars for hire. Suites from $240-$560.

Sheraton Langkawi Resort, Teluk Nibong. ☎ 9551901, fax 9551968. 231 rms. 3 restaurants including Captain's Grill, popular Black Henry Night Club with live band, swimming pool, tennis, water sports facilities. $140 S/D, suites from $242.

Sheraton Perdana Resort, Jl. Pantai Dato' Syed Omar, ☎ 9662020, fax: 9663097. 204 rms. Only 1km from the jetty, Magnificent views of the sea. Complete excellent sports facilities, including salt and freshwater swimming pools, jogging track, bicycles, gym, squash. $168 S/D, suites from $432.

High Intermediate

Burau Bay Resort, Telok Burau, ☎ 9551061, fax: 9551172. In a picturesque bay backed by rainforested mountains. Cabana-style chalets with fridges, TV and tea-making facilities are scattered around beachside forest. Restaurant, bar, pool and watersports center. $76 S, $88 D, family cabanas from $156.

Langkawi Holiday Villa, Pantai Tengah. ☎ 9551701, fax 9551504. 258 rms. Large swimming pool, seafood, Japanese, Italian restaurants, watersports, tennis, squash. $94 S/D, suites $154.

Langkawi Village Resort, Pantai Tengah. ☎ 9551511, fax: 9551531. All rooms have bathtubs, restaurant by the seafront serving buffet & BBQ, lounge, swimming pool, tours can be arranged, car hire. $62 S/D, $74 seafront, suite $200.

Low Intermediate

Beach Garden Resort, Pantai Cenang, ☎ 9551363, fax: 9551221. 13 rms. On the beachfront. Thatch-roofed, marble-floored, spotlessly clean. Run by a friendly German couple. Rates include a huge breakfast. Excellent value at $50 S, $58 D.

Delima Resort, Kuala Muda, ☎ 9551801, fax: 9551811. 100 rms. Malaysia's largest beach resort, very spread out. The rooms are new with all mod cons. Huge pool, tennis courts, hawker center, karaoke lounge. $24 S/D, suites from $110.

Langkawi Seaview Hotel, Jl. Penarek, ☎ 9660600, fax 9660620. 143 rms. Within easy access of shops and seafood, comfortable rooms, karaoke, swimming pool, good restaurant. $40 S/D.

Nadias Inn, Pantai Cenang, ☎ 9551401, fax: 9551405. 99 rms. AC with TV and bathroom. Not on beachfront, has swimming pool. Good restaurant and hawker center in the evenings. $48 S/D.

Budget

Pantai Cenang and Pantai Kok are full of budget chalets. One of the original at Cenang is **Langkawi Sandy Beach Motel**, ☎ 9551308, fax: 9551762. 36 rms. Still good value. $14 for chalet with bathroom, $12 with shared bathroom, AC rms $40. Other favorites are **AB Motel**, ☎ 9551300, and **Grand Beach Motel**, ☎ 9551457. At Pantai Kok, **Kok Bay Motel**, ☎ 9551407, has basic beachside chalets run by friendly Malay family. $12 D with fan. **The Last Resort**, ☎ 9551046. 12 rms. Good beach for sunsets, great bar, friendly staff. Rms are $12-34. You could also try **Inapan Mama**, ☎ 9551352.

DINING

Seafood is Langkawi's specialty and the most popular local spot is **Restoran Labu Labi** which specializes in Thai-style cooking at the **Medan Selera**, the eating stalls in Kuah on the town side of the bridge. More expensive, but in an unmatched location is the up-market **Sari Seafood Restoran** built on stilts beside the small town jetty and sharing the complex with Kraftangan, the government-run crafts store. Many Chinese restaurants in Kuah and all the big resorts also serve seafood. **Sangkar Ikan** on Jl. Pantai Penarak in Kuah, has a great view of fishing boats and the fish farm, and serves excellent Chinese-style seafood. Malay food is found in dozens of hawker stalls around Kuah, particularly along the main road on the seaward side. Check out the Langkawi specialty of *mee gulung*.

For western food, nowhere beats the **Beach Garden Resort** where the German hostess supervises the kitchen. It's worth the splurge for an evening meal under the palms at sunset. Shark steaks, buttered potatoes, herbed salad, waffles and cream and coffee – a typical meal – although the menu changes nightly – costs around $27 for two. Huge $5 breakfasts – inclusive with room rates – are a main meal with eggs, German sausages, cheese, rye toast, coffee and fresh juice. Also check out **Backofen Restaurant** and **Bon Ton Restaurant** on Pantai Cenang for a great mix of East and West. The Barn Thai Jazzaurant on Kampung Belangga Pecah is at the end of a beautiful 1.5km walkway through nicely-lit mangrove forest. It serves excellent Thai food with jazz music in the background, and sometimes features live bands. **Charlie's Place** at the Langkawi Yacht Club near the jetty dishes up good Western food, particularly lamb chops, offers great views of the Kuah harbour.

SHOPPING

Langkawi is billed as a duty-free shopping paradise, but this is mainly for the locals as there's not much to interest international tourists. However, here you find the cheapest liquor and cigarettes in the Peninsula; note that you can only bring back to mainland one bottle of liquor and one carton of cigarette after 72 hours of stay on the island. Keep your ferry/bus/plane tickets as proof. Other buys are Indonesian batik, *air gamak* – a traditional "cure-all" medicine made from sea slugs, cashew nuts and cheap T-shirts for souvenirs. The main shops are in Kuah.

SERVICES

Four local bus companies operate within the state, and from the bus station in Kangar run shuttle services to Padang Besar, Arau, Kuala Perlis, Alor Setar (Kedah), Jitra (Kedah), Chuping, Kaki Bukit, and services to all the states.

Information

Langkawi Tourist Information Center, Jl. Persiaran Putra, ☎ 9667789.

Banking

Langkawi banks operate according to Kedah hours closing on Thursday afternoons and all day Friday. Banks including Maybank, Bank Rakyat and Public Bank are around the Jl. Pandak Mayah area in Kuah. For money changers, try Seeni Mohamed at 4A Arked Teratai.

TOURS

Packages. Most tour agencies organize 3D/2N packages to Langkawi and 5D/4N combined Langkawi/Penang tours. You could also take a 3D/2N tour from Penang by air or ferry, which includes accommodations and a city tour.

DIVING

Pro Dive, ☎ 9553739, fax: 9553475 have a PADI Instructor Development Center in Pantai Cenang, which runs all-day trips for snorkeling and diving to Pulau Payar (50 mins away). Dive courses and equipment hire available. They also run scheduled trips from KL.

Langkawi Coral have a glass-bottomed observatory pontoon at Payar and an AC luxury catamaran to ferry guests there. Activities include snorkeling and diving. Lunch, refreshments and equipment available. Book at the jetty, ☎ 9667318.

Perlis

GETTING THERE

By Air

Malaysia's smallest state, in the extreme northwest, has no airport, but travelers can fly to Alor Setar and take a taxi from there to Kangar, the state capital, about a 45-minute drive from the airport. Fares are about $1.60 per person for a "share" taxi, or $6.50 for a chartered taxi.

By Train

The Langkawi Express from Kuala Lumpur runs daily to Arau, Perlis' royal capital. Fares from Kuala Lumpur are 1st class $31, 2nd class $13. This train also stops at Alor Setar.

By Road

Express buses run daily to Kangar from Kuala Lumpur, $8.50, from Butterworth, $2.50 and Alor Setar, $0.90.

LOCAL TRANSPORTATION

Four local bus companies operate within the state and from the bus station in Kangar run shuttle services to Padang Besar, Arau, Kuala Perlis, Alor Setar (Kedah), Jitra (Kedah), Chuping, Kaki Bukit, and services to all the states other towns. "Share" taxis to the border town of Padang Besar and other major towns are best organized at the taxi stand near the bus station. Taxis can also be chartered for trips to Gua Kelam at Kaki Bukit, and to other attractions in the state, and prices are reasonable as the distances are small.

ACCOMMODATIONS

The amount of visitors that Perlis attracts is evidenced by the lack of hotels. Apart from the few hotels in Kangar, there is only one hotel in Kuala Perlis and none in the rest of the state. **The Kangar Travelodge** (44 rms), Persiaran Jubli Emas, ☎ 9767755, fax: 9761049, is the only "up-market" hotel in Kangar. Relaxed, friendly place, with swimming pool. Restaurant serves fine Chinese cuisine. $80 S, $120 D, suites $144. **Pens Hotel**, Kuala Perlis, Tel: 754122/754125. A short walk from the Pulau Langkawi jetty. Excellent value when it first opened, but now standards have dropped. Deluxe rooms have good views. Non AC $14 S, $16 D; AC $22-28 S, $26-32 D. **Federal Hotel** (42 rms), 104 Jl. Kangar ☎ 766288, is a Chinese-style hotel conveniently close to downtown with both fan-cooled and air-conditioned rooms. $14-$25. **Malaysia Hotel** (25 rms), 65 Jl. Jubli Perak, ☎ 761366, is close to banks and shops. Basic rooms from $10. The cheapest place in town is Hotel Ban Cheong, 76 Jl. Besar, ☎ 761184, where rooms start from $5.

DINING

Perlis food is basically the same as in Kedah. Breakfast specialties are *roti canai* and *nasi lemak*, and the main meal is at lunch when most restaurants serve curries and rice – *nasi campur*. Noodle dishes, including the northern favorite – *laksa* – are often eaten for the evening meal. Night markets – *pasar malam* – are a great place to sample local delicacies. Kangar's *pasar malam* is on Wednesday nights, Kuala Perlis on Tuesday, and Arau on Friday. Food stalls serving cheap food around the bus and taxi station in Kangar's downtown and good Malay food at the Gerai Medan Dato' Jaafar on Jl. Tun Abdul Razak, and Gerai MARA on Jl. Kuala Perlis. **The Federal Hotel** has a reasonable Chinese restaurant, and a local favorite for good Chinese noodles is the Soo Guan Restaurant at 96 Jl. Kangar. Thai food, including tom yam is served at Ramlah Restoran, 344 Taman Mutiara, Jl. Pengkalan Asam, and at Sawadee Restoran, 275 Jl. Baru. Diana Fed Chicken, 14 Lorong Seruing, off Jl. Raja Syed Alwi, is good for snacks and fast-food.

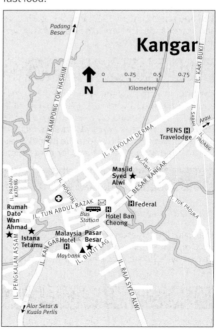

5 Terengganu PRACTICALITIES

Since eastern Terengganu is one long beach, driving allows you to stop anywhere you fancy for a dip in the sea and a snooze in the sun. The coast is well geared for tourism, and has plenty of charming accommodations from budget class to luxury resorts. Inland, Kenyir Lake, also adequately equipped for tourism, provides a quieter alternative. *Prices in US dollars. S=Single: D=Double: AC=Airconditioning. Telephone code 09.*

Kuala Terengganu

GETTING THERE

Sultan Mahmud Airport, 18km north of Kuala Terengganu, has daily Malaysia Airlines flights from Kuala Lumpur ($42) and Kuantan ($26). MAS office, 13 Jl. Sultan Omar, ☎ 6221415. Airport ☎ 6664204. Taxi to downtown costs $6. Express buses from Kuala Lumpur's Hentian Putra, opposite The Mall on Jl. Putra, cost $8. From Kota Bharu the fare is $3; from Penang $9.40; and from Singapore's Lavender Street terminus $9. Long-distance share taxis from Kota Bharu cost $5, from Kuantan $6, from Penang $24 and Kuala Lumpur $16. All buses, both local and express, operate from the Central Bus Station on Jl. Syed Hussain.

LOCAL TRANSPORTATION

The best time for sight-seeing is early morning and late afternoon when it is pleasant to walk around. Trishaws are still extremely popular –the town was once known as Malaysia's Trishaw Capital. Cheap ferries ply across the river to Pulau Duyung; they can also be hired for river trips.

SERVICES

Information

The Tourist Information Center is in Wisma MCIS, 2243 Jl. Sultan Zainal Abidin, ☎ 6221553. Hours: Saturday–Wednesday 8am–5pm, Thursday 8am–12.45pm.

TOURS

Most agencies do tours around the city, with vari-

ations such as cultural tours, (about $60 per person) and a river cruise to Pulau Duyung and the museum. There are also trips to Redang and Kapas, Rantau Abang for turtle watching, Sekayu and other waterfalls, and Kenyir Lake.
MAS Golden Holidays ☎ 7463000 has a 3D/2N package from KL to Kuala Terengganu which includes a city tour, and optional tours to Sekayu Waterfall and Kenyir Lake.

ACCOMMODATIONS

Like most places along the East Coast, prices drop substantially during the annual monsoon season (Oct-Feb). **Primula Parkroyal** (249 rms), Jl. Persinggahan, ☎ 6222100, 8008878 (toll-free), fax: 6233360, overlooks Batu Buruk Beach, 1km from town. Great sea views, a landscaped swimming pool, grillroom by a waterfall, tennis courts, car rental, island and waterfall excursions. $87/D, suites from $184. **Permai Park Inn International** (131 rms), Jl. Sultan Mahmud, ☎ 6222122, fax: 6222121, 500m from the beach, swimming pool, gym, restaurants Malay and Eastern fare. $74 S/D, deluxe $100. **Motel Desa** (20 rooms), Bukit Pak Apil, ☎ 6223033, fax: 6223863, sits on top of a hill overlooking town. Good views, swimming pool, and large well-appointed rooms, but is difficult to get to without a car. $36 S/D. The cheap and intermediate-priced hotels are downtown. Jl. Sultan Ismail houses several medium-priced hotels including the **Seri Hoover** at No. 49, ☎ 6233823, fax: 6225975, and the **Sri Terengganu Hotel**, at No. 120, ☎ 6234622 which have AC rooms with hot showers and TV for around $23 S/D. **Seri Indah Resort**, 898 Jl. Haji Busu, at Batu Buruk Beach, ☎ 6221598, fax: 6239933, is rather expensive, but the chalet-type rooms are clean with AC, TV, hot shower and phone. There is also a restaurant and swimming pool. Quiet location on the beach and close to good food stalls. $55 S/D.

The most popular place for budget-travelers is **Ping Anchorage**, 77A Jl. Dato' Isaacs, just past Jl. Tok Lam, ☎ 6220851, fax: 6228093, with clean rooms, rooftop restaurant and bar. They also organize island and inland tours. Rooms are all non-AC. Dorms $2.40, $6 D with shared bath. For peace and quiet at a budget price, **Awi's Yellow House**, ☎ 6231741, across the river on Pulau Duyung is a great alternative. Dorm beds cost $2.50 and rooms are slightly more. Cooking facilities and tea and coffee are free.

DINING

Terengganu's famous *Nasi Dagang* ("travelers' rice") is served everywhere. Comprising glutinous rice cooked in coconut milk and served with fish curry, the best is supposed to be at a roadside stall at Chendering, 2 km from the Kuala Ibai bridge. For a good cheap breakfast walk east on Jl. Sultan Zainal Abidin to stalls. Other good stalls are upstairs at the market. For lunch, try **Sofinaz Restoran**, 38 Jl. Masjid Abidin, opposite the mosque, which specializes in *nasi padang Sumatra*. For Chinese food, **Restoran Cheng Cheng**, 224 Jl. Bandar, has a cheap buffet of rice and noodle dishes. **Restoran Golden Dragon** on the same street serves delicious chicken rice and roast duck. Batu Buruk Beach, east of town, has outdoor restaurants, excellent for reasonably-priced Malay seafood dishes.

SHOPPING AND SOUVENIRS

For a fine selection of Southeast Asian crafts, jewelry and textiles, check out **Teratai**, 151 Jl. Bandar, which also boasts limited edition prints by renowned watercolour artist Chang Fee Ming. The **Sutera Semai Centre** at Chendering has a nice collection of silk, batik, songket, copper and brassware.

Merang and North

GETTING THERE

Four daily local buses, and a mini-van service run from the bus station on Jl. Masjid Abidin along the coastal road via Merang to Penarik. Travelers coming from Kota Bharu can get off at Permaisuri on the main East Coast highway and catch a local bus to Penarik. Share taxis from Kuala Terengganu also ply this route.

ACCOMMODATIONS

Beside the beautiful beach at Merang is the **Merang Beach Resort**, ☎/fax: 6239018, with

A-frames with shared bathrooms on the beach for $20, and rooms with attached bath in the hilltop guesthouse for $24. The more upmarket **Sutra Beach Resort**, ☎ 6231111, fax: 62696410 in the Rhu Tapai fishing village has traditional architecture with suites clustered in landscaped gardens overlooking the sea and islands. $72 S/D, suites $260.

Pulau Perhentian

GETTING THERE

Take a SKMK bus No. 3 from Kota Bharu to Pasir Puteh, then change for No. 96 to Kuala Besut via Kertih. Share taxis from Kota Bharu cost $2, from Pasir Puteh 80c. From Kuala Terengganu, buses are $2.20, and taxis, $4. From Kuala Besut, the 2-hr boat trip to the islands costs $6 one way. Organize for the boatman to pick you up for the return trip if it's off season.

ACCOMMODATIONS

In Kuala Besut there is only the **Primula Besut Beach Resort**, ☎ 6971563, on the quiet beachfront with swimming pool and restaurant, S $36, D $44, suites from $56. On Pulau Perhentian Besar, the **Perhentian Island Resort** (34 rms), ☎ 6910946, KL (03) 2480811, fax: 6977562, to the right of the jetty has comfortable chalets for $13, bungalows $21 with attached bath and AC, and dorms $5. **Coral View Island Resort** (40 rms), ☎ 6956943, fax: 6910943, has chalets for $24 S/D non-AC, $48 S/D AC, a restaurant, snorkeling and diving. All the budget accommodation is north of the jetty and costs under $10. Boats will either drop you at the beach – you'll have to wade in – or it's a 20-min walk from the main jetty. **Coco Hut's** A-frames, ☎ 011-972085; **Rosli Chalet's** dorms and rooms, ☎ 6910155; **Cozy Chalet**, ☎ 011-326822, 010-3309717; and **Flora Bay**, ☎ 011-977266, 6977266. Pulau Perhentian Kecil also has budget accommodations. All have basic facilities, washing from wells, and no electricity. Kerosene lamps are provided. Food is the main problem, there are places to eat but little variety. Water is also sometimes a problem. **Isabella Coffee Shop** at the jetty is good for mee goreng, fresh squid and drinks. Tiny **Coral Cave Cafe** on the beach has good food, and a marvelous ambiance but incredibly slow service.

TOURS

Ping Anchorage, ☎ 6220851, fax: 6228093 has a 3D/2N trip departing Kuala Terengganu for $152, including snorkeling. **KTM Berhad**, ☎ (03) 2757267/9, fax: (03) 2736527, has a 5D/4N rail package which includes AC or non-AC accommodation, meals, boat transfer and snorkeling from $160 per person. Only between Mar-July.

Pulau Redang

GETTING THERE

The 3-hr journey from Merang costs $10-$16/person or $112/boat; from Besut $20/person, $220/boat. Passenger boats also leave the jetty in Kuala Terengganu or the Chendering Fisheries Complex south of town, but it's often a long wait.

ACCOMMODATIONS

Redang Beach Resort, ☎ 6238188, fax: 6230225, or KL ☎ (03) 2015079, fax: (03) 2015075, has 3D/2N packages from Kuala Terengganu for $160 D, including boat transfer, 3 meals and snorkeling. Extra activities include jungle-trekking, candat sotong (squid fishing), fishing. Diving: Redang Aquatic Adventures, leisure dives available. **Coral Redang Resort**, ☎ 6236200, fax: 6236300; reservations, call ☎ 011-972174. Has 40 AC chalets, swimming pool, coffee house, bar, snorkeling and diving. Accommodation and 3 meals: $74 D, deluxe $86. A 3D/2N dive package with 4 dives is $252. **Redang Lagoon**, ☎/fax: 8272116 has 20 clean wooden chalets with fans and attached baths, restaurant with Chinese food, water activities, diving Scuba Quest: ☎ 011-333070. $32 D, $40 triple. 3D/2N package including transfers from Merang, 10 meals and snorkeling $112/person. **Redang Bay Resort**, ☎ 6236048, fax: 6228190, does 3D/2N packages for $180 D, including transfer, 4 meals, and snorkeling. Diving and equipment hire available. Chalets are AC with bathroom attached. There is also a canteen and swimming pool, and a campsite on the island. At the nearby Pulau Lang Tengah is the **Blue Coral Island Resort**, contact Ping Anchorage ☎ 6220851, fax: 622809.

DIVING TOURS

A 3D/2N dive package goes for about $200 from Kuala Terengganu, including transfers, accommodation and food. Equipment can be hired. **Ping Anchorage**, ☎ 6220851, fax: 6228093, organizes trips with chalet accommodation. Snorkeling included, diving nominal charge for air. Camping trips are about half the cost, and include meals. Sole agents for Pulau Lang Tengah. **Pro Dive** has a PADI Instructor Development Center in Merang, ☎/fax: 6242495 or KL ☎ (03) 2737317, fax: (03) 2738317. Daily dive and snorkeling trips to Redang and Lang Tengah. They also offer 4 or 5-day beginner dive courses. **Redang Aquatic Adventures** ☎ 6238188, fax: 6230225. PADI instruction and 2D/1N to 4D/3N tours from Kuala Terengganu, with accommodation at Redang Beach Resort or camping. Outings can be arranged to Lang Tengah, Perhentian and Yu. Leisure trips are offered by **Borneo Divers**, ☎ (03) 7173066, fax: (03) 7184303; **Scuba Point**, (4D/3N from Jertih) ☎ 7747288, fax: (03) 7754288;

Marang And South

GETTING THERE

Local buses from Kuala Terengganu cost 40c, chartered taxis $5, and share taxis $4 per cab for the 15 km journey to Marang. The accommodations, eating places, jetty, and markets are a short walk from the main highway.

ACCOMMODATIONS

Marang has plenty of basic budget accommodation for around $2.40 a dorm bed, and under $10, a room or chalet with shared baths. Among them, **Marang Inn** (10 rms), ☎ 6182132, fax: 6228093, and **Island View Resort**, ☎ 6182006 north of town, overlooking the lagoon (38 rms). Just past here is **Kamal's** (15 rms), ☎ 6182181, the original and best-known budget resort. At the top of the hill behind Kamal's is the **Marang Guesthouse** which has its own restaurant, and good views. **Marang Resort & Safaris** (100 rms), Batu 17, Jl. Dungun/Marang, ☎ 6182588, fax: 6182334. Chalets with attached baths and hot water from $48 S/D, deluxe $100 D. River cruises, day tours to Pulau Kapas, and waterfalls including Sekayu. South of town is the **Anguilla Beach House Resort** (52 chalets) in Kampung Rhu Muda, ☎ 6181322, fax: 6181322. Verandahs, attached baths, recreation room, garden shelters, restaurants, laundry, boat service. AC $32, non-AC $24.

DINING

The cheapest food is at the stalls beside the market. Most guesthouses have their own restaurants and Marang Inn is well-known for its tasty fare. The best *nasi dagang* is at a roadside stall on the way south from Kuala Terengganu to Pantai Chendering after Kuala Ibai (where there is a beautiful 'floating' mosque).

Pulau Kapas

Wooden passenger boats make the 6km crossing from Marang jetty for $3 one way. Hiring a boat costs $24 upwards. Boats are easy to organize from the guest houses or the boat offices in the main road. The boats also service another smaller island next to Kapas called Gemia.

Primula Kapas Island Beach Resort, ☎ 6236110, is comfortable although expensive, with swimming pool, restaurant, bar, and facilities for snorkeling, scuba-diving, wind-surfing and fishing. Traditional Malay-style chalets with AC and attached bath cost $56 S, $64 D, and family bungalows are $112. The best of basic chalets is **Zaki Beach Chalet**, ☎ 6220258, which has clean A-frames with shared bathroom, and chalets with bathroom and fan for $10-$15. Order food in advance if you dislike slow service, and bring snacks and fruit from the mainland. **Gem Isles Resort** on Pulau Gemia has 52 AC chalets with views of the alcove and Pulau Kapas. Offers snorkeling, diving, non-motorized water sports, deep-sea fishing and squid fishing (*candat sotong*). Opportunities to watch turtles hatch at its turtle hatchery. $S/D. Contact **Ping Anchorage**, ☎ 6220851, fax: 6228093, for Gemia snorkeling and dive tours from Kuala Terengganu.

Sekayu Waterfalls And Kenyir Dam

Local buses and share taxis run from Kuala Terengganu to Kuala Berang. It is 15km further to the waterfalls and the same distance in the other direction to the dam. Hire a taxi for around $12 for either trip. Taxis also run directly from the Kuala Terengganu airport to the lake ($24). Buses go daily from KL's Hentian Putra station to the floating restaurant at the Pengkalan Gawi jetty in Kenyir ($9.50). At the jetty, boat rentals and chalet bookings and transfers can be arranged. The Tourist Information Centre, ☎ 010-9340101, there opens from 9am-5pm (Saturday to Wednesday) and closes at lunch, and opens 9am-1pm on Thursday and Friday.

For accommodation at **Sekayu Resthouse**, $12-16 per room, make reservations through the Kuala Berang District Office, ☎ 6811259. **Primula Kenyir Lake Resort**, ☎ 010-9836105, has 40 comfortable AC rms, hot showers, restaurant, and water sports, and sits on an island right across from the jetty. $37 S/D, deluxe $53 D. Other accommodations are further in and isolated from each other. Other than water and trekking activities, the concept is very much back to basics, which means no TV or even telephones. All meals are included in prices. Among the operators in approximate order of distance from the jetty are, **Tan's Kenyir Lake Resort** (73 chalets), ☎ 51466002; **Kenyir Woods** (15 chalets), ☎ 6238188; **Nature Lodge** (22 chalets),

☎ 673809 or KL (03) 7638877; **Muping Island Resort** (22 rms - floating) ☎ 6811348, fax: 6812197; **Little Traveller** (12-rm boathouse), ☎ 6229564; **Musang Kenyir** (22 chalets), ☎ 010-9837886; and **Remis Rakit** (45 rms - floating), ☎ 6811348. **Kenyir Boating Holiday** has 3 boathouses that go around the lake, ☎ 6230170. **Ping Anchorage**, ☎ 6220851, fax: 6228093, offer a full board 3D/2N tour on a double-decker houseboat at $76 per person (min. 10 people) which goes into Taman Negara. They also have floating chalets.

Rantau Abang

Local buses from Kuala Terengganu's main bus station cost $1.20, chartered taxis are $10 or $2.50 per seat for the 58km journey south. The bus stop is at the Turtle Information Center which is open daily except for Friday, during the season (May to September). From KL, the 7-hr journey costs $8.60 ($16 taxi). Pelangi Airways fly daily from Kuala Lumpur to the oil town of Kerteh ($50). Airport ☎ 8261187. Taxi to Kerteh town is $4. From there, Rantau Abang is easily accessible by bus and taxi.

Rantau Abang Visitor Centre, Km 20.8, 1km north of the information center, has traditional-style wooden houses overlooking a lagoon. The large rooms sleep six, have overhead fans and attached bathrooms. AC $40, non-AC $24 S/D. The prices vary according to turtle nesting seasons. If there's a turtle sighted, the management wake you and take you to where it's nesting. The nearest food is at the Malay restaurants near the information center. Cheap accommodations close to the information center includes **Awang's**, ☎ 8443500, with a restaurant and chalets on the beach for $5, and similar prices apply to the neighboring **Ismail's**, ☎ 8441054, and **Dahimah's**, ☎ 8452843, south on the highway, a popular budget hostel with a good restaurant. **Tanjung Jara Beach Hotel** (100 rooms), ☎ 8441801, fax: 8442653, is 9km south of Rantau Abang, at Km 12.8, Dungun. This elegant resort with award-winning Malay architecture is a delight in which to unwind. They also organize turtle-watching. Rooms all AC with TV, IDD phone, hot showers, $80 S, $92 D. **Great Value Holidays**, ☎ 2483257, fax: 2613630, has a 3D/2N package with a Kuala Terengganu city tour. Golfers can tee off at the five-star **Awana Kijal**, ☎ 800-8228 (Toll-free), fax: 8641688, midway between Dungun and Kemaman. All 308 rooms face the sea, and cultural and snorkeling/scuba-diving tours can be organized. $104 S, $116 D, suites from $160. Pelangi Air, ☎ (03) 2624446, has a 3D/2N package from Kuala Lumpur.

5 Terengganu

Kelantan PRACTICALITIES

6

Getting around Kelantan is cheap and easy. The kampungs are the places to head for, some of which are accessible by local bus, although only a tourist guide can bring you to the cottage industries. There are no luxury hotels, but plenty of beach chalets; dress sensibly: the populace is of strong Muslim belief. Also brush up on your Bahasa Malaysia, you really need it here. The Islamic fasting month (Ramadhan) and monsoon period (Nov-Feb) are generally very quiet. The best time to visit is during the Carnival in July/August. *Prices in US dollars. S=Single: D=Double: AC=airconditioning. Telephone code 09.*

Kota Bahru

GETTING THERE

By Air

Malaysia Airlines flies daily from Kuala Lumpur ($42) to Kota Bharu's Sultan Ismail Petra Airport. Pelangi Airways flies there once a week from Kuala Lumpur (ask about the Kota Bahru/Kuala Lumpur night fare), Penang ($35), and Alor Setar ($28). Taxis cost $4 for the 8km ride to town, less if you share. MAS office, ☎ 7447000, is opposite the clock tower on Jl. Gajah Mati. Airport ☎ 7737000.

By Train

Two daily express trains run from Kuala Lumpur and Singapore to Wakaf Bharu, about 7km from Kota Bharu. The journey from Gemas in Johor is often slow, but the rainforest scenery is balm for the soul. The express departs Kuala Lumpur at 8.20pm and arrives at Kota Bharu at 7.13am the following day; 1st class $31, 2nd $18, 3rd non AC $9. Fares from Singapore (in Singapore dollars) are 1st class AC $36, 2nd AC $16. Trains also run from Thailand. The station is at Golok, just over the border from Rantau Panjang a 90-min bus ride from Kota Bharu on Bus No 29.

By Road

Express buses run to Kota Bharu from all major towns and cities. From Singapore's Lavender Street terminal, buses cost $18. From Kuala Lumpur buses depart from Hentian Putra, opposite The Mall on Jl. Putra. Fares are as follows: from Kuala Lumpur $10, Penang/Butterworth $7.60, Johor Bahru $13, Alor Setar $8. Express buses leave Kota Bharu from either the Langgar Bus Station on Jl. Pasir Puteh or the Jl. Hamzah station. **Share taxis** to Kota Bharu cost $16 from

Kuala Lumpur and $17 from Butterworth. For travelers arriving by **car** there are three possible routes. The East-West Highway from the West Coast which starts at Grik is 224km from Kota Bharu. Grik can be approached from either Kuala Kangsar in Perak (108km), or Sungai Petani in Kedah (117km). From Kuala Lumpur take either the Karak highway to Kuantan and then travel up the East Coast Highway (630km), or the more winding route (474km) linking Kuala Lipis in Pahang with Gua Musang in the south of Kelantan.

LOCAL TRANSPORTATION

Kota Bharu is easy to walk around and alternatively there are plenty of trishaws. Agree on

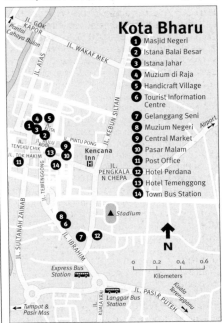

Kota Bharu

1 Masjid Negeri
2 Istana Balai Besar
3 Istana Jahar
4 Muzium di Raja
5 Handicraft Village
6 Tourist Information Centre
7 Gelanggang Seni
8 Muzium Negeri
9 Central Market
10 Pasar Malam
11 Post Office
12 Hotel Perdana
13 Hotel Temenggong
14 Town Bus Station

a price before boarding. A 10-min ride shouldn't cost more than $1. **Bicycles** are a great way to see the town, the beaches and the cottage craft areas. They can be rented cheaply from most travelers' hostels. The state-run SKMK runs local **buses** from the Central Bus Station on Jl. Padang Garong. Number 10 bus for Pantai Cahaya Bulan (30 min) leaves from Central Market or in front of the Kencana Inn at Jl. Padang Garong every 20 minutes. It also runs past the Perdana Resort and returns from HB Village making it feasible to stay out at the beach and commute cheaply to town. For Tumpat and Pantai Seri Tujuh take No. 43; for Pantai Irama (Bachok) No. 23 or 39; For Pantai Sabak and the Airport take Nos 8 or 9. **Taxi** rates hourly are $6, daily $30. For **car rentals**, check at the airport. Avis is also at Perdana Hotel, ☎ 7484457.

SERVICES

Information

The Tourist Information Center on Jl Sultan Ibrahim, ☎ 7485534, fax: 7486652, is open from Sunday to Thursday 8am–4.45pm, closed for lunch 1–2pm. Tours and tourist guides can be arranged here too. The **Gelanggang Seni (Cultural Center)** is open from March to October and has different performances on different days. Check with Tourist Information for the latest updates and times. Basically, the programmes are as follows: Saturday: *rebana ubi, silat, gasing, wau*; and dances and traditional music (night); Monday: *rebana, silat, gasing, sepak*, Wednesday: *kertuk, silat, sepak raga*; and *wayang kulit* (night). Admission is free. Sights in the **Cultural Zone** are open daily from 10.30am–5.45pm except Friday. The exciting **Carnival** in July/August is held outside the stadium and sees plenty of action in traditional game competitions.

TOURS

Wilderness Experience, ☎ (03) 7822377, fax: (03) 7822387, organizes a 4D/3N whitewater rafting trip to Sungai Nenggri in Gua Musang.
SA Tours, ☎ (03) 2429155, fax: (03) 2429420 has a 3D/2N package from KL, which includes flights, meals, snorkeling, jungle trekking and Kota Bahru city tour.
KTM Berhad, ☎ (03) 2757267/9, fax: (03) 2736527, has a 5D/4N rail package to the scenic Stong Hill (Gunung Stong), which includes accommodation at the Perdana Stong Hill Resort and meals.

ACCOMMODATIONS

Room rates plunge during the annual monsoon, when it can be sunny for days on end, but the rain when it comes can last for weeks and you may find that the only way out is by air. Kota Bharu has no luxury class hotels, but there are ample accommodations from first-class rooms and chalets by the sea, to a competitive range of backpackers' hostels.

High Intermediate

Hotel Perdana, Jl. Mahmood, ☎ 7485000, fax: 7447621. 136 rms. Kota Bharu's only "fancy" hotel is close to the Cultural Center, and 1km from Central Market. Swimming pool, tennis and squash courts, gym. Rooms have mini bar, IDD phones, TV and in-house videos. $88 S, $95 D, suites from $180.
Perdana Resort, Jl. Kuala Pa' Amat, Pantai Cahaya Bulan, ☎ 7744000, 8008840 (toll-free) fax: 7744980. 120 rms. Resort overlooking the beach. The chalets have verandahs with sea views, private bathrooms, TV, IDD telephones and mini-bars. Excellent restaurant, swimming pool, tennis courts, and watersports center. AC chalet $78 S, $88 D.

Low Intermediate

Temenggong Hotel, Jl. Tok Hakim, ☎ 7483844, fax: 7441481. 37 rms. 5-storey, in town center close to all sights. Popular with Malaysians and often full. AC, attached baths $38 S/ D.
Dynasty Inn, Jl. Sultanah Zainab, ☎ 7473000, fax: 7473111. 47 rms. Central, rooftop coffeehouse that overlooks river, seafood restaurant, friendly. $36 S, $40 D, riverview $62 S, $66 D, including breakfast.
Kencana Inn, Jl. Padang Garong, ☎ 7447944, fax: 7440181. 52 rms. Close to all sights and buses stop at the door, lounge, karaoke, all rooms with private bathroom, AC, fridge, TV. $20 S/D, deluxe $28.
Kencana Inn City Center, Jl. Doktor, ☎ 7440944, fax: 7440181. Close to buses, with restaurant serving Thai and Malay food, all rms with AC, attached baths, hot water. $22 S/D, deluxe $28 (3-4 people).

Budget

H.B. Village, Pantai Cahaya Bulan, ☎ 7734993, fax: 7741006. 24 rms. A-frame chalets and cabins in a quiet location 1.5km from Pantai Cahaya Bulan. Town bus stops at the door. Great location for wandering around kampungs and checking out handicrafts. Restaurant has good local food. They also run boat trips and rent bicycles. Non-AC chalet $20 S/D, AC chalet $24 S/D.
Long House Beach Motel, Pantai Cahaya Bulan, ☎ 7731090, fax: 7473664. 21 rms. Original "beach of passionate love" hostelry. Run-down rooms that sleep five people have huge beds, horizontal mirrors at bed level. But the location right on the sand is great; restaurant serves Malaysian food. Price per room, non-AC $26, AC $32.

Rebana Hostel, opp. Istana Kota Lama, up an alley off Jl. Sultanah Zainab close to the silversmith workshops in Kampung Sireh. Malay-style house with friendly hosts 1km from downtown. 40 rms. Dorm $2, S $5, chalets and garden rooms $10.

Ideal Traveller's Guest House, off Jl. Pintu Pong, ☎ 7442246. 52 rms. Popular and often full, centrally-located with nice garden. Dorm $2, rooms with bath $10.

Rainbow Inn Hostel, near Royal Thai Consulate on Jl. Pengkalan Chepa (32 rms) is an old traveler's favorite with gardens and interesting hosts. Dorm $2; rooms around $10.

DINING

Kota Bharu is one of the best towns in Malaysia for cheap street cuisine. At breakfast, coffee shops serve various types of rice with accompaniments wrapped in banana-leaf packages. The favorite is *nasi dagang* – "trader's rice" – an unbleached rice with a sweet curry sauce, and is best at **Kedai Kopi White House** opposite the State Mosque on Jl. Sultanah Zainab. Other coffee shops, including Razak Restoran on the corner of Jl. Datok Pati and Jl. Padang Garong, serve Indian Muslim breakfasts of *roti canai*, *murtabak*, and even an Indian favorite toast and *kaya* – coconut jam. For lunch, upstairs at Central Market there are dozens of stalls. At dusk the night stalls opposite **Central Market** provide probably the best eating in Malaysia.

SHOPPING & SOUVENIRS

The things to buy are traditional handicrafts and cheap goods from Thailand. Jalan Temenggong is the main shopping area or visit the kampungs. For silver, Kampung Sireh, Kampung Marak or Kampung Badang; *songket*, Kampung Penambang; batik, Kampung Puteh, Kubor Kuda, Kampung Badang; *wau* (kites) along the road to Pantai Cahaya Bulan.

Pahang's northern beaches are among the most popular in Malaysia and are crowded on weekends and public holidays. Otherwise they are lovely, well-developed for all ranges of tourists, and easily accessed by reliable and cheap public transport. Ask about packages. Quiet during the monsoon months at the end of the year.
Prices in US dollars. S=single: D=double: AC=air conditioning. Telephone code 09.

Kuantan

GETTING THERE

Malaysia Airlines fly direct to Kuantan airport, 15km west of downtown on the main road to Kuala Lumpur, from Kuala Lumpur ($30), Kuala Terengganu (($26) and Singapore ($78). Pelangi Airways fly there once a week from Pulau Tioman ($32). Taxis charge around $6 from the airport to town. Several daily express buses run from Kuala Lumpur's Putra Bus Station, opposite The Mall in Jl. Putra for $4.60; from Kota Bharu for $6.40; Butterworth $11.6, and Singapore $7. Share taxis are also prolific from Kuala Lumpur $10, Butterworth $25, Kota Bharu $12, and Johor Bahru $12.

LOCAL TRANSPORTATION

All the downtown hotels, restaurants, sights, post-office, banks, etc., are within a few blocks of each other and are an easy walk. Tourist information is in the Kompleks Terantum at the southern end of Jl. Mahkota, ☎ 5133026. A host of car rental companies is at the airport. Hertz Rent-A-Car is also beside the Samudra Hotel on Jl. Besar, Orix is at the Grand Continental, Jl. Gambut, and Avis and National are also at Jl. Teluk Sisek.

ACCOMMODATIONS

Kuantan's most luxurious hotel is out at Teluk Chempedak, but the fanciest lodging downtown is the **Samudra Hotel River View** (70 rms), Jl. Besar, ☎ 555333, fax: 5130618. Comfortable rooms with TV, AC, hot showers. $56 S/D. Another mid-price hotel close by is the **Classic Hotel** (33 rms) Jl. Besar, ☎ 554599. All rooms have AC, TV, IDD phones, hot-water baths. $86 S/D, family $132. **Hotel Pacific** (60 rms), Jl. Bukit Ubi, ☎ 5141980, fax: 5141979, with helpful staff, all rooms with AC, hot showers, TV, $39 S/D, suite $56. Coffee house serves local cuisine. **Seri Malaysia Kuantan** (100 rms) Jl. Teluk Sisek, ☎ 553688, fax: 5531118, has decent rooms with AC, attached baths, coffee house. $40 S/D with breakfast. **Sin Nam Fong Hotel** (20 rms) 44 Jl. Teluk Sisek, ☎ 521561, has rooms for $20 but the cheapest lodging in town is at **Hotel Min Heng** (10 rms) 22/24 Jl. Mahkota, ☎ 5134885, with swing doors, wooden floors and an arched verandah which hasn't changed in decades. $5 S, $6 D, $7 triple.

DINING

The Taman Selera food stalls on Jl. Mahkota just north of Jl. Masjid have good Chinese food and beer. Opposite there is an open-air fruit market. There are also stalls along the riverbank walkway south of the Samudra River View Hotel which serve excellent seafood.

SERVICES

The Tourist Information Center is at Jl. Mahkota, ☎ 5133026. Banks are close by.

Teluk Chempedak

GETTING THERE

Taxis ply the 5km to Teluk Chempedak, Kuantan's closest seaside beach, or take bus No. 39 from the main bus station on Jl. Besar or the stand near the corner of Jl. Mahkota and Jl. Masjid.

ACCOMMODATIONS

The beachside **Hyatt Regency** (340 rms), Teluk Chempedak, ☎ 5131234, 8008181 (toll-free), fax: 5137577, has luxurious rooms, restaurants, a disco, boutiques, tennis courts, water sports center, and swimming pool. $120 S/D, suites from $220. The best value at the bay is the **Hotel Kuantan** (25 rms), Tel/fax: 5130026, opp. the Hyatt, an impeccably clean, 60s style, 2-storey hotel. $15 non AC with bath, $22-30 S/D AC and bath, $35-40 family. The cheapest lodgings, popular with backpackers is **Asrama Bendahara**, which has an outdoor restaurant and nice atmosphere. Dorm beds $3, $6 S, $7 D. There are more reasonable accommodations in the street behind the restaurant strip.

DINING

Everyone from Kuantan goes to Teluk Chempedak for a night out. The **Hyatt** has a varied, but expensive buffet, good for a splurge, and **Hugo's** is the region's only gourmet restaurant. The **Pattaya,** an outdoor restaurant on the promenade is popular for seafood, as is the **Katong Seafood Restaurant** on the main road which specializes in fishhead curry. **Nisha's** nearby serves good North Indian. The cheapest food is at the food stalls at the end of the promenade.

Beserah

GETTING THERE

From Kuantan's Jl. Besar bus station, take a Balok bus No. 30, Sungai Karang No. 28 or Kemaman No. 27 which all stop on the main highway at Beserah, 10km north of Kuantan; alternatively flag down a taxi that will cost about $5 per cab.

ACCOMMODATIONS

On Jl. Pantai, halfway between the highway and the beach, is **Belia Perkasa Hotel** (15 rms), ☎ 5448178, fax: 5448179, a hostel with clean, fan-cooled dorms for $4 and above, and 4-bed rooms for $30. Cooking facilities cost $3 per day. Heading north from Beserah is **Duta Sands Resort**, Km 8, ☎ 5448101, fax: 5448291, which has caravans on the beach complete with kitchenette and microwave ovens $55 (triple-share), rooms $46 S/D, chalets $50 S/D. Cafetaria, swimming pool, bicycles, kayaks. Walking distance to restaurants and stalls. **Gloria Maris Resort**, ☎ 5447788, fax: 5447619, has attractive wooden chalets by the beach, a restaurant serving homestyle Thai, Western and Malaysian food and wholemeal bread. $98 AC, fridge with bath. **Le Village Beach Resort** (130 rms), ☎ 5447900, fax: 5447899, in Sg. Karang offers both hotel rooms and traditional

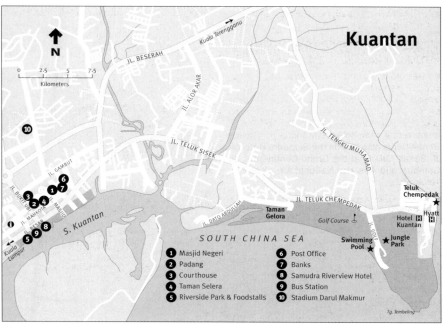

Kuantan

JL. BESERAH

Kuala Terengganu

JL. ALOR AKAR

JL. TELUK SISEK

JL. GAMBUT

JL. TENGKU MUHAMAD

JL. TELUK CHEMPEDAK

Taman Gelora

Golf Course

Teluk Chempedak

Hotel Kuantan

Hyatt

JL. BUKIT BESAR

JL. MAHKOTA

JL. MASJID

JL. DATO ABDULLAH

JL. GOLF

S. Kuantan

Kuala Lumpur

SOUTH CHINA SEA

Swimming Pool

Jungle Park

Tg. Tembeling

❶ Masjid Negeri	❻ Post Office
❷ Padang	❼ Banks
❸ Courthouse	❽ Samudra Riverview Hotel
❹ Taman Selera	❾ Bus Station
❺ Riverside Park & Foodstalls	❿ Stadium Darul Makmur

N

0 2.5 5 7.5
Kilometers

Pahang 7

timber chalets. Facilities include a gym, restaurants, swimming pool and car rental. Beach chalets are $64 D, $112 family, rooms are $64 D, suites $100.

There are food stalls along the highway serving Malay food including rabbit satay at the first place from Kuantan on the left. There is also excellent Chinese seafood, and an excellent stall, just down from Belia Perkasa Hotel towards the beach which opens early.

Cherating

From the main Kuantan bus station take a Kemaman No. 27 bus for the one-hour journey, and then walk the short distance to the beach from the road, or get a share taxi from Jl. Besar.

There is no problem with cheap accommodations here – at least a dozen choices of thatched-roof chalets and homestays, and more are springing up all the time. Favorites are **Mak Long Teh's** (12 chalets) ☎ 5819290, and **Mak De's** (16 chalets) ☎ 5819396, homestays, next to the bus stop on the highway where full board is available. Ranges from $8-$10. As for the other budget accommodation, walk around until you find something that catches your fancy. Upperclass resorts are further north. Just before Club Med is the luxury **Legend Resort**, ☎ 5819818, 8008866 (toll-free), fax: 5819400, 248 rooms. Beachfront villas and large selection of water sports. Airport transfer from Kuantan can be arranged. $100 S/D, suites from $240. Next door, Cherating **Holiday Villa** (138 rms) ☎ 5819500, fax: 5819524, has Steak House, 2 swimming pools, tennis, squash, sauna, watersports. Chalets $66 S, $78 D, suites from $88. Right after Club Med is the **Impiana** (121 rms) ☎ 5819000, 800-8828 (toll-free), fax: 5819090, with its lovely wooden architecture. Offers outdoor and water sports activities, as well as local tours. $74 S/D, 2-rm suite at $300. **Ombak Beach Resort** (30 rms) ☎ 5819166, fax: 5819433. AC rooms with own terrace and carpark, BBQ dinners. $47 S/D. **Club Mediteranee**, Batu 29 Jl. Kuantan/Kemaman, ☎ 5819133, fax: 09-5819524. 600 rms. Family entertainment concept with organized activities including tennis, squash, watersports, trapeze, rock-climbing and archery. There is also a disco, health center, swimming pool. 3D/2N full board $197. **Residence Inn**, Sg.

Karang, ☎ 5819333, fax: 5819252. 74 rms. Two minutes' walk to the beach; chalets perched on the outer zone. Pool and jacuzzi, restaurants, disco, karaoke, jungle-trekking. $70 S, $78 D, suites $86 S, $94 D; chalets $78 S, $86 D.

Pekan

Buses run from the main bus stand several times daily or get a share taxi from Jl. Besar for the 44km journey. The town is small and easy to walk around. At the Sultan Abu Bakar Museum pick up the brochure which has an excellent map with all the sights marked. To get to the Silk Weaving Center and Tun Razak's Birthplace take a taxi from the stand in front of the market on Jl. Sultan Ahmad. There are couple of old Chinese hotels in the downtown with basic rooms for $4, but the only place to stay with atmosphere, albeit rather rundown, is the **Pekan Resthouse**, ☎ 421240, on Jl. Sultan Abu Bakar where huge rms cost $7. You can have Malay style meals here; alternatively there's a good variety of food stalls beside the market.

Tasik Chini

Travelers with their own car can drive to Chini, an oil-palm plantation town. On the Karak Highway, turn off at Gambang onto the Kuantan/Segamat highway and then follow the road 8km till a right turn-off to the Lake Chini Resort. Chini buses leave from Kuantan's main bus station for the 2-hour trip. From Chini you'll have to organize a lift or get a taxi to the resort. The best way to get to Tasik Chini is by boat from Kampung Belimbing on the Sungai Pahang. To get there take a Maran bus along the main Kuala Lumpur highway and get off at the turnoff 56km from Kuantan. Then you'll have to hitch a ride to the riverside kampung. Return day trips from here by 4-seater wooden longboat cost $16 per boat, and overnight trips $28. There are parking areas for cars here. The only place to stay is the **Lake Chini Resort**, ☎ 4567899, fax: 4567898, a quiet wooden place amongst the rainforest. Chalets $24 S/D, deluxe AC $40, dorms $6, camp sites for RM1.20 per person. The restaurant serves good local food. Alternatively day-trips are organized by the Tourist Information Office, Kuantan hotels, and chaletowners in Cherating which start from around $16. **MAS Golden Holidays** ☎ 7463000, has a 3D/2N package to Kuantan from KL, with an optional tour to Tasik Chini including a boat ride and visit to an Orang Asli settlement. The Kuantan sector includes a village tour around Beserah.

Prices in US dollars. S=single: D=double: AC=airconditioning. Telephone code 09.

PREPARATION

All rainforest areas are difficult to reach during the annual Nov-Jan monsoon season when the rivers get dangerously high. Taman Negara is closed from Nov – Jan. Except for early mornings and evenings, or at high altitudes, the rainforest is hot and humid, so loose cotton clothing is best. If you plan on hiking make sure you have good hiking boots or jogging shoes – but canvas shoes dry out the quickest. Long pants and sleeves protect against sharp rattans, mosquitoes, and from the sun on river trips. Leeches can be a real problem; if you're really squeamish about them don't bother to do any hiking. Keep your trousers tucked into your socks and boots laced tight. Calico "leech socks" can be purchased from the Malaysian Nature Society (MNS), 34, Jl. Bakar Idaman, Batu Caves, ☎ (03) 6165259, fax: (03) 6165258, for $3. Poncho-style raincoats, water bottles, first-aid kits, and a torch are helpful. Carry everything in plastic as glass is not permitted in the park.

Taman Negara

GETTING THERE

Jerantut, the jump-off town for Taman Negara, 194km northeast of KL, is reached by either road or rail. If you are driving, take Route 2 to Mentakab, then Route 98 (3–hr drive). Share taxis leave from KL's Puduraya station ($8). Buses depart from Perhentian Pekeliling on Jl. Tun Razak several times a day. The 3-hr return trip costs $4. Travelers coming from Singapore should take the train: it stops not only at Jerantut, but at Tembeling Halt, a half-hour walk to the boat jetty for Taman Negara. Make arrangements in advance for the train to stop at this station. A local bus and taxi service ply the 16km stretch between Jerantut and the Kuala Tembeling jetty. The only way from Kuala Tembeling to Kuala Tahan, the headquarters

base at Taman Negara, is by boat. Boats leave at 9am and 2pm daily and return from the park at the same time. Depending on the river level, the boat journey takes 3-4 hours and costs $7 –$60, depending on the number of passengers.

SERVICES

Information

Park permits must be purchased upon arrival at Kuala Tahan and cost 40c. Fishing permits $4, camera $2. At the reception center, organize and pay for guides, porters, accommodations at overnight hides and fishing lodges, boat trips within the park. For further information and bookings contact Department of Wildlife and National Parks, Km 10, Jl. Cheras, KL, ☎ (03) 9052872, fax: (03) 9052873.

TOURS

Wilderness Experience, ☎ (03) 7822377, fax: (03) 7822387, tailor-made trips, including the challenging hike up Gunung Tahan; they also run a 3D/2N whitewater rafting trip in Sungai Tembeling. **Asian Overland Services**, ☎ 45291100, fax: 4529800 have a 4D/3N package departing three times a week from KL.
KTM Berhad, ☎ (03) 2757267/9, fax: (03) 2736527, offers a 5D/4N rail package including accommodation at the resort, meals, jungle trekking, canopy walkway, and all transfers, from $168 per person.

ACCOMMODATIONS AND DINING

The two main accommodation facilities are at Kuala Tahan and Nusa Camp. At Kuala Tahan, the **Taman Negara Resort**, ☎ 2663500, fax: 2661500 / KL, ☎ (03) 2455585, fax: (03) 2455430, has 87 AC rooms, bungalows, a 16-rm guesthouse, and 64-bed dorms. Two 10-rm lodges are located away from the main resort. There are 2 expensive restaurants serving buffet meals, and a lounge. Book at any travel agent. You can also arrive at the park and organize everything from there. Hostel rooms with shared bathroom and cooking facilities cost $14 per bed. Chalets with AC, own bathroom and hot shower cost $70, standard guesthouse rooms are $50, and deluxe rooms $104. Campsites at Kuala Tahan are $1.20 per night. Elsewhere, camping is free.

All hides, except for Bumbun Tahan have sleeping facilities for 6-8 people, and a bathroom. There are no cooking facilities and it is advisable to bring in pre-cooked food to maximize your chances of spotting wildlife. If you must cook, do it away from the hides. There are visitor lodges at Kuala Trenggan and Kuala Keniam with beds, bedding, eating utensils, kerosene stove, and water. The fishing lodges at Lata Berkoh and Kuala Perkai have beds and mattresses but bedding and cooking equipment must be brought in ($3.20). Camping and hiking gear can be rented from the reception center. The restaurant near the reception center has cheaper local fare and they also pack take-away meals for treks. A small shop sells tinned food and basics like batteries and insect repellent.

Nusa Camp is further upriver past several rapids. For a 3D/2N package, A-frame chalets start at $21 S, $47 D; dorms $33; Malay kampung house, $66 D. Package includes boat transfers and breakfast. Full packages are also available. ☎/ fax: KL (MATIC) (03) 2627682. There is plenty of cheap lodging at Jerantut. Try the **Resthouse** ☎/ fax: 2664488, which has 12 rms. With AC, showers and a restaurant. $16 S/D.

HIKES AND BOAT TRIPS

Guides are a good idea for long treks. They cost about $30 per day and are organized through the reception center where you can pick up a good booklet outlining all the trails, boat trips, fishing, etc., with trail maps. Trails are signposted with approximate walking times. Organized daily hikes, with lunch included, from Kuala Tahan or Camp Nusa, cost $20. Camp Nusa packages include treks. A short 20 mins from Kuala Tahan is the world's longest canopy walkway, 25m above the ground. Closed on Sundays. One easy trek to do is to Bukit Teresek and Tabing Hide, then take a boat to the rapids at Lata Berkoh and hike back to HQ. Another goes to Bukit Indah, then by boat through the rapids to Kuala Trenggan and then hike back. Boat trips to Lata Berkoh, Kuala Trenggan, and further afield to Kuala Keniam and Kuala Perkai are cheaper if the four-seater boat is full. Expect to pay around $28 per boat for the shorter journeys. There are also numerous caves to explore, and whitewater rafting. The beautiful but challenging hike up Gunung Tahan takes about 7 days; there are campsites and fresh water en route.

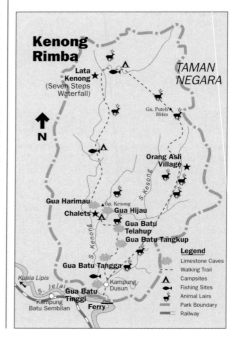

Kual Lipis And Kenong Rimba

GETTING THERE

Kuala Lipis, the former capital of Pahang, in the northeast of the state is 171km from Kuala Lumpur. By road take the KL/Kuantan highway to Bentong (Route 8), then turn off via Raub and Benta. Buses run daily services from Putra Bus Station, KL, or from Kuantan and Kota Bharu. Share taxis also run from these towns. Kuala Lipis is on the east coast railway line and is a good stopover for travelers en route to Kota Bharu. Get a park entry permit from the District Forest Officer, Kuala Lipis Government Office Complex, ☎ 3121273. To get to Kenong Rimba take the early morning local train from Kuala Lipis to Batu Sembilan. From the nearby jetty, motorized longboats (20-min trip) run to Kenong Rimba. Visitors are only allowed to enter the park if they are accompanied by a registered local guide. Each guide can take a maximum of 10 visitors at a time. Guides to Gunung Tahan charge $120-$200 per week. Some cheap hotels organize trips into the park. **Wilderness Experience**, ☎ (03) 7822377, fax: (03) 7822387, organizes day runs and a 2D/1N whitewater rafting tour at Jeram Besu in Kuala Lipis.

ACCOMMODATIONS AND DINING

There are a few wooden chalets inside the park at Gunung Kesong, but take your own bedding. If you go with a tour this is taken care of. If hiking past the park, bring your own tent. A tiny store at Kampung Dusun beside the park sells basic foodstuffs but if traveling further bring your own foodstuffs and cooking equipment. The best place to stay in Kuala Lipis is the hilltop **Resthouse** (Rumah Persinggahan Kuala Lipis) on Bukit Residen, 1km south of town, ☎ 3121599. It has an in-house museum, great views, and the restaurant serves excellent Malay-style food. Rooms cost $16-20 S/D and have bathrooms and AC. Most backpackers stay in the cheap downtown hotels. On the main street, the **Hotel Paris** and **Hotel Central** have basic rooms for under $10.

Endau-Rompin

As this proposed state or national park is only being developed at the present, there is no organized transport system into Endau-Rompin and only very basic accommodations at Kuala Jasin; however more is being planned. The best way to get to Endau-Rompin is with a tour company which can fully organize a camping trip. Wilderness Experience run a fully guided 4-5 day trip from Kuala Lumpur for $260, inclusive of food, camping equipment, and travel.

Melaka PRACTICALITIES

INCLUDES NEGERI SEMBILAN

Melaka, extremely popular with Singaporeans, is packed on weekends—especially with large tour groups and bridal couples. Hotels impose a surcharge on weekends and public holidays. Always ask about packages, especially on weekdays. There are charming and distinctively Melakan accommodations. Jonker's Street is an excellent place to buy Asian curios.
Prices in US dollars. S=single: D=double: AC=airconditioning. Telephone code 06.

Melaka

GETTING THERE

By Air

Pelangi Air runs three weekly flights from Singapore ($44), and Ipoh ($40). There are also Friday flights from Sumatra. The airport is at Batu Berendam, 9.5km from town and taxis to town cost $8. Airport ☎ 3174175. MAS office Contact Pelancongan Kota Malacca, ☎ 247728, or Atlas Travel, ☎ 220777.

By Sea

Express ferries run daily between Melaka and Dumai, Sumatra. The boat takes 4 hrs and leaves Melaka at 9.30am, and Dumai at 12pm. $32 single, $60 return. Contact **Madai Shipping**, 321-A, Jl. Tun Ali, ☎ 2840671, **Tunas Rupat Utama Express**, 17A Jl. Merdeka, ☎ 2832506.

By Road

The fastest way from Kuala Lumpur is by share taxi from Puduraya taxi station for $7; Butterworth $25; Johor Bahru $9. AC express buses run frequently from Kuala Lumpur's Puduraya for $2.70; Ipoh $6.40, Butterworth $9.60; Singapore $4.60; Kuala Terengganu $8.60.

By Train

Nearest train station to Melaka is at Tampin, 38km north of town. For train schedules phone Melaka Railway Office, ☎ 2823091, or Tamping Railway Station, ☎ 411034. Train fares are: from Kuala Lumpur $6.80; Singapore $10.80.

LOCAL TRANSPORTATION

Walking is by far the best way to see Melaka, as many of the town's attractions are centered within the heart of old downtown. Ask for a Heritage Trail map at Tourist Information. Trishaws are the second-best mode of transport and are excellent for getting to slightly out-of-the-way places like St. John's Fort, and the Portuguese Settlement. They charge about $8/hr.

Buses are cheaper than trishaws, although not as pleasant. The bus station is at Jl. Tun Mamat, off Jl. Hang Tuah in the north end of town, but there are convenient bus stops throughout the downtown area. Bus No. 17 goes to the Portuguese Settlement, and close to St. John's Fort (get out at the jail). Bus No. 19, goes past the new State Mosque to the recreation area at Ayer Keroh where Mini Malaysia, the jungle recreation park and other theme parks are located. For the seaside drive northwest, past Klebang to Pantai Kundor, take a Pat Hup Bus No. 51. To get to Umbai for boats to Pulau Besar, and also for Merlimau and Muar, take an Aziz Co. bus from the central terminal. **Ferries** to Pulau Besar leave from Umbai jetty. Return fare is $4, but this is for a full boat load of 8 persons. To charter a boat costs around $32.

Melaka is a beautiful state to drive around and there are many picturesque villages with outstanding examples of traditional architecture which are not easily accessible by bus. Car rentals can be organized at Avis Rent-a-Car at 124 Jl. Bendahara, ☎ 2846710, or further down at National, 36 Jl. Laksamana, ☎ 2848871.

SERVICES

Information

Melaka Tourist Information Centre, is in the Town Square, ☎ 2836538. Open daily from 9pm.

Banking

Banks are open 5 days a week and half day on Saturdays. Hongkong and Shanghai Bank is on Jl. Kota and next door is Bank Bumiputra. Overseas Chinese Banking Co is on Jl. Hang Jebat. There are plenty of money changers around especially close to the historical center.

TOURS

Ask any travel agent for half-day **city tours**, which average $12. Try Stadhuys, 151 Jl. Bendahara ☎ 2846373, or Cammy, 311 Jl. Ong Kim Wee, ☎ 2827244. Tours usually cover the main sights in the city or go out to the plantations (2 hrs each) or can be planned according to personal itineraries (4hrs - $20). **Riverboat cruises** up the Melaka River start from jetty behind the Tourist Information Center and cost around $3 for a 45-min trip. Check at the center for departure times (usually hourly at high tide from 10am). Boats also depart from here to Pulau Besar if there are 12 passengers. Most tour agencies have a 3D/2N package to Melaka from KL, which include accommodations and city tour.

ACCOMMODATIONS

Melaka is a popular tourist destination all year round, and has a wide variety of lodgings ranging from luxury hotels to cheap dorms. Accommodation is always available, but on public holidays up-market hotels are often full.

Luxury

Century Mahkota Hotel, Jl. Merdeka, ☎ 2812828, fax: 2812323. 617 rms. Sitting on reclaimed land on the waterfront, near shops and historical hub, large landscaped swimming pools, tennis, squash, golf, international eateries, activities for children. Rm $120 S/D, 1,2 and 3-bedrm suites from $140.
Renaissance Melaka Hotel, Jl. Bendahara, ☎ 2848888, 8004146 (toll-free), fax: 2849269. 295 ms. The original luxury hotel. Centrally located, good views of Melaka River and the Malay village. Luxurious, well-appointed, comfortable rooms, restaurants, sauna, swimming pool, Utan fun pub with tropical decor. $112 S, $124 D, suites from $144.
Paradise Melaka Village Resort, Ayer Keroh, ☎ 2323600, 8008797 (toll-free), fax: 2325955. 510 chalets. 10km from downtown. Traditional Malay-style wooden buildings or modern apartments, beautifully-landscaped grounds, swimming pools, tennis courts, golf, Malaysian, Chinese and Japanese restaurants. $80 S/D, suites from $112.
Riviera Bay Resort, 10 km Jl. Tanjung Kling, ☎ 3151111, fax: 3153333. 450 rms. 10 km or 20 minutes' drive from Melaka town. Roman-inspired architecture, sea-facing suites in 1, 2 and 3-bedroom. combinations. Chinese and Italian restaurants, fun pub, karaoke, tennis, squash. $145-$300.

High Intermediate

Shah's Beach Resort, Tanjung Kling, ☎ 3153121, fax: 3152088. 50 rms. Overlooking the straits, 10km north of town, this wooden Malay-style resort

Melaka
Environs SELAT MELAKA

has character, cane chairs on the verandahs, bamboo blinds, a Malay/Western cuisine restaurant, small swimming pool and tennis court. AC rms with bath S/D $46, suites $65.
The Emperor Hotel, 123 Jl. Munshi Abdullah, ☎ 2840777. 250 rms. Central and comfortable, Chinese restaurant with dim sum, swimming pool, lounge. Rm rates include breakfast. $100 S/D, suites $156.
The City Bayview, 20 Jl. Tun Sri Lanang, ☎ 2839888, fax: 2836699. 182 rms. Good views. Near St. Peter's Church and town attractions. Pool, TV, in-house videos, Chinese, Western restaurants, $130 S/D, suites $207.
Ayer Keroh Country Resort, Ayer Keroh, ☎ 2325311, fax: 2320422. 50 rms. Next door to Mini Malaysia. Quiet location with jungle trees with tracks, pool, restaurant. Car rental available. AC with own bathroom, TV. $54 S/D motel room, $92 chalets.
Tanjung Bidara Beach Resort, Tanjung Bidara, ☎ 3842990, fax: 3842995. 45 rms. Beside the Strait's best swimming beach, but hard to get to without own transport. $60 S/D AC with own bathroom, TV.

Low Intermediate

Heeren House, 1 Jl. Tun Tan Cheng Lock, ☎ 2814241, fax: 2814239. 7 rms. Colonial guesthouse with river view, and excellent cheesecake. Peranakan and Portuguese lunches. $40-48 S/D, Alberquerque Suite $72-80.
Air Keroh d'Village, Ayer Keroh, ☎ 2328000, fax: 2327541. 240 rms. 20 mins from town, choice of motel room or chalets, swimming pool and children's wading pool, restaurant, pub, bicycle hire. $52 motel room, $64 chalet.
Baba House, 125-127 Jl. Tun Tan Cheng Lock, ☎ 2811216, fax: 2811217. Picturesque Peranakan house in the middle of the historical area. $34 S/D, $38 deluxe with bath and AC.
Hotel Portugis, 12 Jl. Melaka Raya 20, ☎ 2924100, fax: 2929300. New, full of character, wonderfully decorated VIP rooms, Portuguese restaurant, food court, karaoke, central location. $71 S/D, VIP rooms $155.
Straits Heritage Lodge, 591-A Taman Melaka Raya, ☎ 2823950, fax: 2823957. Clean, homely rooms open out to a charming Melakan open air fountain courtyard. Portuguese bistro and restaurant. $40 S/D, $50 family room.

Budget

Majestic Hotel, 188 Jl. Bunga Raya, ☎ 2822367. 22 rms. Old colonial era hotel with high ceilings and fans. Located beside the Melaka River. Non AC $11 S, $21 D; AC with bath $15 S, $25 D.
May Chiang Hotel, 52 Jl. Munshi Abdullah. 8 rms. Very clean, centrally located. AC with bath $16 S/D.
Chong Hoe Hotel, 26 Jl. Tukang Emas, ☎ 2826102. In the heart of Chinatown, opp. Kampung Kling

Mosque. Clean and basic. $6 S, $7 D non-AC with shared bath; $11 with AC and attached bathroom.
Kancil Guest House, 177 Jl. Parameswara. In an interesting old shophouse area about 1km from town. Quiet, spotlessly clean, safe, charming, simple meals, bicycle hire. $6.40-$14 S, $7.20-$16 D. There are guesthouses along Jl. Parameswara and also in Taman Melaka Raya, south of this road. However, be careful which ones you choose, especially if there are lots of girls hanging around outside. Dorm beds and rooms are generally under $10.

Melaka is well-known regionally for its cheap, tasty food, and the majority of famous food spots are unnamed hawkers' stalls.

Chinese

Chinese food freaks start with a dim sum breakfast – steamed delicacies served with Chinese tea – at the coffee shop opp. **Masjid Kampung Keling** on Jl. Tukang Emas. Around mid-morning to lunch, a tiny shop at 4 Jl. Hang Jebat (just near the bridge) is famous for its chicken rice with the rice shaped in billiard-size balls, and home-made barley drink. Further up Jl. Hang Jebat, on the corner of Jl. Lekir, a satay seller makes Melaka's best pork satay throughout the afternoon. For refreshing *chendol* – a coconut-milk based drink – try shop on the corner of Jl. Hang Jebat and Jl. Hang Kasturi. For dinner, **Madame Fatso's Restoran Bunga Raya** at Glutton's Corner, the hawker stalls along Jl. Merdeka, serves baked crab and Chinese-style steamboat. Nonya food, or Straits Chinese cuisine, a blend of Chinese and Malay, is good at Taman Melaka Raya, particularly **Ole Sayang Restaurant**, at No. 198/199; and at the **Peranakan Restaurant**, in a restored Baba villa at 317 Kelebang Besar. **Jonkers Melaka Restoran**, in a revamped Baba townhouse on Jl. Hang Jebat, does a set nonya-style lunch.

Malay

Malay food is good at **M. Annuar Catering**, a small shop next to the food stalls on Jl. Taman facing the Padang. Their delicious *nasi briyani* – spicy rice with chicken or mutton – comes with tasty *rojak* and pickles. The stalls either side serve cheap nasi campur – rice with curries at lunch – and Malay-style soups and noodle dishes. For excellent albeit pricey Melaka-style Malay fare and very spicy *sambal belacan* and *masak asam pedas* dishes, go for a small restaurant at 35 Jl. Merdeka. Out of town, and well worth the trip to Klebang Besar, 8km north, is a group of outdoor restaurants overlooking the Melaka Straits which specialize in satay, and baked fish – *ikan bakar*. Portuguese cuisine, which is similar to Malay, but slightly more Mediterranean, is good at the square in the Portuguese Settlement. Recommended places include **Restau-**

rant D'Lisbon, **Restoran De Portugis**, and the San Pedro opp. the square. Their baked fish and "devil" curry is good, and the small deep-fried fish, known as *gading-gading*, are delicious as a snack with beer.

Indian

Indian food shops are centered around the Jl. Temenggong and Jl. Bendahara. Sri Lakshmi Vilas Restaurant in Jl. Bendahara and **Restoran Veni** in Jl. Temenggong serve delicious South Indian pancakes – delicate *thosai* with curry sauces. Also in this area are plenty of coffee shops selling *roti canai* and *murtabak*.

Western

Western food is best and expensive at **Summerfield's Coffee Shop** in the Ramada Renaissance Hotel, Jl. Bendahara. Its other outlet, Caper's, features Mediterranean fare. Other major hotels and resorts also serve western cuisine. The small restaurant in the **Majestic Hotel**, Jl. Bunga Raya does reasonably-priced steak and lamb chops. On Jl. Laksamana, **Restoran Kim Swee Huat**, serves "travelers" food – porridge and muesli breakfasts – and is popular with backpackers. The **Tai Chong Hygienic Ice Cafe** on Jl. Bunga Raya has a large menu of drinks and desserts including peaches and ice-cream. **Taberna Faial** opp. the Straits Heritage Hotel, is owned by a Portuguese, and has authentic Portuguese recipes and wines, which are also available at the bistro/tavern of the same management beneath the hotel.

Negeri Sembilan Seremban

GETTING THERE

Seremban, is 64km south of Kuala Lumpur, a 45-min drive on the North-South Expressway. Regular buses from Kuala Lumpur run from Puduraya terminal ($1.20), and share taxis can be hired upstairs ($4.80). Trains, although much more infrequent than the buses, also stop at Seremban's old colonial-style railway station; fares from Kuala Lumpur are $5.20 AC, and from Singapore $12 AC. The air-conditioned KTM Komuter swiftly and comfortably covers the distance in 1 hr 10 mins for $2.28.

LOCAL TRANSPORTATION

Seremban's attractions are easily seen by foot; however to get to the Cultural Handicraft Complex/State Museum, which is out of town on the link road to the expressway, catch a taxi from the bus and taxi station at Jl. Sungai Ujong. It is also feasible to hire a car from Kuala Lumpur, where the rates are more competitive, make a 2-day trip to Seremban and Sri Menanti, and then take the coast road via Port Dickson to Melaka.

ACCOMMODATIONS

Intermediate

Allson Klana Resort, Jl. Penghulu Cantik, Taman Tasik, ☎ 729600, fax: 739218. 224 rms. Seremban's only up-market hotel, close to the lake, swimming pool, gym, Japanese and Chinese restaurants. $82 S, $90 D, suites $176.

Carlton Star Hotel, 47 Jl. Dato' Sheikh Ahmad, ☎ 7625336, fax: 720040. 34 rms. Central, Chinese restaurant, fitness center, karaoke, AC rooms with bathrooms are $62 S/D.

Lakeview Hotel, ☎ 7630994, fax: 7635355. 48 rms. Overlooking the Lake Gardens on Jl. Tetamu off Jl. Za'aba. Motel-style rooms overlook the pool. Quiet and comfortable. AC, hot showers. $62 S/D.

Mee Lee Hotel, Jl. Tunku Hassan, ☎ 7630162. 17 rms. Right in town close to food and transport. Showers, AC rooms. $16 S, $20 D.

Milo Hotel, Jl. Dato' Abdul Rahman, ☎ 7623451. Central but quiet, double bed, hot showers, Chinese restaurant downstairs that also serves Western and Malay and buffets. 35 rms. $15 S, $24 D, suite $72.

Seremban Inn, 39 Jl. Tuanku Munawir, ☎ 7617777, fax: 7637777. Central and close to shops and bus

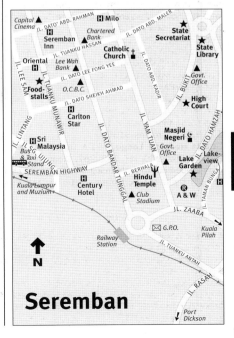

Seremban

N. Sembilan

9

terminal, bakery downstairs, next to hawkers; AC and hot showers. $38-$50 S/D.

Budget

There is a host of cheap Chinese hotels which all offer very basic facilities for under $10 including **The Oriental Hotel** (18 rms), 11 Jl. Tuanku Munawir, ☎ 7630119, and the **Wah Seng Hotel**, (9 rms) 110 Jl. Dato' Bandar Tunggal.

DINING

Negeri Sembilan food follows the traditions of the Minangkabau from Sumatra and the cuisine is tasty, but very hot and spicy. The cheapest and best place in town is the hawker center on Jl. Tuanku Munawir. More up-market Malay cuisine is served at **Flamingo Inn**, 1A Jl. Za'aba. Indian Muslim food – curries, and *roti canai*, and *murtabak* – are good at **Bilal Restaurant**, 100 Jl. Dato' Bandar Tunggal. Recommended Chinese restaurants include **Suntori Restaurant**, 10/11 Jl. Dato' Sheikh Ahmad, and the **Happy Restaurant**, 1 Jl. Dato' Bandar Tunggal. Tasty banana-leaf curries cooked in the South Indian style are aplenty along Jl. Yam Tuan where there is also an **A&W** near the lake opposite the Seremban Parade shopping center.

Sri Menanti and Kuala Pilah

GETTING THERE

Catch share taxis to the royal town of Sri Menanti, 33km west, and to Kuala Pilah from the Seremban bus and taxi station in Jl. Sungai Ujong for $1.60. Local buses run frequently.

ACCOMMODATIONS AND DINING

There is no hotel in Sri Menanti, but Kuala Pilah, 6km further northwest, has a hilltop Resthouse (Rumah Rehat Kerajaan) with 14 rooms on Jl. Bukit. The Minangkabau food here is more authentic than in the capital. The hawker center at the corner of the roads to Seremban and Tampin has a good variety of dishes. There are also a number of cheap Chinese and Indian coffee shops in town.

Port Dickson

GETTING THERE

By car take the Port Dickson exit on the North/South Expressway and then follow the main access road from Seremban. Share taxis from Kuala Lumpur's Puduraya station cost $4.80, from Melaka $4, and from Seremban $1.50. Express buses from Kuala Lumpur (Puduraya) cost $2 and frequent local buses depart from Seremban for 65c. To get around the Port Dickson region hail a share taxi anywhere along the beachfront road, or catch local buses to Blue Lagoon. Walk in to Tanjung Tuan, or to the megaliths at Pengkalan Kempas.

ACCOMMODATIONS AND DINING

The entire Jl. Pantai stretch is packed with accommodations. Seafood is definitely PD's forte, and just about any eating stall or restaurant on the way or in PD itself serves fresh food. Weekend rates are higher.
Bayu Beach Resort, Km 7, Jl. Pantai, ☎ 6473703, fax: 6472507. 189 rms. Water sports, pool and jacuzzi, gym, sauna, golf, Chinese/Western restaurant, hawker stalls. 1, 2 and 3 bedroom suites from $80.
Ming Court Beach Hotel, Km 12, ☎ 6625244, fax: 6625899. 164 rms. Top range beachfront hotel. Comfortable rooms, TV, IDD phones, swimming pool, tennis courts, restaurants. Weekdays are cheaper $64 D.
Regency Hotel & Resort, Km 8, ☎ 6474090, fax: 6475016. 217 rms. Traditional Minangkabau architecture, Chinese restaurant, pool and lobby lounges with live band, water sports, golf, gym. $72 S/D, suites from $168.
Delta Paradise Lagoon Hotel, 3.5 km Jl. Pantai, ☎ 6477600, 8008575 (toll-free), fax: 6477630. 201 rooms. Sea-facing rms, man-made lagoon, sports and water facilities, restaurant. $96 S/D, suites from $168. The mid-priced **Si Rusa Inn**, Km 12, ☎ 6625233, fax: 6625332, a 1960s-style "motel" where AC rooms with bath cost $20 D, to $36 per family. A number of cheap, Chinese-run guesthouses get very noisy on weekends, but are quiet through the week, including **Pantai Ria Hotel**, Batu 8, Jl. Pantai, ☎ 405265, $16 AC S, $20 AC D; **Lido Hotel**, Batu 8, Jl. Pantai, ☎ 6625273, $10 S, $12 D. There are good seafood restaurants, Malay-style, with economical prices, on the beachfront at Pantai Bagan Pinang, and at Teluk Kemang. At the former, there is a small food center which serves excellent Malay-style breakfasts. For a splurge, the buffet at the poolside coffee shop in the **Ming Court Hotel**, is excellent. They also serve western cuisine, and snacks and cakes.

Johor PRACTICALITIES

INCLUDES DESARU AND PULAU TIOMAN

Johor's biggest visitors are Singaporeans, who flood in every weekend. A car is the best way to get to the mainland beaches, fishing villages and seafood corners, but in town itself, leg power works well. Public transport is plentiful to the jump-off points for the islands, and tours can easily be arranged at the capital. Accommodation is no problem, and the whole gamut is available, from beachside chalets to luxurious resorts. *Prices in US dollars. S=single: D=double: AC=airconditioning. Telephone code 07, except Muar 06.*

Johor Bahru

GETTING THERE

By Road

Malaysia's southernmost major town, fondly known as JB, is usually visited either coming or going to Singapore, 1km across the Causeway, a half-hour drive from downtown. AC express buses shuttle from Singapore's Rochor Rd. terminus (S$1), or the regular bus No. 170 from Queen St. stops along the way. Share and charter taxis also depart from Queen St. for $4 a seat. Johor Bahru has a much better range of express bus and long-distance taxi services than Singapore, and many travelers to Malaysia merely get across the border and make onward travel arrangements from Johor Bahru. The taxi station is on Jl. Wong Ah Fook, and the bus station on Jl. Gertak Merah. The Kuala Lumpur/Singapore train passes through JB.

By Air

Malaysia Airlines fly to the airport in Senai, 15km from town, from Kuala Lumpur ($37), Penang ($71), Kota Kinabalu ($139), Kuching ($68) and Sumatra. Pelangi Airways flies twice a week from Kuala Lumpur and once a week from Ipoh ($64) and Sumatra. MAS office, Menara Pelangi, Jl. Kuning, ☎ 2229348. Airport, ☎ 5994737. An AC coach service runs between the airport, JB (Puteri Pan Pacific Hotel) and Singapore (Novotel Orchid Hotel), bookings through MAS.

By Sea

Ferrylink operates daily between Changi Point near the Singapore airport and Tanjung Belungkor in Johor. Vehicles are driven on board.
Most of JB's downtown attractions can easily be seen on foot, or taxis can be hailed from the road-

side. For **car rentals**, check the airport. Avis is also at Tropical Inn, ☎ 2237971; Orix, Johor Information Center, ☎ 2241215; Hertz, Johor Information Center, ☎ 2237520; Mayflower, Wisma Tan Chong ☎ 2241357; National, Jl. Ibrahim, ☎ 2230503.

ACCOMMODATIONS

Hotels are more expensive in JB than in most other Malaysian towns, mainly because of the demand by Singaporeans, and decent rooms are hard to find on weekends.
Hyatt Regency, Jl. Sungai Chat, ☎ 2231234, fax: 2232718. 406 rms. Fronting the Straits of Johor, 10 minutes away from town and near the

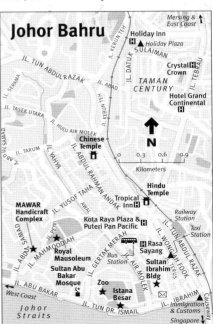

Johor Bahru

Sultan's Palace. Luxurious, four restaurants, two-tier swimming pool, tennis, fitness center, Roman spa. $140 S/D, suites from $400.

Puteri Pan Pacific Hotel, Jl. Salim, ☎ 2233333, fax: 2236622. 468 rms. A luxury hotel beside Kota Raya shopping complex in the heart of downtown with silver-service restaurants, swimming pool, fitness and business centers. $88 S/D, suites from $180 D.

Holiday Inn Crowne Plaza, Jl. Dato Sulaiman, Century Gardens, ☎ 3323800, 8001021 (toll-free), fax: 3324000. 2km north of town. Swimming pool, health club, and Szechuan and Italian restaurants, $136 S, $148 D, suites from $220.

Crystal Crown Hotel, Jl. Tebrau, ☎ 3334422, fax: 3345505. 248 rms. Right in the commercial area. Restaurants, coffee house, health center. $72 S, $80 D, studio from $100.

Merlin Inn, 10 Jl. Bukit Meldrum, ☎ 2237400, fax: 2238690. 132 rms. 4-star hotel 10 mins from city center. Malay restaurant, swimming pool, pub. $60 S/D.

Tropical Inn, Jl. Gereja, ☎ 2247888, fax: 2241254. 160 rms. AC, mini bar, hot showers, views of Singapore, 24-hour restaurant and room service. $50 S, $54 D, including buffet breakfast.

Hotel Grand Continental, Jl. Dato' Abdullah Tahir/Jl. Tebrau, ☎ 3323999, fax: 3321999. 288 rms. In town with views of Tebrau Straits and Singapore. Chinese restaurant, karaoke, swimming pool, money changer. $48 S, $56 D, suite $120.

Heritage JB, 69 Jl. Ibrahim Sultan, ☎ 2228228, fax: 2221710. 10 mins walk from town, easy bus access, near restaurants, rms AC with attached baths. $28 S, $32 D.

Hotel Straits View, 10 Jl. Skudai, ☎ 2241400, fax: 2242698. 30 rms. Out of town overlooking the straits. Huge beds, hot showers, TV, IDD phone, and renowned seafood restaurant. $42 S/D.

Fortuna Hotel, 29A Jl. Meldrum, ☎ 2233210, fax: 2236243. 50 rms. Cheap and clean, with AC, attached baths, and eateries opposite. $20 S, $31 D.

Hotel JB, 80A Jl. Wong Ah Fook, ☎ 2234788. 33 rms. Central, basic with fan, shared bath for $16 S/D, $20 with own bath and AC.

DINING

JB is well known for its excellent and cheap food. For the best Johor-Malay cuisine, head for **Tepian Tebrau food center**, Jl. Abu Bakar, for seafood steamboat, nasi briyani – spiced rice with mutton or chicken, *ikan bakar* – fish grilled in banana leaf, the delectable Wahid *mee rebus* family recipe. Another favorite with locals is **Capati Corner**, which serves home-made capati – Indian bread, and curries, on Jl. Kolam Air (parallel to Jl. Skudai). Good up-market restaurants include **Rang Mahal**, 68 Jl. Padi Satu, Bandar Baru Uda, ☎ 360888, which specializes in

North Indian cooking good for naan and Tandoori chicken. **Manhattan Grill**, Level 5, Plaza Kota Raya, does prime ribs, stews, steaks, salads and mouth-watering desserts. Recommended seafood restaurants include **Jaws 5**, at the Straits View Hotel, Jl. Skudai, which has delicious tiger prawns, and traditional dance performances. **Midland Garden**, 11 Jl. Skudai, does excellent grilled fish dishes, "drunken" prawns and shark's fin soup. **Prawn House**, Jl. Kebun Teh, is a converted bungalow with tables in the open, serving seafood and specializing in yam cake. On the same road, **Briyani House** dishes up the Johor special of *briyani gam* – rice with mutton and chicken, served with acar.

SERVICES

Information

The Johor Information Center is at Jl. Ayer Molek, ☎ 2223591, The Dept. of Tourism Johor is at The Fort, Bukit Timbalan, ☎ 2234935.

Muar

From Melaka to Muar, 45km south, take a share taxi or bus from the main bus station. From JB, taxis depart from Jl. Wong Ah Fook or buses from Jl. Terus. Car hire can be organized in Melaka or from JB. Muar has an old-world **Resthouse** (18 rms) on Jl. Sultanah, Tanjung Mas, ☎ 9527744, close to the rivermouth, AC. $11 S, $13 D with own bathrooms. More upmarket is the **Hotel Sri Pelangi**, 79 Jl. Sisi, ☎ 9518088, fax: 9522786. Overlooks the river. 80 comfortable rms with TV, IDD phones. S/D AC $34-$42. There are plenty of basic, cheap, Chinese hotels for under $10 like the **Lee Wa Hotel**, 75 Jl. Arab, ☎ 9515995. The town gourmet specialty is rojak petis – fruit salad with peanut sauce – at the Tanjung food stalls on the riverside. Cheap Chinese restaurants are found in Chinatown (downtown). Malay food is good at the riverside stalls in town.

Batu Pahat

Catch a local bus, or a share taxi from JB (126km), Melaka (98km), or Muar (53km). Buses and taxis can also be stopped anywhere along the Muar/Batu Pahat road. **Hotel Carnival**, 2 Jl. Fatimah, ☎ 4315122, fax: 4310611, 60 rms, is the classiest hotel in town, and has a Chinese restaurant, coffee house, comfortable rooms. $26-$35 S/D. Near the roundabout where Route 5 goes to Pontian, is the **Resthouse**, 870 Jl. Tasek, ☎ 4341181, with 14 large rooms for $13 with own baths and a good

10 Johor

restaurant. Cheaper rooms for under $10 can be found in the old-style Chinese hotels like the **Fairyland Hotel**, Jl. Rahmat, ☎ 4341777.

Batu Pahat has a great variety of eating spots and some of the tastiest and cheapest eating on the peninsula. For Chinese food, especially pork satay and oyster omelets, try **Glutton's** Corner beside the river at the end of Jl. Rahmat. West along the riverbank are Malay satay and grilled fish stalls. Opposite the Immigration Department on the Pontian road are the best fried bananas in Malaysia – served with a hot soy sauce sambal. The food center north of the bridge on the Muar road, serves delicious Malay curries and rice.

Pontian/Kukup

No one really stays in Pontian – they just drive through on the way to Kukup, or further south to Tanjung Piai, to eat seafood. To get to Pontian, take a share taxi or local bus from JB (61km), or Batu Pahat (73km). Most visitors to Kukup either come by tour bus from JB or Singapore or drive their own cars. However, you can catch a local bus from Pontian (19km) or hail a share taxi. Kukup has a wide variety of seafood restaurants, but the best for atmosphere are those with large dining areas built out over the water. The best-known is **Restoran Makanan Laut Kukup** – great for prawns and crabs; also well-known is **Restoran Tong San** – good for grilled fish and **Restoran Zaiton Hussin** – good for Malay-style seafood. At Tanjung Piai, the tip of the Asian mainland (hard to get to without your own transport) is **Atan Seafood Restaurant** – atmospheric cheap eating with marvelous views. Go through Pasir Gudang to Pasir Putih where there is a cluster of restaurants on stilts by the seaside for fresh fish Malay style – cooked with sambal, and for other seafood delicacies.

Kota Tinggi

Local buses and share taxis ply the 42km from JB to Kota Tinggi. To get to Lombong Waterfalls take a No. 23 bus. At the waterfalls, the **Kota Tinggi Waterfalls Resort**, ☎ 8836222, has chalets set amongst the rainforest ($50 D) as well as hotel rooms ($32), AC, showers, TV. There is also a restaurant serving Malay food. In town there are only basic, old-style hotels. The best is **Hotel Bunga Raya**, ☎ 8833023 opp. the bus station, triple share non-AC $10, AC $18. To get to Johor Lama is difficult without your own transport, but you can hire a taxi in Kota Tinggi.

Gunung Ledang

Catch a bus or share taxi from JB. If you are dri-ving, turn off the North-South Highway at Tangkak and head towards Sagil. Turn left at a sign which says 'Air Terjun' (waterfall). There is a waterfall and a trek up the mountain which takes all day. KTM Berhad offers rail tours, which include accommodation in AC chalet or a rough hut, meals, transfer from the Segamat station, and ranger service up the mountain. A 2D/1N trip from JB is $80. Min.4 passengers. ☎ (03) 2757267/9.

Desaru

Catch a bus or share taxi from Kota Tinggi, or alternatively from Singapore a ferry service plies between Changi Point and Penggerang and from there you can catch a taxi north to Desaru. There is no cheap accommodation at Desaru, and on weekends, rooms are usually booked out despite rates being very much higher. The hotels are all along the same stretch of beach. **Desaru View Hotel**, ☎ 8221221, fax: 8221237, has 134 rms going for $48 S/D, deluxe $60, Chinese restaurant, swimming pool. A private resort company owns the next three properties. There is a campsite at **Desaru Leisure Camp**, ☎ 8222777, while **Desaru Chalet**, ☎ 8221211, fax: 8221937 has 35 units. AC, hot showers, facing the ocean, 50-100m from the sea, restaurant. Book two weeks ahead for weekends. $57 D, $103 (four people), suites $132 with cooking facilities. Guests may access resort facilities next door. **Desaru Golden Beach Resort**, ☎ 8221101, fax: 8221480. Beachside, restaurant serving Malay, western, seafood, new swimming pool for water polo, water sports. $60 S/D, $80 family, suites $140, villas (bungalows with 4 doors) $68 each door (twin-share).

For most meals, guests rely on the pricey hotel restaurants. Further south there are newly-built chalets along the seafront at Sungai Musuh, but you must have your own transport, and there are also a few Chinese hotels in Sungai Rengit, and good seafood restaurants at the latter. **Sebana Golf & Marina Resort**, ☎ 8252411, is further down the road, and faces a marina. Restaurant, swimming pool, karaoke, bicycles, golf, archery, water sports, fishing, tours. Boat hire from $32 per person per hour; cruises from $120. $108 S/D, suite $128. A better and quieter beach is Teluk Mahkota (Jason's Bay) which has chalets; it is close to Tanjung Balau, where there is a Fishing Museum.

Mersing

The jump-off port for all the islands except Sibu, Mersing is located 186km south of Kuantan, and 137km north of JB. Buses and taxis connect from both towns and the local station is on Jl. Sulaiman, beside the river. Share taxis cost $4.50

from JB, and $6 from Kuantan. Boats for Sibu and some boats for Tinggi depart from Tanjung Leman. To get there, head south instead of north to Mersing at Jemaluang from the winding Kluang road, or go all the way down and turn off at Kulai from the North-South Highway and head north on Route 3 towards Kota Tinggi.

ACCOMMODATIONS AND DINING

Mersing is a pleasant town with an interesting riverside and if you have to wait overnight for a boat to the islands there is plenty of accommodation and restaurants. The nicest place to stay is the **Mersing Rest House**, ☎ 7992102, about 1km from downtown on the seafront. 18 huge rooms overlook the sea and distant islands. Book ahead as it is always popular. $14 S/D, with Western breakfasts, lunch and dinners. Malay food is cheap and good at the food stalls next to the bridge particularly the satay in the evening. Sri Mersing Cafe on Jl. Sulaiman is good for tea and cakes and the Taj Mahal Restoran on Jl. Abu Bakar has delicious North Indian food.

SERVICES

Information and Tours

The friendly staff at the **Mersing Tourist Information Center**, ☎ 7995212, fax: 7993975, just before the jetty in front of the mini stadium, has comprehensive information on the islands and on day tours. Open daily 9am–4pm, except Saturday, half-day, and Sunday and public holidays. They also organize day trips to Pulau Besar, Pulau Tengah and Pulau Hujung for $64 (12 persons), including snorkeling and picnic. Fishing trips can also be arranged for 1, 2 or 3-day trips. Most island resorts have offices at the jetty where you can enquire about boats, prices and accommodation and there's always plenty of touts and boatmen around that are knowledgeable and easy to talk to about island information.

Banking Bank Bumiputra in Jl. Ismail changes travelers' checks, and you can change money at the goldsmith's on Jl. Abu Bakar.

Pulau Tioman

GETTING THERE

Pelangi Air has daily flights from Kuala Lumpur ($56), Kuantan ($32) and Singapore ($S115). Berjaya Air, ☎ (03) 2452828, flys daily from Kuala Lumpur ($58). Silk Air also flys from Singapore. The landing at the airport in Tekek (☎ 4146301), surrounded by mountains, can be somewhat hair-raising, but the sea and landscapes along the way are marvelous. Buses from the Berjaya Tioman Beach Resort meet all flights. The jump-off point to the island is Mersing. Most boats leave in the morning, but depend on the tide. Trips take 1-2 hours, cost $10-12 one way, and stop at Tekek, Ayer Batang, Paya and Salang. For boats to Mukut (south), Teluk Nipah and Kg. Genting (southwest), ask around. Passenger ferries also run from Singapore to Pulau Tioman, enquire at the tourist information office in Singapore.

LOCAL TRANSPORTATION

A path runs from Tekek north to the end of Ayer Batang. The only road goes from the airport to just south of the Berjaya resort. The cross-land walk from Tekek to Juara takes 3 hrs. Sea Bus boats make daily trips between Tekek, the Berjaya Resort, Ayer Batang and Salang; twice-daily service operates to Juara for $6, and a daily round-the-island trip, including a stopover at the Kampung Mukut waterfall, costs $12. Just ask at any jetty. Many resorts also organize boat trips to Pulau Tulai (Coral Island) the best diving spot.

ACCOMMODATIONS AND DINING

Avoid Singapore and Malaysian public holidays as the most popular places are often booked out and the main beaches are quite crowded. During the annual monsoon (Nov-Feb), there is usually more rain, wind change and maybe rougher seas. Travelers have an incredible range of budget accommodation to choose from, many of which are upgrading and moving into the mid-price range. The luxury **Berjaya Tioman Beach Resort** (379 rooms), ☎ 4145445, fax: 3135718, south of Tekek, has comfortable chalets, pool, a watersports center for scuba gear and windsurfers, a golf course, tennis-courts and horse-riding. AC rooms and chalets from $136. The restaurant serves good, but highly-priced western and Malaysian cuisine. There are dozens of small chalet-type resorts with restaurants, all along the beachfront at Tekek, and further north at Ayer Batang, fondly known as ABC, and Salang. Likewise on the other side of the island at Juara. Teluk Nipah in the south is far quieter. All accommodations have AC options and attached baths, but no hot water. Prices range from $10 non-AC, to $44-72 AC. Walk along the beach and go for whichever grabs your fancy.

SERVICES

General

There are grocery shops, but prices are high. Batik and souvenirs can be bought. There is one Telekom phone card public phone, and a mini post office.

TOURS

Tour packages are usually 3D/2N affairs including return air travel and twin-share accommodation from $185. **Pelangi Airways**, ☎ (03)-2624446, flys from Kuala Lumpur, Kuantan and Singapore. Accommodation at the Berjaya Tioman Beach Resort, breakfast included. **SA Tours**, ☎ (03) 2429155, fax: (03) 2429420 stay at Tioman Paya Resort and offer road travel option. 5 meals and snorkeling.

DIVE OPERATORS

Tioman's waters are a wonderland of reefs rich in life, including hawksbill turtles. Best scuba-diving spots are Tulai (popular for snorkeling too), Labas, Cebeh, Sipoi, Jahat, Renggis and Pulau Jahat, all accessible by short boat rides. A 4D/3N package with around 7 dives, is about $276, including food and chalet accommodation. Arrangement can be made to stay at the Berjaya Resort. Walk-in leisure dives are $16-22. Gear hire is $8-12. **Scuba Point**, ☎ (03) 7747288; fax: (03) 7754288 also offers a 5-day PADI dive instruction package for $355, without food. The facility is in Tekek. The other outfit at Tekek is **Tioman Reef Divers**, and at the Berjaya Resort. **Borneo Divers** ☎ (03) 7173066, fax; (03) 7184303 ties in with Dive Asia at Salang for its openwater instruction/leisure trips. Other outfits at Salang are **B&J** and Fisherman. **Bali Hai Divers** operate at Penuba.

Pulau Rawa

Owned and run by **Rawa Safaris Island Resort**, ☎ 7991204, fax: 7993848. 52 chalets. Their office is at the Mersing (to the left of the jetty). Round trip by boat costs $5.20 round trip. Closed from Feb – Nov. Comfortable, shaded, chalets cost $52 (twin), $55 (quad), no-AC, shared baths; $74 (twin), $69 (quad) AC, attached bath. Excellent restaurant and bar and watersports facilities. Diving is $40 per dive, and $120 extra for a divemaster.

Pulau Besar

Most of the resorts here have offices near the jetty at Mersing that can advise of boat times, and accommodation availability. This island is popular with weekend trippers as it's only one hour by boat from Mersing, $10 return. Through the week it is often deserted. **Radin Resort & Safaris**, ☎ 7994152, fax: 7991413 just north of the jetty have 50 chalets, twin and triple share, AC, fridge, hot showers, starting from $48, a restaurant, bar, jungle trail, visits to nearby islands, snorkeling and water sports. There are several other smaller accommodations on the island include **Nirvana**, ☎ 7995979; **Sun Dancer Re-**

sort, **Sun Tan Beach Resort**, ☎ 7994995; and **Pulau Besar Chalet**, ☎ 010-7736586. **Hill Side Chalets**, ☎ 7994831, has chalets with great views overlooking the sea. Chalets are $32 upwards.

Pulau Tinggi

Enquire at the Tanjung Leman jetty for boat times. **Nadias Inn Tropical Resort**, ☎ 7995582, fax: 7995797; KL (03) 4519353, fax: 4518909. Has 58 rms starting from $52 S/D, restaurant serving local meals, swimming pool, karaoke, snorkeling. Diving pre-book and groups only. Rooms have hot shower, telephones. Suites from $190. **Tinggi Island Resort**, ☎ 7994451, fax: 7994452. Has 26 chalets, restaurant, disco, island tours. $46 S/D. **Tanjung Balang Chalet**, ☎ 011-784064 has a 10-room longhouse at $60 per room (6 persons) but caters to groups.

Pulau Sibu

Another favorite island with weekenders with a good range of accommodation The beaches are clean and quiet, and there is also a nice kampung atmosphere. Boats run from the jetty at Tanjung Leman for $8 return between February and November. **Sea Gypsy Village Resort**, ☎ 72228642, fax: 2387305, has 23 Malay wooden chalets with attached bathroom for $14, and a restaurant, bar (with wines), and shop. Dive center offers instruction and leisure dives. $82 S, $118 D, full board. Further along the coast is the **Sibu Island Cabanas**, ☎ 3317216, fax: 3311920. Has 18 comfortable chalets and good restaurant. $76 S, $106 D, including 4 meals. Both Sea Gypsy and the Cabanas have dive centers, which offer instruction, equipment nire and charge $56 for 2 dives. The cheapest island accommodation is O & H Kampung Huts, ☎ 7995096 or 011-354322, where basic 'A' frame chalets with shared bath are $10 and chalets with bathroom $26 D. Other facilities on the island are: Twin Beach Resort, ☎ 9848866; Waterfall Hillside Chalets, ☎ 2236554 Sibu Coconut Village Resort, ☎ 553592; and Rimba Resort, ☎ 2231494.

Pemanggil and Aur

The smaller islands of Pemanggil and Aur cater only for groups of 10 and above, for fishing and diving tours. Contact: Pemanggil Holiday Heaven, ☎ 7994360; Pemanggil Baru Chalet, ☎ 7992363; Pulau Pemanggil Mini Resort, ☎ 7992660. At Aur, contact: Aur Samudera Holidays, ☎ 7994407; Aur Holiday Resort, ☎ 7994072; Mahmood's Chalet, ☎ 7994217; Teluk Batai Chalet, ☎ 7994870; Friendly Waters Chalet, ☎ 4472108.

11 Singapore PRACTICALITIES

Singapore is one of the most readily accessible tourist destinations worldwide. Island tours can be booked at any travel agent or major hotel. But it is more fun to simply explore the city state on your own; 2 or 3 days are generally sufficient to cover most of the sights and attractions. If arriving from a northern climate, remember that it takes time to adapt to the tropical heat. An entire day spent wandering around can be very exhausting, so plan early morning outings. The early afternoon, when the weather is hottest, is best spent in an airconditioned restaurant or at the poolside. The late afternoon and early evening are pleasant for shopping, and most stores in Singapore's Orchard Road shopping district stay open until 9–9.30 pm, though they open late, around 10 am. *All prices in US dollars unless noted: Singapore telephone code is 65. S=single: D=double: AC=airconditioning.*

GETTING THERE

By Air

Arriving in Singapore by air is an immensely positive travel experience. Changi International Airport was repeatedly voted the world's best airport (i.e. by the magazine *Business Traveller*). The airport with its two terminals houses about 100 shops, 20 restaurants, 75 dayrooms, two business centers, two fitness centers and a number of other service centers.

The airport is linked to all major destinations worldwide. A few of the airlines operating from Changi include United Airlines, Delta Airlines, Thai Airways, Qantas Airways, Cathay Pacific Airways, Lufthansa, British Airways, Air India, Air Canada, Garuda Indonesia, Japan Airlines, Malaysian Airlines Systems and Air France.

Singapore Airlines, considered as one of the best and most profitable carriers, has long-term equity arrangements with various other airlines, providing an extensive route network that connects Singapore with numerous countries. Singapore Airlines has daily flights to and from Montreal, Toronto, Auckland, London, Los Angeles, San Francisco and New York. Additionally, Singapore Airlines and Malaysian Airlines jointly operate a regular shuttle between Changi Airport and Kuala Lumpur's Subang Airport with about a dozen flights daily, at a third cheaper than scheduled flights.

Taxis ply the 20- to 30-minute route to town for $14 to most hotels. There is also an AC city bus, No. 390, from Changi Airport to Orchard Rd. Many hotels offer mini bus and limousine services. There is also an airport coach service, AIRBUS, which operates luxurious buses from about 9 am to 11 pm between the airport and the city with many stops

in the Orchard Road and tourist belt area. Singapore Airlines is at SIA Building, 77 Robinson Rd, (1800 223-8888, 1800 223-6030), and ticket sales counters are at Mandarin Hotel, 333 Orchard Rd, and Raffles City Shopping Centre, 252 North Bridge Rd. Travel agents give cheaper fares than airline offices and are easily found in shopping arcades.

By Sea

Singapore is the busiest port in the world in terms of shipping tonnage and there can be as many as 700 cargo ships in port at any one time. All passenger cruise ships arrive and depart at the World Trade Centre Terminal, a 10-minute taxi ride from downtown, and at the Tanah Merah Ferry Terminal. Singapore's fantastic port can be viewed from luxurious catamarans, or the traditional wooden junk or *tongkang*, restored and reconditioned. Harbor and river cruises depart from the World Trade Centre, Clifford Pier, Clarke Quay and Raffles Place.

By Train

Singapore Railway Station on Keppel Road, a 5-minute taxi ride from most hotels, takes travelers from Singapore to Bangkok, Thailand, through Kuala Lumpur and Butterworth, Malaysia, and vice versa. Customs and immigration are on the premises. Singapore to Bangkok, S$195 (1st class AC), S$91.70 (2nd class AC). To Butterworth (Penang), S$127 (1st class AC), S$60 (2nd class AC). To Kuala Lumpur S$68 (1st class AC) and S$34 (2nd class AC).

By Bus

A number of buses also arrive at Singapore from

Malaysia. Customs and immigration points are at the joint border. From Johor Baru to the Rochor Road Terminus costs about S$1 or S$2.10 for an express bus. Long-distance buses to Malaysia depart from the Ban San Terminal (corner of Queen and Arab streets) and from the corner of Lavender Street and Kallang Bahru: Mersing S$11, Melaka S$11, Kuala Lumpur S$17, Butterworth S$30, Kuantan S$16.

ACCOMMODATIONS

Singapore boasts a string of major award-winning hotels whose special character reflects the island republic's unique Asian appeal. Visitors can choose from a wide range of accommodations—from luxuriously upscale to moderate to low budget. Room rates are for single occupancy standard rooms, and do not include the 10% service charge or 4% government tax. Booking hotels through a travel agent is usually cheaper than walking in off the street.

Luxury ($200 and up)

Shangri-La Hotel Singapore (823 rooms) 22 Orange Grove Road, Singapore 258350. ☎ 737-3644. Fax: 737-3257. Routinely voted among the world's top 10 hotels. 5 mins from Orchard Road, among lush landscaped greenery. $240.

Raffles Hotel (104 suites), 1 Beach Road, Singapore 189673. ☎ 337-1886. Fax: 339–7650. Conveniently located in the heart of the business and historic district, the Raffles is Singapore's most famous hotel. All suites have a spacious parlor, bedroom, dressing room and bath. $451.

Goodwood Park Hotel (235 rooms), 22 Scotts Road, Singapore 228221. ☎ 737-7411. Fax: 732-8558. One of the most unique hotels in Singapore, set in lush gardens in the fashionable Scotts Road district. $267.

The Oriental Singapore (518 rooms), 5 Raffles Avenue, Marina Square, Singapore 039797. ☎ 338-0066. Fax: 339-9537. 5 mins from the business center, located in Marina Square, Southeast Asia's largest shopping and hotel complex. Full exercise facilities, meeting and convention rooms. $250.

The Marco Polo Singapore (600 rooms) 247 Tanglin Road, Singapore 247935. ☎ 474-7141. Fax: 471-0521. 5 mins from the Orchard Road shops and adjacent to the Botanic Gardens. Renowned for top quality food and service. $209.

Hilton International Singapore (423 rooms) 581 Orchard Road, Singapore 238883. ☎ 737–2233. Fax: 732-2917. Rooftop pool with an incredible view. Health club with a gymnasium. $222.

Hyatt Regency Singapore (693 rooms) 1—12 Scotts Road, Singapore 228211. ☎ 738–1234. Fax: 732-1696. On Scotts Road, near the intersection with Orchard Road. $292.

Singapore Marriott Hotel (371 rooms) 320 Orchard Road, Singapore 238865. At the busy intersection of Orchard and Scotts roads. ☎ 735-5800. Fax: 735-9800. $264.

Mandarin Singapore (1,200 rooms) 333 Orchard Road, Singapore 238867. ☎ 737-4411. Fax: 732-2361. Classic Chinese decor with a rooftop revolving restaurant. $236.

Westin Plaza (793 rooms) 2 Stamford Road, Singapore 178882. ☎ 339-6633. Fax: 336–5117. World's tallest hotel surrounded by a shopping complex which houses 60 stores. $236.

Royal Crowne Plaza (493 rooms) 25 Scotts Road, Singapore 228220. ☎ 737–7966. Fax: 737-6096. Beautiful landscaped garden terrace and an excellent business center. $229.

The Regent of Singapore (441 rooms) 1 Cuscaden Road, Singapore 249715. ☎ 733-8888. Fax: 732-8838. Breathtaking atrium lobby; 5 mins from Orchard Road. $243.

Imperial Hotel Singapore (600) 1 Jalan Rumbia, Singapore 239616. ☎ 737-1666. Fax: 737-4761. 5 mins to Orchard Road and 25-min drive to airport. $230.

Orchard Hotel Singapore (680 rooms) 442 Orchard Road, Singapore 238879. ☎ 734-7766. Fax: 733-5482. Rooftop pool and sundeck. $202.

Intermediate $100-199

Albert Court Hotel (136 rooms) 180 Albert Street, Singapore 189971. ☎ 339-3939. Fax: 339-3252. Close to Little India. $125.

Plaza Hotel Singapore (350 rooms) 7500A Beach Road, Singapore 199591. ☎ 298-0011. Fax: 296-3600. Minutes away by bus from Marina shopping district. $160.

Concorde Hotel (515 rooms) 317 Outram Road, Singapore 169075. ☎ 733-0188. Fax: 733-0989. Located near the Singapore River. $132.

The Boulevard Hotel (521 rooms) 200 Orchard Boulevard, Singapore 248647. ☎ 737-2911. Fax: 737-8449. $153.

Furama Hotel Singapore (356 rooms) 60 Eu Tong Sen Street, Singapore 059804. ☎ 533-3888. Fax: 534-1489. 24-hr room service and free shuttle service available. $139.

Hotel Phoenix Singapore (309 rooms) 277 Orchard Road, Singapore 238858. ☎ 737-8666. Fax: 732-2024. $174.

Cockpit Hotel (176 rooms) 115 Penang Road, Singapore 238460. ☎ 737-9111. Fax: 737-3105. Nestled on the fringe of the Orchard Road shopping area. $132.

Ladyhill Hotel (180 rooms) 1 Ladyhill Road, Singapore 258670. ☎ 737-2111. Fax: 737-4606. Lovely poolside coffee shop. One of the best-kept secrets in Singapore. $118.

Garden Hotel (216 rooms) 14 Balmoral Road, Singapore 259800. ☎ 235-3344. Fax: 235-9730. $111.

Low Intermediate ($55-$90)

Singapore's budget hotels aren't so cheap by international standards due largely to the strength of the Singapore currency.

Strand Hotel (130 rooms) 25 Bencoolen Street, Singapore 189619. ☎ 338-1866. Fax: 336-3149. Reasonably priced hotel near Orchard Road.

Lion City Hotel (166 rooms) 15 Tanjong Katong Road, Singapore 436950. ☎ 744-8111. Fax: 748-7622. Close to Malay Village and Paya Lebar MRT station.

Hotel Supreme (86 rooms) 15 Kramat Road, Singapore 228750. ☎ 737-8333. Fax: 733-7404.

Inn of the Sixth Happiness Hotel (48 rooms) 33–37 Erskine Road, Singapore 069333. ☎ 223-3266. Fax: 223-7951. Small, picturesque hotel in a shophouse-type building in Chinatown.

The **YMCA International House** at 1 Orchard Road (☎ 336-6000) in the central tourist district has comfortable AC rooms, own bathroom and TV. The **Fort Canning YWCA** on 6 Fort Canning Road (☎ 338-4222) is also located near the Orchard Road shopping belt. The **Sloane Court Hotel** at 17 Balmoral Road (☎ 235-3311) is a pleasant little hotel with some ambience within walking distance of Orchard Road.

Budget ($45 and below)

Rooms at the **Pasir Panjang Guest House** near the University of Singapore on 404 Pasir Panjang Road (☎ 778-8511) come with attached bath and AC. The **Metropolitan YMCA is** at 60 Stevens Road (☎ 737-7755).

Good bargains include the **New 7th Storey Hotel** at 229 Rochor Road (☎ 337-0251) and the **San Wah Hotel** on 36 Bencoolen Street (☎ 336-2428), which has great character and offers rooms with AC and communal bath.

For very cheap accommodation try **Peony Mansion Traveller's Lodge,** 46A Bencoolen Street (☎ 338-5638). 28 rooms. Easy access to Orchard Road, Bugis Village, CHIJMES and Little India.

GETTING AROUND

Walking. Generally a sweaty experience over 100 m. Best to walk in early morning or after 5 pm.

Buses. Singapore has a superb city bus network. All major places of interest and residential areas are accessible by bus. Singapore Bus Service (SBS) and Trans-Island Bus Service (TIBS) operate regular and inexpensive services. Regular buses run between 6am and about midnight with fares starting at 55 cents (S) to S$1.35. The Singapore Explorer ticket provides the traveler with unlimited local bus use for one day (S$5) or three days (S$12). Available at leading hotels. Bus guides are sold at bookshops. The Singapore Trolley bus service runs between the Orchard Road area, Tanjong Pagar and the World Trade Centre. S$9 for adults, S$7 for children. Operates from 9 am to 10 pm.

Trishaws. A fascinating way to view the down-

town area. Most trishaw rides are organized by tour groups though individuals can hire one after agreeing on the destination and fare. Allow the tour operator to negotiate.

Mass Rapid Transit. The Singapore MRT is quite simply the most advanced underground and urban train system in the world. Fully completed in early 1990, various MRT routes cover nearly the entire island, with fares ranging from 60 cents (S) to S$1.60. The squeaky clean polished marble stations, complete with works by local artists, are tourist attractions in themselves. The system operates between 6 am and 11.40 pm and is simple and easy to use. Warning: **Fines** exist for littering and smoking (S$500), as well as eating and drinking (S$200). A Transitlink fare card (minimum S$12) will pay for your fares on both bus and MRT train.

Taxis. The easiest and coolest way to see Singapore is to take one of the more than 10,000 taxis that are all over the island. They are readily available and cheap by international standards. Fares recorded on the meter are S$2.40 for the first 1.5 km, and 10 cents (S) for every additional 240 meters covered up to 10 km. After 10 km, the fare rises 10 cents for every 225 meters or less. For waiting, the fare is 10 cents for every 30 seconds or less. Additional charges not recorded on the meter include S$3 for every trip from the airport; a Central Business District surcharge of S$1 for a taxi trip inside the designated restricted zone at peak hours; a 50% surcharge of the metered fare between midnight and 6 am; a S$2.20 surcharge for taxis booked by phone and an additional S$1 surcharge for every booking at least half an hour in advance. Station wagon taxis and London cabs cost an extra S$1, and the recently introduced Mercedes taxis command generally steeper fares.

Car Rentals. International companies are prevalent in Singapore but rates are high, about $100 a day. Most of the country's six taxi services rent vehicles with a driver for an hourly and daily rate. A few of the many rental agencies include: Avis Rent A Car, ☎ 1800–7379477; Hertz, ☎ 734-4646, 542-5300; Ace Tours & Car Rentals, Tel. 235-4433; Ken-Air, ☎ 737-8282; Happy Car Rentals & Tours, ☎ 473-9071; Budget, ☎ 339-4388; City Car Rentals & Tours, ☎ 733-2145; Blue Star Car Rentals & Tours, ☎ 253-4661; Falcon-Air Car Rental, ☎ 452-0880; CTS, ☎ 734-2445; San's Tours and Car Rentals, ☎ 734-9922; Orix Car Rentals, ☎ 469-1455; RMG Tent-A-Car, ☎ 2351311. Rates for chauffeur-driven cars start at S$40 an hour, with a 3-hr minimum, and a daily rate of between S$220 and S$400. Rates for self-driven cars are between S$75 and S$225 a day and between S$360 and S$1,200 a week with a mileage charge of 60 (S) cents per kilometer.

Central Business District. An important thing to remember is the Area Licence Scheme, which is designed to alleviate traffic congestion during peak hours (7.30 am to 7 pm, Mon–Fri; 7.30 am to 2 pm, Saturdays). Under the scheme a S$3 sticker must be purchased and displayed each day. The taxi driver is entitled to ask you to pay the $3 fee for a trip into the CBD during peak hours, if he does not have one.

TOUR AND TRAVEL

Most travel agents and hotels offer air conditioned coach tours of Singapore's major sights. Tour operators pick up at all hotels and the cost for an 3.5-hr day tour is about $27 for an adult and $14 for a child under 12. The coach passes Elizabeth Walk, Supreme Court, City Hall, the Singapore River and Merlion Park; proceeds towards Chinatown where it stops at the Sri Mariamman Temple; then continues on to Haw Par Villa and stops for the Instant Asia Cultural Show; then drives past the Queenstown Housing Estate and proceeds to the Botanical Gardens where the tour ends.

The operators of the tour are Singapore Sightseeing/Tour East, ☎ 332-3755; Singapore Explorer, ☎ 339-6833; RMG Tours, ☎ 220-1661; and SH Tours, ☎ 734-9923. Other major tour operators include Holiday Tours and Travel, ☎ 738-2622 and Malaysia and Singapore Travel Centre, ☎ 737-8877/235-5133. All of the mentioned operators offer more specific packages to Singapore's tourist destinations.

There are daily tours of Sentosa, the most developed and organized of Singapore's offshore islands, organized by Sentosa Discovery Tours (☎ 277-9654) and other tour operators.

DINING

Located at the crossroads of Asia, Singapore is a melting pot of cuisines of every conceivable kind. A dizzying array of affordable cuisines are available from the casual, open-air hawker center to Cantonese dim sum and exquisite French. All major hotels offer several specialty restaurants as well as a coffeeshop with both international fare and Asian delicacies. All hotels levy a 10% service charge and a 4% government tax.

Chinese

House of Blossoms, Marina Mandarin Hotel, 5 Raffles Boulevard, Marina Square. A beautifully decorated Cantonese restaurant renowned for its lunchtime dim sum. A moderately priced set menu is available for groups between four and ten. ☎ 331-8540.
Mooi Chin Palace Restaurant, B1-03 Funan Centre, 109 North Bridge Road. Located in a modern shopping complex near the Central Business District, it serves Hainanese cuisine and is especially noted for its spicy hot Sambal Pomfret fish.

☎ 339-7766.
Crystal Jade Palace Restaurant, #04-19 Ngee Ann City, 391 Orchard Road. Top-quality food is served in this restaurant in Singapore's most posh shopping center. Recommendations: Hong Kong seafood, pigeon, shark's fin and porridge.
Ming Jiang Sichuan Restaurant, Goodwood Park Hotel, 22 Scotts Road. Elegant Szechuan restaurant in one of Singapore's most stylish old hotels. ☎ 737-5337.
Happy Realm Restaurant, #03-16 Pearl Centre, next to People's Park complex. The very best Chinese vegetarian fare in Singapore at cheap prices. ☎ 222-6141.

Malay/Indonesian

Aziza's Restaurant, 180 Albert Street, #02-15 Albert Court. Singapore's most stylish Malay restaurant well known for its spicy Beef Rendang. ☎ 235-1130.
Sanur Indonesian Restaurant, #04-17 Centrepoint, 176 Orchard Road. Very popular with the local crowd. ☎ 734-2192.
Tambuah Mas Indonesian Restaurant, #05-14/27 Shaw Centre, 1 Scotts Road. Famous for curry fish head, beef and tahu telor. ☎ 733-3333.
Rendezvous Restaurant, #02-19 Raffles City Shopping Centre, 252 North Bridge Road. Excellent Indonesian Padang food served cafeteria-style at reasonable prices. Located in one of Singapore's swankiest shopping centers. ☎ 339-7508.

Japanese

Nogawa Japanese Restaurant, #03-101 Le Meridien Singapore, 100 Orchard Road. Top-quality Japanese food such as kaiseki, sushi and Japanese noodles. ☎ 732-2911.
Hoshigaoka, #03-45/46 Centrepoint, 175-180 Orchard Road. Right in the middle of an Orchard Road shopping center, Japanese fare at reasonable prices. ☎ 734-0259.
Inagiku Japanese Restaurant, The Westin Plaza, 2 Stamford Road. An old Japanese chain expanded into Singapore, the Inagiku is famous for its tempura. ☎ 431-5305.
Nadaman Japanese Restaurant, Shangri-La Hotel, 22 Orange Grove Road. Probably the best, most authentic Japanese restaurant in Singapore, but you pay for it. Excellent food. ☎ 737-3644.

Seafoods

UDMC Seafood Centre, East Coast Parkway. Eight large restaurants in one enormous complex by the sea offering moderately priced seafood. ☎ 444-7967/448-2020.
Palin Island Seafood Restaurant, 220 Stadium Road, Kallang Park. Reservations required. Specialities are pork ribs in red wine, black pepper crab and red garoupa in a special sauce. ☎ 346-0211.
Golden River Restaurant, 26–27 Boat Quay.

Seafood by the Singapore River. Black pepper crab, lobster and spicy duck can be recommended. ☎ 535-9009.

Ponggol Hock Kee Seafood Restaurant, Harbour Promenade, #01-124 Maritime Square. Try pepper crab, mee goreng or gold coin bean curd. ☎ 274-3500.

Indian

Muthu's Curry, 79 Race Course Road. A functional, air-conditioned southern Indian restaurant with spicy hot food served on banana leaves. Not for the faint-hearted. ☎ 293-2389.

Our Village, 4th and 5th story, 46 Boat Quay. North Indian cuisine by the river. ☎ 538-3058.

Annalakshmi Restaurant, #02-10 Excelsior Hotel and Shopping Centre, 5 Coleman Street. Fine Indian Vegetarian cuisine. ☎ 339-9993.

Rang Mahal, Imperial Hotel, 1 Jalan Rumbia. North Indian food in an elegant atmosphere. Floor show at night. ☎ 297-0400.

Komala Vilas Restaurant, 76/78 Serangoon Road. Southern Indian vegetarian, very cheap, very good. Located in the heart of "Little India." ☎ 293-6980.

French

La Brasserie, Omni Marco Polo Hotel, 247 Tanglin Road. Elegant French brasserie with superb food. ☎ 378-1861.

Restaurant Latour, Shangri-La Hotel, 22 Orange Grove Road. Impeccable atmosphere and impressive menu featuring such dishes as pan-fried venison and sauteed deep-sea scallops. ☎ 737-3644.

Les Amis Restaurant & Wine Bar, #02-16 Shaw Centre, 1 Scotts Road. ☎ 733-2225.

La Cascade French Restaurant, 7 Ann Siang Road. French cuisine in Chinatown. ☎ 324-1807.

Italian

Prego, The Westin Plaza, 2 Stamford Road. A large range of pastas, moderately priced, in a cheerful atmosphere. ☎ 431-5155.

Pete's Place, Hyatt Regency Singapore, 10/12 Scotts Road. Italian specialities and a good salad bar. ☎ 738-1234.

Il Piccolo, #01-06/07 Crown Centre, 557 Bukit Timah Road. ☎ 468-5837.

Paladino Di Firenze, 7 Mohamed Sultan Road. Italian food of the highest quality. Try the *antipasti* or the lamb with herbs. ☎ 738-0917.

American

Ponderosa Steakhouse, Picnic Foodcourt, Scotts Shopping Centre, ☎ 336-0139. Raffles City Shopping Centre, 334-4926.

Steeples Deli, #02-05 Tanglin Shopping Centre, 19 Tanglin Road. New York deli favorites in a bright atmosphere. ☎ 737-0701.

Hard Rock Cafe, 50 Cuscaden Road #02-01. Huge helpings of American food amid rock

memorabilia. ☎ 235-6256.

Thai

Thanying Restaurant, Amara Hotel, 65 Tanjong Pagar Road. Features a chef imported from a Thai royal household. Sophisticated Thai cuisine in a casual atmosphere. ☎ 222-4688.

Baan Thai, 391 Orchard Road, #04-23 Ngee Ann City. Try grilled fish, baked king prawns or fried rice noodles. Nice ambience but expensive. ☎ 735-5562.

Klongtan Ping Restaurant, 46 Lorong Mambong. Located in fashionable Holland Village, high quality Thai/Chinese seafood but a fairly limited menu. ☎ 469-2762, 468-5668.

Street Food

Eating at a hawker center is one of the highlights of any visit to Singapore. Unlike many other Asian countries, cleanliness is not a problem as stringent health regulations are strictly enforced. Hawkers are often conveniently housed in centers attached to fresh produce markets. All types of local food— from Malay Muslim through the entire spectrums of Chinese and Indian — are represented. Over the past few years many have moved upmarket into shopping complexes and are attractively designed and air-conditioned, though not as authentic.

Free seating is the norm, so you are never obligated to order from any one particular stall. Order from several stalls and pay for the food as it arrives. No tipping, please. Hawker centers to try include: **Newton Circus,** the largest and most famous hawker center in Singapore. Good-quality food with a wide range and specializing in seafood. While some stalls are open in the morning, it doesn't really get rolling until the early evening and goes through the night. Near Newton MRT.

Bugis Square, Foch Road (off Lavender Street). Noted for its Chinese food. Also busiest at night. **Lau Pa Sat Festival Market.** Right in the heart of the Central Business District, this recently renovated Victorian filigree structure houses a variety of stalls and is open 24 hours a day.

If you're at the **World Trade Centre** en route to Sentosa, just across the street is one of Singapore's finest. Serves the entire gamut of Singapore food from lunch to midnight.

Hill Street Centre, 64 Hill Street. Good cheap food, open from morning till dinnertime. Also recommended is the **Chinatown Complex** in South Bridge Road.

If ever there was a shopper's paradise, it has to be Singapore. Because of its location at the crossroads of Asia and its duty-free status, prices are often—but not always—cheaper than in their country of origin. The shopping centers along Orchard Road are among the most modern in the world. Unlike many other Asian countries, bargaining is discouraged in many places and in department stores. There is a fantastic range of goods to be found, from Japanese consumer electronics to American computers and compact discs to gems from Sri Lanka and silk from Thailand and China. The Good Retailers Scheme established by the Singapore Tourist Promotion Board ensures high quality goods and service in shops displaying the red Merlion symbol.

One-Stop Gift Shopping. Orchard Road and the immediate outlying area are riddled with air-conditioned, ultra-modern shopping centers. Here is just a sampling: **Tang's Department Store**, corner of Orchard and Scotts Roads. Five floors stuffed with a variety of household goods, fashion and electronics. Has an excellent souvenir shop. **Takashimaya Shopping Centre/Ngee Ann City**, Orchard Road. This is probably Singapore biggest and poshest shopping center, all clad in brown Italian marble. It houses a big Japanese department store and a cornucopia of individual shops. A city in itself. **Marina Square**, 6 Raffles Boulevard. Another huge shopping center, it is the size of seven football fields and has three floors of shops with two department stores, Metro and Tokyu. **Liang Court**, between River Valley Road and the Singapore River. This attractive retail complex is home to the Japanese Daimaru department store as well as scores of small specialist shops and bookstores. Other noteworthy shopping centers along Orchard Road include Far East Plaza, Scotts, Centrepoint, Lucky Plaza, Wisma Atria and Forum The Shopping Mall.

Antiques. Tanglin Shopping Centre, 19 Tanglin Road. With four floors of valuable antiques shops, it houses Singapore's only specialist in antique maps and the renowned Hassan's Carpets.

Other areas replete with antique shops include Smith and Temple Streets in Chinatown. Peter Wee's **Katong Antique House** on 208 East Coast Road also has bargains. The **Chinese Cloisonne-Ware Centre** in Raffles City, 2 Stamford Road, offers a complete selection of cloisonne-ware pots, vases and decorative items.

Jewelry. At the top of Arab Street near North Bridge Road are goldsmiths and jewellers in tiny shops selling sets of gold worn by Malay brides. Similar items can be found in the Geylang Serai area of town. Precious gems can be found at virtually all of the many shopping centers. In Orchard and Scotts roads try Tanglin Shopping Centre, Orchard Towers and Far East Plaza, where some shops make items to order. Pidemco Centre in South Bridge Road houses Singapore's Jewellery Mart. Other areas for jewellery are New Bridge Road, Arab Street and People's Park Complex in Chinatown.

Arts and Crafts. Local art can be found in galleries such as Sun Craft, Tanglin Shopping Centre; Decor Arts, Wisma Atria; or at Orchard Gallery in Orchard Point. For arts and crafts with true ethnic character, Arab Street and the nearby streets are the ultimate. Tiny shops abound carrying basketry, camel skin bags, Indonesian and Malaysian textiles and batik.

Tailoring. Delivery is generally fast and the price reasonable. Tailors are in nearly every shopping center and most hotels with an excellent selection of fabrics. Try Coleman Street, Selegie Road, North Bridge Road, Orchard Road and Tanglin Road.

Electronics. Sim Lim Tower and Sim Lim Centre, on Jl. Besar, offer some of the best deals for consumer electronics. Always bargain, test the equipment purchased and insist on a receipt. Best Connection with its various outlets (i.e. Ngee Ann City, 5th floor) is also reasonable and reputable. Pertama and Electric City (i.e. at the Heeren Shops) also have various outlets and fixed prices

Computers. Funan Centre, 109 North Bridge Rd. Good for personal and notebook computers, printers, accessories and software. Also recommended is Sim Lim Square.

PHOTOGRAPHY

One-hour processing is the norm, and shops can be found all over Orchard Road and many other places. Camera shops offer excellent deals in such places as Albert Photo in Orchard Towers and Cathay Photo Store in Peninsular Plaza on North Bridge Road.

NIGHTLIFE

Singapore is not quite a 24-hour city—but it's going in that direction. Nightclubs, discos and bars get going at around 10 pm and continue till the wee hours (3 am, that is). The vast majority of nightlife centers on or around Orchard Road, but there are also pockets outside the district.

Prices vary widely depending on the entertainment offered. Most bars and lounges do not impose a cover charge, but the fee for entering a disco is about $20–25, inclusive of the first drink. Like restaurants, many establishments charge 10% for service and 4% tax. Dress is almost always informal, but you will feel out of place in many establishments in jeans and T-shirt, so smart casual is recommended.

Bars

Brannigan's, at the Hyatt Regency Singapore, 10–12 Scotts Rd., is probably Singapore's most famous pub. Also referred to as a "singles" bar, it offers good rock-pop music (live band). **Club 392**, #01-21 Orchard Towers, 400 Orchard Rd. Sleazy but popular bar with wall-to-wall cigarette smoke and scores of bar girls on offer. **Elvis' Place**, 1A Duxton Hill. A nostalgic tribute to Elvis, with a DJ spinning discs from the 50's and 60's. **Anywhere**, #04-07 Tanglin Shopping Centre, 19 Tanglin Rd. The resident band, Tania, is a Singapore institution and part-owner of the bar. Well worth the experience. **5 Emerald Hill Cocktail Bar** in quaint Emerald Hill Road attracts expats and locals alike.

Music Clubs

Saxophone, 23 Cuppage Road. Wonderful local Jazz and Blues bands with other musicians sitting in. One of Singapore's most famous bars, popular with expats and run by the Belgian Fabrice, who also owns **Fabrice's World Music Bar** in the basement of the Marriott Hotel: ethnic music and live bands from all corners of the world. **Somerset's Bar**, Westin Plaza Hotel, 2 Stamford Rd. International bands play Jazz and Chicago blues. **Ginivy,** #02-11 Orchard Towers, 400 Orchard Rd. Authentic and sleazy Honky Tonk bar featuring Texas swing and country music.
Coco Carib, Boat Quay; Caribbean music and ambience by the Singapore River. A good place to sit, dance and unwind.
Hard Rock Cafe, Cuscaden Rd. Original Rock 'N' Roll memorabilia lines the walls of this hard-driving club. Excellent American food is served.

Discos

Studebakers, Pacific Plaza, Scotts Road. American ambience and one of the "in" discos.
Xanadu, Shangri-La Hotel. Hi-tech hangout with laser displays and pop videos. **Zouk,** 17-21 Jiak Kim St. incorporates a disco, restaurant, bar and cafe.
Top Ten, #04-35 Orchard Towers, 400 Orchard Rd. A converted cinema, with live band and DJ. Popular with lonely expats and the girls you meet in Brannigan's earlier on in the evening. **Sparks,** Ngee Ann City. A huge discotheque in Singapore's marble shopping complex.

Nightclubs

Lido Palace Nite-Club, #05-01 Concorde Hotel Shopping Centre, 317 Outram Road. Chinese banquet cuisine in plush atmosphere with beautiful Chinese hostesses and flashy dance floor.
Dallas Theater Lounge and Nite Club, #05-01 Amara Hotel, 165 Tanjong Pagar Road. Spectacular nightclub floor show featuring Chinese pop stars.

CULTURAL EVENTS

Singapore is an astonishing variety of races and cultures and there is much to see and do.

At Tang Dynasty Village, Jurong, go back to 7th-century China at one of Asia's largest cultural and historical theme parks. Visitors can see replicas of the Silk Road and the Great Wall, as well as take in cultural films at any of the three film studio blocks. Haw Par Villa, on Pasir Panjang Road, is world-famous for its colorful statues and the Spirits of the Orient Theater.

Plays are staged at the Drama Centre, at Fort Canning and at the Victoria Theater, Empress Place. Chinese street opera takes place all over the island during the Festival of the Hungry Ghosts, usually August or September.

Multi-cultural and multi-religious Singapore celebrates festivals and holidays throughout the year and they are always colorful events with food and mystique.

Starting with the Western New Year on Jan 1, the southern Indian festival Thaipusam follows in Jan/Feb, and then Chinese New Year, fixed on the lunar calendar, is held in late Jan or Feb. Twice a year, in Feb and Oct, Chinese mediums in trance celebrate the Birthday of the Monkey God. The Muslim fasting month of Ramadan falls in December and January, with believers consuming nothing during daylight hours until the feasting day of Hari Raya Puasa, which marks the end of the fasting month. Vesak Day in May commemorates the Buddha's birthday. The annual Dragon Boat Festival in June honors ancient Chinese poet and statesman Qu Yuan. The Chinese Hungry Ghosts Month falls between Aug and Sep, while the Chinese Mooncake Festival is held Sep/Oct. In Oct, Hindu temples offer classical dances during the Festival of Navrathri. Fire walking to celebrate the Hindu Thimithi Festival takes place end of Oct.

The Festival of the Nine Emperor Gods is celebrated in Oct and the Hindu holiday Deepavali is end of Oct or in Nov. Singapore then finishes the year off with impressive illuminations and decorative displays during Christmas.

MUSEUMS

The **National Museum and Art Gallery,** Stamford Rd, houses a fascinating display of artifacts and ethnology tracing Singapore's development, together with a wide array of Southeast Asian treasures. Displays include the Haw Par jade collection, one of the world's largest; the History of Singapore Gallery, with its ornate history and artifacts. Admission S$3, adults, S$1.50, children.
The **Asian Civilisations Museum,** 39 Armenian Street, combines treasures of the past with present-day technology. The first wing of the Museum houses the Permanent Display on Chinese Civilisation. Admission is S$3 for adults and S$1 for children.
The **Singapore Art Museum** is housed in a beautifully restored school building on 71 Bras Basah Road, the former St. Joseph's Institution, whose cornerstone was laid in 1855. It contains Singapore's national art gallery. Adults, S$3; children, S$1.50.

MEDICAL SERVICES

Singapore's healthcare facilities are the best in Southeast Asia and of Western standard. Pharmaceuticals are readily available. Most hotels have their own doctor on 24-hour call. Other doctors are listed under Medical Practitioners in the Yellow Pages. The Tanglin Medical Clinic, #05-28 Tanglin Shopping Centre, has an excellent reputation for competent, reasonably priced service.

There are nine government facilities and several private hospitals. Singapore General Hospital on Outram Road is very efficient and competent. However, be ready with identification and cash or credit cards, as a foreigner you will likely be asked for money upfront before admission. For an ambulance, dial 995.

POST & TELEPHONE

Singapore probably has the best telecommunications system in the world. Virtually all hotels have fax machines and International Direct Dialing. Public pay phones are all over the island and cost 10 cents (S) for 3 mins. Public phones designated for international calls are clearly marked and operate using special phone cards costing S$2–S$50; they are sold at post offices and some shops. The Singapore postal system is generally quick and efficient and most hotels provide postal service.

VISA FORMALITIES

With just a few exceptions, a valid visa, onward travel reservations and adequate finance are all the traveler needs to enter Singapore. However, citizens of Cambodia, China, Laos India and the Commonwealth of Independent States are required to produce a visa. You will automatically be given a 14-day tourist visa upon entering Singapore, though 30-day visas are readily available upon request, especially when entering the country by air.

CUSTOMS

Singapore is essentially a free port; however, some consumable items are dutiable. These include alcoholic beverages and tobacco products. Each incoming traveler is allowed one liter of spirits and one liter of wine or beer. Prohibited items include chewing gum, chewing tobacco, endangered species of wildlife and controlled drugs and psychotropic substances.

The penalty for drug trafficking (defined by the quantity of drugs carried, including "soft" drugs like marijuana) is death. Any traveler possessing pharmaceuticals must be able to produce a valid prescription.

LANGUAGES

Four official languages—Mandarin, Malay, Tamil and English. The latter is the language of busi-ness and administration, and is widely spoken and understood. Most Singaporeans speak English as well as their mother tongue.

TAX, SERVICES AND TIPPING

Tipping is not expected. It is prohibited at the airport and discouraged in hotels and restaurants that have a 10% service charge.

Airport tax is S$15 for all destinations, with the exceptions of Malaysia and Brunei.

ELECTRICITY

The electrical supply in Singapore is extremely reliable and is on the 220–240 volt, 40 Hz system. Most hotels have transformers for 10–120 volt, 60 Hz appliances.

TIME ZONE AND OFFICE HOURS

Singapore is 8 hours ahead of Greewich Mean Time. Business hours at government departments and international agencies are generally from 9 am to 5 pm, and from 9 am to 1 pm on Saturdays. Banks are open from 10 am to 3 pm on weekdays, and from 9 to 11.30 am on Saturdays. Closed Sundays.

EMBASSIES & CONSULATES

Australia, 25 Napier Rd. ☎ 737-9311. **Belgium,** 10 Anson Rd. #09-24 International Plaza ☎ 220-7677. **Britain,** Tanglin Rd. ☎ 473-9333. **Canada,** 80 Anson Rd. IBM Towers, ☎ 325-3200. **Denmark,** 101 Thomson Rd. #13-01/02 United Square, ☎ 250-3383. **France,** 5 Gallop Rd. ☎ 466-4866. **Germany,** 545 Orchard Rd. #14-01, Far East Shopping Centre, ☎ 737-1355. **India,** 31 Grange Rd. ☎ 737-6777. **Indonesia,** 7 Chatsworth Rd. ☎ 737-7422. **Ireland,** 298 Tiong Bahru Road, #08-06 Tiong Bahru Plaza, ☎ 276-8935. **Italy,** 101 Thomson Rd. #27-02/03 United Square, ☎ 250-6022; **Japan,** 80 Anson Rd. ☎ 235-8855. **Malaysia,** 301 Jervois Rd. ☎ 235-0011. **Myanmar,** 15 St. Martins Drive, ☎ 735-0209. **Netherlands,** 541 Orchard Towers, #13-01 Liat Towers, ☎ 737-1155. **New Zealand,** 391A Orchard Rd. ☎ 235-9966. **Norway,** 16 Raffles Quay, #44-01 Hong Leong Bldg. ☎ 220-7122. **Philippines,** 20 Nassim Rd. ☎ 737-3977. **Sweden,** 111 Somerset, #05-08 PUB Bldg., ☎ 734-2771. **Switzerland,** 1 Swiss Club Link, ☎ 468-5788. **Thailand,** 370 Orchard Rd. ☎ 737-2644. **USA,** 27 Napier Rd. ☎ 476-9100.

Further Reading

This selection is intended to provide an introduction to Peninsular Malaysia and Singapore and the books listed below are both readable and informative. Many books were written in English during the British colonial days, and some have been reprinted by Oxford University Press in Singapore and Kuala Lumpur available at Times and MPH bookshops. Select Books in the Tanglin Shopping Complex, Singapore, specializes in books on the Southeast Asian region. Many of the best journals on history and culture were written and published through the Malayan Branch of the Royal Asiatic Society, referred to as JMBRAS. Reprints are available at selected bookstores.

HISTORY

Andaya, Barbara Watson, Leonard Y. (1982) *A History of Malaysia*. Excellent and readable, with a non-colonial contemporary viewpoint similar to current local interpretations. The best book in the field for a comprehensive, unbiased coverage.

Bellwood, Peter (1985) *Pre-history of the Indo Malaysian Archipelago*. A revolutionary view of where the region's first inhabitants came from. Detailed and fascinating reading.

Brown, C.C. (Translator) (1953) *Sejarah Melayu* or "Malay Annals", JMBRAS. The finest Malay literary work which traces the geneology of the Melakan Sultanate. Vivid narrative, and superb story-telling of the Malay's 15th-century "Golden Age".

Butcher, J.G. (1979) *The British in Malaya, 1880-1941. The Social History of a European Community in Colonial South-East Asia*. Interesting, and written in a lively style.

Coates, Austin (1968) *The Commerce in Rubber: The First 250 Years*. The definitive work on the crop that changed the face of Malaya. Starting with its discovery in Brazil, then its growth, booms and slumps in Southeast Asia.

Gullick, J.M. (1987) *Malay Society in the Late Nineteenth Century, The Beginnings of Change*. An in-depth look at how this traditional Islamic society adapted to a different world.

Linehan, W. (1936) *A History of Pahang* MBRAS. Scholarly, and sometimes difficult going, but nonetheless a fascinating look at the historical development of the Peninsula's largest state.

Wheatley, Paul (1964) *Impressions of the Malay Peninsula in Ancient Times*. An absorbing look at pre-16th century history according to Chinese, Indian and Arab sources. This is the synthesized version of his more scholarly tome *The Golden Khersonese* (1961).

Windstedt, R.O. (1935, reprint 1982) *A History of Malaya*. Rather dated colonial viewpoint, but is well written and easy to read.

BIOGRAPHIES & REMINISCENCES

Chapman, Frederick Spencer (1949, reprint 1983) *The Jungle is Neutral*. A true tale of the author's three and a half years spent hiding from the Japanese in the Malayan jungle. One of the classic tales of World War II.

Coope, A.E. (Translator) (1967) *The Voyages of Adbullah*. A journey up the little-known East Coast in the early 19th-century by Abdullah bin Abdul Kadir, former scribe to Raffles.

Hill, A.H. (Translator) (1955) *The Hikayat Abdullah* JMBRAS. Abdullah bin Abdul Kadir's autobiographical tale of 19th-century Melaka and Singapore. Tells of the coming of Raffles, and many other first-hand reminiscences.

THE ARTS

Couillard, Marie-Andree (1980) *Tradition In Tension: Carving in a Jah Hut Community*. A look at these indigenous wood sculptors and their work.

Edwards, Norman and Keys, Peter. (1988) *Singapore - A Guide to Buildings, Streets, Places*. Not a travel guide, but an intensive street-by-street compilation of Singapore's architecture. A must for architecture buffs.

Lim Jee Yuan (1987) *The Malay House*. Profusely illustrated, large-format work on the indigenous Malay house. Contains house-building styles, regional variations, and an interesting look at the economic reasons behind the demise of the traditional home.

Werner, Roland (1973) *Mah Meri, Art and Culture*. The only authoritative book on the sculptures and lifestyle of this west coast Orang Asli group.

CULTURE & RELIGION

Carey Iskandar (1975) *Orang Asli: the Aboriginal Tribes of Peninsular Malaysia*. Good introduction to the peninsular's indigenous people.

Khoo Kay Kim (1992) *Malay Society: Transfor-*

mation and Democratisation. A stimulating and discerning study of the evolution of Malay society from the time of the Melakan Sultanate to the present by the nation's leading authority.

Lat. *Kampung Boy, Town Boy, Mat Som, Best of Lat.* Malaysia's best-known cartoonist gives his humorous and highly-accurate account of contemporary life and politics.

Mahathir bin Mohamad (1970) *The Malay Dilemma.* A controversial, but interesting theory by Malaysia's Prime Minister on the background behind the nation's racially-dominated economy.

Schebesta, Paul (1928, reprint 1973) *Among the Forest Dwarfs of Malaya.* This classical work on the so-called Negrito peoples of the Malay Peninsula has an introduction by Geoffrey Benjamin.

Winstedt, Richard (1947, revised 1981) *The Malays - A Cultural History.* The pre-history is outdated, but it is a good introduction to the beliefs, religion, and the political, social, legal and economic systems of the Malays.

LANGUAGE

Coope, A.E. *Macmillan's Malay-English, English-Malay Dictionary.* Pocket-sized and concise, revised in the new Malay spelling.

Hamilton, A.W. (reprinted 1985) *Malay Made Easy.* Lives up to its title, but its colonial-style phrases are incredibly dated, albiet amusing. There are commands for ironing collars correctly, and getting the syce to exercise your horse, among others.

Sulaiman, Othman (1990) *Malay for Everyone: Mastering Malay Through English.* Probably the most up to date, teach-yourself book. Set out in a series of lessons and good for anyone wanting a thorough grounding of the language.

LITERATURE

Fauconnier, Henri. *Soul of Malaya* (1931, Oxford reprint 1965). Evocative, semi-autobiographical novel written by a French rubber planter. This sensitive portrayal of the Malays won the Prix Goncourt in 1930.

Han Su-yin (1956) *And the Rain My Drink.* A novel about life in the Emergency—the communist-terrorist uprising—set in a New Village.

Maugham, W. Somerset (1933, reprint 1986) *Maugham's Malaysian Stories*, and *Ah King and Other Stories.* Short stories by the master English novelist which brings to life the colonial era. Many tales were of true characters and events, thinly-disguised, which scandalised Malaya's early expatriate society.

Rehman Rashid. (1993) *Malaysian Journey.* Incisive, witty treatise – if rather opinionated – on contemporary Malaysia by one of the country's most brilliant writers.

Winstedt, Richard (revised 1992) *A History of Classical Malay Literature.* A collection of the best works. Excellently compiled.

NATURE

Cubitt, Gerald, and Payne, Junaidi (1991) *Wild Malaysia.* Large-format book profusely illustrated with high-quality photographs.

Strange, Jeyarajasingham (1993) *A Photographic Guide to the Birds of Peninsular Malaysia and Singapore.* Nice colour plates, comprehensive.

King, Ben, Woodcock, Martin and Dickinson, E.C. (1975) *Birds of South-East Asia.* The definitive guidebook for all birdwatchers. Profusely illustrated.

Morrel, R. (1960) *Common Malayan Butterflies.* Well-illustrated guide for both laymen and lepidopterists.

Shuttleworth, Charles (1981) *Malaysia's Green and Timeless World.* An aborbing account, and excellent introduction to the flora, fauna, and indigenous peoples of the rainforests.

Tweedie, M.W.F. and Harrison, J.L. (1981) *Malayan Animal Life.* Well-illustrated introduction to the Peninsula's diverse fauna.

GUIDES AND TRAVELOGUES

Bird, Isabella L. (1967) *The Golden Chersonese, Travels in Malaya in 1879.* This intrepid Victorian adventuress give a perceptive and beautifully-descriptive account of her travels through Singapore and the peninsular west coast in the days when the British were just starting their push into the interior.

Falcon Press (Publisher) *Petronas Heritage Mapbook of Peninsular Malaysia.* Easy to follow guide for motorists in a mapbook form. Covers many off-the-beaten-track attractions.

Harrison, Cuthbert Woodville (1923, reprint 1985) *An Illustrated Guide to the Federated Malay States.* The first real guidebook to the Peninsula covers "Notes for Travellers", "Hints for Motorists", and sections on big-game shooting, museums, mining, and an informative appendix. Although very dated, some of his countryside scenes are still the same and the British colonial-style writing makes for a great read.

Lloyd, R.Ian and Moore Wendy. (1987) *To Know Malaysia.* Large-format book with informative essays. Superbly photographed by one of the region's top photographers.

Wheeler, Tony, etc. *Malaysia, Singapore and Brunei.* Lonely Planet's travel survival kit is good for getting around and budget accomodation. Take the opinionated comments with a grain of salt, however, as these are often biased taxi-driver's tales.

About the Authors

Barbara Watson Andaya has a Ph.D from Cornell University and is currently Lecturer with the Department of History, University of Auckland, New Zealand. Her research focuses on the Malay-Indonesian archipelago.

Hashim Awang A.R. holds a Ph.D in medical anthropology from University of Hawaii-Manoa, and is an Associate Professor at the Department of Malay Studies, University of Malaya. His major research is in Malay medicine and he has published many articles on this subject.

Peter Bellwood is a Reader in Prehistory at The Australian National University, specializing in Southeast Asian and Pacific prehistory. His books include *Man's Conquest of the Pacific* , *Prehistory of the Indo-Malaysian Archipelago* and *The Polynesians*.

Geoffrey Benjamin studied at Cambridge but has spent most of his adult life in Singapore, where he is Associate Professor in Sociology at the National University. Since the 1960s he has been studying the Temiars and other Orang Asli.

Shane Callahan, a regular contributor to regional magazines, writes on culture, travel and food. His unique Eurasian Singaporean background gives him a multi-cultural insight.

Geoffrey Davison is a biologist who received his Ph.D from the University of Malaya and has lived and worked in the country since then. He now works for WWF Malaysia. His particular interests include animal behavior.

Mohd. Kassim bin Haji Ali was born in Melaka, and first joined the Museums Department in 1962. During his museum tenure he has held various posts including Curator of Ethnology and is is currently the Senior Assistant Director for Education and Exhibitions. Kassim has written several catalogues and reference books.

Yahaya Ismail has written over 30 books on politics, culture, literary criticism, fiction and tourism and has been appointed the royal biographer to the present King of Malaysia. In his varied career, he has been a teacher, research officer, lecturer, and chief editor of a newspaper.

Kiew Bong Heang is a well-known Malaysian naturalist currently lecturing at the Department of Zoology, University of Malaya. He has over 20 years of field experience and has been involved with numerous expeditions. He regularly contributes to a number of publications.

Ku Zam Zam Ku Idris is an Associate Professor at the Department of Malay Studies, University of Malaya, lecturing on ethnomusicology and Malay culture. Her numerous articles in English and Bahasa Malaysia, on traditional Malay music, culture and expressive arts can be found in several academic journals and books.

Lee Kam Hing obtained his M.A. from the University of Malaya and his Ph.D from Monash University, Melbourne. He currently holds the post of Associate Professor in the History Department, University of Malaya, where he teaches Southeast Asian history, but researches mainly in Indonesian and Malaysian history.

Zuraina Majid, a Professor at Universiti Sains Malaysia in Penang, obtained her Ph. D from Yale. Archaeology is her main research area and among the major sites she has excavated are the Niah caves, Sarawak, and Kota Tampan in Perak. She has written several books and articles based on her research.

Wendy Moore, a freelance writer and editor, born in Sydney, Australia, has traveled extensively. In 1984 she was based in Singapore, then moved to Malaysia in 1986 where she has lived and worked ever since. She is a frequent contributor to many publications and has written a number of travel-related books.

Fiona Nichols, a travel writer and photographer, has been based in Singapore for the last 10 years. Her work includes the first photographic book on Phuket, and photography for a book on the Taj Mahal.

Said Halim Said Nong, a lecturer at the Language Center, University of Malaya, has published books on television drama, literary text analyses, a collection of folk tales and children's stories.

Ilsa Sharp is a British-born freelance writer who has lived in Singapore for the past 25 years. A Chinese studies graduate, she has worked for the *Far Eastern Economic Review* and the Straits Times newspaper group. She currently specializes in the environment and wildlife, as well as Southeast Asia.

Morten Strange, a Danish national, retired from his career as a petroleum engineer in 1986 to pursue a lifelong interest in birds. He has birdwatched and photographed all over Asia, in particular Peninsular Malaysia. In 1992 he wrote and photographed a guide to birds of Peninsular Malaysia and Singapore.

Yeow Mei Sin, a Singaporean freelance writer specializing in travel and culture, has contributed articles to many regional magazines.

Index

Map Index